Before the Nation

Asia-Pacific: Culture, Politics, and Society

Editors: Rey Chow, H. D. Harootunian, and Masao Miyoshi

A STUDY OF THE WEATHERHEAD EAST ASIAN INSTITUTE

SUSAN L. BURNS

Before the Nation

Kokugaku and the Imagining of Community

in Early Modern Japan

DUKE UNIVERSITY PRESS

Durham and London

2003

© 2003 DUKE UNIVERSITY PRESS
All rights reserved. Printed in the United States of
America on acid-free paper ⊚ Typeset in Quadraat
by Tseng Information Systems, Inc. Library of Congress
Cataloging-in-Publication Data appear on the last printed
page of this book.

STUDIES OF THE WEATHERHEAD EAST ASIAN
INSTITUTE, COLUMBIA UNIVERSITY
The Weatherhead East Asian Institute is Columbia
University's center for research, publication, and teaching
on modern and contemporary Asia Pacific regions. The Studies
of the Weatherhead East Asian Institute were inaugurated in
1962 to bring to a wider public the results of significant new
research on modern and contemporary East Asia.

To Hannah

Contents

Acknowledgments

This book has its origins in a seminar paper I submitted to Professor Harry Harootunian and Professor Tetsuo Najita in 1986, my first year of graduate school at the University of Chicago. During the past sixteen years as I have worked—and at times struggled—to complete this project, I have been reminded again and again of how much I have learned from them. I continue to be profoundly grateful for the vital intellectual community they created at the University of Chicago during my years there and for the support they have provided me since then. I am indebted as well to Koyasu Nobukuni, now Professor Emeritus of Osaka University. During the two and half years I spent at Osaka University, Professor Koyasu allowed me to participate fully in his graduate seminar. He and his students, especially Miyagawa Yasuko and Higuchi Kōzō, made it possible for me to engage with the kokugaku canon in ways that would not have been possible on my own. William Sibley guided my first early efforts to read Norinaga's work, while Naoki Sakai patiently endured my stumbling early efforts to read the work of Fujitani Mitsue.

I owe much to the colleagues and friends who carefully and critically read the manuscript in its many postdissertation forms and forced me to rethink, reformulate, and refine my ideas and my prose. These include Leslie Pincus, Herman Ooms, Peter Nosco, and Anne Walthall, as well as my dear former colleagues at the University of Texas at Austin, Edward Rhoads, Margherita Zanasi, and Cynthia Talbot. The members of the Kinsei Shisōshi Kenkyū-kai, based in Kyoto, provided a much needed forum for me to test out my work, and I benefited greatly from their comments and suggestions. Thanks to Barbara Brooks and Sally Hastings for their friendship, encouragement, and support, and to Carol Gluck and Madge Huntington, who guided me through the process toward publication. I am grateful as well for the help of Reynolds Smith, Justin Faerber, and the others at Duke University Press for their help during the publication process.

The research for this work was conducted with the support of a Fulbright-Hays Dissertation Research Grant in 1989–1990 and a Japan Foundation Dissertation Grant in 1990–1991. A Whiting Foundation Grant supported a year of dissertation writing in 1991–1992, and a grant from the Center for East Asian Studies at the University of Chicago provided support in the summer of 1992. The support of the National Endowment for the Humanities and the Japan Society for the Promotion of Science made it possible for me to complete my revisions in 1998–2000.

I am profoundly grateful to my family for their love and support during the long years of this book's gestation. Thanks to my parents, Frank and Shirley Burns, for teaching me the value of hard work and determination and for being exemplary grandparents, and to my sister, Barbara, for managing my affairs each and every time I depart for Japan. Finally, thanks to my daughter, Hannah, for being a great kid and my inspiration. This book is for her.

Introduction

Between Community and the Nation

In 1764 in the town of Matsuzaka in Ise province, a physician and part-time teacher of poetry and poetics took up the study of a then obscure work. His name was Motoori Norinaga (1730–1801), and the text that came to consume him was the Kojiki (*Records of Ancient Matters*). Dated to 712, the Kojiki tells of the creation of the Japanese islands by heavenly deities, the sun deity's command that her grandchild rule over these islands, and the process by which his descendants established and extended their rule as emperors. Today the Kojiki is regarded as a legitimating device produced by the early imperial court, but Norinaga argued that this work, the earliest extant text written in Japan, recorded oral transmissions handed down from the formative moment of his country and thus revealed the reality of an original and authentic Japan. For more than thirty years he labored over the exegesis of the Kojiki, moving character by character, line by line, producing an annotated version of the text that he called the Kojikiden (Commentaries on the Kojiki). In the Kojikiden, Norinaga argued that the Kojiki, correctly read, revealed that Japan—or sumeramikuni (the imperial land) as he termed it—had once been a harmonious community in which subject and ruler had lived in perfect communion with each other and with the deities, with no need for laws, institutions, principles, doctrines, or norms. This natural community gradually disappeared, however, after the beginning of cultural contact with China led to the introduction of flawed forms of knowledge in the form of Confucianism and Buddhism. Exposed to ethical principles and political theories, the Japanese people "lost" the capacity to relate to one another immediately and authentically. The result of the new self-consciousness that emerged was a society marked by discord and conflict, in which social relations were founded on coercion and force. Norinaga asserted that by stripping away these alien influences, it would be possible to recover the "real" Japan, the idyllic community of the past.

The *Kojikiden* sent shock waves through the intellectual circles of late Tokugawa Japan, which included Neo-Confucianists, Ancient Studies Confucianists, Shintoists associated with the Suika and Yoshida schools, and practitioners of what was known as *wagaku* or "Japanese studies." From the time chapters of this work began to circulate in the 1780s, and even more so after 1790, when its publication began, Norinaga met with both criticism and acclaim. His readers were astounded by his knowledge of the *Kojiki*, even as they were intrigued, confused, or angered by his claims about its meaning. Critics were many, but so too were converts. At the time of his death, Norinaga's school in Matsuzaka, known as the Suzuya, had almost five hundred students drawn from forty-three provinces, and he was recognized as the leader of the new intellectual practice that had come to be called *kokugaku* (the study of our country), a term coined to differentiate it from *kangaku* (Chinese studies).[1]

Like Norinaga, those who associated themselves with this new discourse took up the study of the handful of texts written in Japan in the eighth and ninth centuries and argued that these were central to understanding the nature of Japan as society, culture, and the source of individual identity. Through repeated acts of interpretation, they attempted to discover the nature of the community that they claimed had existed before writing, history, and memory. Thus kokugaku discourse unfolded through the process of textual exegesis, philological study, and grammatical explication, and the interrogation of issues of language and textuality was at the center of this practice. As a consequence, the conclusions of the kokugaku practitioners emerge through a complex network of annotated texts, not as straightforward expository prose. But the difficulty of this form should not obscure the issues that concerned them: What is "Japan"? How did it emerge and how is it maintained? What binds those within it together?

It is through the articulation and exploration of these questions that "Japan" began to be constituted as the primary mode of community, one that transcended and subsumed other sources of identity, such as status, occupation, religion, region, village, and city. To this point in Tokugawa Japan, philosophical discussions of community had, for the most part, been framed by Confucian theory, which explained human society as a network of interlocking hierarchical social relationships—ruler and subject, parent and child, husband and wife, teacher and student, and so on—that ideally were to be infused with benevolence from the superior and respect, even reverence, from the inferior. When individuals in these various social roles acted in conformance with the ethical requirements of their position, community took form. In Confucian analysis, "Japan" had no clearly defined status beyond a set of geographical borders: it was nothing more than a set of superficial "local" variations of universal and transcendent norms, although these norms were considered by many to be best exemplified in China. Norinaga and other kokugaku scholars began to question this understanding of the community by making "Japan" the locus of their discussions.

My use of the term "community" here and throughout this work is informed by the work of scholars such as Cornelius Castoriadus and Etienne Balibar. Castoriadus has argued that community takes form as the product of a regime of representation. He uses the term "social imaginary" to describe the domain of significations, the array of signifieds, practices, and symbols, the production of which allows a society to represent itself as a community of shared interests, beliefs, and ideals.[2] Similarly, Balibar has stated that community "is based on the projection of individual existence into a collective narrative, on the recognition of a common name, and on traditions lived as the trace of an immemorial past (even when they have been fabricated and inculcated in the recent past)."[3] Following Castoriadus and Balibar, I conceive of community as something that is "imagined" and thereby constituted through multiple acts of signification, representation, and narration. The goal of this study is to explore this process of production in relation to a distinct historical moment. In eighteenth- and nineteenth-century Japan, kokugaku discourse was not an exercise in antiquarianism, nor an expression of nostalgia, as some accounts have suggested. Rather, it was a moment of social formation in which one set of representations, one "imaginary," was beginning to fail and another was taking form.

The context of this transformation is the subject of the first two chapters, in which I explore the social, political, and intellectual context that gave rise to kokugaku discourse. Chapter 1 examines the "crisis of community" that began in the second half of the eighteenth century, as economic transformation, famine, and unrest made the politically authorized social divisions of samurai, merchant, artisan, and cultivator and the geographic divisions of domain, city, and village increasingly difficult to maintain. As popular unrest in the form of urban riots and rural uprisings increased, the response of the bakufu (the government of the Tokugawa shogun) and the domainal governments of his chief retainers was to attempt to shore up the boundaries upon which their authority depended. But both the dissolution of status and geographic constraints and the popular questioning of political claims to be governing ethically proved difficult to curtail.

Implicated in this moment of material and ideological crisis were the intellectual transformations that occurred in the eighteenth century. Chapter 2 explores this issue by examining how and why the *Kojiki* and *Nihon shoki* (*Chronicles of Japan*), the two texts that record the "Divine Age narrative" of Japan's mythic beginnings, were read in the Tokugawa period. In the early Tokugawa period, whether viewed as a metaphysical treatise or as a history, the Divine Age narrative was taken up in ways that affirmed the conceptions of social and political order that emanated from the political authorities, the shogun and his vassals, the daimyo. However, in the eighteenth century, a new awareness of history and a concern for language began to call into question such interpretations of the narrative. As a result, the *Kojiki* and *Nihon shoki* began to be regarded as works that offered a glimpse into a time and place very different from the Tokugawa world.

In his work *The Order of Books*, Roger Chartier explores the cultural impact of the circulation of books in early modern Europe. He argues that the rise of print literature led to the formation of new "communities of readers" and that these communities came to "transform forms of sociability, permit new modes of thought, and change people's relationship with power."[4] Chartier's notion of the "community of readers" is a useful one for understanding the nature of kokugaku as a social practice. The *Kojikiden* established the *Kojiki*, in particular, but the other early Japanese texts as well, as important new objects of analysis. As a result, kokugaku practice came to be centered around the act of reading and analyzing the ancient texts and the related processes of producing, circulating, and acquiring commentaries on them. Today, the *Kojiki*, *Nihon shoki*, the poetic anthology called the *Man'yōshū* (*The Ten Thousand Leaves*) and the other texts that preoccupied the kokugaku scholars are canonical works. They are the "classics" of Japanese literature and thus are available in authoritative standard texts by noted scholars. But in Tokugawa Japan, these texts were still of shifting and indeterminate value. Even the question of how to pronounce the Chinese characters that comprised them gave rise to prolonged and heated debate.

In chapters 3 through 6, I examine how the *Kojiki* and other early Japanese works were read by four very different kokugaku scholars. My point of departure is of course Norinaga's *Kojikiden*, the seminal work that was a consistent point of reference for all practitioners of kokugaku in the Tokugawa period. From there I turn to explore a series of texts written in the wake of and in explicit response to the *Kojikiden* by Ueda Akinari (1734–1809), Fujitani Mitsue (1767–1823), and Tachibana Moribe (1781–1849). Like Norinaga, these authors took as their object the *Kojiki* and the other ancient texts and through their exegesis sought to explain "Japan" by interrogating the nature of political authority in relation to the world of the Divine Age narrative and by describing what cultural identity as "Japanese" meant for the individual subject. Some scholars have characterized the kokugaku of the late eighteenth and early nineteenth century as either politically unengaged or as consistent with the Tokugawa social and political order, but I argue that in this period kokugaku scholars were profoundly implicated in questioning the distribution of power within their society.[5]

For those familiar with the modern Japanese literature on kokugaku, the decision to focus on works by Akinari, Mitsue, and Moribe will undoubtedly seem an odd one. In the major works on kokugaku produced in modern Japan, these authors do not figure greatly, if at all. Overwhelmingly, studies have focused on the work of what were termed the "great men" of kokugaku. Adopting a narrative of "development" or "evolution," the modern histories of kokugaku describe how in the mid-Tokugawa period Keichū (1640–1701) and Kada no Azumamaro (1669–1739) began to study the early Japanese texts in the midst of an intellectual world dominated by Confucianism.[6] However, it was not until the *Man'yōshū* studies of Kamo no Mabuchi (1697–1769) that Confucian paradigms of interpretation, in which history and literature were evaluated in light of their ethical value, were set aside. Then, in his work on the *Kojiki*, it is said, Norinaga finally succeeded in resurrecting the pre-Confucian worldview of the ancient Japanese, which was then popularized and politicized by his self-proclaimed student, Hirata Atsutane (1776–1843), in the 1830s and 1840s.

As this genealogy suggests, there is an important and ongoing national narrative in which kokugaku is valorized as the intellectual movement that marked the emergence of Japanese national consciousness in the late eighteenth century. As a consequence, the early modern discourse has come to be profoundly implicated in the modern Japanese discourses on the nation and nationness. This understanding of kokugaku began to take form in the late nineteenth century in the aftermath of the Meiji Restoration of 1868, the political revolution that overthrew the Tokugawa shogun, returned the emperor to power, and marked the beginning of Japan's transformation to a modern nation-state. For figures such as Haga Yaichi (1867–1927) and Mu-

raoka Tsunetsugu (1884–1946), scholars who began to define the content and
method of the modern academic disciplines of national literature and intellectual history in the late Meiji period, Norinaga's work marked the point of
beginning for the modern humanistic study of the nation, a study in which
they themselves were also involved as professors in Japan's new universi-
ties. They praised the "objectivity" and rigor of his analysis and embraced
the objects of inquiry that he defined. The result was the acceptance of the
problematic notion that an original and authentic Japan was recoverable as
a set of unique and enduring cultural values, including reverence toward the
imperial house based upon its claim of divine descent and a "national character" that was different from and superior to that of any other people. In
the 1930s and during the war years, the privileging of kokugaku reached new
heights in the hands of Yasuda Yojūrō and the other members of the Japan
romantic school, who engaged in a "revolt against the West" by celebrating
the uniqueness of Japanese culture, which Norinaga was said to have redis-
covered and preserved.[7]

In the aftermath of World War II, the centrality of kokugaku in intellectual discourse on national identity continued, but now some scholars identified it as the source of Japan's descent into militarism, war, and defeat. The
most influential of these critiques was Maruyama Masao's *Nihon seiji shisōshi
kenkyū* (Research on Japan's Political Thought, 1952).[8] In this work, Maruyama traces the intellectual character of the modern emperor system back
to eighteenth-century kokugaku and argues that the antirational impulses
he perceives as ordering this discourse prevented a truly critical intellectual
ethos from developing in Japan. This failure, Maruyama asserts, ultimately
contributed to Japan's descent into fascism. A similar argument is made in
Saigō Nobutsuna's *Kokugaku hihan* (A Critique of Kokugaku, 1948). Saigō argues that the method of Norinaga's *Kojikiden* was characterized by a set of
philological, historical, and ethnological fallacies that produced and sustained a "passive," "antiprogressive," and "conservative" political subject.[9]
In the same vein, Matsumoto Sannosuke has stated that "kokugaku thought
was an important source for the imperial ideology of the nation. I think that
the notion of politics in kokugaku and the logic which supported it is the
model for the politics and logic of national ideology after the Meiji period."[10]

Writing in the 1970s, however, Haga Noboru, the pioneering social historian of kokugaku, criticized the perspectives of Maruyama and Saigō. According to Haga, only by "making the study of kokugaku independent from
'politics' "—that is, from the political uses to which it was put in the pre-

World War II period—and placing it back within "popular history" (minshū-shi), does the true meaning of the discourse become apparent. Haga states, "In fact, kokugaku was not only a movement that occurred in Japan. It took form within the context of the ethnic movements for independence and the movements against colonization in East Asia in the second half of the nineteenth century."[11] As this statement suggests, Haga's interest is in the kokugaku of the so-called Bakumatsu period, the final decades of Tokugawa rule that followed the forced "opening" of the country in 1854. In contrast to the "unpolitical" kokugaku of Norinaga, Haga characterizes Bakumatsu kokugaku as "political" but in terms very different from Maruyama and Saigō: it was not "narrow" and exclusionary" but rather a "modern" and "humanistic" popular movement for ethnic self-determination.[12]

What unites both prewar and postwar scholarship on kokugaku then is the assumption of continuity and therefore explanatory power vis-à-vis modern Japanese national identity. Of course, the assessment of the ethicality of this nationalism has changed dramatically, from natural and beneficial before the war, to abnormal and virulent in its aftermath, and then in Haga's work, to modern and enlightened once again. My decision to approach kokugaku by abandoning the genealogy of "great men" and the narrative of development it instantiated is tied to the second purpose of this work. In addition to exploring the political meaning of kokugaku in the late eighteenth and early nineteenth century, I also reconsider the relation between the kokugaku discourse on "Japan as community" and the modern Japanese sense of nationness.

The origin of national identities is of course an issue that has long been pursued by historians, sociologists, and political scientists. In 1882 Ernest Renan delivered a talk before the Sorbonne, "What Is a Nation?" that still reverberates through contemporary discourse on the nation and nationalism. In it, Renan moved methodically through the various deterministic explanations of the formation of national communities then current in late nineteenth-century Europe. Race, language, dynastic principles, religious affinities, economic interests, and geographical boundaries are taken up, but each is dismissed in turn by means of reference to specific nations, the histories of which call into question any attempt to identify a general principle of nation formation. Renan concluded that "a nation is a soul, a spiritual principle. . . . [It is] a large-scale solidarity, constituted by the feeling of the sacrifices that one has made in the past and of those that one is prepared to make in the future."[13] In recent years, authors such as Eric Hobsbawm,

Benedict Anderson, and Homi Bhabha have focused on the "constituted" nature of the nation, by analyzing the processes by which the nation as a form of community and a mode of individual identity is produced and inculcated as real by means of specific political, social, and cultural practices in the context of the modern nation-state.[14] Thus Anderson explores the role of the print media in producing what he calls the "imagined community" of the nation, Hobsbawm examines the use of "invented traditions" to create a sense of a shared past and common culture, and Bhabha writes of the power of narrative to create a sense of nationness.

The notion that Japanese national identity was constituted in the modern period and then that moment of production was forgotten, hidden, or silenced, has oriented much recent work on Meiji Japan. In her study of Meiji ideology, Carol Gluck analyzes the role that nongovernmental figures, the civil (*minkan*) ideologues as she terms them, played in the production and diffusion of national identity in the late nineteenth century.[15] More recently, Takashi Fujitani has focused on the immediate post-1868 period and explored the role that state rituals, ceremonies, national holidays, and public buildings played in creating and inculcating mass nationalism. While Fujitani suggests that there may be early modern antecedents to the modern nation, citing in particular Harry Harootunian's work on kokugaku, he describes this phenomenon as an "inchoate and scattered sense of identity" that was transformed or "channeled" by the Meiji leadership into a modern nationalism.[16] My work departs from that of Fujitani and follows that of Harootunian in that it is precisely the discourse on Japanese identity that predates modern nationalism that I seek to interrogate. Prasenjit Duara has criticized the many recent studies of nationalism that deploy the terms "invented" and "imagined" to describe the nation in order to suggest that modern national consciousness necessarily represents a "radical discontinuity" with the past.[17] Duara describes such works as "ahistorical" and argues instead that there are complex and multiple relations between premodern representations of community and the modern nation precisely because "modern nationalism seeks to appropriate these pre-existing representations into the mode of being of the modern nation."[18] In his study of the formation of the modern Greek nation, Stathis Gourgouris makes a similar point when he states that "the nation goes so far as to borrow from [the] *archegonous* 'prehistorical' narrative precisely those elements that . . . make possible the notion of 'the national community,' the political hypostasis of modern nation and state."[19]

One scholar who has articulated the importance of prenational aspects of community for the formation of the nation is Etienne Balibar. The study of these elements, he suggests, would allow for the writing of the "prehistory" of the nation. Balibar succinctly delineates the difference between such a "prehistory" and the writing of the linear history of the nation:

> First, it consists of a multiplicity of qualitatively distinct events spread out over time, none of which implies any subsequent event. Second, these events do not of their nature belong to the history of *one* determinate nation. They have occurred within the framework of political units other than those which seem to us today endowed with an original ethical personality. . . . And they do not even belong to the history of the *nation*-state, but to other rival forms (for example, the "imperial" form). It is not a line of necessary evolution but a series of conjunctural relations which has inscribed them after the event into the prehistory of the nation form.[20]

It is as a "prehistory" of the nation form, in the sense that Balibar uses that term, that I view the kokugaku discourse of the late eighteenth and early nineteenth century. The "Japan" of which the kokugaku scholars spoke and the forms of community they envisioned do not evolve into, or produce, or explain modern Japanese "nationness." It is precisely to foreground the lack of linearity that I use the term "Japan as community" to describe the object of Tokugawa kokugaku practice, even at the risk of some awkwardness. Beginning in the 1880s, modern scholars would insist that the "Japan" of which Norinaga spoke was the nation-state Japan had become, and thus they termed kokugaku a discourse on Japan as nation, but I want to maintain a sense of distance and unfamiliarity. On the other hand, I do not mean to deny that there is a relationship between this discourse and that on the nation that emerged in the 1880s. As we shall see, the kokugaku discourse of the Tokugawa period provided a new vocabulary and a new set of epistemological strategies that were used to "think the nation" in the Meiji period.[21]

The project of writing the prehistory of Japanese nationness requires the disruption of the genealogy of "four great men" that has ordered so much of modern scholarship on kokugaku and which made possible the production of the narrative of development that is at its center. It was with this aim that I chose to juxtapose Norinaga's *Kojikiden* with the work of what are generally regarded as minor or marginal figures. Ueda Akinari, Fujitani Mitsue, and Tachibana Moribe are kokugaku scholars who appear for the most part as footnotes and asides in the major modern studies, but their status in the modern histories is at odds with their stature in their own time. Akinari, best known today as the writer of the collection of supernatural tales *Ugetsu monogatari* (*Tales of Moonlight and Rain*), was the student of one of Kamo no Mabuchi's favored disciples. In addition to writing studies of the *Kojiki*, *Man'yōshū*, and other texts, he engaged Norinaga in a widely discussed and publicized debate over how to interpret the Divine Age chapters of the *Kojiki*. Fujitani Mitsue was a well-known figure in Kyoto intellectual circles. His work of *Kojiki* exegesis, *Kojiki tomoshibi* (Illuminating the *Kojiki*), called into question every premise of Norinaga's textual practice. Tachibana Moribe too produced a series of exegetical texts that challenged Norinaga's conception of the *Kojiki* and the understanding of the Divine Age he produced from its reading. A prominent figure in and around Edo, in the 1840s his fame rivaled that of his now better known contemporary, Hirata Atsutane.

Akinari and the others lectured to students and wrote texts that were widely read and discussed. Like Norinaga, they declared themselves to be practitioners of kokugaku, even as they subjected Norinaga's work to a series of penetrating critiques. However, the designation in the modern period of Norinaga's work as the "mainstream" of kokugaku required that this other body of texts be dismissed as flawed, marginal, and hence without significance.[22] The rationale employed to effect this effacement took the form of a comparison between these textual traditions and that which was posited as "true" kokugaku. This comparison allowed these works to be characterized as tainted by extraneous influences or flawed in either their method or their results. Modern commentators have accordingly described Akinari's work as ordered by the rationalism of the Confucian tradition and thus at odds with the ethos of belief said to characterize kokugaku. Mitsue's work has been characterized as subject to any number of aberrant influences, including Taoism, Yoshida Shinto, Jōdo Buddhism, and medieval poetics. Tachibana Moribe, some have said, was a poor scholar whose philology was no match for that of Norinaga and whose theories derived from those of Hirata Atsutane.

Such characterizations are problematic on both theoretical and factual grounds. The arguments regarding influence are flawed not only in their attempt to posit some "pure" kokugaku that is free from deviance but also because even the most careful accounting of sources does not become an explanation or an analysis. Even more troubling is the relation of centrality and margin that such characterizations sustain. It was only the judgment of what kokugaku meant in the modern period that allowed historians to decide which works were significant and which were not. But this initial act of interpretation, which authorized the acts of selection that followed, has not been sufficiently interrogated. The modern understanding of kokugaku took form in the Meiji period, the time during which, as Gluck and Fujitani have noted, Japanese nationness was being produced and popularized both within and outside of government. It is at this moment that Norinaga's work came to be rendered canonical. Thus the genealogy of great men that took form is a cultural artifact that reveals much about Meiji notions of Japan as nation and far less about late Tokugawa concepts of Japan as community.

I am not the first to question the usefulness of the genealogy of great men for understanding the place of kokugaku in Tokugawa society. It has been critiqued before, most notably by Uchino Gorō, writing in 1970s.[23] Like Haga Noboru, Uchino wanted to "rescue" kokugaku from its associations with wartime ultranationalism. To this end, his work focuses on the so-called Edo school, kokugaku scholars associated with Kamo no Mabuchi, who took up poetry and poetics rather than the analysis of the Divine Age narrative. He made these scholars the point of origin for what he called *bungeishi* (the history of art and literature). In other words, against the politicized genealogy of the "four great men," he attempted to find another kokugaku that was purely literary and thus untainted by ideology. What is problematic of course is the easy opposition of the literary and the political. My analysis of the work of Norinaga, Akinari, Mitsue, and Moribe suggests that this opposition cannot be maintained, because discussion of poetry, poetics, and fiction was implicated in interrogating the Tokugawa political order. A more productive critique of the genealogy of great men is Harry Harootunian's *Things Seen and Unseen*.[24] While Harootunian comments on the work of Mabuchi and Norinaga, his focus is on that of Hirata Atsutane (1776–1843) and its reinterpretation in the hands of his rural disciples in the mid-nineteenth century. Harootunian uses figures such as Suzuki Shigetane, Mutobe Yoshika, and Miyauchi Yoshinaga to explore how kokugaku became a discourse that rendered the agricultural village a divinely authorized mode of community.

While my debt to Harootunian's analysis is apparent throughout this work, I take a different approach. The scholars I examine are not members of the same "school," that is, disciples of the same teacher, nor does a single privileged site such as the "village" thematically link their work. Rather, they represent disparate forms of kokugaku that, unlike the work of Atsutane's disciples, were not directly implicated in the Bakumatsu movement to bring down the Tokugawa bakufu. What allows me to bring them together is their interest in the Divine Age narrative and their determination to use the texts that inscribe it, the *Kojiki* and *Nihon shoki*, to construct new visions of community. My strategy of "reading from the margins" is not, however, meant to minimize the impact of Norinaga's work. Akinari, Mitsue, and Moribe all wrote in response to the *Kojikiden*, and it is this work that defined the terms of the discussion of Japan, but this dialogic relation does not mean that their work is unimportant. Rather, it is these heterogeneous and discontinuous textual traditions that together provide a point of access into what kokugaku was in the late Tokugawa period.

This discourse on the nature of Japan was ordered around a number of common themes. No single issue concerned Norinaga and his critics more than the nature and significance of the language of the ancient texts. Their discussions of etymology, morphology, phonetics, and syntax may strike modern readers as tedious and antiquarian, but questions of language were profoundly implicated in their discussions of community. In a society, where every act of speech and writing was shaped by variables such as gender, genre, dialect, status, and so on, the ideal of an original, authentic, and enduring "Japanese" language was a powerful means to explain and thereby constitute cultural identity.

To early Tokugawa scholars, the *Kojiki* appeared to be a work in Chinese, albeit a peculiar and corrupt Chinese. Norinaga, however, argued that the network of Chinese characters that comprised the text was in fact a sophisticated method of inscription meant to preserve the orality and immediacy of the archaic language. The recovery of this language was for him the means to resurrect what it had meant to be "Japanese" in the archaic period. Thus in the *Kojikiden* he abandoned the standard system of diacritical markers and pronunciation glosses used by earlier annotators and rewrote the *Kojiki* in the phonetic script known as *kana* in a feat of linguistic bravado so skilled that the "Chineseness" of the text ceased to be an issue for many. Jean Luc-Nancy has argued in his discussion of community that "nothing is more common to the members of a community, in principle, than a myth, or a group of myths. Myth and community are defined by each other."[25] In just such a way, it is this founding myth of an authentic Japanese language—so patently belied by the text of the *Kojiki* itself—that gave rise to and sustained much of the kokugaku discourse on Japan.

Issues of language reverberate through the work of Akinari, Mitsue, and Moribe, each of whom grappled with the idealization of orality upon which

Norinaga relied. What they all questioned, albeit from different perspectives, was the notion that the *Kojiki* narrative was transmitted orally within Japanese society unaltered from the Divine Age until that moment in the eighth century when it was finally inscribed. For Akinari, the notion of a text that preserved orality could not be sustained, and he eventually abandoned the analysis of the Divine Age altogether. In contrast, Mitsue and Moribe embraced language as a mode of cultural identity, but not on Norinaga's terms. Rejecting Norinaga's claim that the oral transmissions needed no interpretation but revealed directly and immediately the reality of the archaic world, Mitsue asked who spoke, to whom, and why. He argued that the *Kojiki* was inscribed in poetic language by the emperor Jinmu, the first emperor of the "Age of Men," who employed a complex system of metaphors to explain how he was able to establish his rule and constitute Japan as a community. Moribe too found Norinaga's conception of orality untenable. He argued that at the moment when the *Kojiki* narrative was passed from the deities to men, it was transformed by the process of transmission as the people of ancient Japan altered and adapted it through the use of metaphor, allegory, and rhetorical embellishment.

For Norinaga, the issue of language was intimately tied to his assertion that in the ancient period the Japanese people had perceived and experienced the world very differently from their descendants in his own time. He argued that before contact with China, the Japanese people had lived "naturally" (*onozukura*) in union with the deities, the emperor, and one another, but with the introduction of Confucianism and Buddhism came ideas, norms, and values that were not "natural" but human in origin. When Norinaga spoke of "returning to the Divine Age," he referred to the recovery of the mode of subjectivity—the form of consciousness that made unquestioning belief in the deities possible and made political institutions unnecessary—that had been lost. Within kokugaku discourse after Norinaga, the consideration of what it meant to "be Japanese" became the discursive site where kokugaku scholars pursued the vertical relations of power that were so much a part of their world. Akinari, Mitsue, and Moribe relentlessly pursued the nature of the relation between the "private" world of the individual subject and the "public" world constituted by political authority, but each questioned the regime of cultural difference that ordered Norinaga's account.

My exploration of the kokugaku discourse on Japan focuses on the period from 1780, when Norinaga's *Kojikiden* began to circulate, up until the 1840s, when Moribe was writing. But the debate over the nature of community did not end then. In the 1850s and 1860s, the kokugaku movement came to be implicated in the growing social turmoil that followed the "opening" of Japan. As criticism of the Tokugawa bakufu grew, some kokugaku practitioners began to call for radical political change, the restoration of the emperor to the political role he had played in Japan a millennium before, a goal many initially believed was achieved in 1868. This kind of kokugaku was termed *fukko* or "restorationist" kokugaku.[26] In the first years of the Meiji period, figures associated with the restorationist kokugaku schools took up positions of influence in the new Office of Shinto Worship, as well as in other offices and bureaus of the new government. But even at this moment, a new vision of Japan as modern nation-state was taking form among Japan's new leaders, many of whom soon grew impatient with the kokugaku practitioners' attempts to define policy by reference to antiquity. As nation building began in earnest in the 1870s, kokugaku visions of Japan as community came to be mediated by new notions of nationness.

Partha Chatterjee has focused on the rise of nationalism within the colonial situation and argued that in Asia, Africa, and Latin America, discourse on nationness has a complexity that distinguishes it from European examples. He argues that for the non-West, nationalism is a "derivative discourse" that involved the implementation of social codes, cultural categories, and frameworks of thought that were other. Moreover, it was implicated in new relations of power at each moment and every level of this process—between the different cultures in question certainly, but also between the intellectuals who accept the new discourse and those who do not, between intellectuals and the mass of people. The consequence of this problematic process has been, in Chatterjee's words, a series of suppressed possibilities and unresolved contradictions for the people of non-Western cultures who have been "seduced, apprehended, and imprisoned" by the specter of the nation.[27] Of course, Japan in the late nineteenth century had a very different political status than did India, the country that is Chatterjee's point of reference. It was a sovereign nation-state, not a colony. Nonetheless, the cultural and political relations of power of which he speaks informed social and political discourse on Japan as nation in the Meiji period.

In chapter 7, I explore the status of kokugaku in this new context, focusing in particular on how historians of thought and literature came to recoup kokugaku as a discourse on the nation. Modern academicians such as Haga Yaichi and Muraoka Tsunetsugu were all too aware of the claims of cultural supremacy that emanated from Europe and America. They worked hard to prove that Japan's indigenous "civilization" was as modern as anything the West had to offer. It was in this context that the genealogy of great men took form in order to demonstrate that kokugaku was both "national" and "scientific." Yet even as a reconstituted "new kokugaku" was transformed into an intellectual orthodoxy, other forms of intellectual practice emerged on the margins of mainstream academia. While relegated to the footnotes of the histories of the nation, the works of Akinari, Mitsue, and Moribe continued to be read. In the hands of intellectuals such as Origuchi Shinobu (1887–1953) and Tsuda Sōkichi (1873–1961), who questioned the theories of Japanese culture emanating from the state in the 1910s and 1920s, this body of texts was used to suggest the possibility of "imagining" a different Japan.

E. J. Hobsbawm opens his influential work *Nations and Nationalism since 1780* with a brief fable about aliens who arrive on earth in the aftermath of a nuclear holocaust that destroyed all life on this planet. The visitors quickly come to the conclusion that the last two hundred years of human history and the cause of the cataclysmic war that ended it are inextricably tied to an institution called the "nation," but they are at a loss to grasp what this term means exactly and why it came to have such a hold on human emotions.[28] Hobsbawm's point is that the idea of the nation is inextricably bound up with the political, cultural, and social exigencies of modern experience, so much so that we have a difficult time thinking beyond the notion of the nation that has come to be embedded in the histories, cultures, and social norms of the countries in which we live. Thinking beyond the nation is something that still eludes me, but in this work I hope to catch a glimpse of a moment before the nation.

Chapter 1

Late Tokugawa Society and the Crisis of Community

Miroslav Hroch, the pioneer social historian of European nation-formation, has argued that "for national consciousness to arise, there must be something for it to become conscious of."[1] His point is that historically the constitution of the nation as a new locus of identity has occurred in the context of a set of socioeconomic transformations that made it possible to begin to think beyond traditional conceptions of community. These transformations include a social or political crisis of the old order that brings rising discontent among many within a society and a loss of faith in traditional moral systems, new forms of social and geographic mobility resulting from the commercialization of agriculture and handicraft production in the countryside, and a high level of social communication made possible by expanding rates of literacy, the formation of schools, and the rise of market relations. Within this kind of social setting, as traditional ties weakened or dissolved, new collective identities began to take form.[2] Significantly, Hroch, while focusing on the social context that gives rise to nationalism, avoids the reductionism and determinism that have characterized some attempts to explain the rise of nationalism. The social changes he delineates are not presented as the "causes" of nationalism, but rather as a set of conditions that contributed to its conceptualization.

Hroch's work focused on European society, but his discussion provides a framework for reconsidering the developments that shaped Japanese society in the late Tokugawa period as the kokugaku discourse on Japan emerged. This was a tumultuous era, marked by economic change, natural disasters, famine, and unrest, but also by new forms of cultural production, spurred by expanding literacy, a burgeoning publication industry, and the creation and diffusion of popular media. It was in this context, as older explanations of how society "worked" became increasingly difficult to maintain, that Norinaga, Akinari, Mitsue, and Moribe began to rethink the political, social, and geographic divisions that ordered their world. The prolonged debate over the nature of Japan in which they engaged is the focus of the chapters that follow, but in this chapter I want to discuss the social conditions that mediated their attempts to explore community.

THE READERS IN QUESTION

The background of the kokugaku scholars themselves provides a window into the complexity of late Tokugawa Japan. While the founders of the Tokugawa political order had envisioned a society in which social and geographic mobility would be limited and in which the *bushi* or samurai as scholar-officials would be at the center of cultural productions, the experiences of Norinaga, Akinari, Mitsue, and Moribe suggest how inadequate this conception had become. They are a heterogeneous group, and the course of their lives defies easy generalization by means of reference to either social or spatial boundaries.

Motoori Norinaga was born in 1730 in Matsuzaka, the second son of a wealthy cotton merchant, Ozu Sadatoshi.[3] After his father's death in 1740, the family's finances suffered, but they were still affluent enough to provide Norinaga with a good education. He was schooled in Confucian texts like many merchant sons of his day and also received lessons in poetry composition, tea ceremony, and *nō* chanting. At the age of sixteen Norinaga was sent to an uncle's shop in Edo as an apprentice, but he returned home after only one year after apparently showing no talent for business. He was then adopted into the Imaida family, paper merchants in Yamada, a town not far from Matsuzaka. However, life with his adopted family apparently did not go smoothly, and he again returned home to Matsuzaka. When his elder brother died in 1751, Norinaga became the head of the family and at that point changed the family name from Ozu to Motoori, a reference to a samurai ancestor of the pre-1600 period. The following year he was sent to Kyoto by his mother to study medicine, with the hope that this would provide him with an occupation.

Norinaga studied in Kyoto for more than five years, and in this city, one of the cultural centers of his day, he quickly became involved in the primary forms of intellectual practice of his day. He studied with Hori Keizan, an eclectic Confucian scholar who was trained in Neo-Confucianism, but who also had a profound interest in the work of revisionist Confucianists such as Ogyū Sorai. At the same time, he actively pursued training in the composition of *waka* poetry and attended many poetry competitions. It was in Kyoto that Norinaga came into contact with the emerging discourse of wagaku, or "Japanese studies," when he happened upon a work by Keichū, a Buddhist monk who wrote on the *Man'yōshū* and other early Japanese works. In 1757, Norinaga completed his medical studies and returned to Matsuzaka where he began to practice medicine, the occupation that would provide his main source of income for the rest of his life. About the same time he also began to read works by Kamo no Mabuchi, another scholar of wagaku, and to offer instruction in poetics and the *Genji monogatari* (*The Tale of Genji*) to acquaintances in Matsuzaka. In 1763 he was able to meet Kamo no Mabuchi for the first and only time and formally enrolled as his student. The following year he began his research on the *Kojiki*.

Ueda Akinari too was raised within a merchant household. Born in 1734 to a "pleasure woman" (*yūjo*) in the brothel district of Osaka, he was adopted and raised in a family of retail merchants who sold oil and paper.[4] He was educated to some extent in the private Confucian academy, the Kaitokudō, which was located near his childhood home in the Dōjima section of Osaka, and also received training in waka and the linked verse form known as *haikai*. In 1755 he took over the management of the family business, but at the same time he was writing prose fiction; he eventually published two popular collections of stories in the mid-1760s. Akinari would later recall that it was around this time that he first became interested in the early Japanese texts when he, like Norinaga, stumbled upon a work by Keichū while in Kyoto, a city to which he often traveled to attend poetry gatherings. He soon began to search for a teacher and in 1766 became the student of Katō Umaki, a samurai and bakufu official who was a disciple and intimate of Kamo no Mabuchi. In 1771 Akinari's home and business were destroyed in a fire, and he turned to the study of medicine. From 1776, he supported himself by practicing medicine, a profession he shared with Norinaga, all the while continuing to teach, edit, and write commentaries on the ancient Japanese texts.

Unlike Norinaga and Akinari, Fujitani Mitsue was of samurai status.[5] At the age of nineteen, Mitsue's father, Nariakira, was adopted into the Fujitani family, samurai who served the Tachibana family, the daimyo of Yanagawa (present-day Fukuoka prefecture). For the generous annual stipend of 200 *koku* of rice, Nariakira and later Mitsue maintained the Kyoto residence of the Tachibana, oversaw the delivery and storage of their tax rice in Osaka, and managed their financial transactions in that city. Nariakira's natural father, Minagawa Nariyoshi, was a dealer in antiques, but he had an interest in scholarship that he conveyed to his children. The Confucian scholar, Minagawa Kien, was Nariakira's elder brother, and Nariakira himself was well known for his scholarship. His most famous works are the *Kazashisho* and the *Ayuisho*, both of which attempted the morphological exploration of the Japanese language. Born in 1768 into this family that valued scholarship, Mitsue was schooled in the most important cultural forms of his age. When he was twelve he began to study the orthodox tradition of waka composition with an aristocrat of the Dōjō school, which emphasized rigid adherence to the poetic conventions of the imperial anthology, the *Kokinwakashū* (Collected Poems from Ancient and Modern Times, 905). He was, at the same time, being tutored in the Confucian classics by his uncle, and in his mid-teens he became the disciple of a noted haikai poet. Mitsue would later recall that it was as a youth of sixteen or seventeen (that is, c. 1784–1785) that he first attempted to read the *Kojiki* and *Nihon shoki* and sought out Norinaga's works as an aid to understanding them.

The early life of Tachibana Moribe, the final figure in this study, stands in sharp contrast to that of Norinaga, Akinari, and Mitsue. He was born in 1781 in a village called Obuke in Ise province, the eldest son of Iida Motochika, the village headman.[6] However, while Moribe was still quite young, his father lost his position as headman and was exiled from the village, a punishment that seems to have been related to a peasant uprising that occurred in Ise during his tenure as headman. In the turbulent decade of the 1780s the Ise region was the site of rural violence, as crop failures following a destructive flood and increased demands from the local lord for corvée labor angered cultivators. Motochika, as headman, may have been held responsible when his fellow villagers participated in the rebellion. In the aftermath of his father's exile, the family fell into poverty. Moribe was passed from relative to relative, sometimes living in Edo, sometimes in Osaka. He seems to have received little formal education, until as a young man he began to educate himself by reading the Confucian classics and works on Chinese and Japanese history. Eventually he was able to support himself by teaching reading and writing to children in his neighborhood. Then, when he was in his late twenties, Moribe began to study the early Japanese texts with Shimizu Hamaomi, a scholar associated with the Mabuchi school.

As these biographical sketches reveal, the kokugaku scholars whose work I explore were the products of very different circumstances. While Mitsue lived a life of privilege and ease, Moribe's youth was marked by poverty. While Norinaga, with the exception of his five years in Kyoto, lived his entire life in the provincial town of his birth, Akinari was the quintessential urban man of culture who moved between Osaka and Kyoto, respectively the second and third largest cities in this period. While both Norinaga and Akinari became physicians, an occupation of not particularly high status or repute, Mitsue held an important domainal post. The involvement of these four figures in kokugaku discourse points not only to the ideologically problematic fluidity of late Tokugawa society, but also to the emergence of a pervasive sense of crisis as people "located" throughout Japanese society began to view the social and political order of the day as flawed.

A WORLD IN DISORDER

Things were not right in the world. Such was the opinion of a man known by the pseudonym Bunyō Inshi, who in the early nineteenth century began to compose what he called *Seji kenbun roku* (A Record of Worldly Affairs Seen and Heard). The title of this work itself is significant because it points to a new concern for recording, describing, and analyzing events of the day that was shared by many of his contemporaries. For Bunyō, the proper state of things was self-evident. Regarding the samurai, he wrote, "The behavior of the bushi is a model for the world, and it is their duty to investigate the good and the bad, the right and wrong of the people, and to bestow punishments and rewards. Therefore they should not be at all extravagant, nor cynical, nor avaricious, but rather should devote their lives to the country and to demonstrating loyalty and filial piety." Peasants, on the other hand, "should always obey the rules of their lords and the fief-holders, perform the corvée required of them, carry out their various duties, and produce the five grains and all the other things the country requires." [7] As these remarks suggest, Bunyō's view of the world was ordered by the status divisions — samurai, peasant, artisan, and merchant — authorized by the Tokugawa political order and infused with the Confucian view that these social groups were functionally tied to each other. When farmers farmed, and samurai ruled, the result was an orderly and harmonious society.

However, Bunyō argued that in his own day samurai and peasants had abandoned their proper roles, clear evidence of which was the immorality, conflict, and confusion he detected everywhere. Why had the world gone so awry? For Bunyō that too was clear:

Recently the policies of the lords and the fief holders are all about profit, and they try to increase taxes, to lend money so as to make a return, and to learn the ways of commerce. The people too learn from such policies and compete to make a profit, and then the lords and the fief holders show favor to those who seek profits and praise them for expanding the wealth of the domains. . . . All have abandoned the rules from ancient times and lost the principles of humane governance.[8]

Clearly, Bunyō regarded commercialization—"the pursuit of profit," in his terms—as a development that was undermining the social and political order of his day. The political system established in the seventeenth century under the Tokugawa shoguns was founded upon the division of the country into discrete economic sectors: the villages were envisioned as subsistence-agricultural economies organized around the production of tax rice, while the castle-towns and the three great cities of Edo, Osaka, and Kyoto were to be sites of artisanal production, commercial activity, and consumption. To some extent, this ideal was always a myth, but it became patently so after 1750, as cultivators in the villages began to participate in an expanding market economy both by producing goods for sale and by buying goods produced elsewhere.

The development of the textile industry is not only a useful case study of the process of rural commercialization; it also had direct implications for two of the kokugaku scholars who figure in this study. Cotton cultivation, which had begun in the seventeenth century in the area around Osaka, gradually expanded throughout much of the country in the eighteenth century.[9] Soon, farmers who were cultivating cotton also began to engage in spinning and weaving. By the mid-eighteenth century, all stages of production, from cultivation to the bleaching of cotton and processing of bleached cloth, were being carried out in rural areas. One important site of cotton production was the Ise area in present-day Mie prefecture, where Norinaga lived most of his life. Both Norinaga and many of those who joined his school, the Suzuya, came from merchant families who sold locally produced cloth as far away as Edo. Silk textiles too began to be produced in rural areas in the late eighteenth century. Beginning in the 1760s, artisans in the Kiryū region (present-day Gunma prefecture) and the area around the city of Toyama mastered the techniques of Kyoto craftsmen and began to produce fine quality silk fabrics. As local artisans' demand for raw silk grew, farmers in these regions began to engage in silkworm cultivation and to spin silk thread. By the early decades of the nineteenth century, the quality and quantity of its silk fabrics was such that Kiryū was known as the "Nishijin of the east," a description that evoked the great textile producers of Kyoto. In the late 1820s, a group of Kiryū merchants began to study kokugaku under Tachibana Moribe; they became his main source of income for the next two decades.

In the mid- and late eighteenth century, other rural areas were similarly transformed by the growth of local industries. For example, in regions where rapeseed had long been grown, villagers began to process this raw material into lamp oil, rather than transporting it to Osaka, a development that was devastating for manufacturers and merchants there. In villages outside of Edo such as Choshi, and later Sawara and Noda, villagers established breweries and began to produce soy sauce for consumers in Edo, to the detriment of long-established producers in Kyoto and Osaka.[10] The effects of this kind of rural commercialization reverberated through Japanese society, causing tension at every level. As villagers turned to the production of such cash crops as cotton, rapeseed, and soybeans, rice yields began to fall and rice prices rose. The urban population as a whole suffered from the inflation that resulted, but especially hard hit were the samurai, most of whom were dependent upon stipends paid in rice out of their lord's granaries.

Economic problems contributed as well to growing tension between the bakufu and the domainal governments, many of which were already experiencing financial difficulties by the mid-eighteenth century. In the 1760s and 1770s, the shogun's chief advisor, Tanuma Okitsuga, alienated many daimyo when he aggressively pursued policies that aimed to improve bakufu finances, such as the confiscation of domainal territory and the selling of monopoly rights to raw materials produced in the domains. Such policies might have improved bakufu's finances, but they caused hardship for the domains involved. When Tanuma's patron, the shogun Ieharu, died in 1786, a group of angry daimyo drove him from office.[11] But their criticisms of Tanuma's policies notwithstanding, daimyo too were experimenting with new financial policies designed to tap the wealth of commercial development. Some domainal governments began to directly market products produced in their domains in Edo and Osaka, while others began to tax goods as they moved from producer to wholesaler or from wholesalers to retailers in the cities.[12] In many instances, domainal authorities simply established monopolies that allowed them to control distribution and retain a large percentage of the profits for themselves. Such policies too became a source of conflict: in some cases angry merchants and commercial farmers, whose profits were being siphoned off by the domainal government, banded together to challenge daimyo authority.

Within the villages, commercialization allowed some villagers access to heretofore inaccessible luxuries such as soy sauce, tatami, and silk. Yet prosperity came at a cost. Increasingly, villagers were divided into two groups: a small land-owning group whose profits from commercial activity allowed them to accumulate land and a much larger group of cultivators who had mortgaged or sold their lands to richer neighbors and thus were left with no land at all or plots too small to sustain their families.[13] For many poor cultivators, life in the cities as a day-laborer or servant was preferable to a marginal existence in their home villages, and they fled to Edo or Osaka. In contrast, affluent farmers and merchants in the emergent "local towns" (*zaigōmachi*) used their new-found wealth to participate in cultural life as never before. They took up the study of poetry and the tea ceremony, bought books, and traveled to and from the cities in increasing numbers. But their new status was fragile. Wealthy villagers needed to keep their land under cultivation in order to pay their taxes on their entire holdings, but agricultural labor was expensive and difficult to obtain. Thus it was all too easy to fall into debt when crops failed or agricultural labor became difficult to procure.

The result of the division of wealth in the villages was growing instability and conflict. Perhaps the best indicator of this trend was a marked increase in the number of peasant uprisings (ikki) after 1750, when commodity production took off.[14] According to the analysis of Aoki Kōji, the number of protests rose from an average of 4.9 per year in the seventeenth century to an average of 14.4 between 1751 and 1800 and to 16.3 between 1801 and 1850. The nature of protests changed as well. They became larger and more disorderly—and had new targets. As Stephen Vlastos has demonstrated, in the early Tokugawa period, rebellions took the form of "peaceful appeals" for benevolence from those above, in which peasants asked for tax relief or disaster aid from the political authorities of their domain. In contrast, the peasant rebellions of the late Tokugawa period were frequently mass demonstrations that involved significant destruction of property. Moreover, the object of much of this violence was not samurai officials invested with political authority, but the wealthy within the villages, village headmen, landlords, and rural merchants, whose homes were subjected to "housebreaking" (uchi-kowashi) by angry mobs. The vulnerability of these groups to such violence was clearly recognized. In 1833, for example, Tachibana Moribe wrote to Yoshida Akinushi, one of the Kiryū merchants who was his student, to report that a riot that had broken out in the post-town of Satte in Musashino, where Moribe had lived for some years before taking up residence in Edo. He noted that in a single evening rioters had looted and burned more than twenty-four merchant houses and urged Akinushi as a merchant and man of means to exercise caution: "since people are aroused in this way, you should be on your guard there as well. During this period, it is best to act with restraint in all things."[15]

Adding to the disorder and strife of this period were a series of natural disasters, bad harvests, and famines. Like Bunyō Inshi, the physician and "Dutch learning" scholar Sugita Genpaku (1733–1817) too recorded and analyzed contemporary events. In the third section of the work he called *Nochimigusa* (Notes for Later Consideration), Genpaku chronicled the unprecedented string of disasters that occurred in the 1780s.[16] In 1782, sustained rains in the spring led to flooding around the country, and in the summer an earthquake struck in Odawara, with many deaths and much damage to property. In the next year, in the Kantō region, heavy rains continued, and it was so cold that people wore their winter clothing well into the spring. Then, the volcano known as Mount Asama became active. Genpaku reported that the major eruption on the eighth day of July buried "more than twenty thousand people and many cows and horses," and spread volcanic ash "as far west as Shinshū and Karuizawa and as far east as Takasaki and Maebashi," killing crops throughout the Kantō area, while in the rest of the country, the cold weather resulted in poor harvests. In the domains in the Tōhoku region where little or no rice was salvaged, every day "one or two thousand people" fled their villages for Edo or other domains, while some who remained behind were reduced to eating corpses. According to one refugee whom Genpaku quoted, in the areas of Matsumae and Mutsu (present-day Hokkaido and Aomori prefectures), there were villages where no living person remained, and corpses lay rotting in the fields.[17] Order was restored to some degree in 1785–1786, as the agricultural situation improved, but 1786 was another disastrous year marked by strong winds, an earthquake near Hakone, and heavy rains, which resulted in flooding "of an extent never heard of before," according to Genpaku.[18] Again, the country experienced the cycle of widespread crop failures, famine, and starvation.

In his recent social history of famine in early modern Japan, Kikuchi Isao estimates that perhaps 300,000 people died of starvation and disease in 1783 and 1784, the peak famine years of the 1780s. Reports to the bakufu from domains in the Tōhoku region on rice yields from this period suggest the extent of the disaster: Hirosaki reported that no rice was harvested in 1783, Hachi-nohe, that of an expected harvest of 20,000 koku, 19,336 was lost; Morioka, that of 100,000 koku, 65,670 were lost.[19] The result was unprecedented rural unrest: in 1783 there were forty peasant uprisings and in 1787, forty-four, figures that were roughly triple Aoki's average for the second half of the eighteenth century.[20] In cities and towns, resources were strained by the large number of refugees from the stricken regions, and the scarcity of rice—and hoarding by speculators—meant huge increases in prices. Genpaku reported that at one point in the spring of 1787, rice prices in Edo had increased more than tenfold.[21] The urban population responded to economic distress with riots that were marked by "housebreaking." Between 1781 and 1788, there was an average of twenty-six urban uprisings per year, more than three times as many as during the peak of the last great period of famine, that of 1732.[22] In 1783, there were riots in Osaka and Kyoto, as well as in rural towns such as Yamada in Ise and Ōta in Iwami, but the next great famine year, 1787, was marked by even greater violence. In the spring of that year, rioters protesting the high price of rice filled the streets of Edo for four days, destroying more than five hundred shops including those of rice merchants, moneylenders, and sake brewers. Finally a bakufu force of three thousand men succeeded in restoring order to the city.[23]

In his account of the famine of the 1780s, Genpaku took note that the beginning of this difficult period coincided with the change of the era name from An'ei to Tenmei in 1781. He commented that from the outset many people found the term tenmei (literally, "bright heaven") inauspicious because of its resemblance to the term "the mandate of heaven" (tenmei), and he noted that as the era progressed events brought to mind the proverb that "heaven has no mouth and so speaks through men."[24] This evocation of the Confucian notion of political legitimacy is revealing of the framework of Genpaku's work. His chronicle of famine, suffering, and unrest was also a critique of the bakufu leadership, particularly of Tanuma Okitsuga, who had forged bakufu policy since 1769.[25] Genpaku viewed these events not as "natural" disasters that were beyond human control but as evidence of the need for "world renewal" (yonaoshi), a term that from the 1780s onward gained currency as a popular demand for social and political change. When Tanuma's son, Okitomo, was assassinated inside Edo castle in 1784, the people of the city heralded his killer as "a great deity of world renewal" (yonaoshi daimyōjin), and those who participated in the Edo riot of 1787 made "world renewal" their battle cry.[26]

THE INFORMATION SOCIETY AND
POLITICAL CRITIQUE

There had of course been crop failures and famines throughout Japanese history. What distinguished the Tenmei famine of the 1780s and next great famine, the so-called Tenpō famine of the 1830s, from earlier ones was that in this period information could be disseminated as never before. The result was an explosion of discourse on famine conditions, the social unrest that accompanied them, and the perceived failure of political authorities to provide relief to the suffering. Kabayama Kōichi has argued that this led to the emergence of new forms of social and political critique, and he has described late Tokugawa society as "a culture born of famine."[27] Just how well informed Japanese were of the events of their time is revealed by records from two villages located in the northern province of Dewa (present-day Akita and Yamagata prefectures), an area far removed from the cultural centers of Edo, Osaka, and Kyoto. Events such as the eruption of Mount Asama, the assassination of Tanuma Okitomo and the ouster of his father soon after, the Edo riots, and the rise of Matsudaira Sadanobu as chief official of the bakufu were all known to the villagers. They also recorded information about the worsening famine conditions, noting estimates of the number of dead in particular areas and the outbreaks of violence in castle towns such Sendai, Yamagata, and elsewhere.[28]

In his home in Matsuzaka where his work on the *Kojiki* was just beginning to bring him fame, Motoori Norinaga too was intimately aware of developments around the country. In his journal entries during the 1780s, Norinaga carefully recorded the rising price of rice and noted the rumors he heard regarding mass starvation in northern Honshu and peasant uprisings throughout the country. His entry for the last day of 1786 stated, "the whole world is suffering from extreme poverty."[29] Entries from the spring of the next year detailed the course of urban uprisings. In the fifth month, Norinaga wrote, "in Osaka there was a great riot, and also riots are occurring one after another without pause in Wakayama, Hyōgo, Okazaki, and various places. From the evening of the twentieth day until the twenty-third or twenty-fourth, there was a great riot in Edo."[30] In the next month he noted a new development in Kyoto: commoners from nearby provinces were journeying to that city to pray at the imperial palace for good harvests.[31]

What accounts for this unprecedented flow of information around the country? To be sure, the eighteenth century saw the burgeoning of Japan's publishing industry, well established since the mid-seventeenth century. The number of works published in Edo alone almost doubled between the 1730s and the 1770s, and publishers in Kyoto and Osaka were flourishing as well. The publishing industry declined in the mid-1780s when new censorship laws went into effect, but it rebounded as these restrictions were relaxed. By the early nineteenth century, there were 917 publishers active in Edo, 494 in Kyoto, and 504 in Osaka. Beginning in the 1780s and 1790s "bestsellers" sold as many as 10,000 copies.[32] This period was also marked by the proliferation of commercial lending libraries or *kashi hon'ya*, which made books available to many who would have been unable to purchase them outright. According to one source, there were 656 "book lenders" in Edo in 1806.[33] And the business of selling and lending books was by no means limited to the major cities. The number of publishers operating outside of the three major cities increased tenfold between the seventeenth and nineteenth centuries.[34] By the early nineteenth century, book peddlers regularly brought books to wealthy farmers and merchants living in the villages outside of the major cities, and even rural towns had lending libraries.[35]

However, the expansion of publishing contributed only partially to the spread of information about contemporary matters. From the late seventeenth century onward, the bakufu forbade the publication of books that contained any reference to the shogun or past shoguns, their vassals, or any matter pertaining to them without permission from the office of the magistrate. In 1722 these restrictions were expanded to include works dealing with "unorthodox matters" and with sexual content. Bookstores and lending libraries succeeded in circumventing these restrictions by circulating works that dealt with forbidden subject matter, political or otherwise, in manuscript form.[36] A case in point is a work entitled *Nakayama monogatari* (The Tale of Nakayama), which dealt with a conflict that emerged between the bakufu and the imperial court in 1789. Authored by a courtier named Nakayama Naruchika, it described in terms favorable to the imperial family the efforts of the emperor Kōkoku (reigned 1779–1817) to bestow the title of *Dajō Tennō*, one traditionally reserved for retired emperors, upon his father, although the latter had been passed over for succession. In a show of power, the bakufu refused to honor the emperor's request. The *Nakayama monogatari* circulated widely through lending libraries until the bakufu banned it and ordered that manuscripts of the work be burned and the rental shops that stocked it, punished.[37] Known as "records of true events" (*jitsurokumono*), works such as *Nakayama monogatari* became a significant part of the stock of the lending libraries, which profited by circulating these works that would not have passed the scrutiny of bakufu censors.

Another means of disseminating information were the broadsheets known as *yomiuri* or *kawaraban*. In the late eighteenth and early nineteenth century these rough, one- or two-page, wood-block prints disseminated news about a wide variety of topics including such things as natural disasters, scandals, riots and uprisings, samurai vendettas, and sightings of foreign ships.[38] Just how important a medium these became can be seen from a work known as *Ukiyo no arisama* (The State of Things in the Floating World), whose anonymous author lived in Osaka. He carefully recorded the events of his day from 1806 until the late 1840s and makes repeated mention of kawaraban as the source of his information.[39] Contributing to the spread of information via kawaraban, as well as letters, manuscript texts, and word of mouth was the establishment of many private networks of express messengers in the late eighteenth century. As commercial activity increased in the late eighteenth century, these messenger services expanded rapidly, increasing the number of places to which they made delivery and the speed of deliveries. By the early nineteenth century, a letter or document could travel from Kyoto to Edo in only two days.[40]

The spread of information via new forms of media and new networks of communication gave rise to what Konta Yōzō has termed an "expanding geographic consciousness," which began to breakdown the regional, domainal, and urban-rural divides that had characterized Japanese society to this point.[41] Konta argues that this geographic consciousness was linked to the rise of popular political commentary and criticism like that which infused the works of Bunyō Inshi and Sugita Genpaku. Attacks on political authorities abound in the jitsuroku, kawaraban, letters, diaries and other modes of popular discourse from this period. In the 1780s, for example, authors of the illustrated books known as *kibyōshi* (literally "yellow cover-books") began to parody contemporary political events and figures. One of the most provocative of these was Hōseidō Kisanji's *Bunbu nidō mangoku dō-shi* (A Sieve for Separating Martial Arts and Letters, 1788), which ridiculed the attempts of Matsudaira Sadanobu to encourage members of the samurai class to cultivate martial skills and scholarly pursuits. Hōseidō set his tale in the Kamakura period in order to pass the bakufu censors, but the thrust of his satire was clearly contemporary: there was no one among the retainers of the shogun who was interested in engaging in either intellectual or physical training. Other kibyōshi dealt with matters such as Tanuma Okitsuga's fall from power, the Tenmei riots in Edo, and Matsudaira Sadanobu's attempts at reform.[42]

Political attacks were expressed in other forms of media as well. Konta notes that the 1780s were marked by a proliferation of *rakushu* and *rakugaki*, satirical verses and jottings that were posted in public spaces, many of which were recorded in jitsuroku-type writings. A verse from the 1780s states, "How stupid they are—the senior councilors." Another, seemingly addressed to the political authorities, is equally straightforward and evokes the concept of "world renovation." It states simply, "Make it better, this world of ours."[43] In the aftermath of a fire that swept through Edo in 1829, it was widely reported in both kawaraban and rakugaki that Matsudaira Sadanobu and his son Sadanaga had killed fleeing commoners who were crowding the streets, so that their escape from the fire would not be hindered. The author of *Ukiyo no arisama* reports that he saw no fewer than four broadsheets reporting this incident. Typical of the rakugaki that took up the rumor is this mocking verse: "The lord of Echigo [Sadanobu] runs away with his sword drawn, and following him, the lord of Echizen [Sadanaga], hiding his face."[44]

Traces of political critique appear in the writings of the kokugaku scholars as well. In 1787 Norinaga was asked by Tokugawa Harusada (1728–1789), the lord of Kii, to provide advice on how to deal with the social disorder of the times. Norinaga's response took the form of an essay entitled *Hihon tamaku-shige* (The Secret Jeweled Comb-Box). When he took up the issue of peasant rebellion, Norinaga's sympathies were clearly with the cultivators. He noted that "the delicious rice they grow is given to those above, and they must live by eating nothing but coarse food, not rice. When one thinks of this, one cannot but feel how pitiful, how miserable are the peasants of this age."[45] He refused to blame the townspeople and peasants for the outbreaks of popular violence, stating that riots and uprisings would not occur unless "things were beyond endurance." Moreover, he was critical of attempts by samurai authorities to crush the rebellions:

> Those above should merely listen and report on the wishes of the cultivators and the townspeople. Even if they should begin to rise up, you should not draw weapons against them. Since these are people who know nothing of warfare, it may seem that it will frighten them into inaction, but if those above become needlessly rigid, those below will needlessly throw away their lives. Even if the riot is such that there are thirty-five cultivators or townspeople for every samurai, it is not the case

that [the samurai] cannot handle this multitude. . . . These are your own people, and if even one of them is injured then it is your loss.[46]

Carefully, then, in light of his audience, Norinaga asked whether "those above" have the right to seize rice from the hungry and subject them to violence when they protest.

In the 1830s, in the midst of yet another famine, Tachibana Moribe expressed similar sentiments. Writing to his student Yoshida Akinushi in 1833, Moribe criticized the official handling of the shortage of rice that sparked the outbreaks of violence: "One would think that in a time such as this the officials would feel some sympathy. . . . [If] only they would respond warmly or take some special measure, but because of their arrogant interference it is difficult for commerce to proceed smoothly, and rice shipments have to be sent by a circuitous route."[47] The situation worsened as year after year of bad harvests continued. Another letter from Moribe to Akinushi, this one from 1837, painted a pessimistic picture of life in Edo. Moribe wrote that the cost of sweet potatoes, a "famine food" eaten when rice was unavailable, had more than doubled in recent days, and that his family, fearing that food prices would rise further, had hurriedly laid in stores of dried turnip and fish, but were unable to find other basic foodstuffs. What could one make of the world at present, Moribe wondered. He noted that every day there were rumors of starvation in Edo, yet the fairs and markets were bustling with entertainers and sightseers, and in Yoshiwara, the brothel district, business continued as usual.[48] When Moribe heard that in Osaka a former bakufu official named Ōshio Heihachirō had, in protest of the bakufu failure to address popular suffering, led a mob of thousands as they burned and looted the merchant warehouses of that city, he was prompted to write a commemorative poem in the archaic form known as the "long poem" (*chōka*).[49] In it, he praised Ōshio as a man "of profound emotions" who "attempted to wake the samurai from their slumber," and he asserted that the rebellion was "not an act of evil."[50]

THE PURSUIT OF ORDER

As this chorus of critical voices suggests, the social and economic tensions of the late eighteenth century were accompanied by a new ideological crisis. Some within Japanese society had begun to question the principle that was the foundation of Tokugawa power: the bakufu, in particular, and, by extension, the samurai class preserved peace and order through virtuous rule and thereby served the interests of the people. The response of the bakufu was a series of reform efforts aimed at reviving samurai authority and prestige, the Kansei reforms (1787–1793), the Tenpō reforms (1841–1843), and the Ansei reforms (1854). The architect of the Kansei reforms, which became a model for the policies of the Tenpō and Ansei eras, was Matsudaira Sadanobu, who became the senior bakufu advisor in 1787. Matsudaira was well versed in the ideas of the major Confucian schools of his day, but it was Neo-Confucianism that most profoundly influenced his view of political community. According to Neo-Confucianism, the orderly operation of society depended upon the proper enactment of transcendent ethical principles that were cosmically ordained. Thus, for Matsudaira, the political, economic, and social well-being of Japan derived from the virtue of its people, but particularly the virtue of the samurai, who as rulers had a duty to function as moral exemplars.[51]

In keeping with this analysis, Matsudaira's reform efforts aimed at encouraging virtue as the means to restore social order. He attacked bribery and corruption on the part of bakufu officials, both in Edo and in the local areas, and exhorted the samurai class as a whole to live frugally, to improve their behavior, and to devote themselves to scholarship and to honing their martial skills. It was the seeming speciousness of this latter policy that made him the target of Hōseidō's work. The new ethos of thrift and frugality was even extended to the residence of the shogun, the expenditures of which were sharply curtailed. Merchant activity too came under scrutiny because Matsudaira believed that merchant associations, which had proliferated during the Tanuma era, had manipulated prices in order to increase their own profits to the detriment of the samurai and commoners who were their customers. Selected associations were abolished, while others were admonished to reduce their prices. The rural villages, many of which were underpopulated in the aftermath of the famine years, were also subject to reform efforts. New controls were enacted to curtail the practices of abortion and infanticide, and in an effort to encourage runaway cultivators to return to their fields, the bakufu announced that they would be provided with money for travel, food, and tools if they agreed to go home. Still other reforms aimed at discouraging immorality at all levels of society. There were ordinances against street prostitution, gambling, mixed bathing, elaborate hairstyles, and gaudy clothing. In order to enforce these new regulations, bakufu agents began to patrol the streets of Edo.[52]

The burgeoning popular media was another object of concern for Sadanobu, who believed that books and kawaraban had contributed to the decline in popular morality. Beginning in 1790 a series of ordinances were promulgated with the aim of controlling the spread of information and curtailing political crititicism. Content, authorship, and circulation were all addressed in these laws. For example, the bakufu banned the discussion of contemporary events in print, as well as works that were "amorous," "depraved," or contained "unorthodox ideas." Similarly, it called for books written in the syllabary (kana) and circulated through lending libraries — that is, those most easily accessible to those with limited literacy and limited means — to be carefully monitored for "baseless rumors." In order to make punishments for infractions easier to assign, the real names of authors and publishers were required to be cited in all new works.[53] These new regulations were carefully enforced by the bakufu magistrates. In the city of Osaka alone, between 1790 and 1804, there were at least fifty instances when works were censored by such methods as the seizure of wood blocks, the refusal of permission to publish, lend, or sell designated works, or the destruction of books and manuscripts.[54] Most of the popular writers of fiction were subject to one form of punishment or another when their works were found to have violated the publishing regulations.[55]

The restrictions on publications were in place throughout the period when kokugaku discourse was taking form. They were even expanded during the Tenpō era, when the outbreak of famine disrupted the relative stability of the preceding two decades. As a result, one finds almost no overt commentary on contemporary political or social matters in the kokugaku texts intended for publication, but even so the potential politicality of the work of Norinaga and the other kokugaku scholars was apparent to officials of the day. Evidence of this comes from the work of Matsura Seizan, the lord of Hirato in Hizen province. Beginning in 1821, Matsura began to keep a private record, called *Kasshi yawa* (Night Tales of the Kasshi Era), of the news that circulated among the political elites in Edo. Matsura was close friends with Hayashi Jussai, the rector of the bakufu-supported school of Confucian studies, and the two shared an intense interest in intellectual matters. The *Kasshi yawa* reveals that Jussai was greatly concerned about the rise of kokugaku discourse. He is quoted as stating that "[Norinaga], the scholar of Japanese learning, died in good time, otherwise he would have become someone really important." About the same time, in a letter directed to the Edo magistrate who was in charge of enforcing the censorship laws, Hayashi urged that Norinaga's works be examined carefully because they contained many dangerous passages. Nothing came of this request because Norinaga's works had been published in Nagoya with the permission of the Owari Tokugawa house.[56] Another kokugaku scholar, Hirata Atsutane, was not so fortunate. In 1841 he was banished from Edo after one of his works caught the eye of the city magistrate.

As Hayashi Jussai's remarks on Norinaga's work reveal, in this period the bakufu was increasingly concerned with enforcing ideological orthodoxy, a trend that began in 1790 when Matsudaira Sadanobu sponsored the promulgation of the "prohibition of heterodoxy" (*igaku no kin*). Addressed to Hayashi Kinpō, then rector of the bakufu's Confucian academy, the ban required him to make Neo-Confucianism the basis of instruction in the college and to cease teaching other forms of Confucianism. While Neo-Confucianism had been one of the sources of bakufu ideology since the early seventeenth century, its influence had waned as new and innovative schools of Confucianism, such as the historicist "ancient learning" schools founded by Itō Jinsai (1627–1705) and Ogyū Sorai (1666–1728), had emerged.[57] Herman Ooms has characterized this unprecedented attempt on the part of the bakufu to unify ideology as a direct response to the perception that society was in a state of disintegration. According to Ooms, the ban revealed that "the ruling elites felt an urgency to develop learning and to reorder the world by redressing men's hearts and minds through cultivating the correct values."[58]

The result of the bakufu's pursuit of order was new and unprecedented attempts to regulate everyday life as officials sought to control what clothing people wore, how many children they had, and what books they read. The official embrace of Neo-Confucianism was implicated as well in the expansion of political authority in this way. The metaphysical conception of ethicality legitimated official efforts to regulate popular behavior: the government could characterize its efforts as motivated by a concern for virtue rather than political convenience. But in the contentious world of late Tokugawa society, official attempts to order everyday life met with opposition and resistance.

FROM SOCIAL HISTORY TO INTELLECTUAL HISTORY

As this outline history of the late eighteenth and early nineteenth century shows, Japanese society in this period underwent a political crisis as economic transformation, famine, and unrest led many to question the efficacy

of bakufu and domainal policy and the virtue of those responsible for formulating it. The result was an ideological crisis as new forms of political
critique emerged in the violence of urban and rural rioters, in the works of
satirical fiction, and in the voices of the anonymous authors of the kawaraban and rakugaki. At the same time, developments in popular media and
innovations in communication networks that were spurred by commercialization made possible as never before the flow of information around the
country. The result was the "expanding geographic consciousness," to borrow Konta's phrase, that found expression in the efforts of Sugita Gempaku,
Bunyō Inshi, Norinaga, and Moribe and others to record and comment upon
contemporary events all around Japan.

The response of Matsudaira Sadanobu and other Tokugawa political officials to these developments was to attempt to rectify not the political ideology but the social and economic transformations that called it into question;
hence, the efforts to reestablish the borders of city and village by sending
runaway villagers home and limiting commerce, to affirm the boundaries of
status via sumptuary laws, and to silence voices not only of critique but of
reportage through censorship. The responses of those who were subject to
political authority varied. Some, such as Bunyō Inshi and Sugita Gempaku,
responded to the "disorder" they recorded by calling upon those with political power to be more "virtuous," a demand that in essence reaffirmed the
bakufu's claim of authority. But the kokugaku scholars whose work is my
topic took a very different stance. They began to articulate alternative conceptions of community, ones that challenged the social and political order
authorized by the Tokugawa authorities by means of the ideology of virtue.
In the next chapter, as a prologue to my analysis of the dialogue of texts
that constituted kokugaku practice, I want to further explore this ideological transformation by examining the status of the Divine Age narrative in the
seventeenth and eighteenth century.

Chapter 2

Before the *Kojikiden*: The Divine Age Narrative
in Early Tokugawa Japan

When Norinaga, Akinari, Mitsue, and Moribe began to explore "Japan" in the
context of the disorder of late Tokugawa society, it was through the earliest
Japanese texts. The founding assumption of their work was that these texts
were the traces of the inaugural moment when community had first taken
form in Japan, and thus they were subjected to multiple attempts at explication and interpretation. The texts in question included such eighth-century
works as the poetry anthology *Man'yōshū* and the government-commissioned
reports on provincial conditions known as *fudoki*, as well as the ritual prayers
and genealogies included in later works such as the *Engi shiki* (Rites of the
Engi Era, 905). But at the center of these efforts to interrogate "Japan" was the
Divine Age narrative. Recorded in multiple forms in the two eighth-century
mythohistories, the *Kojiki* and the *Nihon shoki*, it relates how the heavenly
deities created the Japanese islands and then dispatched one of their own to
become the ruler of this "middle world."

In this chapter, I want to explore the context of the event that was the
Kojikiden by examining the status of the mythohistories in the period before
Norinaga's work transformed how and why they were read. Even a cursory
comparison of any of the modern versions of the *Kojiki* with the *Kojikiden*
reveals immediately how indebted their editors and annotators are to the
eighteenth-century text. In their guides to pronunciation, as well as their
explanatory notes, the modern texts rely upon Norinaga's work, albeit with
occasional asides that take issue with minor points while leaving the interpretive framework itself unexamined. Thus the notions that the *Kojiki* is older
than the other mythohistory, the *Nihon shoki*, that its language is more purely
Japanese, and that the very purpose of writing this work was to record and
therefore preserve the "original" Japanese language—assertions put forth in
the *Kojikiden*—have all but achieved the status of fact.

But Tokugawa readers in the first half of the eighteenth century understood the *Kojiki* and the *Nihon shoki* in terms very different from Norinaga. For one, it was the *Nihon shoki* that was the more important text. Long the object of court-supported scholarship, the *Nihon shoki* was the focus of early Tokugawa readers, while the *Kojiki* was taken up as a supplement or variant work. Moreover, unlike Norinaga, who made the language of the *Kojiki* into the privileged signifier of an authentic Japanese identity, early Tokugawa readers did not analyze the text in terms of the opposition of "Japanese" and "other." Similarly, while kokugaku scholars would insist that the Divine Age narratives spoke of experiences, ideas, and social relations that were specifically and inherently "Japanese," early Tokugawa readers had aligned the *Kojiki* and *Nihon shoki* with a series of Chinese Confucian works and perceived no great disjunction.

To understand why these works were not figured as specifically Japanese, it is necessary first to consider the relation of two linguistic styles, *wabun* and *kanbun kundoku*, that shaped discursive production in this period. *Kanbun kundoku* refers to the method whereby one "read" a text inscribed in "Chinese" writing (*kanbun*) by inserting a set of diacritical markers known as *kaeriten* to indicate how the textual surface should be converted to "Japanese" when the text was read, a procedure made possible by the ideographic nature of the characters.[1] However, the "Japanese" thereby produced was not that of the vernacular speech of the eighteenth century; rather, it was an amalgam of linguistic styles comprised of the traces of lexical and syntactical constructions of the language of earlier periods. For uninitiated readers who had not mastered the norms of kundoku, this "Japanese" could be almost as opaque as the original "Chinese" writing. Kundoku had originated as a means to enable Japanese readers to read Chinese texts more easily, but the diacritical markers came to be routinely applied not only to texts imported from China but also to those authored by Japanese writing in "Chinese." As this suggests, writing in kanbun was invested with a certain kind of cultural prestige, and those involved in scholarly pursuits wrote in kanbun with the knowledge that their readers would read in kundoku.

But there was another system of writing as well, wabun or "Japanese writing," which intermixed characters and the native syllabary. As kokugaku began to take form, one's decision to write in wabun rather than kanbun became a marker of where one stood on a range of issues, epistemological, aesthetic, and political. However, until the late eighteenth century, the division of linguistic styles was understood in what might be termed functional terms. Writing in kanbun was considered appropriate for certain kinds of discursive practices; wabun for others. One wrote in kanbun kundoku when one engaged in discourse defined as official or public in nature, while wabun was the linguistic realm that instantiated "private" discourse. Gender too played a role: educated men learned to write in kanbun, educated women in wabun. This linguistic divide would eventually come under attack by the kokugaku scholars, but in fact the opposition of "Japanese writing" and "Chinese writing" was always fluid and subject to interpretation. For example, questions of readership could intercede. Thus the innovative Confucian scholar Kaibara Ekiken (1603–1714) produced a work in wabun on the tenets of Confucianism (*Yamato zokkun*, "Precepts for Japanese Daily Life") that was prefaced with the explanation that it was intended for the common people.

When Tokugawa scholars first took up the *Man'yōshū*, the *Kojiki*, and other ancient texts that dated from a time before the native phonetic scripts known as kana had developed, they entered a linguistic labyrinth that confounded the opposition between kanbun and wabun. These works were inscribed entirely in Chinese characters, but while some passages were easily understandable as kanbun, other sequences were oddly irregular. In some instances, characters were used as phonetic symbols to spell out the names of actors and places within the narrative, a function sometimes demarcated via interphrasal annotations (*warichū*). Most confusing of all were the characters that seemed to signify the grammatical functions of a syntax unknown to seventeenth- and eighteenth-century readers. To early Tokugawa readers, the *Kojiki* appeared to be inscribed in kanbun, albeit a peculiar and corrupt kanbun, and as such it naturally became subject to the kundoku operation. But even the designation of the text as a work of kanbun generated questions for its readers.

These difficulties related to the fact that kanbun kundoku itself allowed for a wide range of stylistic differences. Although the conventions of the kundoku method gradually became more standardized, there was always the possibility of "reading" any given text in a plurality of ways, a fact that is perhaps best illustrated by comparing the various kundoku versions of the Chinese works produced by Confucianists in the Tokugawa period. The gap between the grammar of "Chinese" writing and "Japanese" reading that the kundoku procedure concealed in fact allowed for plural "readings" of a single work.[2] Reading in kundoku required the "translator" to make a series of choices. Should meaningful differences that existed in wabun—of tense, for example, or degrees of politeness—be introduced into the new kundoku text? Should characters grammatically necessary in Chinese but not in Japanese be pronounced, even at the cost of producing unwieldy or unnatural Japanese? Such considerations were never merely or even mainly stylistic or rhetorical in nature. In making these kind of choices, the editors of texts who inserted the diacritical markers inscribed differences of interpretation as well as differences of tone and register into the text, even while maintaining the appearance of similitude.

Those who explored the language of the Nihon shoki and the Kojiki in seventeenth- and eighteenth-century Japan did so from within well-established paradigms of discursive practice, most particularly Neo-Confucianism, the predominance of which had given rise to Confucian-Buddhist and Confucian-Shinto syncretism. As they confronted the labyrinth of characters that comprised the Kojiki, these readers tended to isolate certain phrases—those that seemed comprehensible in light of the system of knowledge within which they worked—and to regard the rest of the text as either irrelevant or hopelessly opaque. Confucian, Buddhist, and Shinto scholars used the logic of metaphor and metonym to render these phrases meaningful in light of the paradigms within which they read. This began to change in the mid-Tokugawa period as a new historicism began to infuse many modes of intellectual practice in Japan. There was a new interest in the writing of history, and for the first time the Kojiki came to be viewed as a history. Implicated, as well, in this transformation was a new concern to historicize contemporary modes of discursive practice. Beginning in the late seventeenth century, scholars such as Itō Jinsai and Ogyū Sorai began to argue that Neo-Confucian principles were the product of a particular historical moment, that is, Song China, not a transcendent theory of how the world worked. Early Japanese works were subject to the same historicizing impulse as scholars such as Keichū, Kada no Azumamaro, and Kamo no Mabuchi began to question whether the early Japanese works did in fact exemplify Confucian norms, with the result that the analysis of the language of the text became implicated in attempts to think beyond Confucianism.

The distinction between kanbun/wabun, China/Japan, metaphysics/history orders the discussion that follows, which traces how the Kojiki was read in seventeenth- and eighteenth-century Japan. The focus of readers throughout the Tokugawa period was the Divine Age section that begins with the formation of the cosmos and ends with the birth of a child who becomes Jinmu, the mythical first emperor of Japan. The crucial opening section of the Divine Age chapters describes the appearance of three primal deities,

Ame no Minakanushi, Takamimusubi, and Kamimusubi, at the beginning of heaven and earth. They were followed by two more deities, Kami-ashikabi-hikoji and Ame no Tokotachi. Next there appear successively seven generations of deities, each consisting of two separate deities. The deities of the seventh generation are Izanagi and Izanami, male and female, whose sexual union results in Izanami's giving birth to the Japanese islands and a host of lesser deities. The last of these is the fire deity, whose birth burns Izanami and causes her death. She then goes to a place called yomi, which is depicted as a subterranean world. Izanagi follows her there and attempts to persuade her to return to the "middle land" they have created, but she refuses, and deities of yomi chase Izanagi back to the middle land. He then washes himself in a river, and this act leads to the appearance of yet another series of deities, the last two of which are Amaterasu and Susanō. Izanagi commands these "children" to rule respectively the heavens and the middle land, but Susanō refuses to descend to the middle land and commits a series of outrages against Amaterasu, until she retreats to a cave to hide from him. She is eventually lured out by other deities, and Susanō is expelled from heaven. He descends to the middle world where his union with the daughter of an earthly deity leads to the birth of Ōkuninushi, the "great master" of the land. When Amaterasu orders her grandchild Ninigi to descend and rule over the middle world, Ōkuninushi is called upon to relinquish his control of the land. Ninigi then marries the daughter of an earthly deity, as do his child and grandchild. The product of this final union is Jinmu, who appears as the first human ruler whose life bridges the Divine Age and the Age of Men.

This outline focuses only on the major elements of the *Kojiki* and the *Nihon shoki*. In fact, the story of the Divine Age is narrated in a manner far more cryptic and elliptical than this summary suggests. Deities appear and disappear without comment, and narrative strands begin but end without closure. Much of the significance of events of the surface plot is conveyed by means of the complex deity names. Tokugawa readers recognized that these were used as signifying devices, but what they meant became the object of ongoing debate. In the discussion that follows I want to explore how Tokugawa readers approached this fragmented and multivocal narrative. My aim is twofold: first, to understand how these ancient texts were read, in terms of theories of language and textuality; second, to discover why they were read, by investigating what questions were posed to them and what meanings found within them.

TEXTUAL STRATEGIES: NEO-CONFUCIANISM

The explosion of interest in the Divine Age narrative in the early Tokugawa period was to some extent the result of new technology. When Toyotomi Hideyoshi and his army returned to Japan in the aftermath of the invasion of Korea in 1592, they brought with them printing presses and fonts of movable type that they had seized as part of the booty of war. The new technology fascinated many among the imperial court and the daimyo, with the result that a wide variety of texts began to be printed. The emperor Go-Yōzei began this boom when he ordered the publication of the Divine Age chapters of the *Nihon shoki* in 1599, as well as the Confucian classics, the *Analects*, and the *Book of Mencius*. In the decades that followed, a number of early works of Japanese literature were printed, including *Ise monogatari* (Tales of Ise), *Heike monogatari* (Tales of the Heike), and the *Hyaku'nin isshu* (Single Poems by One Hundred Poets). It was in this context that the *Kojiki* appeared in print in 1644, perhaps in response to the interest generated by the earlier printing of the *Nihon shoki*.[3] This text, produced in Kyoto, subsequently became known as the *Kan'eiban Kojiki*, named for the era in which it appeared.

The increased availability of both the *Nihon shoki* and the *Kojiki* itself created new questions for their readers, many of whom pondered the relationship between the two works. The preface to the *Kojiki* dates it to 712, and the *Nihon shoki* was compiled in 720, but in spite of the mere eight years that separate them, the form of the two texts is very different. While the *Kojiki* presents a more or less unitary narrative, the *Nihon shoki* brings together a number of variant forms of the story of Japan's mythic past. One of these is privileged as the so-called *honden* or "main narrative," but each section of the *honden* is followed by one or more variant versions (*issho*) of the story. As many readers recognized, some sections of the *Kojiki* were included in the *Nihon shoki* as issho. Further complicating matters was the fact that while the *Nihon shoki* had traditionally been regarded as one of the "Six Histories" recognized by the imperial court, and subject to court-sponsored scholarship, the *Kojiki* was new textual territory.

Unlike the various medieval manuscripts of the *Kojiki*, one or more of which must have served as its base, the *Kan'eiban Kojiki* reveals a new concern for the language of the text. While the medieval manuscripts contain only rudimentary markers, in this work kaeriten as well as *furigana* (pronunciation glossers) and *okurigana* (kana used to indicate syntactical elements) have been attached to most of the text.[4] These innovations were probably necessary because the printing of the *Kojiki*, as well as the *Nihon shoki* before it, allowed for the emergence of a new readership, a readership that, unlike the courtier-scholars and those associated with medieval Shinto sects, would have had no direct knowledge of the ancient texts and how they had traditionally been read. It was probably for the benefit of the intended new audience that the editor attempted to provide guidance for the kundoku operation, if only to a limited degree.

The opening passage of the *Kojiki* text in the *Kan'eiban Kojiki* offers a window into how the language inscribed in the early texts was understood in the early Tokugawa period.[5] In this transcript and others in this chapter, italics are used to indicate aspects of the kundoku text that are problematic or innovative.

> Ametsuchi *no hajimete hirakuru toki*, Takamanohara ni *nariizuru kami wo* Ama *no* Minakanushi *no kami to mōsu*. Tsugi ni Takamimusubi no kami. Tsugi ni Kamumimusubi no kami. Kono mihashira no kami ha *narabi ni hitori kamu narimashite, mi wo kakushimasu*. Tsugi ni kuni *wakakushite ukaberu haragomori no* kurage nasu tadayoheru toki ni, ashikabi no gotoshi kizashi noboru mono ni yo-te, *nariizuru kami wo* Umashi-ashikabi-hikoji *no kami to mōsu*. Tsugi ni Ama no Tokotachi no kami. Kono futahashira no kami *tarashi mata hitori kamu to narimashite mi wo kakushitamaeri*.[6]

This passage suggests that the editor of the *Kan'eiban Kojiki* did not conceive of any difference between the language of ancient Japan and that of the contemporary kanbun kundoku style. For example, although the Chinese characters that are used mitigate against such a construction, he read the first sentence using the phrase *to mōsu*, a typical kundoku construction. Unlike many of the commentators that followed him, he did not attach the honorific *mi* to nouns such as "name" (*na*) and "body" (*mi*), although these terms are used in relation to a deity. Curiously, though, the honorific verb-ending *tamau* is inserted into the final sentence. Thus the kundoku reading is a strangely unstable mixture of verbal registers.

But what is most striking is the interpretations of particular words that enter the text by means of the pronunciation glosses (*furigana*). For example, the character *naru*, which means "to become," is glossed as *nariizuru*, "to be born" or "to grow." Similarly, the characters that literally mean "floating oil" are read instead as *haragomori*, literally, "inside the womb." These kinds of explicitly interpretive moves seem to suggest that the editor had some kind of plot in mind as he moved through the text. But what was the nature of his understanding? The answer probably lies in the interpretation of the Divine Age narrative that took form in the wake of the publication of the Nihon shoki, both within new forms of Shinto practice such as the Suika Shinto sect of Yamazaki Ansai (1618–1682) and the revived forms of others, particularly the Yoshida Shinto associated with the Yoshida Shrine in Kyoto.[7] For example, Ansai's *Jindai no maki fūyōshū* (Wind and Leaves Collection of the Divine Age Chapters), Watarai Nobuyoshi's *Jindaikan kōjutsushō* (Oral Transmissions on the Divine Age Chapters), and Yoshikawa Koretaru's *Jindaikan kaden monjo* (Documents on the Received Understanding of the Divine Age Chapters) were all written by relying on the printed Nihon shoki.

Not surprisingly perhaps, these new readings of the Nihon shoki were profoundly influenced by Neo-Confucianism, the dominant intellectual paradigm of the seventeenth century. In the hands of Ansai and others, Neo-Confucianism came to be employed as an interpretive sieve that allowed the reader to distinguish the seemingly meaningful passages of the Divine Age narrative. By delineating a set of principles that were said to originate in nature and be manifest in all things, Neo-Confucian scholars sought to establish the essential unity of natural law, physical existence, and human conduct and asserted the continuity of universal principles in spite of the appearance of historical change or cultural difference. Beginning in the mid-seventeenth century, Japanese scholars began an ambitious attempt to validate the universalist claims of Neo-Confucianism through a reading of the Divine Age narrative. Ansai, for example, argued that the Nihon shoki was analogous to the Eki kyō (in Chinese, Yijing, "The Book of Changes") in that both revealed the workings of the Neo-Confucian concepts of ri (Chinese: li), the "fundamental moral principle" that permeated all things; ki (Chinese: qi) the "ethereal" substance of existence that simultaneously gave form to and corrupted ri; in and yō (Chinese: yin and yang), the building blocks of ki, and so on.[8]

The nature of the Neo-Confucian–Shintoc amalgam put forth by Suika scholars is suggested by their understanding of the opening passage of the Divine Age narrative. For Ansai, the central interpretive device was the Neo-Confucian assertion that "the universe consists of a single principle." Thus the opening invocation of the Nihon shoki version of the narrative—"when heaven and earth were not yet separate"—becomes an expression of the inherent unity of all things, the cosmic as well as the social. Ansai and his followers argued that the next "event" of the text, the emergence of the "seven generations of heavenly deities," was an expression of the processes involved in the transformation of primal ri into physical existence, that is, the gradual production of the material world. According to Ansai, the narrative describes this in terms of a movement from a state "before life" to the "transformation by means of ki," to the "acquisition of form," and finally to "the acquisition of moral consciousness." Moreover, this process, which resulted in the production of the world, was reenacted again and again through the processes of human birth and death. Other Neo-Confucian principles were also inserted into the narrative. The sexual act of Izanami and Izanagi that appears on the surface narrative and results in the "birth" of the Japanese islands, rivers, wind, and so on, was described as a representation of the productive power of the fusion of yin and yang and the emergence of the basic elements of existence: fire, water, wood, metal, and earth.[9]

As this summary suggests, the Suika Shinto scholars attempted to understand the Divine Age narrative as a metaphorical representation of the central concepts of Neo-Confucian metaphysics. Within this hermeneutic, there was little concern for a true linguistic analysis of the ancient texts. Indeed, Ansai and his students referred consistently to the *Nihon shoki*, an accepted kundoku version of which had existed from the Heian period, and thus the articulation of the text did not become an issue. Their analysis focused on words within the narrative and took the form of the construction of certain speculative etymologies with the aim of "finding" Neo-Confucian concepts in the ancient Japanese texts. In one well-known example of this strategy, Ansai tied the word *tsuchi* (earth) to *itsutsu* (five), to the name of the fire deity, *Kagutsuchi*, to *tsuzumaru* (firm, as in "to be resolved"), and to *tsutsushimu* (to be reverent of). Reading in this way, he managed to find "proof" of the Confucian five elements, one of which was earth, in the *Nihon shoki* and to link this reference to a Neo-Confucian virtue and to the problem of ethical behavior.[10] But more often the Suika analysis relied on the establishment of certain kinds of analogical relationships between elements of the Divine Age narrative and Neo-Confucian concepts. One strategy was to forge a series of metonymical links between isolated words drawn from the text and Neo-Confucian concepts; for example, a relation was established between Izanami and Izanagi and the concepts of yin and yang by means of reference to the gendered nature of these deities and the associations of yin and yang with the qualities of "maleness" and "femaleness." Another strategy was to understand the events of the plot itself in allegorical terms. Thus the sequence of deities who appear and disappear within the text was understood as signifying the generative process that united ri and ki.

It is clear that the *Kan'eiban Kojiki* circulated among the adherents of the new and revived sects of syncretic Shinto. Some forty years after its publication, another version of the *Kojiki* was printed in Ise. Known as the *Gōtō Kojiki* (The *Kojiki* with Notes, 1687), this was the work of Watarai Nobuyoshi (1650–1690), one of a hereditary line of priests who served in the Outer Shrine of the Ise Jingū. Like Yamazaki Ansai, Nobuyoshi had made a name for himself as the author of a number of works of Neo-Confucian–Shinto syncretism. However, he portrayed his reediting of the text as motivated by textual concerns, not issues of interpretation. In his postscript, Nobuyoshi suggested that he found the *Kan'eiban Kojiki* seriously flawed and therefore was moved to reedit the text: "Editions of the *Kojiki* printed in recent times have many mistaken characters, and there are many passages where the meaning is difficult to grasp. Why does no one lament that the ancient history is like this? Instead of relying on these unreliable texts, I sought good versions from old families and used them to correct the miscopied characters, restore the passages that had been omitted, delete superfluous phrases, and add diacritical markers."[11]

Nobuyoshi's explanation of his own method presents a model for textual reconstruction, but in fact his most important points of reference were not the extant manuscripts of the *Kojiki* (the Shinpukuji, Ise, and Urabe texts) but rather the *Nihon Shoki* and a work known as the *Kujiki*. The latter, a third version of the Divine Age myth, was already considered by many to be a forgery, but Nobuyoshi accepted its veracity.

Nobuyoshi went far beyond merely correcting printing mistakes and significantly revised the kundoku reading of the *Kan'eiban Kojiki*. He also hinted at a new understanding of the text via the diacritical markers and glosses he inserted. According to the *Gōtō Kojiki*, the opening passage of the *Kojiki* should be read as follows:

> Ametsuchi *hajimete hirakuru* toki, Takamanohara ni *naru kami no mina ha,* *Ame no Minakanushi no kami*. Tsugi ni Takamimusubi no kami. Tsugi ni, Kanmimusubi no kami. Kono mihashira no kami ha *narabi ni hitori kami narimashite, mi wo kakushimasu*. Tsugi ni kuni ishiku ukaberu *abura no gotoku ni shite* kurage nasu tadayoheru toki ni, ashikabi no gotoku kizashi noboru mono ni yorite *naru kami no mina ha* Umashi-ashikabi-hikoji no kami. Tsugi ni Ame no Tokotachi no kami. Kono futahashira no kami *mo mata hitori kami to narimashite, mi wo kakushimasu*.[12]

Here Nobuyoshi dropped some of more obviously speculative glosses, preferring *naru* to *nariizuru* and eliminating the insertion of *haragomori*. And when the syntax of the original language obviously deviates from typical kan-bun usage, he tried to reflect this in his kundoku: thus the phrase *to mōsu* has been replaced by *kami no mina ha*, a reading that Norinaga would eventually accept and follow. Similarly, Nobuyoshi makes limited use of honorific language. But his criticism of the *Kan'eiban* editor notwithstanding, Nobuyoshi too resorted to some speculation in the glosses he provided. For example, the phrase written as *kuni wakaku* (when the land was young) was read as *kuni ishiku* (when the land was beautiful).

The term *Gōtō* in the title means "headnote" and refers to another of Nobuyoshi's innovations: his attempt to explicitly engage in an exegesis of the *Kojiki*, albeit in a partial and rudimentary way. For the most part, these head-notes take the form of selections from other early texts, the *Nihon shoki*, the local gazetteers known as fudoki, and so on, which are cited to clarify the names of deities, sites, and events within the *Kojiki*. While the notes do not put forth a unified and cohesive analysis of the *Kojiki* narrative, they are suggestive of Nobuyoshi's efforts to contextualize the work by establishing a new set of intertextual relations. When Nobuyoshi aligned the *Kojiki* with the fudoki, works that had never been utilized by either Buddhist or Confucian syncretic schools of Shinto, he was establishing a new textual register. Significant too is the fact that the terms from the text that become the subject of the headnotes are precisely those that had little place in the metaphysical readings undertaken by scholars of the Suika school. They had been regarded as the random as opposed to meaningful aspects of the text and hence had largely been ignored to this point. The creation of the headnotes signaled a new concern for previously unexamined aspects of the *Kojiki*.

It was only in the aftermath of the publication of the *Gōtō Kojiki* that the *Kojiki* narrative itself became the object of a sustained attempt at interpretation. The text in question was the *Kojiki densetsu* (The Transmitted Understanding of the *Kojiki*, late seventeenth century). Little is known of the author, Fujiwara Isei, except that he seems to have been a priest associated with the Buddhist-Confucian-Shinto syncretic sect known as Yoshida Shinto and had access to Nobuyoshi's work. The *Kojiki densetsu* is an analysis of the first two sections of the *Kojiki* and includes not only an annotated text of its narrative but also a section called *sōron*, a "comprehensive theory" of the text, written in kanbun. In his annotations, Isei, like Nobuyoshi, situated the *Kojiki* within a new intertextual space, although one that differed substantially from that of Nobuyoshi. Most of his citations are to medieval works on Buddhist-Shinto syncretism. As this referencing suggests, Isei argued that the Kojiki revealed a Buddhist "truth": its "great significance" (taigi) was that the reign of the imperial line was established and maintained by the Buddhist virtue of compassion, which it exemplified.[13] The Kojiki densetsu has an ambivalent place in the textual history I am constructing. While it was the first attempt to interpret the Kojiki as an integral text distinct from the Nihon shoki, it also represents one of the final "new" attempts to read the Divine Age narrative in metaphysical terms derived from Buddhism or Neo-Confucianism. In the eighteenth century, scholars would continue to explore the Kojiki and the Nihon shoki, but from a very different perspective. No longer would the Divine Age narrative be understood only as an allegory that metaphorically represented a set of a priori concepts. Rather, it began to be viewed as a history.

TEXTUAL STRATEGIES: HISTORICISM

Tetsuo Najita has identified historicism as an important intellectual force in Japan from the late seventeenth century onward. He characterizes it as a response to a growing sense of "discordance" on the part of many intellectuals as the vision of society embraced by the founders of the Tokugawa bakufu— agricultural self-sufficiency, the functional division of society into discrete status groups, limited geographic mobility—began to clash with the reality of everyday life as urbanization and commercialization emerged as potent forces of social change. As scholars pondered why things had begun to go awry, the exploration of historical change became an important mode of inquiry. Through the study of the past, Tokugawa intellectuals sought to move beyond the present to discover the knowledge that would enable them to understand and resolve the problems of their day.[14] To be sure, the study of history was authorized by Neo-Confucianism itself, which held that the universal cosmological principles of ri and ki were verifiable through the observation of both nature and the human realm. Thus, Hayashi Razan and his son Gahō, Neo-Confucian scholars who enjoyed the patronage of the bakufu, composed a history of Japan called Honchō tsugan (A Comprehensive Mirror of Japan), which traced Japanese history from the time of Jinmu, the legendary first emperor, to the end of the reign of emperor Go-Yōzei in 1611. However, in the eighteenth century, historicism gave rise to a new skepticism about the Neo-Confucian metaphysic itself—and eventually to a questioning of the transcultural claims that oriented Confucian practice in Japan.

The Kojiki became implicated in the new historicism in relation to another attempt to construct a comprehensive history of Japan. In 1657 Tokugawa

Mitsukuni (1628–1700), the daimyo of Mito and the grandson of Tokugawa Ieyasu, ordered the compilation of a work that came to be called *Dai Nihon shi* (The History of Great Japan). It was finally completed only in 1906, by which time it filled 397 volumes. Mitsukuni was deeply influenced by Neo-Confucianism, and his history was begun with the aim of illuminating the proper relationship between ruler and subject through an examination of the entirety of Japanese history. The Mito scholars were committed to following the positivist historical method employed by the Chinese historian Sima Qian, which began with the assemblage, comparison, and evaluation of existing textual evidence. As a result, large numbers of scholars came to participate in the project, so that the interest in historical inquiry that motivated it spread far beyond the immediate confines of Mito.[15]

As part of the preparations for the compilation of the *Dai Nihon shi*, Mitsukuni authorized the editing of many of Japan's early texts, with the intention that they would serve as source materials. The *Kojiki* was one of these texts, and the Mito scholars produced a version of the *Kojiki* entitled *Sankō Kojiki* (Reference *Kojiki*). Unlike other Tokugawa editions of the *Kojiki* produced before and after it, the *Sankō Kojiki* contains no diacritical markers of any sort. There are however numerous headnotes, of the sort found in the *Gōtō Kojiki*, that correlate terms from the *Kojiki* with those in later histories and thus with the realm of historical events. Many of these headnotes reproduce the annotations of the Nobuyoshi text, indicating that the Mito school had access to this work, but there are new ones as well that draw upon an expanded network of texts that included the *Man'yōshū*, *Engi shiki*, and *Shaku Nihongi* (The Annotated *Nihon Shoki*).[16] The *Sankō Kojiki* was probably never seen by anyone not connected with the *Dai Nihon shi*, but the same refiguring of the *Kojiki* as a historical source orients the work of Arai Hakuseki, a scholar who worked at the periphery of the Mito project.

Hakuseki (1657–1725), although a man of humble origins, rose to serve in the bakufu, first as tutor to Ienobu, who would be the sixth shogun, and later in a variety of advisory capacities, both institutional and informal. As an official, Hakuseki probably had access to the Mito library, and certainly he was well aware of the Mito goal of writing a history of Japan. Hakuseki himself produced two historical works on ancient Japan, *Koshitsū* (A Comprehensive History of Ancient Times) and *Koshitsū wakumon* (Questions on the *Koshitsū*), both of which were completed around 1716. He explicitly rejected the view of the various Shinto schools that the *Kojiki* and *Nihon shoki* expressed metaphysical principles and argued that "these two works are histories, of the same nature of the Chinese histories. How can there be anything mystical in historical writings?" [17] Based upon this stance, he constructed a new interpretive framework that had the capacity to transform the understanding of the Divine Age narrative.[18]

Unlike the Mito historians, Hakuseki was interested in the language of the ancient texts, in particular, in the relation between the written symbols and the system of sounds these symbols represented. He argued that "when we look at the works that inscribe the events of ancient times of this country, we must not be concerned with the characters that inscribe them but rather seek the meaning that lies between the characters." [19] When deployed as an interpretive strategy, this declaration came to mean that the significance carried by certain key ideographs could be ignored in favor of exploring the meaning of the "Japanese" words they were used to convey. The justification for this strategy was Hakuseki's assertion that the scribes who wrote the ancient histories were often not concerned with the meanings of the character themselves but used them solely for their phonetic values. As an example, Hakuseki pointed to the use of the word *kami.* Although written with the character for "deity," he asserted that it referred to those who are "above" (*jō, kami*), that is, the rulers of ancient communities. Similarly, Hakuseki argued that *ama*, the pronunciation attached to the character for "heaven" (*ten, ama*), should be understood as "sea" (*ama*). And, while the home of the "deities" was inscribed using characters that literally mean "the high heavenly plains" (*Takamagahara*), this is, in fact, a reference to the land of Taka located near the sea in Kyushu. By carrying out a series of displacements of this kind, Hakuseki succeeded in transforming the Divine Age narrative from a a story of deities in a heavenly kingdom to one of powerful men vying for political hegemony at the time of the founding of the Japanese imperial court. Thus, Hakuseki's approach is essentially euhemeristic in nature: he viewed myth as the allegorical representation of actual historical events and persons.[20]

Hakuseki's second interpretive strategy was his assault on the notion of textual integrity that had guided the earlier readings of the Divine Age narrative. Unlike earlier readers who had privileged the *Nihon shoki* as the canonical account or his successors who would valorize the *Kojiki*, Hakuseki held that no single work should be regarded as definitive, for all contained omissions and distortions. He argued that all the texts should be critically examined, in order to isolate those elements that relate the real events of the past. This move, which in the nineteenth century would be adopted by both Hirata Atsutane and Tachibana Moribe, allowed Hakuseki to discard those aspects of the narrative that did not mesh with the history he was constructing. His theory of inscription was similarly motivated. The assertion that the written language of the text had to be interrogated carefully became a license to create pseudo-etymologies, in a manner not so different from that of the Suika scholars of whom Hakuseki was very critical. And like the Suika scholars, Hakuseki offered a selective reading: he chose certain key characters from the narrative and "translated" them, while leaving other portions of the texts unexplained. But his rejection of the notion of textual unity provided a justification for this, and thus Hakuseki's new interpretation is characterized by a kind of theoretical closure that earlier accounts lacked. There is a thematic closure as well. To borrow Hayden White's terminology, the "moral" of this historical narrative is clear.[21] By recasting the story of the Divine Age as a tale of the transfer of authority from one ruling line to another, Hakuseki succeeded in validating the Confucian notion of the mandate of heaven while deconstructing the concept that the imperial line, because of its divine origins, was ultimately the source of political authority in Japan.[22]

TEXTUAL STRATEGIES: LANGUAGE

The Buddhist monk known as Keichū was another scholar who worked on the fringes of the *Dai Nihon shi* project. He took up the study of the poetic anthology *Man'yōshū* by order of Tokugawa Mitsukuni. In the memoirs he wrote in the 1790s, Norinaga recalled how, as a young man studying medicine in Kyoto, he stumbled upon a work by Keichū, whom he recognized at once to be a "great scholar."[23] His contemporary Ueda Akinari also recalled an encounter with Keichū's work as the event that led him to become involved in kokugaku. Feeling "restless" and "confused" by Keichū's ideas, he began to seek a teacher who could explain them, eventually becoming a student of Katō Umaki.[24] Keichū's approach to the ancient texts was fundamentally different from readers such as Yamazaki Ansai and Arai Hakuseki who had isolated specific words and phrases and used them to interpret the Divine Age narrative. It was the ancient language itself that became his object of analysis.

The *Man'yōshū* was inscribed largely in Chinese characters that were used to represent the phonemes of the Japanese language, a method of inscripture that came to be termed *man'yōgana*. Keichū, in attempting to understand how these strings of characters should be read, realized that the use of the kana (*kanazukai*) differed greatly not only from contemporary seventeenth-century usage but also from the orthography put forth by Fujiwara Teika in the thirteenth century, which had subsequently become the accepted method for inscribing wabun.[25] Already by Teika's time, there was a wide gap between the kana orthography and the sounds of spoken Japanese, with multiple kana being used to inscribe a single sound. For example, the sound \i\ could be written with the symbols for *i, wi,* and *yi* and the sound \e\ could be written by *e, we,* and *he.* Teika attempted to impose some order upon kana usage by delineating a set of rules based upon the notion of "pitch." He took as his standard the inscription of words in the poetic anthologies of the Heian period and argued that distinctions in kana usage arose out of attempts to represent the differences in pitch that occurred in speech.

Keichū was trying to read a work that employed an unfamiliar vocabulary and syntax, and an understanding of the relation of symbol and sound was necessary to decipher its grammar. Based upon his own study of the *Man'yōshū,* Keichū soon recognized that Teika's rules could not explain the orthography of the ancient texts. He dismissed Teika's reliance on the notion of pitch to explain disparities of kana usage and instead undertook a rigorous comparison of earlier and later texts in order to trace the process of euphonic change. His work, *Waji seiran shō* (A Treatise on the Correct Inscription of Japanese Words, 1693), takes the form of a lexicon in which the "correct" form for writing "Japanese" is taken up a single word at a time, based upon the orthography of the eighth-century texts. As the use of the word "correct" here and in the title of Keichū's work suggests, the reconstruction of the ancient orthography had "moral" as well as philological value. Keichū asserted that the ancient kana usage revealed the Japanese language in its pristine, original state, and he characterized the differences that separated the language of the past and that of the present not as the result of inevitable historical change but in terms of decline and loss.

The *Kojiki* was but one of the many works Keichū relied upon in his reconstruction of the ancient language, but there is some evidence that he also produced a text of the *Kojiki* complete with pronunciation guides and annotations, although this work is not extant.[26] However, Keichū did take up the poems contained in both the *Nihon shoki* and the *Kojiki* in a work called *Kōgan shō* (An Impudent Treatise, 1691), and his preface to this text contains comments that suggest how he viewed the mythohistories:

> This country is the Divine Land. Therefore, even in the histories, public affairs are related by speaking first of the deities and then of men. In

ancient times the world was ruled only by making reference to the way of the deities. And because things were not yet complex, there was not yet writing, and everything was passed on by word of mouth. Therefore the way of the deities does not explain things in the manner of the Confucian classics or the Buddhist texts. The *Kujiki*, *Nihon shoki*, and *Kojiki* are all written beginning with the Divine Age.[27]

Keichū's characterization of the work as "impudent" suggests his expectation that his understanding of the ancient language would not find easy acceptance. The notion that not only language but also a set of ontological differences distinguished the early Japanese texts from those of China was a radical departure from the universalistic assumptions that had shaped the Suika discourse on the mythohistories and the history of Arai Hakuseki.

Further evidence of the emergence of the new belief that language is the key to detecting historical and cultural "difference" can be found in the work of Itō Jinsai and Ogyū Sorai, who successively founded new philosophical and philological schools of Confucianism in the late seventeenth century. Both began as students of Neo-Confucianism but eventually became known as the pioneers of a new form of Confucian practice known as "ancient learning" (*kogaku*). The starting point for their work was the assertion that an awareness of linguistic and discursive change must be the foundation of any exegetical enterprise. This led them to reject the tenets of Neo-Confucianism, with the charge that these were the result of misreading the ancient Confucian texts using "today's words," to borrow Sorai's phrase. Both Jinsai and Sorai used philological methods to "recover" what they regarded as the original meaning of Confucianism before it came to be fundamentally reinterpreted by later scholars. Sorai, however, went one step further than Jinsai and turned his critical eye on the practice of Japanese Confucian scholars of using kundoku to read Chinese texts. Describing the procedure as akin to "an attempt to scratch one's itchy feet with shoes on," he argued that kundoku was a barrier that stood between the reader and the language of the Confucian texts and prevented a correct understanding of the "ancient way" of the sage kings.[28] In keeping with this perspective, Sorai tried to understand the early Confucian texts in light of the language of ancient China.

The historicism that infused Jinsai and Sorai's understanding of the language of the ancient Confucian texts resulted as well in a new skepticism toward the entirety of the Neo-Confucian metaphysic with its emphasis on timeless and unchanging moral absolutes. Both were still concerned with issues of ethicality, but they no longer accepted the notion that human virtue originated with and manifested the cosmic principle of ri. As they reconsidered the nature of virtue, both Jinsai and Sorai showed a new concern for human agency. Jinsai concluded that the individual was endowed with the capacity to develop his innate potential for virtue, but that its development depended upon his own effort. Sorai went even farther and historicized virtue itself so that it became a product of human endeavor and intention. For Sorai, the message of the ancient Confucian texts was one of social genesis. He argued that in the ancient world, heroic kings or *sen-ō* had created the rites, laws, ethical norms, poetry, and song that brought peace and well-being to their people. In other words, culture itself was the product of human endeavor.[29] As we shall see, the interrogation of human agency would become an important theme within kokugaku discourse, but it was detached from the concern for ethicality. For Norinaga and those who followed him, the question of how the subject became virtuous was abandoned in order to explore how subjects came together to form community.

TEXTUAL STRATEGIES: CULTURAL DIFFERENCE

Modern scholars, as well as those of the late Tokugawa period, would argue over which came first, Keichū's work or that of Sorai, but ultimately the problem of chronology—or of influence and reception—is less important than the fact that from the late seventeenth century onward there emerged a series of attacks on the transculturalism and transhistoricism that had been the intellectual norm. Within this new context, the opposition of "Chinese" and "Japanese" came increasingly to be understood as an important and meaningful distinction. Among those who participated in the new discourse on linguistic, cultural, and historical difference was Kada no Azumamaro, the second son of a family of priests that traditionally served the Inari Shrine in Fushimi, near Kyoto, and the man whom Norinaga's self-proclaimed successor, Hirata Atsutane, would declare to have been the first scholar of kokugaku in the 1840s.

In addition to founding a school where he lectured on Shinto theology, ancient history, and poetry, Azumamaro also served as a consultant to the bakufu on a broad range of antiquarian matters.[30] The influence of the work of Jinsai and Sorai on Azumamaro is unmistakable, revealed in the constant reiteration of terms such as "ancient meanings" and "ancient words" that

had served as their maxims, but his analysis of the *Man'yōshū* reveals his debt
to Keichū's *Man'yō daishōki* (A Stand-in's Chronicle of the *Man'yōshū*) as well.
However, in the post-Sorai era, the declaration that "the interpretation of
words is the foundation of the learning of our country" had a significance
that was lacking when Keichū was writing some forty years before.[31] It began
to define, in a preliminary way, the boundaries of a new discourse founded
on the assumption that the ancient language inscribed in the ancient texts
would reveal a system of ideas and values fundamentally different from those
of the present.

The new concern for language, however, had an ambiguous place in the
work of Azumamaro. It has been said that he privileged the *Nihon shoki* over
the *Kojiki*, and this is true to the extent that, within his oeuvre, it was this
text that most often became an object of study. When the two texts offered
differing accounts, Azumamaro always designated the *Nihon shoki* version as
the "correct explanation." However, it would be more accurate to note that
he perceived a functional difference in the editorial intentions that shaped
the two works. This is perhaps best illustrated by remarks he made in regard
to the preface of the *Kojiki*. According to Azumamaro,

> We must understand that Yasumaro did not write this entire preface by
> referring to the ancient matters of foreign countries, but rather com-
> posed it by carefully choosing everything from among the ancient mat-
> ters of the Divine Age and the *Nihon shoki*. Therefore, one should not be
> confounded by the meaning of these sentences. Since it was written by
> broadly drawing on the ancient matters of Japan, there are many places
> impossible to understand if one thinks too much about the meaning of
> the sentences.[32]

Here Azumamaro speaks only of the *Kojiki* preface, but these remarks
seem to reflect his view of the text in its entirety. He approached the *Kojiki* not
as a narrative but rather as a repository of "ancient matters." In other words,
his analysis focused not on the level of plot but on words and phrases that
he found significant. Azumamaro's *Kojiki sakki* (Essential Elements of the
Kojiki, 1729), one of only two works he wrote on the *Kojiki*, takes the form of
a lexicon, a list of words and phrases extracted from the *Kojiki* and explained.
These explanations, however, are quite different from those that appeared
in the *Gōtō Kojiki*, which dealt only with the proper nouns associated with
deities, sites, and objects that appear within the text, and for the most part
merely indexed these names with those that appeared in other texts. Azu-

mamaro's lexicon was made up of words that encompassed the full range of grammatical functions. A typical entry is his examination of the term *katatsu-kuni*, which appears in the passage that describes the confrontation between Susanō and Amaterasu following Susanō's refusal to rule his assigned domain and his request instead to go to *katatsukuni*. The term is inscribed with the characters that mean "hard" or "strong" and "land," prompting Azumamaro to explain that "since this is the place that is a foundation, a place that is unchanging, it is called the 'hard land.' "[33] This explanation, which attaches no negative connotations to the word, is very different from that of Norinaga, who would argue that *katatsukuni* was a reference to yomi, the foul subterranean world, and cited Susanō's desire to go there as evidence of his evil nature. It is precisely this kind of explanatory mode, which relies on internal references to the narrative itself, that Azumamaro avoided in the *Kojiki sakki* in favor of etymologically derived meanings.

Within *Kojiki sakki*, little attention is paid to the problem of kundoku, but this is probably because Azumamaro had already produced another version of the text, the *Hitten Kojiki* (A Secret Reading of the *Kojiki*, 1724), the title of which suggests that this work was circulated only among Azumamaro's disciples. It is a copy of the *Kan'eiban Kojiki* that has been altered by the inclusion of numerous editorial comments: characters are changed, diacritical marks altered, and pronunciation glosses amended. In all, Azumamaro made more than seven hundred changes, although some of these reiterate the notes of the *Gōtō Kojiki*.[34] According to Azumamaro, the opening passage of the *Kojiki* was to be read as follows:

> Ametsuchi *hajimete wakareshi* toki, Takamanohara ni *naru kami no mina wa, Ame no Minakanushi no kami to nazukemōsu*. Tsugi ni Takamimusubi no kami. Tsugi ni Kamumimusubi no kami. Kono mihashira no kami ha *mina hitori kami to narimashite, mi wo kakushitamau*. Koko ni kuni *ishiku ukaberu abura no gotoku ni shite*, kurage nasu tadayoheru toki ashikabi no gotoku kizashi noboru mono ni yorite *naru kami no mina ha*, Umashi-ashikabi-hikoji no kami. Tsugi ni Ame no Tokotachi no kami. Kono futa-hashira no kami mo *narabi ni mata hitorikami to narimashite, mi wo kakushi-tamau*. Kami no *kudan no* itsuhashira no kami ha *sunawachi*, amatsukami nari.[35]

Here Azumamaro differed from Nobuyoshi in his concern for the insertion of honorific language in the relation to the deities. He attached honorific prefixes to nouns, so for example *na* (name) became *mina*, and he retained the

Kan'eiban's use of the honorific verb *tamau* to describe actions by the deities. He also left many of the earlier editors' problematic attempts at kundoku in place. For example, the *Kan'eiban* editors use of the phrase *to mōsu* in the opening sentence is retained, as is Nobuyoshi's reading of the phrase *kuni wakaku* (when the land was young) as *kuni ishiku* (when the land was beautiful). There are also a number of new interpretive moves. A case in point is the final sentence in the passage quoted above, which contains the notoriously difficult to interpret sequence of the characters *betsu, ten, shin*. The *Kan'eiban* text had arbitrarily assigned the reading of *kotoamatsukami* to this phrase, which offered no clue to its meaning. However, Azumamaro obtained a more lucid reading only by declaring the character *betsu* to be a misprint of the character *soku*, the kun-reading of which is *sunawachi*, so that the sentence came to mean that "the five deities above are, in other words, the heavenly deities."

These attempts to alter the textual surface would be comprehensible if they were imposed in order to construct a new understanding of the Divine Age narrative. However, they appear to be scattered comments that do not point to the construction of a meaning that radically departs from the syncretic Confucian-Shinto formulations already in place; this in spite of Azumamaro's many declarations to the effect that "the Divine Age chapters are all one needs to know the way" and that "their message differs from that of later Confucian writings." [36] As Peter Nosco has indicated, in constructing his cosmology Azumamaro made use of the notions of ki and the five elements in order to argue that the Divine Age myth relates the transformation of the pure and the immaterial to the impure and material, an obvious echo of the Neo-Confucian paradigm. [37] The stability of this interpretation suggests that the relation of grammatical explication to exegesis had a very different status in the work of the early kokugaku figures, compared to the interpretive endeavors of the revisionist Confucian schools of Itō Jinsai and Ogyū Sorai. While Jinsai's and Sorai's concern for language was implicated in the rethinking of Neo-Confucianism, efforts to delineate the "difference" of the early Japanese language did not immediately call into question the established interpretive modes.

Issues of language were central to the work of three other scholars who were working in the mid-eighteenth century: Kamo no Mabuchi, Tanigawa Kotosuga (1709–1776), and Tayasu Munetake (1715–1771). A well-known teacher in Edo where he resided, Mabuchi attracted a large following among samurai and commoners alike. He was Norinaga's acknowledged "master," and the latter attached great significance to the famous "one night in Matsuzaka" that took place in 1763, the first and only meeting of the two men. In his memoirs, Norinaga described their conversation at some length. He states that when he told Mabuchi of his desire to annotate the *Kojiki*, Mabuchi responded,

> I too originally had the intention to explain the Divine Text, but first it was necessary to cleanse my heart of *karagokoro* (the Chinese mind), so that I would be able to return to the sincere intentions of the ancient period. But to know the mind of the ancients, it is necessary to understand the ancient language. To understand the ancient language, it is necessary to study the *Man'yōshū*. Therefore, while I was trying to clarify the *Man'yōshū*, I grew old. The rest of my life can only be a few years, not enough to explain the Divine Text.[38]

As Norinaga told the story, Mabuchi then charged him with carrying out the important work of analyzing the *Kojiki*. The truthfulness of this account of their meeting cannot be ascertained, but some aspects are clearly contrived. The term *karagokoro*, for example, was very much Norinaga's phrase. Moreover, Mabuchi had in fact done substantial work on the *Kojiki*, and in correspondence between the two in the 1760s, Norinaga asked several times for access to his work. In addition, during this same period, Mabuchi was urging several of his students to take up the *Kojiki*. One of these was Katō Umaki, a bakufu official who later became the teacher of Ueda Akinari; another was Tayasu Munetake, the second son of the shogun Yoshimune, who became a student and patron of Mabuchi.

Mabuchi, who began to study with Azumamaro at the age of thirty-six, gained fame for his analysis of the *Man'yōshū*, which was subject of his first great work, the *Man'yō kō* (A Theory of the *Man'yō*, 1758). Like Keichū before him, Mabuchi's encounter with the ancient poems led him to consider the other early texts as well. From the beginning the sheer difficulty of the language of the *Kojiki* and *Nihon shoki* seems to have both fascinated and baffled Mabuchi. He once wrote, for example, "I assembled [the works of] the people who related the ancient meanings and ancient sentences, and I read and analyzed the *Kojiki* seven times and reread the *Nihon shoki* three times, but although I have thought a great deal, still I have not succeeded [in understanding them]."[39] In works such as *Koku i kō* (On the Meaning of Our Country) and *Kotoba i kō* (On the Meaning of Words), he attempted to conceptualize the "difference" of the ancient language by enlarging upon Keichū's theory of the Japanese phonetic system, albeit with a significant difference. While Keichū's privileging of the "sounds" of the ancient language had relied upon a comparison of "original" Japanese with that of the later periods, Mabuchi provided an explanation for the "loss" of the former: the introduction of alien sounds via the adoption of Chinese characters.

Mabuchi argued that the original Japanese language was far superior to that of the Chinese, because the fifty sounds of the Japanese syllabary had been sufficient to speak of the myriad acts and things of the world. Moreover, these sounds, he asserted, were derived from heaven and earth and thus indicated the simplicity, directness, and naturalness that characterized life in ancient Japan before the introduction of Chinese culture. With cultural contact, however, there came different sounds—sounds derived not from nature but from men—and a seemingly endless stream of written characters that fundamentally altered the seamless relation of man/nature/sound that had characterized existence to this point. And as a result, life in Japan came to be characterized by division, distinctions, and distortion as the original unity was lost.[40] For Mabuchi, the possibility of recovering this original mode of experience rested upon recovering the language of the ancient period, and he began to argue that the *Kojiki* preserved this language and the *Nihon shoki* did not:

> In investigating the ancient histories, go first to the *Kojiki* and next to the *Nihon shoki*. The *Nihon shoki* assembles the various works of the ancient period, but the Confucianist Ki no Asaomi no Toneri [editor of the *Nihon shoki*] muddied the transmissions with Chinese writing and so there are many differences with the facts of the ancient period. . . . The *Kojiki* is the true history of our country during the ancient period. It is mainly concerned with our country's language, and so there is nothing better for recognizing the customs of the ancient period, knowing the ancient words, and understanding the ancient sentences.[41]

The emphasis on "understanding the ancient sentences" is significant. For Mabuchi the necessity to produce a "Japanese" text was motivated by an epistemological claim that differed fundamentally from those of the scholars who preceded him. Mabuchi never attempted to elucidate a cosmology from the Divine Age narrative, nor was he interested primarily in reading it as history. Although he described the *Kojiki* as "the essential history of our country's ancient age" and stated that one must study it "to know the way of the divine emperors," his analysis was focused not on verifying facts or identifying principles but on exploring the level of the text that he denoted as *fumi* or *bun*, the linguistic expressions, the phrases and sentences that comprised the textual surface.[42]

It was in the fumi, according to Mabuchi, that one could discern the qualities that had characterized existence in the ancient period. The attempt to conduct such an analysis is the topic of Mabuchi's work *Bun i kō* (On the Meaning of Fumi), which opens with the assertion that "in the sentences of the ancient age, there was nothing like 'style.' The many bothersome things that characterize the writing of men in later ages cannot be seen in the fumi of the ancient age."[43] As an example of the elegance, directness, lack of artifice, and strength that he asserted characterized the fumi of the *Kojiki*, Mabuchi took up the passage that describes the struggle between the sun deity Amaterasu and her brother, the deity of the "middle world," Susanō. He focused particularly on the words *takebi* (to act bravely) and *nigibi* (to be gentle) that were used to explain the actions and attitude of Amaterasu: "We should think deeply [about the use of these words]. Although this is a female deity, when the occasion demands it, she acts bravely and governs using her august majesty. But always she possesses a gentle heart. This is the foundation of the way of the gods: to watch and to listen and thereby to manage all matters. This is the teaching that should be used to manage the country and the family."[44]

Ultimately for Mabuchi, it was on this level—that of word choice and sentence structure—that the meaningfulness of the *Kojiki* was constituted. He urged his students to master the vocabulary and syntax of the *Kojiki* in the belief that it was this that would allow for the recovery of the "spirit" of the ancient people. As a result, many of Mabuchi's students began to experiment with writing in the style of ancient wabun. Ban Kōkei, for one, produced two manuals for those who aspired to write in the ancient language. In *Kunitsubun yoyo no ato* (Traces of Japanese Sentences from Each Age, 1777) he provided a list of model sentences drawn from classical texts, and in *Yakubun warabe no satoshi* (A Child's Guide to Translated Sentences, 1794), he discussed how to "translate" vulgar prose into elegant wabun.[45]

Mabuchi produced two versions of the *Kojiki*, the *Kojiki tōsho* (The Edited Kojiki, 1757) and the *Kanagaki Kojiki* (The Kojiki Written in Kana, 1765), both of which had the goal of correcting and standardizing the pronunciation of the text. The *Kojiki tōsho* was Mabuchi's attempt to improve upon the printed texts, the *Kan'eiban* and the *Gōtō Kojiki*. It takes the form of a copy of the *Gōtō Kojiki* to which Mabuchi attached editorial comments that took issue with Nobuyoshi's revisions, pronunciation guides, and interpretive annotations.

However, Mabuchi came to feel that this preliminary effort to improve upon the reading of the Kojiki did not go far enough. An inscription in the text suggests the cause of his dissatisfaction: "In the eighth month of 1757, I read this work while ill. I have corrected the meaning of the kun-readings, but still there are many old mistakes that are [founded upon] the reading of Chinese works. Later I will change it completely and perhaps make it into the language of the imperial court."[46] In the next years he held a series of seminars with his students in which they focused upon the problem of reading the Kojiki. It was these meetings that resulted in the production of the first "pure" wabun version of the text, the Kanagaki Kojiki. In this work Mabuchi abandoned the convention of kundoku—the insertion of the diacritical markers into the "Chinese" text—and in what seems to be an attempt to master the fumi of this work rewrote the text in a mixture of kana and Chinese characters according to the grammar of ancient Japanese as he understood it.

According to Mabuchi's "Japanese" Kojiki, the opening passage of the narrative should be read as follows:

Ametsuchi *no hajimete hirakuru toki,* Takamanohara ni *narizuru kami no mina ha,* Ame *no* Minakanushi *no kami.* Tsugi ni Takamimusubi no kami. Tsugi ni Kamimusubi no kami. Kono mihashira no kami ha, *narabi ni hitori kami narimashite, mi kakurimashinu.* Tsugi ni kuni ishiku, *ukaberu abura nashite* kurage nasu tadayoheru toki ni, ashikabi nasu kizashi noboru moni ni yorite *narizuru kami no mina ha,* Umashi-ashikabi-hikoji *no kami.* Tsugi ni Ame no Tokotachi no kami. Kono futahashira no kami *mo hitorigami narimashite, mikakurimashinu.* Kami no kudari no itsuhashira no kami ha kotogoto ni amatsukami nari.[47]

What is most immediately striking about this version of the Kojiki is how little it reflects the work of Azumamaro, a curious disjunction in light of the narrative of development that is usually used to frame the relation of the Azumamaro, Mabuchi, and Norinaga. Headnotes to the text suggest that Mabuchi had knowledge of the Kojiki *sakki*, but in his reading of the text he departed significantly from Azumamaro's work and quite often followed that of Nobuyoshi, in spite of his explicit criticism of the latter. For example, he rejected Azumamaro's insistence on attaching the honorific suffix (*tamau*) to the verbs that describe the actions of the deities and used instead the neutral *masu*. Moreover, unlike Azumamaro but like Nobuyoshi, he read the narrative as a series of completed actions, by carefully inserting the auxiliary verbs *tsu* and *nu* into the text. Perhaps the best evidence of Mabuchi's explicit goal of producing a purely "Japanese" text is his treatment of the phrases that in earlier texts had been read as *ashikabi no gotoku* (like reed-shoots) and *uka-beru abura no gotoku* (like floating oil), readings that reflect the usual kundoku treatment of the "Chinese" syntax of this passage. Instead, Mabuchi read these phrases as *ashikabi nasu* and *ukaberu abura nasu*, using the verbal suffix *nasu* that means "to be like." The close attention both to the textual surface and to the syntax and vocabulary of ancient Japanese are revealing of Mabu-chi's concern for what he called fumi.

Language has a different status in the work of Mabuchi's student and patron, Tayasu Munetake. Munetake had become involved in kokugaku prac-tice when, in 1742, he commissioned Arimaro, the son of Azumamaro, to produce a treatise on the origin, function, and method of the Japanese poetic form, waka, which has thirty-one syllables in the pattern of 5-7-5-7-7. The text Arimaro produced, *Kokka hachiron* (Eight Theories of Japanese Poetry), began a debate on poetics that continued into the nineteenth century. Ari-maro argued that poetry had no social or political function to serve but was merely an amusement or pastime, an enjoyment of words that could lift the spirit. Munetake, a good Confucianist for all his antiquarian interests, was outraged and composed a rebuttal of Arimaro's position, *Kokka hachiron jogen* (A Preface to the *Kokka hachiron*), in which he argued that poetry illustrated the workings of ri, the moral force that infused and ordered the social and natural worlds, by indicating that virtue was rewarded and bad behavior pun-ished. Secondly, citing the preface to the tenth-century poetic anthology, the *Kokinwakashū*, which stated that poetry had the power "to move heaven and earth, and soothe the gods and the demons," Munetake held that poetry could serve as an emotional outlet for man's passions and therefore be an aid to governance.

In addition to producing his own critique of Arimaro, Munetake also sought out the opinions of Mabuchi, who interjected his voice into the debate by means of his work *Kokka hachiron josetsu shūi* (Gleanings from the Preface of the *Kokka hachiron*). Mabuchi agreed with Tayasu's assertion that poetry had a political function: he argued that it expressed the emotions of the speaker and thus could allow the ruler to grasp the sentiments of his subjects.[48] This was a position Munetake could support, and in 1746 he became Mabuchi's patron and student. Like his teacher, Munetake too became intensely inter-ested in the Kojiki. In the early 1760s, the same period in which Mabuchi was writing the *Kojiki tōsho* and *Kanagaki Kojiki*, Munetake began his own exegesis of the text, which resulted in the work called *Kojiki shōsetsu* (A Detailed Explanation of the *Kojiki*).⁴⁹ The *Shōsetsu* consists of an annotated text in three chapters, to which have been attached two supplemental chapters that attempt to elucidate difficult or significant passages. An explanatory note inserted in the work by Munetake's retainer, Nagano Kiyoyoshi, suggests the author's attitude toward the *Kojiki*,

> Not only did he think that *Kojiki* was first among the various histories of our country but also that it contained true explanations that cannot be seen in the other histories, and thus my lord thought first that this work must be edited. Although there are various versions of the work available, that edited by Nobuyoshi was for the most part acceptable, and therefore he took this up and edited it. . . . Although it was for the most part correct, he believed that the diacritical makers had to be revised.⁵⁰

The valorization of the *Kojiki*, as well as the concern for how to read the text, suggests the influence of Mabuchi, but from this shared problematic, Munetake produced a substantially different *Kojiki*.

One point of departure was their treatment of the issue of kundoku. Unlike Mabuchi, Munetake did not rewrite the text in wabun; instead, he followed the convention of inserting diacritical markers and pronunciation glosses into the original text. But more than any of the earlier readers of the *Kojiki*, Munetake demonstrated his awareness of the problems involved in trying to vocalize this network of Chinese characters. He was particularly concerned with the status of those characters that functioned as pronominals, conjunctions, particles, and the like. These kinds of words had a particularly ambivalent status within the text: some were necessary in terms of Chinese syntax but were not easily "translated" into Japanese; others rendered the sentence incomprehensible as Chinese and thus seemed to signify some aspect of the ancient language. In a gesture that foreshadowed Norinaga's work, Munetake focused on these problematic characters and paid particular attention to their operation within the text. According to the *Kojiki shōsetsu*, the opening passage of the *Kojiki* should be read as follows:

> Ametsuchi *hajimete hirakeshi toki*, Taka-amabara ni *naru kami no mina ha*, Ame no Minakanushi no ōmikami. Tsugi ni Takamimusubi no ōmikami. Tsugi ni Kamimusubi no ōmikami. Kono mihashira no ōmikami ha *narabi ni hitori kami to narimashite, mi wo kakushimashiki.* Tsugi ni kuni *ishiku ukaberu abura no goto nareba*, kurage nasu tadayoheru toki, ashikabi no goto kizashi noboru mono ni yorite *narimaseru ōmikami no mina ha*,

Umashi-ashikabi-hikoji no ōmikami. Tsugi ni Ame no Tokotachi no ōmikami. Kono futahashira no kami mo hitorigami narimashite, mi wo kakushimashiki. Kami no kudari no itsuhashira no ōmikami ha wakite amagami nari.⁵¹

An example of Munetake's concern for the characters that expressed
grammatical functions is his treatment of the third character of the original
text, which some of the earlier editors, including Mabuchi had read as *no*.
Munetake argued that this *no* is grammatically unnecessary in wabun and
dropped it. The same kind of careful attention to the workings of the ancient language is evident in his discussion of the proper articulation of the
character *ten* (heaven), which earlier commentators had read sometimes as
ame and sometimes *ama*. Munetake argued that it should be read as *ame* unless it became part of a compound noun, when euphonics required it to be
pronounced as *ama*.⁵² The articulation of certain key reoccurring nouns also
come under scrutiny. For example, the character for "deity" is consistently
read, not as *kami*, but as *ōmikami*, with an honorific prefix attached.

What was the relation between this careful attention to the syntax of the
text and the extraction of meaning from its narrative? The construction of
meaning was carried out within the *Shōsetsu* itself by inserting a series of interpretive glosses parenthetically into the text. In addition, certain passages
were treated at greater length in the supplemental volumes (*bekki*). Munetake's commentary reveals that, like Hakuseki, he relied upon a set of euhemeristic strategies. The relocation of the narrative within the human sphere
is revealed in the first of Munetaka's bracketed comments: he explains the
term *Taka-amabara* (usually read as *Takamagahara* [the heavenly plain]) by stating that "*Taka-ama* means august, and *hara* means large, so *Taka-amabara*
refers to what is later called the imperial capital."⁵³ He goes on to explain
that the deity name Ame no Minakanushi was an appellation applied to the
first lord of capital, that is, the emperor, while that of Takamimusubi referred to the crown prince. The description of the land as "like floating oil"
referred to the confused state of the country after the death of the ruler at a
time when his successor was too young to rule effectively. The sprouting of
the reed shoots was a metaphor that conveyed how quickly the child-ruler
matured, so that the restoration of order soon followed.⁵⁴

As these comments on the opening passage suggest, Munetaka transformed the Divine Age narrative into a description of the early imperial court.
Like Hakuseki's *Koshitsu*, the *Kojiki shōsetsu* rejected the potential of any cos-

mological significance of the *Kojiki* narrative. But unlike Hakuseki, whose analysis functioned to cast doubt upon the imperial family's claim to genealogical integrity, Munetaka attempted to turn the text into a handbook for rulers that exemplified the various kinds of problems that could beset an emergent dynasty. Significantly, Munetaka's concern for language had but little to do with the production of this new meaning. None of his syntactical revisions, or his alterations of the vocalized text, are implicated in the etymologies and the metaphors he constructs in order to read the text in terms of this new narrative.

The continuing power of the Confucian paradigms can be seen as well in the work of Tanigawa Kotosuga, a contemporary of Norinaga and one with whom he had much contact.[55] Like Norinaga, Kotosuga was a native of Ise, which had become a stronghold of Shinto faith and scholarship due in part to its proximity to the Ise Shrine, where the deity Amaterasu is worshipped. Twenty years older than Norinaga, he was already an established figure when Norinaga, as a student in Kyoto in the early 1750s, first became interested in the emerging discourse on Japan. In 1732 Kotosuga formally became a student of Yamazaki Ansai's school of Suika Shinto, but he soon evinced a concern for the language of the ancient texts that was at odds with the reliance on questionable etymologies that characterized much of the scholarship produced within the Suika school. Kotosuga was in Kyoto studying medicine in the 1720s when prominent Neo-Confucian scholars in that city were first coming under the influence of Sorai's "learning of ancient words and texts" and when Keichū's works on the *Man'yōshū* were being circulated among the various schools of waka composition and poetics.[56] He soon distinguished himself from other Suika scholars, by analyzing not only the Divine Age chapters of the *Nihon shoki* and the so-called Five Classics of Shinto — the usual province of the Suika scholars — but also other early Japanese works, the *Man'yōshū*, the gazetteers known as fudoki, as well as the prose narratives of the Heian period.

The new concern for the language of the ancient texts that his expansion of the Suika canon suggests is apparent in Kotosuga's *Nihon shoki tsūsho* (A Compendium Treatise on the *Nihon shoki*, completed c. 1748, published in 1762). The *Nihon shōki tsūsho* was simultaneously a collection of *Nihon shoki* scholarship, an analysis of the *Nihon shoki* narrative, and an attempt to revise the kundoku of this text. As an appendix to the first chapter, Kotosuga attached a text he called *Wago tsūon* (A Compendium of the Sounds of the Japanese Language), a work that inserted his voice into the expanding debate on the orthography, phonology, and syntax of the ancient Japanese language. In it he attempted to account for the relationship between the phonemes of early Japanese and the Chinese characters used to inscribe these sounds by delineating the various characters used to represent what seemed to be a single phoneme.

Kotosuga's interest in kana usage was tied to a number of grammatical issues. He was particularly concerned with analyzing the inflection of verbs in ancient Japanese. What, he wondered, was indicated by the phonetic changes seen in a single verb such as *ta* (to stand) which became *tachi*, *tatsu*, *tate*, and *tato* when linked to certain auxiliary verbs that indicated tense, negation, politeness, and so on? In order to account for such changes, Kotosuga charted a variety of verbs against one another and demonstrated that the vowel sounds involved were stable and unchanging. He then speculated that these phonetic modifications were expressive of a set of meaningful differences. For example, Kotosuga argued that the sound \i\ expressed an action not yet completed or fulfilled; \o\ indicated an action that occurred spontaneously, of itself, and so on. This, according to at least one modern scholar, was the first attempt to construct a metalevel grammar of the Japanese language.[57] In the aftermath of the publication of the *Wago tsūon*, Kamo no Mabuchi too would approach similar problems in his *Go i kō* (On the Meaning of Words, 1769), as did Fujitani Nariakira, the father of Mitsue, in the *Ayuisho*. Norinaga too read this work: there exists a copy of the *Wago tsūon* in Norinaga's hand dated to 1755.

Kotosuga's revision of the *Nihon shoki* was not based solely on kana usage or syntactical revision; he also made use of etymological studies as the basis for a philological reconstruction of the lexicon of ancient Japanese. After the completion of the *Nihon shōki tsūsho*, these notes were compiled into a dictionary-encyclopedia entitled *Wakun no shiori* (A Guide to Japanese Words).[58] In its final form, the *Wakun no shiori* contained almost 21,000 words and made reference to Korean, Chinese, and even the Ainu language in its attempt to record and explain the vocabulary of Japanese. All of this reveals Kotosuga's very real concern for language, as do his efforts to make contact with first Mabuchi and then Norinaga in the decade of the 1760s, efforts that led Mabuchi to write with some irritation, "Recently there is someone named Tanigawa Tansai [i.e., Kotosuga] who has annotated the *Nihon shoki*. . . . Whenever his son-in-law or students come [to Edo] they approach me and ask questions directly."[59] Yet these morphological and etymological pursuits ultimately had little impact on how Kotosuga understood the narrative of the Divine Age. Indeed, he ends the *Wago tsūon* with a quotation from a Chinese Confucianist that indicates how firmly he continued to adhere to the essential hermeneutical claim that ordered the discourse of Suika Shinto: "Although characters are created by men, in fact they originate in nature and their meaning is of nature. Therefore, as for what the sages entrust to words, although [these works] are separated by distance, sounds, and writing, if one interprets them, the meaning is the same."⁶⁰ The form of the *Nihon shoki tsūsho*—the manner in which it assembles and orders the interpretations of previous exegetical texts—is modeled upon that of the *Nihon shoki* itself. In the *Nihon shoki*, the insertion of multiple alternative versions after the "main narrative" created a series of overlapping and contesting narrative streams, the relation of which is never made explicit. In mimicking the *Nihon shoki* form in the organization of his compendium, Kotosuga avoided the need to explicitly delineate a new meaning, even as he assumed a critical stance toward certain contemporary efforts to situate the narrative within a new interpretive register.

For example, Kotosuga was incensed at the decision of the editors of the *Dai Nihon shi* to ignore the contents of the Divine Age chapters and begin their story with the exploits of Jinmu, the first "human" ruler:

> If one does not write of the origins of the imperial line, then how can one know of the nature of the lineage of Jinmu and those who follow him? What about the notion that the continuity of the imperial line for ten thousand generations is different from the vulgarity of the rulers of China and so on? The Confucianists of our country cling to that which they can see and hear, and they do not discern the profound mysteries of Shinto and fall into the shallow learning of China.⁶¹

This kind of criticism of "Confucianists" would seem to suggest that Kotosuga had begun to think in terms of a meaning of the text that was specifically "Japanese," but if so, this meaning is not made explicit in the *Nihon shoki tsūsho:* he continues to deploy the Neo-Confucian concepts of ri and ki, yin and yang, and the five elements unquestioningly. This continued reliance on these categories came under repeated attack from Norinaga in their correspondence. But Kotosuga held firm, stating in one letter,

> I have received your repeated instructions on the concepts of yin and yang, and heaven and earth, and your belief that for those whose eyes are dazzled by Chinese works it is difficult to perceive the true mean-

ing of the way of the deities. Even if this is so, . . . since the preface of the Kojiki and the Divine Age chapters [of the Nihon shoki] are of the same meaning, then I wonder how one can believe that only the Kojiki contains the mysterious truth of the great way of ancient times.[62]

Kotosuga's response then was to argue that the ancient texts did indeed reveal universal principles and that this proved the validity of the Suika reading. Norinaga replied by asserting that the Kojiki was written precisely to preserve the "truth" of the Divine Age from the pernicious influence of China.

TOWARD THE KOJIKIDEN

My discussion has relied upon a chronological ordering of Kojiki and Nihon shoki scholarship, but this does not imply that these textual practices superseded one another in time. Rather, many of the meanings that the Divine Age narrative had acquired over the course of the preceding decades were still current in the 1760s when Norinaga began his work on the Kojiki. For example, Yamazaki Ansai's conception of the narrative as an exposition of the workings of the Neo-Confucian principles of ri and ki was taught widely by the more than a thousand disciples Ansai acquired in his lifetime. Embraced by many of the priests at the Ise Shrine, it had become a kind of orthodoxy by Norinaga's time. Similarly, as Tayasu Munetake's work suggested, Hakuseki's argument that the narrative, correctly read, revealed real historical events was widely embraced by other scholars, who debated such issues as whether Takamagahara, which Hakuseki had located in Kyushu, was located instead in Nakatsu, Yamato, or elsewhere. Significantly, although very different, both these paradigms functioned to reify the Tokugawa social and political order. While Ansai found in the Divine Age narrative "proof" of the cosmological underpinnings of virtues such as "loyalty" that supported bakufu and domainal authority, Hakuseki had made the narrative into an exposition of the legitimacy of Tokugawa rule through his reference to the "mandate of heaven."

The discourse on the ancient language that took form in the work of Keichū, Azumamaro, Mabuchi, and Kotosuga was ordered by notions of cultural and temporal difference that seem to contest the universalism of Confucianism upon which the work of Ansai and Hakuseki was founded. Each rejected the "sieve" approach by which Ansai and Hakuseki identified certain terms as significant and dismissed others as irrelevant and began to explore ancient Japanese as a unique linguistic system. However, the new ideological value attached to language did not itself lead to a new understanding of the Divine Age narrative. In fact, until Norinaga, no one succeeded in producing an interpretation of the Divine Age narrative that radically departed from the Confucian paradigms of metaphysics or history. Thus, Kotosuga affirmed the Suika reading, Azumamaro appropriated its terms, and Mabuchi never attached a specific meaning to the Divine Age narrative itself but only deployed its language as a sign of the "spirit" of the ancient period.

In contrast, Norinaga would make the claim to have recovered the ancient language in its completeness the foundation of a new reading of the *Kojiki*. It allowed him to reject the universalist claims of Confucianism and to transform the ancient language of Japan into the privileged signifier of Japanese cultural identity. This was the foundation of his discussion of Japan as community. While Ansai, Hakuseki, and even Kotosuga assumed that "Japan" had not differed significantly from China, for both were ordered by the transcendent ethical force that was ri, Norinaga would argue that Japan was inherently both different and superior.

Chapter 3

Motoori Norinaga: Discovering Japan

In the late 1970s Kobayashi Hideo, one of the most influential literary critics in postwar Japan, wrote a best-selling biography of Motoori Norinaga.
In this work, Kobayashi described Norinaga's stance toward the *Kojiki* in
terms that evoke a sense of direct, almost palpable, contact between reader
and text:

> First of all, the notion of explaining from "here" a story that is "over
> there" never occurred to [Norinaga]. Rather, there is no doubt that for
> him, to listen to the narrative was to feel expectation and excitement as
> he was drawn into the incomprehensible story. Within the act of anno-
> tation that requires selflessness and reticence, he encountered some-
> thing unknown, the oral transmissions [recorded in the *Kojiki*], and at
> some point he became intimate enough to converse with his partner,
> and that is all there was to it. We can say that what they spoke of were
> the facts regarding the ancient people's experience with the deities. . . .
> What Norinaga touched directly was the body of the narrative, what he
> heard directly were the words it expressed, its naked heavy voice.[1]

I begin with Kobayashi's words because they convey so succinctly Norinaga's own depiction of the process by which he read the *Kojiki*. Late in life,
Norinaga characterized the *Kojikiden* in the following terms: "My goal in explaining the [ancient] way was not to insert even the slightest degree of my
own pretensions of knowledge, but just to read the Divine Text exactly as
it was written. If you compare [my work] with other annotations, you will
know this."[2] In this way Norinaga argued that the *Kojikiden* was not an "interpretation" (*kaishaku*)—the term for him implied the imposition of external
theories upon the text—but merely an exposition of the language of the text
that added nothing.

This linguistic claim was the foundation of Norinaga's discourse on Japan and Japaneseness. He argued that in the *Kojiki* he had discovered *Yamato kotoba*, the original language of Japan that had existed before cultural contact with China. Yamato is the name used to refer to the early Japanese state in the eighth-century texts, while kotoba means "language." Norinaga made Yamato kotoba into the signifier of the "difference" of the ancient Japan, culturally in relation to the other that was China and historically in relation to the other that was the Tokugawa world. His study of the *Kojiki* rested on the assertion that the *Kojiki*, read "correctly" as Yamato kotoba, revealed a mode of consciousness that allowed Japan to take form as a "natural" community, one in which laws, institutions, and ethical principles had no place. Thus community became something not produced from "outside" its members or by them but rather constituted from within them. In Norinaga's conception, Japan took form as the expression of an innate Japaneseness.

The "discovery" of Yamato kotoba was Norinaga's great achievement. As Kobayashi Hideo's description of Norinaga hearing the "naked heavy voice" of the text suggests, the notion that there is something that can be named Yamato kotoba and that it is recoverable still reverberates in contemporary discussions of Japanese culture. Koyasu Nobukuni has spoken of Yamato kotoba as "Japan's *imago*," the continuing source of the modern ideology of Japanese identity.[3] In contrast, in the late Tokugawa period, Norinaga's description of Yamato kotoba and the theory of community it supported were attacked by Akinari, Mitsue, and Moribe in their own analyses of the Divine Age narrative. They recognized that Norinaga's conception of the ancient language was intimately tied to an interpretive project.

But if there were critics, there were also many in Tokugawa Japan who embraced the vision of Japan that took form within Norinaga's work. In 1764, when he began the *Kojikiden*, Norinaga had authored only a few scholarly works, *Ashiwake no obune* (A Small Boat Breaking through the Reeds, 1756) and *Isonokami no sasamegoto* (Personal Views on Poetry, 1763), two treatises on poetics, and *Shibun yōryō* (Essentials of Murasaki's Work, 1763), a study of the *Genji monogatari*. In the 1780s, as chapters of the *Kojikiden* began to circulate, Norinaga quickly gained a local reputation as a scholar, and as the *Kojikiden* began to be published in the 1790s, he became the center of a network of disciples scattered all over Japan.[4] In 1783, Norinaga had 87 students, all but 10 of whom lived in Ise. By 1794, he had 354 students, 167 of whom came from outside of Ise. And the school he called the Suzuya continued to grow: at the time of his death in 1801, Norinaga's students numbered almost 500.[5] To explore the vision of Japan that Tokugawa readers embraced, I want to analyze in depth the Divine Age chapters of the *Kojikiden*, the most influential and controversial section of this massive work.

THE *KOJIKI* AS CANONICAL TEXT

The *Kojikiden* begins with a prolonged discussion of a series of methodological issues. In the long opening section, Norinaga explains and justifies his focus on the *Kojiki*, analyzes the method of inscription used within it, and discusses how he was able to uncode the language of the text.[6] This is surely the most widely read part of the *Kojikiden*, and many readers never get beyond it, but the relationship between this statement of methodology and the body of the work that follows has not been sufficiently interrogated.[7] For example, Tokumitsu Hisanari, the author of a history of *Kojiki* studies, began his discussion of the *Kojikiden* with the declaration that "a shortcut to knowing the whole of the *Kojikiden* is to examine the contents of the first chapter, which can be viewed as a summary."[8] In fact, this opening chapter is not an objective description of what is to come but rather a series of ideological statements that were consistently compromised in practice. In the gap that opens up between Norinaga's description of his method and the actual process of explication that follows, it is possible to discern the strategies that allowed Norinaga to impose a new text upon the *Kojiki*.

Norinaga began his opening chapter by putting forth a history of the earliest Japanese texts, the goal of which was to demonstrate the special nature of the *Kojiki*. This was a strategy that would be followed by later kokugaku scholars who, like Norinaga, would attempt to demonstrate the canonical nature of their chosen object of study. But in exploring how and why the ancient texts were written, the kokugaku scholars had scant evidence with which to work. The *Nihon shoki* and the *Shoku Nihongi* (The Chronicles of Japan Continued, compiled 869) contain only four references to the writing of historical works, and no mention is made of the *Kojiki*. The only evidence of when the *Kojiki* was compiled comes from its preface, which gives the date of 712. Norinaga used this date to declare that "among the ancient texts that have been passed down, the *Kojiki* is the oldest."[9] Still, this declaration alone did not allow him to privilege the *Kojiki*. The fact that the *Kojiki* was not mentioned in the *Nihon shoki* had been cited as evidence that the work was not regarded as significant by the court of eighth- and ninth-century Japan. Norinaga wanted to demonstrate that the *Kojiki* was not a "flawed" early text discarded with the compilation of the *Nihon shoki*, or merely an early manuscript of one of the variant texts (issho) included in the *Nihon shoki*. He asserted that it was compiled with a very specific intention and embodied a mode of inscription different from that used in the *Nihon shoki*. Describing the circumstances of the *Nihon shoki*'s compilation, Norinaga wrote:

> It was a time when officials were increasingly infatuated with Chinese learning, so they thought that the *Kojiki* was a very trifling thing, because when one compared it to the histories of China, it was very straightforward, without rhetorical embellishments. Therefore they added a wide variety of events and established a system of dating, and even attached a lot of Chinese-sounding language and composed sentences in the Chinese style in order to make it seem like a history from over there.[10]

Norinaga argued that, unlike the *Nihon shoki*, the *Kojiki* was a conscious and purposeful attempt to retain "how things actually were in the ancient times, by taking the ancient language as its object and not attempting to embellish the words of its prose."[11]

In this statement from the first page of the first chapter of the *Kojikiden* Norinaga began to establish the claim that underlay the entirety of the project that followed: that only the *Kojiki* recorded the ancient language and therefore the reality of the ancient age. The relation Norinaga constructed between the language of the *Kojiki* and the "real" of the past is made explicit in what is perhaps the most often quoted passage of the *Kojikiden*:

> Words, ideas, and objects are things that are in accord with one another, so that the ancient period had its words, ideas, and things, and the later periods have their words, ideas, and things, and China had its words, ideas, and things. But the *Nihon shoki* took the words of a later age and wrote of the ancient period, and took the words of China and wrote of the imperial land, and therefore there are many places that are not in accord. However the *Kojiki* added no pretentious elements but just inscribed what was passed down from the ancient age, and so its words, ideas, and things are in accord with one another, and everything reveals the truth of that age.[12]

Norinaga's assertion was that "words"—that is, language or verbal expression—directly reflected not only the workings of the human mind but also the "reality" of things as experienced by that mind. Over the course of time or across cultures, languages differed, reflecting differences in the way human beings viewed and organized experience. Therefore, Norinaga argued, to understand the ancient age one must interrogate the language of the early texts. Similarly, to write about the past, Norinaga came to believe, one had to adopt that mode of expression. Consequently, in the *Kojikiden* and elsewhere, he began to make use of a new style of writing, which has come to be termed "imitation ancient style" (*gikobun*). Norinaga criticized the students of Mabuchi, many of whom in attempting to imitate the fumi of the ancient texts often did little more than insert an ancient vocabulary into contemporary syntax. In contrast, Norinaga called for grammatical rigor. The gikobun he wrote took the vocabulary of eighteenth-century Japanese, often inventively rendered into kun or "Japanese" readings (as opposed to those derived from Chinese) and then embedded it into the syntax of the ancient Japanese language. Norinaga became a master of gikobun, and he created a prose style marked by lucidity and great rhetorical power.

On the face of it, Norinaga's statement on the relation of words, ideas, and things appears to be a recognition of the linguistic constitution of experience. Changes in language, he argued, were never merely superficial but were expressive of significant transformations in the modes of organizing and perceiving the world. However, other statements by Norinaga suggest that his conception of language was never as rigorously historicist as the language/ideas/reality equation suggested. Like Mabuchi before him, Norinaga did not view the differences between the ancient language and that of the present purely as the product of historical change. Rather, the elements of linguistic change that he discovered in the language of his own time were inevitably characterized as "mistakes," "corruptions," and "vulgarities." For example, in *Kotoba no tama no o* (On Linking Words, 1785), he stated in regard to the use of the grammatical particles *te*, *ni*, *wo*, and *ha*, "In the beginning of the Divine Age, the use of [these particles] in the language of men was naturally established, and thus even though no one paid attention, they were correct. No one studied or discussed them. But in the later period, language gradually became more vulgar, and as the elegant language became more distant, there were many mistakes."[13]

In this way, Norinaga argued not only that the ancient language he found in the ancient texts was different from that of the present but also that it was superior. As a result, a strongly programmatic impulse ordered Norinaga's work on language. He did not merely want to understand the language of the past but to recover it through his own work.

It was in light of this understanding of language that Norinaga developed his criticism of the *Nihon shoki*. He argued that the editors of this text, in abandoning the ancient language in order to incorporate Chinese words, concepts, and syntax, had disrupted the representational value of the ancient language, so that the "reality" of the text was not the "reality" of the ancient period. As an example, Norinaga pointed to the opening passage of the Nihon shoki which stated, "Long ago when heaven and earth were not yet separated and the yin and the yang not yet divided, there was still a primal chaos." What he found problematic about this passage was not merely the inclusion of words of Chinese origin such as "yin," "yang," and "chaos." He argued also that they represented the rise of an epistemology that was alien to ancient Japan. According to Norinaga, "to change the male and female deities into male and female principles is not just a difference of words."[14] Rather, these "words" represented a new way of perceiving the world, one "in which people think in terms of concepts [kotowari] and, using them, explain things." Before the introduction of these concepts from China, the ancient Japanese understood the world in very different terms: "Heaven and earth were just heaven and earth, men and women were men and women, fire and water were fire and water, each with its own nature and form."[15]

However, Norinaga asserted that the inclusion of such concepts as yin and yang within the Nihon shoki was not only a problem of the eighth century, the period in which the text was inscribed. As time passed, these organizing categories were diffused throughout Japanese society, so that little remained of the "ancient way" of perceiving the world. Norinaga labeled the consciousness (kokoro) ordered by such ideas the "Chinese mind" (karagokoro) and believed that it was an all but insurmountable barrier to the recovery of the "original" language and "authentic" reality of the ancient period:

> As for the Chinese mind, this does not refer just to liking Chinese customs or respecting China. Rather, the tendency of people of this age to want to discuss everything in terms of good and bad, right and wrong, and to want to speak of the principles of things has its foundation in the Chinese classics. It is not just the people who have read the Chinese classics who do this. It is the same even with those who have never read a single book. . . . Since the custom of learning from China has continued for more than a thousand years, naturally the Chinese mind has permeated our society and penetrated deeply into people's hearts. . . . When one thinks that "this is not the Chinese mind, but is just commonsense," then one is after all not yet able to distance oneself from the Chinese mind.[16]

The distinction between the "Chinese mind" and the "ancient way" is one of the most productive of the interpretive devices deployed in the annotations of the *Kojikiden*. Norinaga consistently labeled the received understanding of the *Kojiki* as "Chinese," while claiming that his own reading of the text was not influenced by these categories and therefore recovered the consciousness of the Japanese people in the ancient period. The question arises, of course, of how Norinaga, a product of the society he himself described as permeated by the "Chinese mind," was able to escape its pernicious influence. He used words such as "cleanse" and "purge" to explain the process of freeing oneself from the "Chinese mind," and he argued that the repeated reading of the *Kojiki* had allowed him to remove these categories from his mind.

It is important to take note of the relation of individual and culture implied in this explanation. Norinaga argued that to recover a "Japanese" consciousness, one need only to strip away the secondary, alien culture of China. His conception of Japan was founded upon a notion of fundamental and distinct cultural identity, and he rejected completely the claim to universality that underlay Confucian practice in Japan. While Japanese Confucianists, of whatever school, had assumed that the surface narrative of the *Kojiki* and *Nihon shoki* could only express principles already constituted within the Chinese classics, Norinaga rejected outright the possibility of similitude. The notion of original cultural identity for Norinaga came to mean that the Confucian evocation of "humanness," as a state that preceded or transcended culture, no longer had any validity. Human beings, he asserted, were born into culture. One could lack awareness of the original Japaneseness, but it was always present—latent and potentially recoverable. It was this conception of cultural identity as innate, rather than acquired, that became the foundation of Norinaga's reading of the *Kojiki*—and the theory of community he constructed.

Within the *Kojikiden*, Norinaga made use of the notion of the "Chinese mind" to define otherness in terms of a set of recognized and discrete operations. Against the "Chinese mind" that was known, he could define what it meant to be "Japanese," a state that came to be understood negatively as that which is "not-Chinese." However, having "proven" that the *Nihon shoki* was a corrupt text, Norinaga still had to demonstrate that the *Kojiki* was the pure inscription of the ancient language he claimed it to be, this in spite of the fact that only eight years separate it from the *Nihon shoki*, the text he himself asserted was written in a society that was wholeheartedly embracing all things Chinese. To accomplish this Norinaga turned again to evidence from the preface of the *Kojiki*, said to be authored by the courtier Yasumaro. Here he found a brief description of how and why the *Kojiki* was compiled. The emperor Tenmu, having heard that the genealogies and stories preserved by the noble families in the form of written records called the *honji* and *kuji* were being altered and false information included, ordered these records corrected so that they could be handed down intact to later generations. A courtier named Hieda no Are was given the task of reading, memorizing, and reciting the imperial genealogies and the stories concerning the ancient times. Then, more than thirty years later, the reigning ~~emperor~~ Empress Genmei, with the goal of correcting the existing records, ordered Yasumaro to reinscribe the records that Hieda no Are was able to recite from memory. This was the origin of the text known as the *Kojiki*.

Norinaga would always refer to that which was recorded in the *Kojiki* as "the oral transmissions from the Divine Age" (*kamiyo kara no tsutaegoto*), but the preface itself relates not the immediate recording of oral transmissions but a very different process of inscription. What was recorded were the *honji* and *kuji* texts that were *read* aloud. In order to maintain the distinction that authorized his privileging of the *Kojiki*, Norinaga had to suppress the role of these earlier texts and questions such as how they were written, when, and by whom. It was by raising these issues that Norinaga had dismissed the *Nihon shoki*, arguing that officials with "private pretensions of knowledge" had produced a flawed work incapable of conveying the reality of the archaic age.

Norinaga dealt with the problem of authorship by inserting a new element into the relation of text and reader defined by the *Kojiki* preface. He asserted that "the emperor with his own mouth read the kuji and made Hieda no Are listen to them. Then she learned to read and recite them just as they had been spoken [by the emperor]."[17] In other words, according to Norinaga, Hieda no Are did not learn the "ancient matters" from written texts but from the emperor, seemingly the only one who still knew the ancient oral transmissions. It was the emperor who was able to teach Are how to move from the written records back to the oral transmissions of the ancient period. Thus the insertion of the emperor into this textual history allowed Norinaga to assert that the *Kojiki* recorded directly and immediately the truth of the Divine Age: "It was the [emperor's] intention that after someone had learned to vocalize [the kuji], they should then be inscribed just as they were spoken. . . . This indeed was the foundation of the learning of our land. If he did not care about the language, but rather was just concerned about principles, then when he ordered the record made, it would have been pointless to first have someone learn to recite."[18]

For Norinaga, establishing the oral nature of the text was an issue of great importance. Unlike writing, which Norinaga viewed as the product of a singular and self-conscious author perhaps acting on personal ambitions and prejudices, orality was regarded as quintessentially "social." The product of the community, it was free from the mediation of individual intentions. Norinaga used the figure of the emperor in order to assert that this kind of orality existed even in the age of writing. For Norinaga, the emperor, whom he viewed as a direct conduit to the deities, became a kind of icon of the primal Japanese community. By inserting the emperor into his textual history, he was able to establish that the narrative of the Divine Age was a story that no single person told and the *Kojiki*, a text that no single person wrote.

The rejection of the possibility of an "author" was essential to Norinaga's hermeneutic. The *Kojiki* had to be regarded as a transparent transcription of the oral transmissions of the Divine Age. Norinaga insisted that "not even the slightest bit of new meaning was added by the editor, rather it was just that which Are had learned and recited." This assertion had consequences for the act of reading as well. Norinaga argued that to understand the *Kojiki*, it was essential "to vocalize the text by seeking out the pure ancient language and to avoid mixing in any of the Chinese style."[19] Much of chapter 1 of the *Kojikiden* was devoted to explaining the process by which the reader could move from the inscribed text to discover the ancient transmissions that Hieda no Are was said to have memorized and preserved.

The problem, of course, was that the *Kojiki* was written completely in Chinese characters. Norinaga recognized that characters within the text were used in three distinct ways: as purely phonetic symbols (kana) that represented a sound derived from the "Chinese" pronunciation (the *on*-reading) of that character, as ideographs that represent meaning but not sound (*masaji*), and as "borrowed characters" (*ateji*) in which a kun or "Japanese" reading was attached to the character without reference to the meaning of the character. An example of kana was the use of the character *an* (peace) to represent the sound \a\. The term Yamato provides an example of masaji: the characters *tai* (great) and *wa* (peace) were used to write it. Arai Hakuseki had characterized the character for "deity" (kami) as a case of ateji, arguing that it was merely "borrowed" to represent "those above." Discerning the status of any particular character in order to attach a pronunciation, however, was merely a preliminary step. The more profound problem, Norinaga asserted, was how to reconstruct the ancient language as it functioned on the level of the sentence: "All of the ancient texts are written in Chinese prose, so when one tries to vocalize the prose, even if one changes the words one by one into the ancient language, the way of connecting them together is still in the style of Chinese, not that of our land."[20]

While Norinaga recognized that much of the *Kojiki* was written according to the rules of Chinese syntax, his analysis focused specifically on a set of peculiarities that disrupt the regularity of this prose. He delineated these carefully. First, there were sentences in which certain words were "spelled out" phonetically in kana. Secondly, there were sentences that made use of what Norinaga termed the *senmyō* style, after the ancient imperial edicts that were recorded in the *Shoku Nihongi*. In this case, the root of a verb would be written in masaji, while the inflected portion of the verb would be written in kana. Thirdly, there were sentences that, although written in Chinese syntax, contained certain irregularities in word order that seemed to reflect the syntax of the ancient Japanese language. For Norinaga, these peculiarities, situated here and there within the stream of characters arranged by means of Chinese syntax, signified the "real" purpose of the text—the preservation of the ancient language. He insisted, "The characters are just borrowed things, applied after the fact, so one should not probe them too deeply. Rather the goal of study should be to think of the ancient words again and again and thereby know the ancient way."[21]

But how could readers supposedly steeped in the "Chinese mind" discover the ancient language buried beneath this complex system of inscription? Norinaga insisted that this was possible, arguing that traces of the ancient language had been preserved in the imperial edicts recorded in the *Shoku Nihongi*, the ritual prayers (*norito*) of the *Engi shiki*, and the poems contained in the *Man'yōshū*, *Nihon shoki*, and the *Kojiki*. "By learning and reciting these earnestly, one could learn the ancient language," and then apply this knowledge to the *Kojiki* in order to reconstruct its language. However, the movement from these texts to the *Kojiki* was not as straightforward as this statement implied. The *Engi shiki* was compiled almost two hundred years after the *Nihon shoki*, which Norinaga had asserted was already permeated with the "Chinese mind." Moreover, certain stylistic conventions characterized the form of both the prayers and the edicts, conventions that did not necessarily inform the narrative style of the *Kojiki*. Similarly, the ancient poems too were characterized by peculiarities of form, which included the poetic convention of alternating lines of five and seven syllables, as well as the rule-governed use of certain particles. Nonetheless, Norinaga believed that "one could discern and discard every bit of Chineseness" and thus gain an understanding of the ancient language.[22]

The teleological logic of this account is apparent: one read the ancient texts to strip away the "Chinese mind," but to read them properly, one must first remove the "Chinese mind." Nonetheless, this process became the supposed foundation for the production of a new *Kojiki*. Against the network of Chinese characters that made up the original text, Norinaga inscribed a stream of kana. Line by line next to the kanbun, he rewrote the *Kojiki* in the ancient language as he imagined it, discarding the convention of the diacritical markers. It is possible to read Norinaga's kana *Kojiki* while ignoring the original text that lies parallel to it. Approached in this manner, the kana *Kojiki* is a masterpiece. Stylistically, its rhythmic prose possesses great rhetorical power. Syntactically, it appears consistent in every detail. But in spite of Norinaga's rigor, even brilliance, it is apparent that the relation of the kana *Kojiki* to the original text is not one of complete and easy similitude.

In an essay published originally in 1957 the linguist Kamei Takashi asked, "Can the *Kojiki* be read?" Kamei's answer took the form of a meditation on the varied meanings of the term *yomu* (to read) in Japanese. He noted that it refers not only to "reading aloud" or articulating a written text (*ondoku*), but also to the process of extracting meaning from a text (*kaidoku*), and thirdly, to the process of *kundoku*, that is, of "reading" a sentence inscribed in "Chinese" as "Japanese." Kamei rejected Norinaga's assertion that the purpose of the compilation of the *Kojiki* had been to record the ancient oral transmissions, noting that except for proper names and poems, the use of Chinese characters as purely phonetic symbols was very limited, even though this form of inscription would seem the obvious choice if "reading" as vocalization was the issue. He argued that the decision on the part of the editors of the *Kojiki* to write in corrupt Chinese syntax (*hentai kanbun*), when this other means of inscription was at hand, meant that their aim was to produce a text that could be "read" in the second and third senses, not the first. He concluded by stating, "For whatever reason, Norinaga—who must have recognized this fact—chose to ignore it, but it must be said that the *Kokun Kojiki* [i.e., the kana *Kojiki*] is really a 'new *Kojiki*.' "[23]

In the wake of Kamei's analysis, several scholars have worked to demonstrate concretely some of the ways in which the kana *Kojiki* departed from the "original" *Kojiki*. Writing in the late 1960s, Kojima Noriyuki analyzed several aspects of Norinaga's attempt to render the Kojiki a purely "Japanese" text.[24] His discussion is particularly interesting in light of Norinaga's assertion that in reconstructing the ancient language, one had to be concerned not only with the correct reading of individual words but also with the style and structure of the sentence. Kojima noted that sentences within the Kojiki seem to fall into two categories: those that run on and on and make use of numerous conjunctive devices, and those that are quite short and seem to be imitative of a typical pattern of Chinese prose, in which two four-character sequences with similar grammatical forms are aligned. Kojima asserted that Norinaga believed the former to be typical of oral transmissions, perhaps based upon his reading of the ritual prayers in which lengthy, sonorous passages are the rule. Thus, as he constructed the kana Kojiki, Norinaga repeatedly inserted conjunctive particles such as *te* and *ba* in order to join seemingly discreet statements to provide "evidence" of orality.

Similarly, Nishimiya Kazutami has argued that the kana Kojiki is marked by the influence of later linguistic forms, which he identified as the wabun style of works of the early Heian period. Like Kamei, he argued that the Kojiki was written with the intention that it be read via kundoku, with the consequence that "if like Norinaga, you ignore kundoku and just do a free translation [*iyaku*] completely into wabun, then the significance of the choices of those who compiled the text is lost in some places."[25] Nishimiya's *Nihon jōdai no bunshō to hyōki* (Prose and Inscription in Ancient Japan, 1988) analyzes some of the methods Norinaga used in rewriting the kanbun surface of the Kojiki as wabun. One of the many instances he took up was Norinaga's treatment of the characters read as the verb *ari* in Japanese (Chinese: *zai* and *you*). In the Kojiki there are many sentences that reflect standard Chinese word order: subject + verb (*zai* or *you*) + object, in which the object designates a place. Nishimiya noted that in "translating" this written statement into the kana text, Norinaga manipulated the syntax of the written statement so that, for example, a sentence with the form of subject + verb + place that in eighteenth-century Japan would have typically been read as *Hito sono kawakami ni ari* (subject + place + verb) instead became *Sono kawakami ni hito ari* (place + subject + verb). What makes this reading difficult to uphold is that in other sentences in the text, the grammar is "corrupt." In other words, these statements took the form of place + subject + verb. Norinaga's reading, however, effaced the syntactical distinctions that exist on the level of the written text. Why? As Nishimiya noted, a sentence such as *Hito sono kawakami ni ari* had the rhythm of a kanbun kundoku sentence. Thus, Norinaga reversed the order of object and subject in order to produce a construction that he could present as more authentically "Japanese."[26]

The construction of the kana *Kojiki* within the *Kojikiden* thus relied upon a complex set of interpretive strategies, operations that are presented as the objective grammatical and morphological reconstruction of "orality" latent in the text. However, as inconsistencies between the original *Kojiki* and Norinaga's kana *Kojiki* reveal, Norinaga relied upon a set of oppositions that were ideological in nature: the *Nihon shoki/Kojiki*, Chinese/Japanese, orality/ writing. While Norinaga was correct in his recognition that the system of in- scription used in the *Nihon shoki* differed from that of the *Kojiki*, this difference did not mesh neatly with these oppositions. The textual history constructed in the *Kojikiden* in fact relied upon a set of problematic conclusions. Norinaga argued that if the *Kojiki* was written in "Japanese" then it must be the older text. Therefore, it escaped the "Chinese mind" that permeated the *Nihon shoki* and transparently recorded the ancient oral transmissions. Because it was more ancient and more oral, the *Kojiki* alone, according to Norinaga, was capable of revealing modes of perception and experience that were distinctly Japanese. The kana *Kojiki* thus aimed to conceal the fact that the *Kojiki* was not pure "orality" but a different kind of writing. It was not Yamato kotoba but a difficult and complex piece of kanbun. Kamei Takashi refused to speculate on why Norinaga would have ignored that which he "must have recognized," but the answer is clear—the claim that an authentically "Japanese" identity was discoverable through language required him to suppress the fact that even this, arguably the earliest Japanese text, was written in Chinese.

ANNOTATION AND THE PRODUCTION OF MEANING

The construction of the kana *Kojiki* was Norinaga's great achievement. It sup- ported his assertion that he was not engaging in an act of interpretation but only revealing meanings already present within the *Kojiki*. It allowed him to argue that there was something that could be called Yamato kotoba, a form of language that predated cultural contact with China and thus was specifi- cally Japanese. Within the *Kojikiden*, the linguistic explanation of the text and the explanation of what specific passages "mean" are intertwined within the lengthy series of annotations that follow each passage. In the challenging Divine Age chapters, two or three lines from the *Kojiki* are often followed by ten or more pages of annotations. Unlike other readers of the Divine Age narrative, such as Hakuseki before him and Tachibana Moribe after him, Norinaga never put forth his understanding of the *Kojiki* in the form of a separate narrative text. Rather, it was expressed within the notes that addressed particular words and phrases within the *Kojiki*. Much of the explanatory power of the *Kojikiden* is the product of this form: the explanation of how a word was to be pronounced and what it meant became part of a seamless whole interspersed within the kana *Kojiki*.

Norinaga's understanding of the *Kojiki* relied upon the constitution of a complex set of intertextual relations. Outwardly, he advocated the abandonment of the search for "original meaning" that had been an important part of earlier wagaku practice. He advised his disciples to attempt to determine the significance of the language of the text by discovering the value of the "word" within the text itself. In *Uiyamabumi* (First Steps on the Mountain, 1798), a handbook of kokugaku practice that he wrote for his students, Norinaga stated, "Etymology is not important. . . . Although scholars always want to know this first, one should not place much weight on it. . . . Rather than thinking of the original meaning of words, you should consider how the ancient people used them within sentences, and then you will recognize that here they used this word to mean this."[27] However, the annotations within the *Kojikiden* reveal the problematic status of this assertion.

A case in point is the way in which the juxtaposition of the *Kojiki* and the *Nihon shoki*—so important for the valorization of the former—functions within the larger body of the *Kojikiden*. As one might expect, often the *Nihon shoki* is taken up merely to be dismissed: the version of the narrative inscribed in this text is compared with the "true" version offered by *Kojiki* and then rejected as the product of the "Chinese mind." But this is not the only way the *Nihon shoki* is utilized. In a significant number of passages the *Nihon shoki* is employed, not as a negative example, but as the means to justify the assignment of a meaning to a particular word or phrase. A case in point is Norinaga's rendering of the opening passage of the *Kojiki*, which I examined in the previous chapter:

> Ametsuchi *hajime no toki*, Takamanohara ni *narimaseru kami no mina ha*, Ame no Minakanushi *no kami*. Tsugi ni Takamimusubi *no kami*. Tsugi ni Kamimusubi *no kami*. Kono mibashira *no kami ha mina hitori gami narimashite, mimi wo kakushitamaiki*. Tsugi ni kuni *wakaku ukiabura no gotoku ni shite*, kuragenasu tadayoheru toki ni, ashikabi *no goto moeagaru mono* ni yorite *narimaseru kami no mina ha*, Umashi-ashikabi-hikoji *no kami*. Tsugi

ni Ame no Tokotachi no kami. Kono futabashira no kami mo *hitorigami
narimashite, mimi wo kakushitamaiki.*[28]

In his voluminous notes on this passage, Norinaga repeatedly drew upon
the Nihon shoki in order to impose a specific meaning upon the Kojiki narrative.
For example, evidence from the Nihon shoki was cited in order to argue that the
opening phrase of the Kojiki should be read *Ame tsuchi no hajime no toki*, rather
than *hajimete hirakuru toki*, the reading that had been adopted by Mabuchi and
others.[29] As Saigō Nobutsuna noted, in making this pronouncement Norinaga acted selectively, ignoring other passages in the Nihon shoki in which the
rejected reading was employed.[30]

A similar strategy can be seen in the passage in which Norinaga delineated the significance of the statement that referred to a time "when the
land was young, resembling floating oil." Norinaga argued that this "floating land" referred not to the Japanese islands—as Hakuseki and Munetake
had claimed—but was in fact situated in the midst of the heavens, and he
used references in the Nihon shoki as evidence to support this claim: "As for
where this thing was floating, you should look in the Nihon shoki where it
states 'in the heavens' and 'in the sky.' "[31] These examples reveal that the
"reality" of the ancient period was not found in the language of the Kojiki
itself, but rather was constituted by means of the production of a new intertextual space. Thus, the notion of the "Chinese mind" was in fact a device
that allowed Norinaga to reject those aspects of the Nihon shoki that were at
odds with the new understanding of the Kojiki he was trying to create and to
incorporate those that would prop it up.

The constructed nature of Norinaga's account of the narrative is revealed
explicitly in another text. Norinaga described this work, the *Kamiyo masagoto*
(The True Language of the Divine Age, 1798), as a rewriting of the Divine Age
section of the Kojiki in kana for the benefit of beginning students. However,
this work was not simply a transcription of the kana Kojiki of the Kojikiden.
In describing his method for compiling this text, Norinaga stated: "When
something was lacking in the Kojiki, I added it from the Nihon shoki, in order
to return to the language of ancient times. Also when there were things that
were missing from these two texts, then I added one or two things from other
of the ancient texts."[32]

In this work, then, Norinaga not only separated his kana version of the
Kojiki from the original kanbun text but also inserted into it passages from
the Nihon shoki, the various fudoki, and other texts. The selection and incor-

poration of these passages could only have been predicated upon an anterior understanding of what constituted the "real" meaning of the Divine Age narrative. It could only be the interpreting reader, Norinaga himself, who decided what was missing from and what must be supplemented to the *Kojiki*, which he had labeled as direct inscription of the oral transmissions of the Divine Age.

The annotations, where the "meaning" of the text was revealed, took a number of distinct forms. Many were devoted to explaining the language of the text and thus dealt with etymological, morphological, and syntactical points. However, a multitude of other notes functioned specifically to define a set of relations between the world of the text and the world of the Tokugawa reader. In this category of annotations, Norinaga attempted to link the deities, objects, places, and even words that appear in the *Kojiki* to the known world of late eighteenth-century Japan. For example, in the note on the placename Onogonoshima, which appears in the section in which the deities Izanami and Izanagi made the land, Norinaga carefully attempted to delineate the location of this island, declaring that it must be a small island located either northwest or southwest of Awajishima.[33] Later, when the deity name Iwazuchibiko no kami appears in the text, Norinaga noted that there exists in the district of Nagaoka in the province of Tosa a shrine called Iwazuchi Jinja.[34] Objects that appear within the *Kojiki* were subject to similar scrutiny. In the note on the "floating bridge" (*ukihashi*) upon which the deities Izanami and Izanagi stood to make the land, Norinaga asserted that it was located at Amanohashidate (literally, "heavenly bridge"), a sandbar in the Japan Sea: "This was a ladder, and when the deities were sleeping, it would be collapsed and left in the sea near the province of Tango."[35] Similarly, words within the *Kojiki* text were also explained in terms that establish a relation with the reality of eighteenth-century Japan. Repeatedly, Norinaga asserted that one word or another continued to survive in dialects spoken in various areas of Japan. For example, in explaining the significance of the word *toko*, which appeared as part of the deity name Ame no Tokotachi, Norinaga asserted that it meant *soko* (bottom), noting that "even now there are times when soko is pronounced as toko."[36]

In gathering this kind of information Norinaga utilized his network of disciples, whom he questioned about local dialects, customs, and traditions. A student in Nagasaki, an important port town, was queried about the physical attributes of the jellyfish, the creature to which the unformed cosmos is compared in the opening sections of the *Kojiki*. A student who lived in Tango

was questioned about the appearance of the sandbar at Amanohashidate. Information about local customs and dialect too was pursued by Norinaga, and
some of this information was included in the annotations that comprised
the *Kojikiden*.[37] The result of this strategy was that the mytho-space of the
Divine Age was linked again and again to the world of Tokugawa Japan so
that places, language, and objects of the present obtained new meaning as
signifiers of the continuity of the Divine Age narrative.

The third category of annotations, and the most significant in terms of revealing the contours of the new narrative constructed over the surface of the
Kojiki, was those that imposed what might be termed ontological constructs
upon the referential system of the text. In these annotations, Norinaga relied
upon a series of explanatory modes, imposing notions of temporality, causality, and intentionality upon the narrative of the *Kojiki*. In order to explore
how this kind of annotation works, I want to look carefully at two pivotal
moments within the *Kojikiden*: the opening sequence and the passage that relates the emergence of the deities Naobi and Magatsuhi. In his annotations
to these sections of the text, Norinaga hinted at the theory of history that
would be made more explicit in other works.

The opening passage of the *Kojiki* describes the emergence of the five primal deities into the space designated as "heaven and earth."[38] Suika Shinto
scholars had argued that this sequence revealed that ri, or "principle," unified the cosmic and the social realms. In contrast, Arai Hakuseki dismissed
this assertion and manipulated the Chinese characters of the text in order
to situate the events of the text into historical time. The *Kojikiden*, however,
established a different problematic from the outset. As I noted above, Norinaga insisted that the first four characters of the text must be read *Ametsuchi
no hajime no toki* (at the time of the beginning of heaven and earth). His concern was to suppress the potential significance of the character *hatsu* that had
been read by his predecessors as *hirakuru* (to open) and *wakareru* (to separate).
According to Norinaga, both these readings, in that they signified the spontaneous emergence of heaven and earth from a primeval chaos, reflected the
influence of the "Chinese mind": "As for the meaning of [this phrase], it just
generally describes first of all the beginning of this world, but it certainly
does not indicate that this was when heaven and earth were formed. The beginning of the formation of heaven and earth is indicated in the next section
of the text."[39]

Here, Norinaga's concern was, in effect, to delay the beginning of the

story of creation. In the surface narrative of the *Kojiki*, the space demarcated as the "earth" (*tsuchi*) appears first, and then only later are the Japanese islands formed. However, Norinaga refigured the temporal syntagm of
the plot, so that the creation of the "earth" and "Japan" appear as coterminous events. The *Kojiki* was thus utilized to support Norinaga's conception
of original cultural identity: in the beginning, there was Japan.

[margin note: Beginning there was Yamato not Japan]

The delineation of Japan as always present was not accomplished without
some difficulty. In the surface narrative of the *Kojiki*, the anterior formation
of the "earth" is signified in a plurality of ways. These include the phrase
that refers to "the 'opening' of heaven and earth," the description of "when
the land was young like floating oil," the emergence of the deity Kuni no
Tokutachi (whose name means "the one who establishes the foundation of
the land"), the sequence of the seven generations of deities that begins with
Uijini no kami and Suijini no kami, whose names contain references to mud,
sand, soil, and so on. Norinaga, however, rejected the potential meaningfulness of these phrases and argued that the land was not formed until that
moment in the narrative when the deities Izanami and Izanagi, acting upon
the order of the "heavenly deities," create the Japanese islands. For example,
in relation to the phrase "when the land was young," Norinaga carefully explained, "Since the land was formed when the great deities Izanagi and Izanami give birth to it, it did not exist yet. So this phrase makes reference to its
later state in order to explain how it was at the beginning."[40] Similarly, regarding the names of the deities Uijini and Suijini, he stated, "In the case of
both the land and the deities themselves, it is not that the form of the deities
when they emerged was as their names implied. Indeed [the names] have
nothing to do with their form. . . . As for the land, until the time of Izanami
and Izanagi, it was still 'like floating oil.' "[41] The collapse of the distinction
between the "earth" and "Japan" did not have the aim merely of privileging
Japan. As he imposed this temporal scheme upon the *Kojiki*, Norinaga also
began to insert the new concept of causality into the narrative.

Causality first becomes an issue in a note on the opening passage of
the *Kojiki*, which discusses the significance of the phrase *tsugi ni* (next) that
demarcates the appearance in succession of the deities Takamimusubi and
Kamimusubi. Norinaga argued that this phrase did not denote a genera-
tional progression; it was not the case that Takamimusubi was the "parent" who produced the "child," Kamimusubi. Rather, these two deities appeared simultaneously, and together they constituted the generative power

that brought Japan into being. In defining the meaning of the term *musubi*
that appeared in both deity names, Norinaga stated, "As for the term musubi,
it refers to the mysterious spirit that produces all things. . . . The existence of
everything within the world, from heaven and earth themselves to all things,
including each and every object and event, all of them were produced by the
mysterious power of the two Musubi deities."[42]

This understanding of the Musubi deities cannot be deduced from the
narrative itself. Nothing distinguishes their appearance from those who preceded them, and they are mentioned only two more times within the *Kojiki*.
Nonetheless, Norinaga insisted that these deities were responsible for the
production of the cosmological, natural, and social worlds. His commentary
on the Musubi deities has long been recognized as one of the most explicitly interpretive moments in the *Kojikiden*. For example, in *Norinaga to Atsutane no sekai* (The World of Norinaga and Atsutane, 1977), Koyasu Nobukuni
states that "for Norinaga [the Musubi deities] were what might be termed an
a priori concept. They were not the result of his exegetical project, but must
be regarded as something that was constituted before it."[43] In the *Kojikiden*,
this understanding of the Musubi deities allowed for the refiguring of the
narrative as a whole. Norinaga situated the story within a regime of causality
and imposed a teleological design upon it.

Here it is useful to look again at Norinaga's collapse of the distinction between the formation of earth and that of Japan. The displacement of the creation of the earth until this moment was motivated by the need to posit these
deities as the intentionality that caused this event and all those that follow.
Thus the potential meaningfulness of such statements as "when the land
was young" was ignored in order to privilege the moment in the text when
the "heavenly deities"—which Norinaga argued signified Musubi deities—
ordered Izanami and Izanagi to create the Japanese islands. Thus, Norinaga
characterized the creation of Japan as an act of purposeful production, rather
than a spontaneous happening.

Norinaga did not insert the concepts of causality and intentionality into
only this single passage but rather used them to order the narrative as a
whole. He argued that the central events of the story must be understood as
resulting from the intentions of the Musubi deities:

> As examples of the traces that reveal the workings of these deities, there
> is the beginning of Izanami and Izanagi's production of the land and
> all the things [within it], which was based upon the command of the

"heavenly deities." These were the five deities we see here. Also when Amaterasu hid herself within the cave, and when her grandson went down from heaven to rule over the land, the deity named Omohigane who served the latter and thought of the way [to lure Amaterasu out of the cave] was the child [of Takamimusubi]. Also Sukunabiko who solidified the land was the child of [Kamimusubi]. Also the deity Toyoakitsu who joined with Oshihomimi to produce the divine descendant [Ninigi] was the daughter of these deities. Also the command to the deities who disturbed the land [to accept the rule of Ninigi] and the descent of the divine descendant were both based upon the command of these deities. So we can know that the emergence of every object and every event in this world is because of the virtue of the Musubi deities. The meaning of everything in the world can be understood by means of these traces from the Divine Age. As for the development of the good and the evil in the world, from the distant past until the present, there is not one thing that differs from the Divine Age.[44]

It is necessary to recognize the constructed nature of the relations of identity being established in this passage, between the Musubi deities and the events of the narrative and, more importantly, between the world of the text and the world of its readers. Norinaga asserted that within the *Kojiki* each of the events listed above—Amaterasu's emergence from the cave, the completion of the "land-making" process, the subjugation of the unruly earth deities, and the birth and descent of Ninigi, the "divine descendant" of Japan's imperial line—was caused by the Musubi deities. But in order to read the text in this way, he had to establish their "presence" throughout the story in ways that are not necessarily comparable or congruent. He pointed to genealogical links between deities, many of which are speculative, in order to "find" them. And he identified vague phrases such as the statement that something occurred by "order of the heavenly deities" as a reference to these deities. Then, having demarcated the deities as the "prime mover" of each of the major events of the narrative, Norinaga declared this to be proof that they continue to act this way throughout history.

A similar kind of operation is apparent in the meanings Norinaga assigned to the deities known as Magatsuhi and Naobi, which are described as emerging as the deity Izanagi purified himself after returning from the "foul" and "polluted" land of yomi. Like the Musubi deities, Naobi and Magatsuhi assume a significance within the *Kojikiden* that far outweighs their role within the *Kojiki* itself. Regarding the significance of Magatsuhi, Norinaga stated that "all of the bad, evil, twisted things in the world, each of them originally arose from the spirit of this deity Magatsuhi."[45] Similarly, explaining the significance of the deity Naobi, Norinaga asserted that "all of the good and lucky things in this world arise from the purifying power of this deity."[46] As in the case of the Musubi deities, there is nothing in the *Kojiki* itself that supports the claim of the ontological significance of these deities. Saigō Nobutsuna has described Norinaga's statements as "exaggerated interpretations" and characterized them as expressive of "a theology created by Norinaga himself."[47] It is important to recognize that the opposition being constituted here between the categories of good and evil did not derive from the Divine Age narrative itself. Within the *Kojiki*, events and actors are never explicitly described in terms of ethical qualities, but Norinaga used terms such as "good" and "evil" to establish new relationships between events within the narrative.

A case in point is the way in which Norinaga used the opposition of these ethical principles to juxtapose the inherent natures of the deities Susanō and Amaterasu. These deities, who emerged during the process of Izanami's purification, are among the most important figures within the *Kojiki*, for it is their grandchild who eventually descends to Japan and becomes the "divine descendant" of Japan's imperial line. Within the *Kojiki*, both Amaterasu and Susanō are initially described as "treasured children" of Izanami, but Susanō is a more ambivalent figure. He is portrayed alternately as mischievous, willful, destructive, wily, and courageous. However, Norinaga argued consistently that Susanō was "an evil deity" (*ashiki kami*), pointing to Susanō's declaration that he wanted to go to the "land of the mother" as revealing an affinity with yomi, the land of death and pollution. According to Norinaga, it was Susanō's evil nature that led him to disobey Izanagi's command to rule over the seas, to clash with Amaterasu, and to force her into hiding with the consequence that disorder and darkness fell upon Japan.

The identification of Susanō as an "evil" deity and Amaterasu as a "good" deity sets the stage for one of the most extraordinary passages in the *Kojikiden*. It begins with Norinaga musing that "there must be some profound reason why the descendants of the child that was produced during the contest between the good deity and the evil deity have ruled over this land for so long."[48] This leads to a reexamination of the events of the Divine Age narrative in light of the categories of "good" and "evil":

The principle that good events and bad events follow each other in constant succession, which can be seen in all of the things within the world, in each generation, in each moment of time, great and small, is based upon intentions in place at the beginning of the Divine Age. The workings of this principle began with the joining of [Izanami and Izanagi], when the islands and all the deities were born, and extended until the birth of the three treasured children and the command that they divide [authority]. From their joining throughout the birth of the deities everything was good, until with the birth of the fire deity, evil things began with the departure of the mother deity. Since the land of yomi is an evil place and the female deity went there, evil began to happen in the world as well. Since the male deity returned to this world, after having had contact with this evil, the world as a whole came to be evil. Therefore, upon his return to the apparent world, he purified himself. First, the Magatsuhi deity appeared from the filth of yomi; then when that filth was purified, cleansed, and rectified, the three treasured children appeared. When Amaterasu ruled over the heavenly plain, then once again everything became good again. This then is the pattern of this world. Therefore think carefully about this progression, and you will understand the principle that guides the production of good from evil and evil from good. Moreover, you will know the principle that even if there is evil, it will not triumph over good in the end.⁴⁹

[handwritten margin note: Ethical reading of good/evil]

Thus, Norinaga, who had argued that he was going to discover the reality of the Divine Age in immediate terms without recourse to the flawed and mediating categories of the "Chinese mind," began to reemploy the ethical categories he had dismissed. He reduced the mythic multivocality of the narrative into a contest between good and evil, the workings respectively of the deities Naobi and Magatsuhi.

To be sure, the delineation of this principle is not wholly unexpected. Norinaga had already described the Musubi deities in terms of agency; now the Magatsuhi and Naobi deities are characterized in similar terms. "Good" and "evil" too are by this point known and recognized categories because Norinaga has made use of them frequently. For example, although within the *Kojiki*, yomi is described not as "evil" but only as a source of pollution, in his annotations to his term, Norinaga situated "pollution" within the larger regime of "evil." Moreover, the very placement of this passage among the annotations that appear so objective—the careful delineation of how each word should be pronounced, the grammatical notes, the references to places, objects, and words that exist in present—served to mask the explicitness of this moment of interpretation.

But why did Norinaga reduce the events of the narrative to the "principle" that "good" and "evil" are manifestations of the presence of the deities Naobi and Magatsuhi? He hinted at the significance of this passage in the declaration that brings it to a close: "This then is the pattern of this world. Therefore think carefully about this progression, and you will understand the principle that guides the production of good from evil, and evil from good." Here Norinaga asserted again the relationship he established throughout the Kojikiden, of continuity between the Divine Age of the story and the present. At this point, it is not objects, places, and words that reveal this continuity but the principle of causality. For Norinaga, the workings of Naobi and Magatsuhi explained not only the events of the Divine Age, but also of everything that followed, up to and including the present. These deities, like the Musubi deities, come to be implicated in a complex meditation on the nature of community.

AGENTS OF HISTORY

It was outside the confines of the Kojikiden's annotations, in a series of essays that included Naobi no mitama (The Rectifying Spirit), Kuzubana (Arrowroot Flowers), and Tamakushige (The Jeweled Comb-box), that Norinaga attempted to explain the meaning of his "discoveries" for the Japan of his own time. These essays took the form of a discourse on Japanese history, as it unfolded after the end of the Divine Age.[50] As I noted in the last chapter, there was an explosion of interest in the writing of history in the mid-Tokugawa period. Works by Hayashi Razan, Arai Hakuseki, and the Mito school historians were modeled on the principles of Neo-Confucian historiography, embodying simultaneously notions of positivist research and the belief that history would demonstrate the workings of the moral principles that permeated man, nature, and society.[51] In contrast, historicist Confucianists such as Ogyū Sorai identified Confucian principles as an ethical system of human creation, one devised to address a specific set of social and political issues. It is against these conceptions of history that Norinaga developed his own. He divided Japanese history into three periods that he labeled kamitsuyo (the first period), nakatsuyo (the middle period), and chikakiyo (the recent period). The first of these began with the Divine Age and ended at a moment that Norinaga located during the reign of the emperor Ōjin when the "Chinese mind" entered Japan via writing. In describing the nature of Japan as community during this age, Norinaga stated:

> As for how the emperor ruled in the first period, there is in the ancient language the phrase "to rule the world following the deities." This means that the emperor took the will of Amaterasu as his own will and in all things followed exactly the pattern that was established in the Divine Age; and in relation to all things, the emperor did not rely upon his own judgment. This was the correct method of practicing the true way. In this period, from the courtiers to the masses of people below, everyone was righteous and correct. Everyone took the will of the emperor as his own will, all were in awe of the throne, and all followed the rules established by those above. Because there were no judgments based upon individual pretensions to knowledge, inferiors and superiors joined together, and the world was at peace.[52]

Here Norinaga argued that Japan in this age existed as a stable and peaceful community, precisely because those within it lacked a sense of themselves as agents. Reaffirming the view of the emperor that appeared in the chapter 1 of the *Kojikiden*, Norinaga asserted that the emperor, as ruler, was simply a conduit for the deities. Thus, government in this age did not take the form of the imposition of individual intentions upon the ruled. The emperor merely followed the deities, and in turn, the people followed the deities by following the will of the emperor. For Norinaga, it was this mode of consciousness that had allowed Japan to exist as a "world at peace."

It was the introduction of writing and with it of "Chinese" modes of ordering experience that brought about the epochal change that marked the beginning of the "middle period" of Norinaga's scheme. Explaining this change, Norinaga stated, "as people unconsciously began to be transformed by the custom of reasoning, everyone began to make judgments based on their personal pretensions to knowledge, and so those above and those below no longer took the will of the emperor as their own, so everything became much more complex and gradually it became difficult to govern."[53] Thus, Norinaga asserted that this age was marked by the emergence of a new form of consciousness as, under the influence of Chinese ideas, people within Japan began to feel that they possessed knowledge and could act upon it. However, for Norinaga, the consequence of the emergence of this new self-consciousness was the disintegration of social order. He pointed to the state of Japan during the Sengoku or "country at war" period of the fifteenth and sixteenth centuries as the best illustration of the social consequences of this transformation.

Norinaga identified Oda Nobunaga's rise to power in the late sixteenth century as the start of the third period. He described Nobunaga's victories over competitors for power as "the suppression of disorder," a process that continued with the rise to power of Toyotomi Hideyoshi after Nobunaga's death. According to Norinaga, "the world showed signs of the coming of spring and the decline of the court began to improve when the regent Toyotomi began to cleanse and purify the world." For Norinaga, Tokugawa Ieyasu, who completed the process of reunification begun by Nobunaga and Hideyoshi, was someone who "more and more showed respect for the court" and created a world that "in its peacefulness was not greatly different from the ancient period." [54] The favorable evaluation of Nobunaga, Hideyoshi, and Ieyasu seems incongruous in light of Norinaga's idealization of the ancient period, but it points to the complexity of Norinaga's call to "return to antiquity." For Norinaga, "return" did not mean the recovery of the political forms of the ancient period. He did not envision the end of the bakufu or direct rule by the emperor. Rather, "return" signified the adoption of the mode of consciousness that Norinaga believed had existed in the "first age," which he termed the "pure mind" (*magokoro*).

The nature of the mode of consciousness that was signified by the term "pure mind" needs to be examined, but first let us continue with Norinaga's theory of history. While he explained the change from the "first period" to the "middle period" as the result of cultural contact, and the second point of transformation as the result of renewed respect for the imperial court, for Norinaga, these events were merely epiphenomena that masked the real forces of change—the workings of the deities Naobi and Magatsuhi. Norinaga argued that figures such as Nobunaga, Hideyoshi, and Ieyasu who were involved in these moments of political transformation cannot be viewed as autonomous agents. His reading of the Kojiki revealed, he asserted, that these human figures were merely conduits through which the deities act upon this world. Thus, in explaining the rise of the "Chinese mind," Norinaga did not fault the scribes and the scholars of the seventh and eighth centuries for not rejecting the "way of the sages." He argued rather that "this happened because the hearts of the people of the realm were confused by the deity Magatsuhi." [55] The decline of imperial power and the formation of the series of warrior-led governments are explained in similar terms: "That the warriors of all the provinces followed the Hōjō and that they were successful was because the Magatsuhi deity became extremely unruly and the hearts of the people of the realm were confused by the deity. The Hōjō too were tricked by its evil designs. It was the same with the Ashikaga." [56] In the same way, Norinaga explained the rise of Nobunaga and the eventual establishment of peace under the Tokugawa, not as the result of their particular virtue, but as evidence of the resurgence of the "good" deity, Naobi. Thus, for Norinaga, history unfolded according to the pattern established in the Divine Age, as the progression from "good" to "evil" and "evil" to "good" based upon the will of the Naobi and Matatsuhi deities.

It is within the context of this discourse on history that the significance of Norinaga's concern for the categories of "good" and "evil" becomes clear. His explanation of the workings of the Naobi and Magatsuhi deities allowed him to separate these ethical categories from the intentions of individuals. No longer could success or failure be characterized as evidence of individual virtue. This assertion was particularly significant in light of the Neo-Confucian explanation of political authority. According to the notion of "the way of heaven" (tendō), ri, the moral force that permeated the world, rewarded those of exceptional virtue by allowing them to rise to positions of power, where they could then act as models for those over whom they ruled. In *Naobi no mitama*, Norinaga had attacked this theory as nothing more than a clever ruse to legitimate power, stating, "The mandate of heaven is a contrived concept that the ancient sages of China thought up to justify the crime of overthrowing the lord and stealing his land." [57]

Norinaga situated all of Japanese history as the continuation of the Divine Age narrative: the deities who act within the story continue to act. This meant that the Divine Age was understood in two distinct ways. Within Norinaga's scheme of historical periodization, it had the status of a moment in the past. However, in that its events were construed as having explanatory power for the present, the Divine Age was a past that is also always present. Just as Norinaga had explained the entirety of that story in terms of the intentions of these deities, so too did he incorporate the events of his own time into this mythic space. He explicitly declared that "the principles of this world all follow the patterns (omomuki) of the Divine Age." Norinaga came to term these principles a "way" (michi), borrowing the Chinese term for a set of moral principles, but he argued that the "ancient way" of Japan was radically different from that of Confucianism and Buddhism.

For Norinaga the most troubling aspect of Buddhism and Confucianism was that, in his view, they assert that human beings could possess a positive knowledge of the world and that this knowledge could become the basis for action. He argued that concepts such as "heaven" in Confucianism and "karma" in Buddhism were founded on the assumption that the principles that underlay the events of this world were regular and stable. Thus they could be known and form a basis for human action. However, according to Norinaga, "The notion that the way of heaven rewards good and punishes evil is something that even a child who knows not a single letter can understand, and so indeed it seems that this is a correct principle. But even if this statement seems quite reasonable, it is not consistent with events. Because there are evil deities in the world, often good is punished and evil rewarded."[58]

Here the past is portrayed as a series of inexplicable events, the progression of which does not mesh with the explanations offered by Confucianism. Norinaga repeatedly remarked on the failure of Confucianism to offer a convincing representation of the world, writing at one point that "one hears that, of the acts of heaven, everything is correct and nothing is wrong, but how can this be when in this world there are so many things that go against this principle?"[59] His response to the perceived randomness of history was to posit agency and intentionality as ultimately resting entirely outside of the human sphere.

I noted above that in reading the *Kojiki* Norinaga carefully reduced the multivocality of the original text in order to insert a teleological design into the plot of the Divine Age narrative, so that everything happened purposefully. When the motivated nature of every event within the narrative was juxtaposed with the apparent randomness of events within history, Norinaga claimed that the meaning of the narrative was clear. Everything could be understood once one grasped the principle that men could not act, but the deities could and do. Within Norinaga's scheme, agency was reserved for the deities:

> Since all of the events within the world are based upon the acts of the deities, the revealed things [*arawanigoto*] are in fact not separate from the hidden things [*kamigoto*]. As for the distinction between the two, it is, to use an example, that the deities make people of this world act as if they were puppets. What is apparent are the movements of the head, neck, and hands of the puppet, but in fact the various movements of the puppet are based upon the actions of another.[60]

It is within this theory of history that Norinaga articulated his notion of "return." He longed to recover not a different political form or a less complex society but the mode of consciousness he labeled the "pure mind," which had existed in the "first period" of history, when people lived with an awareness of the role of the deities in their life. As yet unconfused by the notions of human agency authorized by Buddhism and Confucianism, they lived "naturally" as part of the community. Within this context, Norinaga's characterization of his own project gains new significance. The insistence that the *Kojiki* was a transparent inscription of the oral transmissions from the Divine Age and that he, Norinaga, did not interpret, but only revealed that which was already written, were part of this larger scheme of rethinking the nature of the subject.

However, the rejection of the possibility of human agency was founded upon the notion that people lived their lives in two distinct spheres: the "public realm" and that which was posed against it, the "private realm." Addressing the idea of "return," Norinaga stated,

> The events of this world are based upon the acts of the good and evil deities, and there are many things that are beyond the power of man. Therefore, to go against the present age and to attempt to return to the ancient way of the deities is itself to go against the way of the deities. . . . Therefore the role of man today is just to follow the rules established by the public realm [ōyake], to follow the customs of the age. Ultimately this is the way of the deities.[61]

Here and elsewhere, when Norinaga spoke of the "public realm" in relation to his own society, he was explicitly concerned with the sphere of political power. He used the term ōyake to refer to officialdom and those aspects of social life over which officials legitimately exercised authority. Norinaga agued that it was the "public realm" upon which the deities acted, and thus he called upon people to adhere to officially defined norms, rules, and laws. Similarly, when Norinaga, in his discourse on history, described the actions of the deities, it was always in relation to the progression of political events. It was, it would seem, historical actors such as the Hōjō regents and the Ashikaga shoguns, Nobunaga, Hideyoshi, and of course Tokugawa Ieyasu who were the "puppets" of the deities.

Norinaga characterized attempts to influence the "public realm" as acts that went against the ancient way. But at the same time, he valorized the "private realm" of emotion and desire as the site where the "return" he envisioned could be realized. He turned again and again to criticize attempts by Confucian scholars to address such things as familial relations, personal conduct, and human emotions in ethical terms: "Propriety, righteousness, loyalty, filial piety are things that the masses of people do not understand and to which they cannot aspire. The nature of these things cannot be taught and must be known naturally."[62] Norinaga called for the rejection of these mediating principles and urged people to recover the consciousness of the ancient Japanese by living their lives "naturally" (onozukara). He argued that attempts to regulate or order behavior according to ethical standards was antithetical to the "ancient way." Evoking the "pure mind" to describe the consciousness of ancient Japanee, Norinaga declared, "To desire delicious food, to desire to wear beautiful clothes, to desire to live in a splendid house, to desire to be respected by others, to desire to live long, all of these things are the 'pure mind.' "[63] For Norinaga, then, to embrace human desire as "natural" was to recover the mode of consciousness that had characterized life in ancient Japan.

The valorization of the "private realm" of emotion and desire had been a part of Norinaga's work even before he took up the *Kojiki*. As a young student in Kyoto, he had written to a close friend who was a student of Confucianism that while he recognized the usefulness of this discourse in terms of "ruling the country, imposing order upon the world, and calming the masses," it had no appeal for one such as him "who would not rule the country or calm the people." In another letter written later he declared his intention "to do nothing but pursue the pleasures of popular pursuits."[64] Some years later, in the series of work that predate his "discovery" of the *Kojiki*, Norinaga identified the "private realm" of experience as the site where the primal Japanese consciousness was maintained. Poetry was the explicit object of these texts, which include *Ashiwake no obune, Iso no kami no sasamegoto*, and *Shibun yōryō*. Like Mabuchi before him, Norinaga's poetic theory was organized by the rejection of the Confucian assertion that poetry was to be an aid to government by inculcating ethical values in the people. He argued that poetry is the embodiment in language of a moment of perception in which someone expressed a direct, unmediated reaction to the social or natural world. Norinaga described this mode of perception as knowing *mono no aware*. In explaining the nature of this "knowledge," he asserted it was to experience the world directly without reference to ethical principles or social norms. To fall in love with an unsuitable partner, to be aware of the ephemeral nature of human existence, to long for things one cannot have—these were emotions of mono no aware that found voice in poetry.

Norinaga found the term *mono no aware* in the eleventh-century narrative *Genji monogatari*, where it was used to denote a state of emotional sensitivity, but he made it into the defining feature of Japanese cultural identity. For Norinaga both mono no aware and the "pure mind" demarcated a realm of experience that was specifically "Japanese" in nature. This designation of their Japaneseness was accomplished by two analytical sleights of hand. First, Norinaga argued that the translation of the "private" experience of mono no aware into poetic form and poetic language in effect generalized it, so that the poem becomes a primordial Japanese voice. This claim rests on Norinaga's assertion that the conventional form of Japanese poetry, the alternation of lines of five and seven syllables, "naturally" expresses the innate and special character of the Japanese language and also of those who speak it. Secondly, Norinaga asserted that an essential difference separated this realm of experience from that ordered by other, alien modes of perception. As Norinaga would have it, Chinese poetry, history, and thought reduced experience to a set of objectified, "rational" principles that distorted the mode of perception called mono no aware.

Based upon his conception of mono no aware, Norinaga defined a realm of private experience within which people were free from the rules and restraints that the "public realm" imposed upon individual experience. As Norinaga began to explore the *Kojiki* he retained this notion of the "private," as well as the theory of language that underlay it. He argued that the people in eighteenth-century Japan could resist the "public realm" ordered by the "Chinese mind" by recovering the language of the ancient world and the consciousness it embodied. Some scholars have characterized Norinaga as "passive" or "unconcerned" about politics, pointing to such things as the fact that after 1798 new students entering the Suzuya school were required to sign a pledge that included the stipulation that "I will not violate official [ōyake] policies and laws."[65] Similarly, in 1787 when the daimyo of Kii, Tokugawa Harusada, approached Norinaga and asked him for advice on how to deal with the riots and peasant protests that followed the Tenmei famine, Norinaga replied not with political or economic advice but with the *Tamakushige*, in which he argued that the public world was controlled by the deities.

It is true that Norinaga never attempted to involve himself in overtly political matters. Indeed, this would have been antithetical to his understanding of the nature of the "public realm." But the "private realm" of human experience he delineated so carefully, and upon which he placed so much emphasis, clearly had political implications. Momokawa Takahito has argued that the theory of mono no aware must be understood as one of a number of forms of cultural practice that emerged in the late Tokugawa period to resist the officially sanctioned Confucian representation of social relations.[66] He aligns Norinaga's work with the culture of the pleasure quarters, the production of a literature of parody and play that mocked orthodox values, and the dramatic representations of the conflict of emotion and duty that appeared in the theatrical forms bunraku and kabuki. The theory of mono no aware, like these other "private" texts, practices, and actions, represented an attempt to question the representations of social order sanctioned by the political authorities. Like the *Kojikiden*'s vision of the "natural" community in which laws and institutions had no place, mono no aware was used to suggest that the divisions that were so much a part of Tokugawa life were not cosmically ordained, natural, and right, but were evidence of the loss of the original community that had once existed.

In this regard, it is important to note that the majority of those who joined the Suzuya were commoners, either townsmen (*chonin*) or those of cultivator status, who resided in the villages. Within the Suzuya, these two groups together outnumbered samurai by a ratio of five to one, a disparity that is even greater when other nonsamurai such as physicians and Shinto priests are considered as commoners. In contrast, even in the private academies of Confucianism of this period, students of samurai status predominated.[67] The cultivators among Norinaga's students were for the most part "elite" villagers, who had the financial resources to engage in scholarship. They were village headmen (*shōya*) or some other kind of village official, or were drawn from the ranks of the so-called *gōnō* or "rich farmers" who were landlords, moneylenders, or merchants in the countryside.[68] Norinaga's townsmen students too tended to be relatively affluent. While their numbers included artisans and retail merchants such as booksellers, pharmacists, tofu-makers, and the carvers of print blocks, many were wealthy merchants of the provincial towns.[69] Significantly, these groups occupied an ambivalent place in the Tokugawa social order. As I noted in chapter 1, in times of economic hardship their relative affluence often made them the target of mob violence on the part of those less privileged. At the same time, the series of "reform" efforts sponsored by the bakufu and domains in the Kansai, Tenpō, and Ansai eras targeted them. For these commoners, who like Norinaga "could not rule," the *Kojikiden* offered a vision of community that made the "private realm" in which they lived their lives important and powerful.

Norinaga's work was politically significant in another way as well. It gave voice, form, and meaning to the expanding geographic consciousness that was both part and product of the questioning of political authority. The category of Yamato kotoba made possible a conception of Japaneseness that transcended not only differences in status but also the divisions of domain and province, west and east, city and village. And in the *Kojikiden*, as Norinaga cited place-names, customs, and instances of dialect, Japan itself took concrete form comprised of these bits and pieces of local existence. As his work became known, Norinaga himself came to regard the geographic expansion of the Suzuya as a measure of the recovery of "Japan." For example, in a letter written to Senge Toshinobu, a priest association with the Izumo Shrine, in 1794, Norinaga stated: "I am overjoyed to hear from you that the study of ancient times is now progressing in your region. Since this is something that occurs when the deities desire it, it will happen naturally. It is something beyond human strength. Now the number of those who revere and believe the ancient way is growing, extending eastward to Ōshū and westward to Kyushu."[70] In 1801, in a letter to another disciple, Norinaga declared triumphantly that kokugaku "has now spread throughout most of the realm. To the west, it is established in Nagasaki and Higo, and to the east, it extends even to Nanbu."[71]

THE PERIMETERS OF DEBATE

Through his exesis of the *Kojiki*, Norinaga succeeded in defining the contours of a radically new conception of community, one that challenged the Confucian vision of society at every level. Rejecting the assumption of transcultural norms, he used Yamato kotoba to establish a theory of original cultural identity that celebrated Japan's "difference." Rejecting the scholarly tradition of deciphering metaphors to discern metaphysical principles and write history, he called for a new ethos of belief in which the reader stood passive before the "Divine Text." Rejecting the principle that "virtue" originated in nature and made the social possible, he held up ethical notions such as benevolence and righteousness as evidence of the loss of an original and authentic community. Against the divisions of power that shaped his world, he put forth a theory of a "unitary" Japan in which ruler and subject alike were characterized by the "pure mind," passive and reverent before the deities. Labeling the language of Confucianism, terms such as *ri* and *ki*, *yin* and *yang*, as both false and foreign, he created a new, ideologically charged set of signifiers: "our Divine land," "the Divine Age," the "oral transmissions," the "Chinese mind," and the "pure mind."

Ichikawa Tazumaro (1740–1795), a student of the "ancient learning" school of Ogyū Sorai, authored one of the first of many Confucian responses to Norinaga's vision of Japan. Ichikawa was an acquaintance of one of Norinaga's disciples and from him obtained information regarding the *Kojikiden*, as well as a manuscript copy of *Naobi no mitama*.[72] In response Ichikawa compiled a text he called *Maganohire* (Exorcising Evil, 1775) in which he attempted a rebuttal of Norinaga's work. The first problem he addressed was the status of writing in the ancient period. Taking issue with Norinaga's valorization of orality, Ichikawa stated, "As for oral transmissions . . . there are many mistakes in what is related, much information comes to be omitted, and many false things are inserted. In every case, we see that in those countries that possess a writing system, events are recorded in writing and therefore one knows clearly how things were in ancient times. This is the virtue of writing."[73]

However, this remark, which failed to address the relationship between writing and orality established in Norinaga's work, was only a preface to Ichikawa's main argument. The focus of his critique was the notion of the "Chinese mind," which Norinaga had used in order to "imagine" what Japan had been. Ichikawa described Norinaga as "someone who wanted to situate our country outside the rest of the world." Drawing upon Sorai's theory of the origin of human society, he stated: "In ancient times, men were just like the birds and the beasts. Then the sages were born one after another, and established the distinctions of ruler and ruled, father and child, husband and wife, elder brother and young brother, young and old. This can be called the teaching of human virtue."[74] Ichikawa borrowed Norinaga's own terminology and argued that his failure to appreciate the transcendental claims of Confucianism was evidence of subjective pretensions to knowledge.

Like Ansai and Hakuseki before him, Ichikawa believed that the "Divine Age" myth could be incorporated within a Confucian paradigm, albeit one defined by Sorai's work. According to Ichikawa, the deities of the *Kojiki* and *Nihon shoki* were merely representations of the early rulers who had functioned in Japan as had the Chinese sages: they were the creators of culture. As for the "way of the deities," it was the invention of these Japanese "sages."

They had instituted the practice of their own worship as a device to inculcate ethical behavior in the masses of people.[75]

But it was not only Confucianists who could not accept Norinaga's vision of Japan as a natural community or the theory of original cultural identity upon which it rested. As the *Kojikiden* began to circulate, other readers who embraced the kokugaku concern for community began to reread the *Kojiki* in light of Norinaga's claims in the *Kojikiden*. They too began by addressing issues of language and text, asking what the nature of the *Kojiki* and *Nihon shoki* was, and how should they be read. And as in the *Kojikiden*, the discussion of a set of exegetical issues became the medium for the exploration of individual and cultural identity. In the work of Akinari, Mitsue, and Moribe, the notion that the *Kojiki* recorded the oral transmissions of the Divine Age in pure Yamato kotoba—the fragile foundation upon which Norinaga's conception of Japan rested—was subject to a series of revisions. Rejecting Norinaga's insistence that the *Kojiki* was not the product of the "Age of Men" but of the deities, Akinari and the others began to explore it as the flawed and complicated product of human time and human authors.

Chapter 4

Ueda Akinari: History and Community

As the *Kojikiden* began to circulate among readers who considered themselves students of "Japanese learning," criticism soon emerged. Many of Mabuchi's followers regarded Norinaga's work to be an outright departure from their teacher's scholarship. For example, Murata Harumi, the disciple of Mabuchi who became the leader of the Edo school after Mabuchi's death, stated that "the master of Agatai [Mabuchi] thought that poetry was the most important thing. He never spoke at all of 'the ancient way,' and it is detestable that Norinaga alone speaks as though the master taught mainly of the way of the Divine Age." Similarly, a compatriot of Harumi, Izumi Makuni, wrote disparagingly of "that sly fox Norinaga" and the "baseless theories" of *Naobi no mitama*.[1]

But of the kokugaku scholars who were Norinaga's contemporaries as well as his critics, none was more virulent, more bitter in his criticism than Ueda Akinari. Attacking Norinaga's reading of the *Kojiki* as based upon a set of flawed assumptions about language, text, and history, Akinari rejected outright the notion that Japan as community took form as the expression of innate cultural identity. He regarded Norinaga's rise to prominence as evidence not of the veracity of his theories but as the result of appeals to the pride and prejudices of his disciples. On the rise of the Suzuya school, Akinari wrote, "There is one who calls his students 'children of the teaching,' and gathers those who come from far and wide. This person has many arbitrary opinions. He is from Ise. He tries to explain the ancient times by taking the *Kojiki* as his canon. I criticize him saying: he wants disciples, even if he must tell lies to get them, even if people call him 'Mr. *Kojiki*.' "[2] Rejecting Norinaga's valorization of the *Kojiki*, Akinari argued that it and the other ancient texts were complicated products of human authors that reflected the relations of power within society. Reading them from this perspective, Akinari began to explore the relationship between political authority and community.

In the 1760s and 1770s, as Norinaga was quietly living in Matsuzaka engrossed in his analysis of the *Kojiki*, Akinari was an active participant in the intellectual life of Kyoto and Osaka. In addition to writing popular fiction, he was a haikai poet who composed with Yosa no Buson and Takai Kitō, the successors of Matsuo Bashō. The linguist Fujitani Nariakira, the Confucian scholar Minnagawa Kien (Nariakira's brother), and the Nakai brothers, Chikuzan and Riken, and Goi Ranjū—three scholars of the Kaitokudō, the Osaka merchant academy—are some of the prominent intellectuals of his time who were his acquaintances but also the objects of his sometimes biting wit. As modern commentators have noted, Akinari was in many ways an exemplar of the eighteenth-century cultural ideal of the *bunjin* or "man of culture" who possessed proficiency in various forms of cultural practice.[3] However, Akinari thought of himself not as a bunjin but as a practitioner of kokugaku, and it was as a kokugaku scholar that he became known to his contemporaries. The Confucian scholar Rai Shunsui, who lived far from the cultural centers of eighteenth-century Japan in Aki (present-day Hiroshima prefecture), knew of Akinari and described him as someone "who lived by studying kokugaku."[4]

In their relation to kokugaku practice—if we define this "institutionally" in terms of the Mabuchi school—Norinaga and Akinari shared a similar position. Norinaga, of course, proclaimed himself to be Mabuchi's successor. Akinari was a devoted student of Katō Umaki, a disciple of Mabuchi who had studied under him far longer and much more intimately than had Norinaga. Umaki, together with Murata Harumi and Katō Chikage, was considered to be among the leaders of Mabuchi's many disciples in Edo. In a letter written to Norinaga, Mabuchi stated, "Here [in Edo] there is one named Fujiwara [Katō] Umaki, who is especially interested in the *Kojiki* and the Divine Age. He has not yet told me his argument, but I am sure he is one who will in the end have something to say."[5] Umaki did in fact begin work on the *Kojiki* but died before he could complete the text he called *Kojiki kai* (Interpreting the *Kojiki*). Akinari studied under Umaki, the man who "opened up the way of ancient learning" to him, for perhaps a decade, from 1766 until 1777, the year of Umaki's death at the age of fifty-seven.[6] However, by 1783, the year in which he began to openly criticize Norinaga's work on the *Kojiki*—evoking a heated response—Akinari had produced only a few brief works: a history of the Kajima Shrine called the *Kajima Jinja hongi* (The True Meaning of the Kajima Shrine, 1774) and a study of the workings of certain particles in haikai poetry, *Yakashō* (Excerpted Examples of *Ya* and *Ka*, c. 1773).

Traces of Akinari's confrontation with Norinaga survive in the text called *Kakaika* (also known as *Ashikari yoshi*, "Cutting through the Weeds," c. 1790), which takes the form of a series of exchanges between Akinari and Norinaga over the meaning and significance of the Divine Age narrative related in the *Kojiki*.[7] I want to look first at these early attempts to interrogate the objectives and principles of Norinaga's textual practice and then turn to examine the series of works Akinari wrote in the aftermath of his celebrated debate with Norinaga. It is in these works that he sought to redefine the relations of "public" and "private," the past and the present, the individual and community that had taken form in Norinaga's exegesis of the *Kojiki*.

DEBATE I: INSCRIPTION, LANGUAGE, AND THE PAST

The context of the debate recorded in the *Kakaika* was Norinaga's rise to a position of prominence in the 1780s. By this time, he had completed his exegesis of the Divine Age chapters of the *Kojiki*, and these chapters, as well as the *Naobi no mitama*, were being widely circulated in manuscript form, precipitating the angry exchange of texts between Norinaga and Ichikawa Tazumaro. In addition, several of Norinaga's philological works had been published, including *Teniwoha no musubi kagami* (A Mirror for the Use of Particles, 1771) and *Jion kana yōkaku* (On the Use of Kana, 1776). It was in 1782 that Akinari, who had no doubt heard of Norinaga by this time, made the acquaintance of one Aragita Sugitomo. A native of Ise and a Shinto priest attached to the Ise Shrine, he was one of the many priests at Ise who had abandoned Suika Shinto for the study of ancient texts with Norinaga. Aragita did not formally became a student of Norinaga until 1784, but it seems that he had access to Norinaga's work and loaned a number of manuscripts to Akinari.

In 1783 Akinari produced a critique of Norinaga's theory of kana usage, which he then circulated among his friends and acquaintances. He gave it as well to Aragita, from whose hands it then passed to Norinaga. Norinaga composed a series of replies to Akinari's criticisms, to which Akinari later responded. Contact between the two seems to have ended in 1783, only to begin again with increased animosity in 1786. In the intervening period, Akinari was able to read several chapters of the *Kojikiden*, as well as another linguistic work, *Kanji san'on kō* ([A Theory of the Three Pronunciations of Chinese

Characters).[8] He had also read Norinaga's response to *Shōkōhatsu* (An Attack on an Eruption of Words, 1781), a work by a Buddhist priest named Fujii Masamichi, who argued that ancient Japanese was influenced by contact with China and the Korean peninsula. Such arguments, Norinaga wrote in *Kenkyō-jin* (Restraints for a Lunatic, 1785), were the product of the "Chinese mind." Akinari inserted his voice into this debate by means of a text called *Kenkyō-jin hyō* (A Review of the *Kenkyōjin*, 1786), a response to Norinaga's critique of Fujii's work. These early texts by Akinari have not survived, but parts of them were later incorporated into Norinaga's two-part response to Akinari. In reply to Akinari's comments on language, Norinaga wrote *Ueda Akinari nan no ben* (A Response to Ueda Akinari's Criticisms, 1787), and on Akinari's work on the Fujii text, he wrote *Kenkyōjin hyō dōben* (A Response to a Review of the *Kenkyōnin*, c. 1787). These two texts were combined by Norinaga to create the *Kakaika* in 1790.[9] Although the *Kakaika* is included in the collected works of both Norinaga and Akinari, it is very much Norinaga's text, in that he carefully edited this account of their exchanges and portrayed himself as the winner on every point.[10] However, even in the fragmented comments attributed to Akinari, it is possible to glimpse the contours of a penetrating critique of Norinaga's work.

Within the modern literature on the *Kakaika*, it is the first section devoted to the meaning of the Divine Age narrative that has received greater attention, but in fact it was questions of language that initially led Akinari to respond critically to Norinaga's work. Modern scholars of kokugaku have typically dealt with these exchanges on language by comparing the assertions of Akinari and Norinaga with the understanding of the ancient Japanese language put forth by modern linguists, with the consequence that, in the words of the author of one such work, "it is clear that in terms of depth of knowledge about the ancient language Norinaga is by far superior."[11] But to focus solely on Akinari's conclusions is to overlook the real significance of his criticisms. Akinari had in fact begun to question some of the founding assumptions of Norinaga's textual practice. In chapter 3, I noted that Norinaga's exegetical enterprise was founded on the assertion that the text of the *Kojiki* preserved intact the oral transmissions that related the events of the Divine Age. Thus, even as Norinaga privileged orality, he also believed that writing could record it, and his *Kojikiden* was an attempt to recover the ancient transmissions through exegesis. It was the necessity to preserve this hermeneutic framework that led to the interpretive maneuver explored earlier, the creation of the kana *Kojiki* that, by seemingly "recovering" the oral transmissions from the Divine Age, exemplified the Yamato kotoba that Norinaga idealized.

The traces of Akinari's comments, which were preserved in the *Kakaika*, reveal that he had begun to question Norinaga's assertion that the *Kojiki* recorded the oral transmissions from the Divine Age, directly and completely. Akinari's immediate concern was for kana orthography, which had become an object of debate beginning with Keichū's *Man'yō daishoki*. Later Mabuchi too had taken up the issue of kana in order to argue that the sounds that comprised the Japanese language originated in nature: combined into words, these sounds—or phonemes, to borrow modern linguistic terminology—were sufficient to speak of all things and revealed the perfect union between man and the world that had existed in ancient times. Mabuchi and later Norinaga argued that the introduction of Chinese words and syntax had disrupted this relationship, bringing into place an artificial system of distinctions, "new" sounds that were not natural but the product of men. Within the *Kojikiden*, Norinaga attempted to restore the "original" system of sounds by excluding from his kana *Kojiki* pronunciations of words that reflected the process of euphonic change (*onbin*). For Norinaga, as for Mabuchi before him, morphological change was understood as the evidence of "decline," "corruption," and "loss." Thus, Norinaga, in his exchanges with Akinari, continually made reference to the "correct" sounds of the past as he attempted to distinguish "original" sounds from those that developed as the result of euphonic change. In contrast, Akinari never employed the correct/incorrect opposition to describe the process of linguistic change. He argued that from the perspective of the speaker, no sound was any more or less natural than any other. Consequently, Akinari tried within the *Kakaika* to demonstrate that sounds Norinaga had labeled as the "corrupt" product of a later age may in fact have existed in ancient times.

But the rejection of the concept of "decline" is only a single aspect of an ambitious critique, the contours of which become obvious in the first exchange of opinions recorded in the *Kakaika*. At issue was the status of the phoneme \n\ in the ancient language. Norinaga had argued in *Jion kana yōkaku* that this sound did not exist in the ancient language and that its emergence in Heian times was the result of the "corruption" of the "pure" sound of \mu\ due to the process of euphonic change. In support of this conclusion, Norinaga pointed out that in *man'yōgana* (that is, Chinese characters used as phonetic symbols), there was no character to represent this sound. In contrast, Akinari argued that \n\ may have existed in the ancient language. He pointed out that within Chinese there is no character that represents this phoneme and suggested that those that represented "similar" sounds such as \mu\, \ni\, and \mo\ were borrowed to represent \n\. The nature of this exchange, in which both Akinari and Norinaga cite numerous textual examples, obscures the difference in their position, but it was a significant difference that transcended the immediate question of the status of a single phoneme. When Akinari argued that \mu\ may have been pronounced as \n\, he was suggesting that there was nothing in the ancient texts themselves that revealed the relationship between the written text and speech. Akinari asserted that it was possible that the written symbols did not exist in a one-to-one relationship with the sounds that comprised the spoken language. Certain sounds, he argued, may have escaped inscripture.

Akinari's point then was that the relationship of writing and speech had a complexity that Norinaga ignored. A similar contention is apparent in another of the exchanges recorded in the *Kakaika.* This concerned the relation of voiced and unvoiced sounds such as \chi\ and \ji\, \ha\ and \ba\. Norinaga asserted that in the ancient language these were distinct sounds, so that differences between them were always strictly maintained in the orthography of the ancient texts. Akinari disagreed. Citing textual evidence, he tried to demonstrate that the ancient people did not think of \chi\ and \ji\, for example, as separate and distinct sounds. He asserted that these phonemes were subject to elision and in speech were frequently interchanged. Akinari insisted that the phonetic distinctions upon which Norinaga placed so much emphasis became stable only after the introduction of writing. As they began to write, the ancient people became aware of differences that had no significance in a preliterate world. In this way, Akinari suggested that the very act of inscription may have produced an ordered uniformity that had been lacking before, with the result that writing became a mediating element, changing that which it was supposed to record.

Norinaga's detailed responses suggest that he recognized that Akinari was questioning the very foundation of the *Kojikiden,* the notion that Yamato kotoba was recorded directly, immediately, and without alteration within the *Kojiki*—and consequently could be recovered through exegesis. Akinari was suggesting the possibility that orality could elude writing or, even more significantly, that writing could alter orality, making the recovery of Yamato kotoba impossible. If this were true, all of Norinaga's careful reconstruction of the ancient language would have been for naught.

The assertion that it might not be possible to discover the ancient language through the examination of texts orders a third exchange as well. In this case, the point of debate was the relation of the characters that were read as \ha\ and \wa\ in the ancient texts. Akinari argued that in ancient times, these two symbols, which seem to represent distinct sounds, at times were read the same way, both as \wa\. In contrast, Norinaga held that the very existence of two characters indicates that these were distinct sounds in ancient times. The source of Akinari's confusion, according to Norinaga, was the fact that beginning in the Heian period \ha\ came to be pronounced as \wa\ in some words due to the process of euphonic change, a process that led to a loss of the distinction between \he\ and \e\ as well. In the *Kakaika*, Norinaga recorded Akinari's objection, a position he rejected as ludicrous. Akinari argued that perhaps it was a mistake to reduce these symbols to mere representations of sound. Could it not be that in ancient times multiple kana were used to represent the same sound in order to signify meaningful differences between homonyms such as "bubble" (written as *aha*) and "millet" (written as *awa*)? Through such examples, Akinari questioned the assumption that writing was capable of accurately and minutely recording the sounds of the ancient language. He tried to demonstrate that for those who spoke the ancient language, distinctions of meaning might have been more important than phonetic differences. By suggesting again the possibility of an alternative explanation for a set of perceived linguistic differences, Akinari implied once more that the orality of the past may not be recoverable through textual analysis.

Akinari's statements, recorded in the *Kakaika*, reveal that his aim was not to produce a positive knowledge of the ancient language, but rather to suggest the problems inherent in Norinaga's philological claims. This skepticism is apparent in another work in which Akinari explored the problem of kana orthography. Entitled *Reigotsū* (A Treatise on the Mysterious Language, c. 1793), it was written a decade after his initial exchanges with Norinaga in the early 1780s.[12] At first, Akinari seems to have retreated from his initial skepticism about the status of "orality" in the ancient texts, for the the work opens with the declaration that "the origin of kana is that the characters were written according to how the words were heard and were read according to how they were written. For example, the word 'plum' was pronounced *ume* and so that is how it is written in the *Man'yōshū*, except in one poem in which it is written as *mume*. This was a mistake, but even so it was written down."[13] But Akinari's point was in fact very different. He went on to question the policy of Norinaga and others of imitating the style of the ancient texts in their own writings, a practice that some, following Mabuchi's theory of *fumi*, regarded as the means to recover the "spirit" of the ancient period. Akinari questioned their reliance on the "imitation ancient style." Is not the imitation of the ancient form of inscripture, he suggested, a curious stance for those who idealize orality?

At the heart of Akinari's argument is his insistence that writing had always existed in an ambivalent relationship with orality. In tracing the history of this relation, Akinari asserted that while "one can speculate that at the beginning there was one character for one sound," it was clear that "as time passed the number of characters increased." Akinari did not believe that this was a peculiarly Japanese phenomenon; he noted that "the case of China is another example in which with each generation there were more characters."[14] While Akinari left this comparison undeveloped, his point seems to have been that writing produced new linguistic distinctions that in fact preceded changes in speech. Even so, he argued, this proliferation of characters was originally not problematic, because people still gave greater weight to speech and made random use of these characters. In a time when speech was privileged, how one wrote was of little importance.

But the primacy of speech began to give way when at some point a "fool" attempted to "cleverly" to distinguish between the redundant characters and invented rules for their use in writing. Akinari argued that those who read the ancient texts must always recognize that rule-governed writing is not the same as the spontaneous and unmediated speech it superseded. Because it is impossible to delineate the point of change, the reader cannot know whether what was recorded was the spoken language of the distant past or a secondary product, the rule-governed, mediated form of writing that replaced it. This led Akinari to dismiss Norinaga's attempt to write in the ancient language: "Whether one relies upon ancient rules or the methods of today, both are the private products of human invention, so how can one argue about which is right or wrong? As for those who worry, 'Shall I rely upon the old or the new?' when writing prose or composing poetry, they should just write as they want."[15]

Akinari argued that to recover the orality of the ancient period, one should not mimic the kana usage of the ancient texts, because to attempt to follow rigidly defined rules was to unwittingly privilege writing over speech. Rather, to inscribe language as it was spoken in the present was a more meaningful kind of recovery in that it signified in practice the primacy of the spoken word that had existed in ancient times.

The *Reigotsū* thus further reveals the critical distance that separated Akinari and Norinaga, a distance already perceptible in the *Kakaika*. Norinaga's
attempt to recover the oral transmissions of the ancient way rested upon
a belief in the capacity of the *Kojiki* to record that orality, and thus the entirety of his exegetical and philological enterprise was focused on proving
the "oral" nature of the text. In contrast, Akinari argued that it was impossible to know what relationship had existed between speech and writing in
the ancient texts. Consequently, he dismissed any attempt to recover orality
through the analysis of writing. The awareness of writing as mediation is,
however, only one aspect of Akinari's critique of Norinaga's work. In the
second half of the *Kakaikai*, Norinaga revealed Akinari's response to the exegetical claims advanced in the *Kojikiden*. Not only did Akinari reject the notion
of original cultural difference with which Norinaga began; he also began to
question whether textual analysis could ever make possible the recovery of
the past.

DEBATE II: HISTORY, TEXT, AND INTERPRETATION

The second half of the *Kakaika* incorporated a series of exchanges between
Akinari and Norinaga that were sparked by the publication of Fujii Masamichi's *Shōkōhatsu*. In this work Fujii characterized the *Kojiki* account of
Japan's origin as fabrication and legend and attempted to demonstrate that
Japan's language and customs derived from the cultures of China and the
Korean peninsula. Both Akinari and Norinaga rejected Fujii's theories, but
each rejected the account of the other as well. The *Kakaika* reveals that the two
had very different views both of the ancient texts and of their significance
for the present.

The first issue taken up was Fujii's assertion that according to his calcula-
tion based on information given in the ancient texts, the Divine Age encompassed a period of 1,791,470 years, which he characterized as an "absurd"
figure that "proves" that the narrative is fictional. Akinari's response was to
assert that Fujii's rigidly quantitative approach was at odds with the "simplicity" of the story it sought to interpret. He declared, "Can anyone understand the principles of the mysterious traces of ancient times?" [16] In other
words, he not only suggested that Fujii's conclusion was wrong but also questioned the attempt to understand the text in quantitative terms. The difficulty
in understanding the ancient texts is the thrust of Akinari's second criticism
as well. He noted, in what seems to be a reference to the multiplicity of vari-

ant texts that comprise the *Nihon shoki*, that there exist many versions of the Divine Age narrative that differ from that of the *Kojiki*. According to Akinari, if one's aim was to prove or disprove the factuality of the text, it would be necessary to examine all of these works, not just a single version. Only this—a step not taken by Fujii—could demonstrate the veracity of one account vis-à-vis all the others.

This criticism, of course, could pertain to Norinaga's work as well—as Norinaga recognized. In reply, he argued that Akinari's stance was as flawed as that of Fujii. According to Norinaga, from one who has indeed grasped the "ancient meaning," the immediate response to claims such as Fujii's would be not to doubt the length of the Divine Age but to question Fujii's characterization of this figure as absurd. In other words, if the "facts" of the *Kojiki* substantiate his figure, it must be accepted as truthful. However, Norinaga sidestepped the issue of how to deal with the existence of variant texts, arguing that to ask which one is correct was tantamount to saying that none of them can be believed. The correct stance of the reader toward the ancient texts was not to question their veracity but to accept them as truthful. Akinari also questioned whether the *Kojiki* was really a recording of oral transmissions that dated from the Divine Age. He pointed out that stylistically many of the poems included in the Divine Age section of the *Kojiki* and the *Man'yōshū* seem to date not from the "Age of the Gods" but from the age of "Asuka and Fujiwara," in other words the period when the texts were compiled. As might be expected, Norinaga was outraged and asserted that Akinari was assuming that the poems were of more recent origin simply because they were relatively easy to understand, in contrast to the main body of the *Kojiki* narrative.

Underlying all of the exchanges in this section of the *Kakaika* were profoundly different views of the ancient texts. Norinaga asserted that the *Kojiki* narrative must be accepted in its entirety, no matter how implausible the story may seem. Apparent inconsistencies are not evidence that the text is flawed or corrupt but reflect instead the limited understanding of the reader. In contrast, Akinari argued that the ancient texts possessed a complexity for which neither Fujii nor Norinaga could account. Thus he raised questions about the relation of one version to another and pondered the problem of how the ancient texts "worked."

The best known exchange of the *Kakaika*, the so-called debate on the sun goddess, further clarifies their differing views. It begins with Akinari asserting that although Norinaga states that the ancient narrative must be believed "as it is written," he in fact interprets certain passages metaphorically. In question was the status of the statement from the *Kojiki* that "Amaterasu shines throughout the six directions." Norinaga argued that this phrase signifies that Amaterasu, the sun deity, is the sun itself that shines over every country. Akinari countered by pointing out that the *Kojiki* makes reference only to Japan. Indeed, in order to incorporate the foreign countries into the Divine Age narrative, Norinaga had resorted to arguing that the passage in the *Kojiki* that describes the departure of the deity Sukunabiko to a place called Tokoyo was a reference to foreign lands. Moreover, Akinari stated, if one inspects European maps, it is clear that Japan is a small land, so how could anyone believe that this land was formed before all the others and that the sun and moon emerged from it? Thirdly, he noted that, like Japan, the foreign lands too have their ancient transmissions that portray their country as the first to be formed. How could one prove that any single account was true and the others false?

By raising these issues, Akinari implied that the assertion that one can understand the ancient texts "as they are written" in fact veiled an interpretive posture that inevitably relied on certain kinds of textual evidence while excluding others. Norinaga's response, however, was to reject the assertion that his understanding of the text was anything but immediate and direct. In order to prove that Amaterasu was the sun itself, he pointed to a phrase from the *Nihon shoki* in which this deity is described as shining "over heaven and earth" and argued that this is a reference to the other countries of the world. Similarly, pointing to another of the variant texts in the *Nihon shoki* in which it is said that "the sun and moon were not yet born," Norinaga argued that this is proof that the sun deity and moon deity were in fact the celestial objects, the sun and the moon.

In addition to citing these pieces of textual evidence, Norinaga made use of a curious explanatory device that indicates the fragility of his stance. Imagine, he said, that a shop in Kyoto has established a branch in Edo. In a certain period in which an epidemic is spreading throughout the country, a letter arrived from the branch manager to the Kyoto office. In it the manager stated, "I hear that you are suffering from this illness. At our shop too everyone is sick without a single exception." "How should we make sense of this letter?" Norinaga asked. Does it mean that only those in the shop are ill, or does it mean that this illness has swept through all of Edo? Any reasonable person would conclude the latter to be the case, according to Norinaga, and he asserted that a similar logic must be used in reading the *Kojiki*. For example, when in the Iwayado section of the narrative, it is stated that "the middle land" became dark after Amaterasu hid in a cave to escape abuse by Susanō, this can only mean that the world as a whole became dark. Clearly, then, Amaterasu must be the sun itself. Thus, in order to demonstrate that his reading of the *Kojiki* does not rely upon metaphor, Norinaga made use of a complex set of metaphorical relations. Not only is his story a metaphor to explain the workings of the text, but the letter of the shopkeeper takes the form of a metaphor in which the store is used metonymically to represent Edo as a whole, and of course the store/Edo relation is posed as an analogy for the Iwayado/world relation. Thus, Norinaga was in the strange position of using a metaphor to explain a metaphor, even as he declared that the *Kojiki* must be grasped "as it was written."

This attempt on the part of Norinaga to answer Akinari's criticism unwittingly highlights the critical power of Akinari's attack. Equally revealing is another of their exchanges, this one over the value of the European map, which Akinari evoked in order to question Norinaga's assertion of Japan's cosmic centrality. Norinaga began his attack with ridicule, stating, "I cannot but laugh when you say grandly that you have seen this map. In these days there is no one who has not seen such things." [17] However, rather than replying directly to Akinari's criticism, Norinaga accused him of suggesting that Japan is inferior to other countries because its small size. In response, Norinaga declared that size is not a determinant of value. A precious stone is worth more than the largest boulder; man is greater than horses and cows. Similarly, Japan is inherently superior to the larger countries, because it was created by the deities and therefore its imperial line is unbroken, its land fruitful, and its people flourishing. What this response failed to recognize is that Akinari had not introduced the European map as evidence of Japan's inferiority, but rather to demonstrate that the Divine Age narrative did not conform to other kinds of information.

It is clear that Akinari recognized the ideological import of Norinaga's understanding of the *Kojiki*. In response to his insistence on the existence of a cultural hierarchy of countries, Akinari argued that these references to Japan's superiority precisely mimic the cultural chauvinism of the Chinese. Rather than escaping from Chinese modes of thinking, he charged, Norinaga continued to act on them. As Akinari pithily put it, "*Yamato damashii* (the Japanese spirit) is just another name for *karagokoro* (the Chinese mind)." Addressing the status of Chinese influence on Japan, Akinari argued that Buddhism and Confucianism must have been appealing and useful to the Japanese people, otherwise the influence of these foreign theories would have been as ephemeral as that of Christianity. However, the "great principle" that allowed for the introduction of these ideas into Japanese culture—the question of what need they filled, what functions they performed—is not perceptible to the "limited knowledge" of men. Significant in terms of his later work is that Akinari explained this "great principle" in terms of the workings of historical change:

> Things and events change naturally, and there is no way to stop this. It may be possible to study and thereby achieve an imitation of the past, but the notion of recovering the past is nothing but the useless theory of scholars. . . . No matter how much we are angered by the evil customs of the present, it is beyond the power of any one man to do anything. My teacher once told me, the ways of the past were good in the past, the ways of the present are good in the present.[18]

Akinari accepted that cultures are subject to transformation over time, a process that transcends human beings and one that they are powerless to change and perhaps even to discern. He labeled this process "natural" and refused to characterize differences between past and present in terms of "loss" and "decline." In contrast, for Norinaga, the origin of cultural change possessed no such ambiguity. It was the workings of the evil deity Magatsuhi and the benevolent Naobi deity that caused things to change for better or worse.

The *Kakaika* was compiled by Norinaga and organized to allow him the last word in every exchange, but even in the somewhat elliptical and fragmented statements and responses attributed to Akinari it is possible to discern the beginning of a penetrating critique.[19] For Akinari the fact that the Divine Age was narrated in a plurality of texts that both overlap and contest one another led to the question of how one could determine the veracity of one account versus another. The issue of textual selection was linked to another issue, that of the representational value of the ancient texts. Is the *Kojiki* a transparent portrayal of the reality of the Divine Age? Is it a composite of fragments of earlier and later works? How does the language of the *Kojiki* work? Can one understand it "literally" (the claim of both Fujii and Norinaga), or must one necessarily read it metaphorically to extract a meaning? By raising these issues, Akinari called into question Norinaga's conclusions as well as his method, suggesting that his vision of Japan derived not from the *Kojiki* but from its reader.

ABANDONING THE PROJECT OF RECOVERY

In the year 1790 Norinaga's rise to intellectual hegemony advanced even further with the first publication of sections of the *Kojikiden*. In this same period, however, Akinari was formulating his own critique of this work. In 1792 he completed a treatise on the study of the ancient texts that he called *Yasumigoto* (Words at Rest). This work was then revised and extended in another work entitled *Otaegoto* (The Stringless Koto, 1803).[20] The titles of both these works suggest their theme, Akinari's skepticism about the recoverability of the past. *Yasumigoto* derives from a phrase that appears near the end of this work, in which Akinari stated that "to let the past rest peacefully as the past and the present as the present is the role of the ordinary man."[21] *Otaegoto* is an allusion to a statement by the Chinese poet Tao Yuanming (Japanese: Tō En-mei, c. 365–427) that Akinari cited in both works:

> I do not seek to force an interpretation on the texts I read. When Yixing first drew the hexagraphs [of the *Yijing*], there were no explanations. Wen Wang and Zhou Gong explained them and wrote the explanatory text [attached to the hexagraphs in the *Yijing*]. Kongzi [Confucius], modeling himself on them, added many words. And each of the works [that followed] claimed to be explaining and added more personal ideas. People speak as if these are the transmissions from the past, but they are all the thoughts of clever men. Taking up a general statement, they sought specifics. This is just like taking a koto [a Japanese zither] without strings and strumming it for one's pleasure. Someone has said, if it is stringless, there is no reason to tune it.[22]

Otaegoto literally refers to the "stringless koto" of this passage, which Tao used as a metaphor to describe the futility of trying to understand the ancient texts. Lacking strings, it cannot produce music, but some people insist upon strumming it anyway. Similarly, the knowledge that would allow the reader to truly understand the ancient texts is missing, but nonetheless attempts at interpretation continue. As both these titles suggest, in these two works Akinari was concerned with exploring the issue of whether textual analysis could ever lead to knowledge of the past. It is in the context of this discussion of history and textuality that Akinari began to explore the categories of "public" and "private" that had shaped Norinaga's discussion of the nature of Japan as community

In *Yasumigoto*, Akinari began his exploration of texuality by examining the

Kojiki, which he characterized as a peculiar work. The stories it records "are very strange, and there are many places that resemble the tales of children. Moreover, its language is straightforward and unembellished."[23] However, rather than taking these characteristics to be evidence of the work's inscription of the oral transmissions, Akinari explained its style and content in terms of the context of its compilation. He pointed out that the preface of the *Kojiki* states that the traditions of the various clans were carefully examined and only those that were correct were recorded in the work. This, he agreed, was an "excellent idea," but "What criteria did they use to distinguish between the correct and the false?"[24] Ultimately, Akinari suggested, the style of the *Kojiki* reflected not the oral transmissions from the Divine Age but a set of arbitrary choices on the part of its editor. Another issue that concerned Akinari was that the *Kojiki* seems to have been ignored by the imperial court that had ordered its compilation. There is no evidence that the *Kojiki* was ever utilized within the court, unlike the *Nihon shoki*, which immediately became what Akinari termed an "official" or "public" (ōyake) history, the object of study within the imperial court.

Having established these facts about the *Kojiki*, Akinari then characterized Norinaga's veneration of the *Kojiki* and his denigration of the *Nihon shoki* as "private" acts motivated by a personal interest in gaining fame as an expert of an unknown text. The notions of "public" and "private" at work here will order the totality of Akinari's work on the ancient texts, so it is useful at this point to examine them carefully. For Norinaga, the term "public" was used to delineate the realm of political authority: it signified rules, laws, policy, officially authorized social norms. In contrast, the term "private" (watakushi) was used in two senses. In relation to the ancient texts, it signified modes of organizing experience that he identified as alien to the original Japanese culture. "Private" knowledge was the use of Confucian and Buddhist concepts that were at odds with the authentic cultural knowledge inscribed in the *Kojiki*. In contrast, when deployed in relation to contemporary society, the "private" became the realm of individual experience, those aspects of life in which it was possible to recover the consciousness of the ancient period and resist the artificial norms imposed from above. In contrast, when Akinari termed the *Nihon shoki* a "public" text, the emphasis was on its official status, not its representational value vis-à-vis the ancient period. In Akinari's work, the *Nihon shoki* was "public" because it was recognized as the "orthodox history" (seishi) by those who held power, the court and later, by extension, the bakufu. In other words, his notion of "public" recognized the authority of those who held power to provide a singular and coherent account of the political realm. Akinari argued that an official history was necessary, in that it provided a unified conception of the past for society as a whole. For Akinari, the quintessentially "private" act was that of Norinaga, who took a text that had no recognized "public" value and declared it to be true.

On the face of it, Akinari's use of the terms "public" and "private" seems to affirm the structure of political power in place. However, Akinari immediately began to redefine this relationship. Like Norinaga, he too was concerned with discovering a "private" realm, one that would be autonomous from the "public" realm of political power and capable of contesting it. He began by attempting to distinguish between the value of the Nihon shoki as the recognized orthodox history and its value as a representation of the reality of the past. In characterizing the Nihon shoki, Akinari sounded not unlike Norinaga: "As for the compilation of the Nihongi, . . . it is an imitation of the histories of China and was compiled in order to impress the Chinese. For this reason, it makes use of [Chinese] idioms and imitates the rhetoric [of Chinese histories], and thus it distorts the ancient language, and there are not a few places where even events are confused."[25]

For Akinari, then, the Nihon shoki was from its inception a political text, compiled to present Japanese history in an appealing light to the Chinese court. But Akinari went on to argue that it was not only Chinese models that had shaped the representation of the events and language of the Divine Age and thus rendered the text an inaccurate representation; more important for Akinari was the context of the act of writing history. He asserted that the Nihon shoki was compiled specifically to suppress certain aspects of the political reality of the past.

Akinari compared the account of the Nihon shoki's compilation that appeared in its preface with those that appeared in other texts. He became convinced that the Nihon shoki was not a neutral or objective account of events, but was profoundly shaped by a political conflict occurring around the time of its compilation. In 672 the future emperor Tenmu and his nephew, the prince Ōtomo, struggled for political hegemony in a conflict that became known as the Jinshin Disorders. Tenmu prevailed over his nephew, the son of the former emperor Tenchi, and went on to become emperor. As emperor, he ordered the compilation of a history of the imperial court. It was Tenmu's son Toneri who compiled the Nihon shoki. Akinari noted that specific references in the Nihon shoki account of the Jinshin conflict are contradicted by evidence from the poetry anthology Kaifūsō (751).[26] The titles applied to Ōtomo and

Tenmu in this work support the notion that Ōtomo had in fact been designated the heir by Tenchi and thereby cast doubt upon the legitimacy of Tenmu's claim to the throne. Akinari asserted that the editors of this work, Ōmi no Mifune and Fujii no Hironari, descendants of Ōtomo, may have attempted in this way to preserve their version of the events of the Jinshin era. Similarly, he argued that those of the Tenmu line crafted the *Nihon shoki* precisely to conceal the evidence of Ōtomo's claim to the throne.

For my purposes, the accuracy of Akinari's account is less important than the conclusions that it enabled. Akinari believed that, like the *Kojiki*, the *Nihon shoki* was ultimately an unreliable text shaped by the political interests of those who wrote it. But this stance did not lead to the assertion that research and analysis would make it possible to separate facts from distortion. Akinari rejected the notion that any textual practice could lead to the recovery of the past, arguing that ultimately exegesis must always make reference to other texts, texts that are also biased. As an example of the problems inherent in the uncritical reliance on textual sources, Akinari took up Norinaga's understanding of the deities Naobi and Magatsuhi. He argued that Norinaga's assertion that these two deities were responsible for producing good and evil and thus controlled the workings of history derived from his readings of certain of the ritual prayers associated with the Nakatomi clan, one of the two clans that performed ritual functions within the ancient imperial court. Akinari stated that Norinaga's attempt to validate his reading by an appeal to the Nakatomi traditions was rendered questionable by the existence of other kinds of evidence. These were the traditions of the other priestly clan of ancient Japan, the Inbe, which were recorded in the *Kogo shūi* ("Gleanings of Old Words," 807). According to Akinari, "The tales of the most ancient age are extremely mysterious, and one should not try to understand them because even the traditions of the Inbe and Nakatomi, who are both practitioners of ritual, are different. How much more so then the oral traditions of the various families that were not recorded in the form of texts."[27]

His conclusion was that there is no way an interpreter can make sense of this heterogeneous body of texts, no criteria by which he, from the perspective of the present, can discover the reality of the past within the network of competing texts. This led Akinari to conclude the *Yasumigoto* with the declaration that "the 'restoration of the past' is just a meaningless phrase. In fact it means nothing more than playing at the imitation of the past."[28] He then urged his readers in the phrase that became his title to let the texts of the past "rest," mute and unimpeachable.

In Norinaga's hands, kokugaku discourse was organized around the reading and interpretation of the ancient texts in the belief that they could reveal
the nature of a pure and unmediated "Japanese" experience. In contrast, Akinari consistently attempted to undermine the modes of textual practice upon
which this enterprise depended. He argued that the philological examination of writing could not reveal orality and that the exegesis of flawed texts
could not reveal the reality of the past. Yet even as he made these statements
Akinari continued to privilege the *Nihon shoki*. He argued that the value of the
text rested not upon its veracity but in the fact that the "public"—the social
world constituted by political power—agreed that this was the account of
the past that would be accepted. Akinari had nothing but contempt for Norinaga whom, he insisted, had created an alternative past based upon spuri-
ous proof and held it up as "truth" and "fact." For Akinari, who rejected the
claims of exegesis, the past could only ever be a construct, validated not by
claims of truthfulness but by tradition and convention.

PLAYING IN THE PAST

In *Yasumigoto*, Akinari's focus was on deconstructing Norinaga's work. In
Otaegoto, a revised and expanded version of *Yasumigoto*, he went beyond mere
critique and began to experiment with a new way of writing history, one that
focused on the power of "play" to produce a new sense of community. The
notion of "play" was introduced early in *Otaegoto*, when Akinari quoted Tao
Yuanming to the effect that clever men take the texts of the past and "strum"
them for "their own pleasure." In other words, they make the texts mean
what they wish. But Tao went on to qualify this critique, quoting "someone"
who stated, "If it is stringless, then there is no reason to tune it." In other
words, what is criticized is the interpreter's pretense that this "koto" has
strings, that is, that his interpretation is in fact the original meaning of the
text. From this opening statement, the *Otaegoto* unfolds as an attempt to construct a mode of reading that does not pose itself as a "recovery" of the reality
of the past.[29]

Akinari turned from critique to delineating his own form of textual practice midway through the *Otaegoto*. The point of departure is his consideration
of a number of poems in the *Man'yōshū* that take as their topic the former
capital of Ōmi, from which the emperor Tenchi had ruled from 662 to 671.
In keeping with the standard practice of this era, Tenchi's capital was abandoned when the new emperor Tenmu ascended to the throne and established

his own capital at a new site, Asuka. Composed by Kakinomoto no Hitomaro and Takechi no Kurohito, the poems are similar in form: they describe
the poet gazing upon Ōmi and the great sadness he feels. Akinari professed
puzzlement at the theme and tone of these poems, pointing out that "since
the time when the imperial capital was established by Jinmu at Kashiwara,
it was moved in each generation, and there is no case in which the desola-
tion of the remains of an old capital was lamented in this way."[30] Akinari
believed that the "orthodox history," the *Nihon shoki*, was very unreliable on
this whole period, so he declared that in considering these poems his approach would be to "imitate one who draws legs on a snake and tell what I
think."[31] The answer, he speculated, may lie in the special relationships between these poets and the Tenchi branch of the imperial family. According
to Akinari, Hitomaro and Kurohito had served the Tenchi branch, the losers
in the Jinshin conflict over succession, and thus they must have come to the
old capital to remember what had been lost and to offer up poems to pacify
the spirits of those who remain here.

   This probing of the context of the Ōmi poems is revealing of the interpretive strategy that became central to Akinari's kokugaku practice. He had
already made use of it in the *Yasumigoto*, when he juxtaposed evidence from
the *Kaifūsō* with the *Nihon shoki* in order to cast doubt upon the veracity of the
Nihon shoki account of Tenmu's ascension to the imperial throne. Similarly,
in the *Otaegoto* Akinari tried to negotiate the inconsistencies he discovered in
the ancient texts. The Ōmi poems, for example, led Akinari to question why
Hitomaro is never mentioned in the *Nihon shoki*, this in spite of his fame as
a poet, clearly demonstrated by his prominence within the *Man'yōshū*. Akinari speculated that Hitomaro, because of his associations with the Tenchi
line, may have been excised from the official history that was compiled by
the Tenmu court, evidence that the political struggle of the Jinshin era reverberated long after Tenmu became emperor. Akinari did not present this
kind of speculation as the "truth" of the past, instead describing it as akin
to drawing legs on a snake. In Japanese, this expression is used to describe
the addition of something redundant or unnecessary. Indeed the compound
dasoku (snake legs) means "superfluous."

   The *Otaegoto* unfolds as an attempt to imagine the "history" that was not
written by probing the disjunctions and ruptures of the *Nihon shoki* narrative.
Another example of this strategy is Akinari's treatment of an earlier episode
recorded in the *Nihon shoki*. In 645 the prince Naka no Ōe, with the aid of
a courtier named Nakatomi no Kamatari, succeeded in crushing the Soga

clan, which had been attempting to usurp the throne. Akinari argued that the *Nihon shoki* narration of the aftermath of this event is strangely opaque. Naka no Ōe, the crown prince who was designated to succeed him, never ascended to the throne. Subsequently, the reigning emperor Kōgyoku abdicated in favor of Kotoku, and then less than ten years later Kōgyoku returned to the throne (an unprecedented event) to rule again under the name Saimei. Naka no Ōe finally began to rule, as the emperor Tenchi, in 661. Akinari attempted to explain this complicated sequence of events as the result of the introduction of Confucian political thought to Japan: "The beginning of the withering away of the imperial way was when people heard or read about the practices of abdication and usurpation, and as a result the desire [to rule] grew stronger and stronger. The teaching of the scholars who came from Kudara [on the Korean peninsula] bearing tribute was a method to incline man's heart toward good, and so anyone would agree it was something for which to be grateful." [32]

Akinari speculated that it was at this moment that a new understanding of imperial rule was introduced from the continent, one in which abdication was a virtue and usurpation a possibility. The result was the transformation of the conception of imperial succession then in place, producing on the one hand the attempt by the Soga to seize control and, on the other, the series of abdications that followed their destruction. However, he refused to criticize Confucianism itself for the events that followed its introduction to Japan — as he noted, "It was something for which to be grateful."

Further complicating matters, according to Akinari, was the simultaneous diffusion of ideas from Buddhism, which according to the *Nihon shoki* was introduced during the reign of Emperor Kinmei. Akinari explained, "Since there were many people, high and low, who despaired of their place in life, the notion that [Buddhism] could lead to limitless happiness and fortune found a place deep within their hearts. Who would not have celebrated this?" [33] But the effect of this newfound faith, he went on to say, was a lessening of respect for the native deities, as the emperor and his court began to worship the Buddha in the hope that this would prove efficacious. At the same time, the reverence with which the ordinary people viewed the court was diminished as they too fell under the influence of Buddhism and began to believe that the Buddha was more powerful than the emperor. Akinari agreed with Norinaga that the introduction of Confucianism and Buddhism had transformed Japanese society. But he did not portray China as the source of malevolent influence, nor are Confucianism and Buddhism characterized as inherently inferior to indigenous beliefs.[34] Akinari's concern was to understand the appeal of these ideas and their effect upon the emotions and sensibilities of the Japanese in the ancient period.

In this way, Akinari attempted to make sense of a set of transformations that do not appear on the surface narrative of the *Nihon shoki.* Like Norinaga, he recognized that over time the way in which individuals perceived and experienced the world had changed. But unlike Norinaga, he refused to characterize these changes in terms of the oppositions of authentic/corrupt or Japanese/Chinese. And unlike Norinaga, Akinari stressed repeatedly the imaginary nature of his own textual endeavors, stating at one point, "I have told this long story [*monogatari*] as I worried over it in my own mind, knowing that there is nothing upon which to depend in this world and that this is something that cannot be known."[35] While Norinaga argued that his *Kojiki-den* revealed the reality of the Divine Age, Akinari emphasized that his musings on the Age of Men cannot be regarded as factual, because ultimately the past is unrecoverable.

In describing the *Otaegoto* as a monogatari (a story or tale), Akinari collapsed the then current distinction between historical writing and the writing of fiction. For the Mito school historians, Arai Hakuseki, and other Confucian scholars, the aim of historical writing was to recover the truth of the past in order to illuminate ethical principles. In contrast, fiction was often described as *gesaku* (literally, "playful writing"), a term that implied entertainment rather than edification. In the Tokugawa period, the term *gesaku* was applied to a variety of popular prose forms including the illustrated books called kibyōshi, as well as *sharebon* (witty books), *kokkeibon* (humorous books), and *ninjōbon* (books of human feelings).[36] Many of the gesaku works were satirical in nature and parodied romantic intrigues within the licensed brothel quarters, the Chinese and Japanese classics, historical heroes and events — and the political figures and policies of the day. Other works were more serious, exploring the emotional toll that resulted from the conflict of social norms and human feelings. For the political authorities, the popularity of these prose forms was a matter of great concern. The Kansei-era censorship laws examined in chapter 1 were formulated largely with gesaku works in mind. Today Akinari himself is best known as a gesaku writer. His most famous works are the two collections of stories he wrote after he took up the study of kokugaku, *Ugetsu monogatari* (*Tales of Moonlight and Rain,* 1767) and *Harusame monogatari* (*Tales of Spring Rain,* 1808). Akinari's evocation of "play" at the beginning of *Otaegoto* was intimately tied to his conception of fictional narrative as "playful writing" — and the belief that it was potentially subversive.

At about the same time he was writing *Yasumigoto*, Akinari produced two works of theory that explore the nature of the monogatari form. The first was *Yoshiya ashiya* (For Good or for Bad), an essay Akinari attached to Kamo no Mabuchi's treatise on *Ise mongatari*, which he edited for publication.[37] In this work, Akinari argued against the traditional view of the *Ise monogatari*, which held that it was an account of the real adventures of the Heian courtier Ariwara no Narihira, and stated that it must be read as a work of *soragoto*, a word that means "fiction," but which Akinari wrote using the compound *gūgen* (allegory). His second work on monogatari was *Nubatama no maki* (The Blackberry Book), a work that takes the form of a fictional narrative.[38] The protagonist is one Muneharu, a Heian courtier who, according to tradition, copied the entire *Genji monogatari*, a work of some length, twenty-four times. In Akinari's account, Muneharu has a dream in which he encounters the poet Hitomaro and with him debates the meaning of the *Genji monogatari*. Hitomaro charges that the work Muneharu so valued was in fact a trivial story, one that the great poet Fujiwara Teika had described as "just playing with words."[39] To this Muneharu objects, making reference to the theme of karmic retribution that is interwoven within the story and arguing that the work thus had the goal of "punishing evil and encouraging good."

It is in response to this traditional view of the function of the *Genji* in particular and prose fiction in general that Akinari, through the figure of Hitomaro, developed his theory of the monogatari. Deploying a developmental scheme, he distinguished historically between poetic expression and narrative. The poetic form, he argued, emerged in the ancient period and reflected the fact that in that time people were able, immediately and without reflection, to respond to their world and express themselves in language. According to Akinari/Hitomaro, the Divine Age section of the *Kojiki* and *Nihon shoki* is marked by the traces of this poetic mode of expression, which had existed once in China as well. This mode of expression was characterized as "natural," and Akinari argued that, "since it emerged from the heart of the one who spoke, one cannot discuss it in terms of truth and falsehood."[40]

The discussion of poetic expression is sketchy, and many of its attributes only become clear in Akinari's discussion of the narrative mode that superseded it. He asserted that the mode of consciousness expressed in poetry — one in which people reacted immediately, without self-consciousness, to their world — was maintained until the reign of the emperor Ōnin, when scribes from Korea arrived with writing. Unlike Norinaga, who characterized writing as the vehicle for the infusion of alien modes of organizing experience into Japanese culture, Akinari situated the emergence of writing within a general scheme of cultural change. In China, as in Japan, with the development of writing came the possibility of social memory, with the result that it was no longer possible to experience the world immediately. Instead, perception was shaped by a new historical consciousness capable of remembering the past and reflecting on the present. It was precisely this new kind of subject who produced the monogatari.

> As for what we call monogatari, in China too there is a similar thing. It is often referred to as fiction [soragoto], and it is said to have no effect upon the real world. However, it is always the authors' intention to deplore the fickleness of the world, to lament the poverty of the country, to ponder the inability to restrain the changing times, to fear the evil of the powerful. They write by taking up the things of the past and thereby strike out in a general way against the reality of the present.[41]

In characterizing the author of narrative, Akinari referred repeatedly to the emergence of a new relation between the subject and the social world that he signified by the term ikidōri, literally "indignation" or "rage."[42] He argued that the writer of monogatari, imbued with a new sense of self-consciousness and agency, could now reflect and cry out against the "public" world that restrains him. The emergence of this new kind of subject meant that the immediacy and naturalness that had characterized poetic expression was no longer possible. Thus, Akinari dismissed the poetry of later ages as shallow and trivial: "The ephemeral birds and flowers were nothing but lies."[43] It retained the form of ancient poetic expression, but nothing else.

This statement—that the writing of monogatari began with the author's awareness of history—was expressed in the *Yoshiya ashiya* as well. In this work, however, Akinari departed from the position that the relation between past and present, subject and community, necessarily gave rise to "resentment." It was also possible to narrate from a perspective of "progress" born of "good fortune." According to Akinari, "The intention of the one who writes has its origin in a feeling of personal misfortune, and he cries out against the world as an expression of longing for the past. Or sometimes he believes that the flowers that bloom in the present are more beautiful and ponders the process of change."[44] However, even as he defined monogatari as an expression of historical consciousness, Akinari maintained that it was distinct from the writing of history. In characterizing monogatari, he spoke of soragoto (fiction) and itazuragoto (playful words) and contrasted it with the nature of historical writing embodied in texts such as the Nihon shoki. Historical works were described by terms such as makoto (truth) and mamegoto (seriousness). The value of the monogatari rested neither upon the assertion of referential truth, the claim of Norinaga in the Kojikiden, nor upon a political truth, the claim of orthodox history. The writing of fiction was the means by which subjects within history tried to render their "private" world intelligible. In the monogatari that Akinari constructed in the Otaegoto, he was concerned with probing the emotions of people like Hitomaro and Kurohito, who were displaced by the Jinshin insurrection, and with understanding how the introduction of Confucian and Buddhism transformed the ethos of the emperors and their courtiers. In each case, it is the exploration of the consciousness of these actors — their awareness of and concern for the events that shape their lives — that is the theme of Akinari's work.

But the delineation of these topics as "private" and of the monogatari form as "playful" and "fictional" did not mean that the writing of narrative did not possess the power to contest orthodox history. While Akinari continually asserted the autonomy of the one from the other and outwardly affirmed the triviality of fictional narratives, he also recognized — indeed embraced — the potential for confusion. He wrote in the preface to Harusame monogatari, "Stories of the past — and of the present as well — have deceived many; indeed, I myself, being unaware that such accounts were lies, have on occasion misled others by repeating them. But what of this? Such stories will continue to be told, and there will always be some who honor them as true history."[45] The possibility of a plurality of pasts necessarily implied that the present too possessed an opaqueness that must be interrogated. Arguing in this way, Akinari attempted to make fiction the form of writing that allowed for the questioning of the "official" representations of the social and political world. Again, the monogatari created in Otaegoto is illuminating. When Akinari explored the emotions of Hitomaro and Kurohito as they gazed upon the abandoned capital of Ōmi, he was — even as he labeled his efforts fiction — expressing the reaction of those who fell victim to political changes beyond their control. Thus the label of "fiction" functioned to mask the potential value of the monogatari form: it could express the perspective of those who are subject to the political power that is legitimated by the writing of "true history."

It was in the ten stories he called Harusame monogatari that Akinari attempted to make the writing of monogatari into a form of kokugaku practice. These stories were written sometime between 1802 and 1806, the same period in which Akinari was completing *Otaegoto* and *Nubatama no maki*.[46] They embody the strategy of writing that he defined in order to counter the claims of both historical writing and the form of kokugaku that Norinaga was practicing. The story entitled "Kaizoku" (The Pirate) is a case in point. Set in the early tenth century, it describes an encounter between Ki no Tsurayuki, one of the courtiers who edited the poetic anthology the *Kokinwakashū* and the author of the *Tosa Nikki* (The Tosa Diary, 934), and a pirate named Funya no Akitsu. Akitsu too was a real historical figure, who appears in the *Zoku Nihongoki* (Later Chronicles of Japan Continued), another of the "Six National Histories," of which the *Nihon shoki* was the first. An aristocrat who served in the court of the emperor Ninmyo, he was implicated in a rebellion against the emperor that broke out in 842. As punishment, he was exiled to Izumo.

The notion that Akitsu became a pirate was Akinari's invention, as was the supposed meeting with Tsurayuki. In fact, Akitsu died more than forty years before Tsurayuki's birth. This clearly is an example of the "fictionalization" of the past that Akinari asserted was the proper method for writing monogatari. Significant as well is Akinari's choice of Akitsu as protagonist.[47] This man, who in the orthodox history appeared only briefly as a rebel and an exile, is at the center of Akinari's story. Tsurayuki too is an interesting figure. The *Tosa nikki* is narrated from the perspective of a woman and written in kana rather than the kanbun that was expected of a male courtier of rank. The temporal framework of the story overlaps with that of the *Tosa nikki*: Tsurayuki, who had been serving as governor of Tosa, departs by ship for Kyoto accompanied by his wife and attendants. According to Akinari's story, however, they were suddenly overtaken by pirates. One of these pirates, later revealed to be Akitsu, at once began to address Tsurayuki: "This is what I wanted to ask you about. In the fifth year of the Engi era, the Emperor ordered an anthology of Japanese poems [the *Kokinwakashū*] to be compiled. I understand that you were in charge of the project. You gave the collection the subtitle 'Man'yōshū Continued,' implying, I suppose, that it's the successor to the original *Man'yōshū*."[48]

Akitsu then chastises Tsurayuki for the explanation he gave of the meaning of the title *Man'yōshū*, focusing on the meaning of the second character *yō*. In the preface to the *Kokinwakashū*, Tsurayuki stated that the character for *yō*, which literally means "leaves," was a metaphor for "words." Understood in this way, the title *Man'yōshū* means "ten thousand words," rather than "ten thousand leaves." According to Akitsu, this arbitrary explanation on the part of Tsurayuki resulted in the formulation of a new word, that is, *koto no ha* or *kotoba* (*ha* is an alternative pronunciation for the character *yō*). The term *kotoba*, coined by Tsurayuki, came to mean "words" or "language."

Thus, obliquely, Akinari made his point: those in positions of authority invent and create language—and culture. Yet he acknowledges as well that for later speakers of Japanese, the word *kotoba* is as "authentic" as any other. The rest of the story unfolds as a repetition of this theme. Akitsu tells Tsurayuki that his theory that there are "six kinds of poems" is at odds with the myriad of emotions that had previously found expression in poetry in ancient times. He argues that Tsurayuki's privileging of love poems in the *Kokinwakashū* does not mesh with the natural sense of morality that had existed in the "ancient Divine Age." And so on. In each case, the point is much the same. For Akinari, it was not the "Chinese mind" that had transformed Japan but the arbitrary acts of men of stature like Tsurayuki.

The rest of the stories that comprise the *Harusame monogatari* are similarly positioned between history and fiction, and from that space Akinari attempted to critically explore the process of historical change from the perspective of the individual within history. In the first story of the collection, "Chikatabira" (The Bloodstained Robe), the person in question is the emperor Heizei (774–824), who succeeded to the throne in 806, only to abdicate three years later.[49] The events recorded in the "orthodox histories" are that Heizei, together with Fujiwara no Kusuriko, his consort, and her brother Nakanari, plotted to regain the throne and raised a military force against his younger brother, who was then reigning as the emperor Saga. The rebellion was crushed, and Heizei was forced to become a monk. In the *Ruijū kokushi* (Classified National History, 892), Heizei is characterized as "envious" and "suspicious." In the *Nihon isshi* (Supplemental History of Japan, 1692), Heizei's reign is portrayed as a time of drought, starvation, and plague.[50] Akinari, however, depicted the reign of Heizei in very different terms. He began his story by portraying Heizei's rule in the laudatory terms used in Chinese histories to describe the reign of a virtuous king:

> Ame no Oshikuni Takahiko no Sumera Mikoto, known to history as Emperor Heizei, ascended to the Throne as the fifty-first sovereign since the beginning of the Imperial rule. Throughout the Five Home Provinces and the Seven Circuits there were neither floods nor droughts. The

people patted their well-filled stomachs and sang of abundant harvests. Beneficial wildfowl could build their nests without hesitating over the choice of a tree.[51]

Similarly, Heizei is described as "good in nature, but yielding and easily swayed" and as "a man with an honest heart" who possessed an "admirably trusting nature."[52] As in his musings on the Jinshin Disorders, Akinari implied that Heizei was characterized in negative terms because the history of this era was written by Saga and his descendants.

"Chikatabira" is an attempt to explore the character of this problematic figure and his relation to the events of abdication and rebellion. Akinari portrayed the emperor as a man no longer convinced of his right to rule. In a dream, Heizei's father, the emperor Kanmu, appears and urges him to abdicate in favor of his brother. Upon awakening, Heizei begins to ponder the meaning of the Confucian term "the mandate of heaven," which put forth the notion that the cosmos, "heaven," authorized a man of virtue to rule, a principle that was in sharp contrast to the Japanese genealogical conception of kingship. At one point Heizei states, "Heaven is the domain of our Imperial Ancestor who shines down upon us every day. Whenever I ask the Confucian scholars, 'Does Heaven refer to the sky?,' they answer, 'No, it is Fate.' Or else they say it means the destiny allotted to a man at birth. They have all kinds of explanations."[53]

Here Akinari returned to that moment in the past that he had pondered in *Otaegoto*, when he took up the aftermath of the destruction of the Soga. In both cases, his concern was to attempt to delineate a moment of historical transformation: what was the effect of the introduction of Confucian and Buddhist ideas upon someone like Heizei?

This concern for the impact of new forms of knowledge upon the individual becomes the theme of the story. Heizei was forced to consider the source of his own authority: is it his divine ancestry as posited by the narrative of the Divine Age, or is it the "mandate of heaven," of which Confucian scholars speak? Akinari described Heizei as looking back with nostalgia to the age of poetry when life was lived immediately, and not remembered and recorded: "Emperor Jinmu, the founder of the Imperial line, took his spear and hand and opened up the whole country for settlement. From then until the reign of the tenth Emperor, Sujin, were there no events worth recording? The Chronicles of Yōrō do not mention any."[54] At the end of the story, Akinari provided no easy answers for the confusing sequence of events recorded in the "official histories." The reasons for Heizei's abdication are left undefined, as is the nature of Heizei's involvement in the plots of Kusuriko and her brother.

BEYOND THE DIVINE AGE

Akinari's concern for actors within history meant that in his kokugaku practice, the Divine Age narrative retained little of the significance that it had had for Norinaga. Indeed, in "Chikatabira," Akinari presented the story of divine descent as merely one of several competing explanations of legitimacy, one questioned by the emperor himself. Akinari's only attempt to take up the Divine Age narrative directly was in a work he entitled *Kamiyo monogatari* (A Tale of the Divine Age, 1808), which was completed one year before his death. That he should call this work a monogatari is significant; it immediately signified that this account cannot be read as a piece of "orthodox history." Encompassing fewer than thirty pages in the most recent edition of Akinari's collected works, the *Kamiyo monogatari* is the antithesis of the *Kojikiden*. Weaving bits and pieces of the variant texts of the *Nihon shoki* together with innovations of his own, Akinari narrated the story of the Divine Age in simple, lyrical Japanese.

True to his definition of fiction, Akinari's *Kamiyo monogatari* is indeed an allegory, an allegory that describes the creative potential of speech. The work begins with a consideration of the meaning of the term *mikoto*, which in the ancient texts is an honorific attached to the names of certain deities. Akinari asserted that mikoto was a reference to speech, a contention he supported by linking mikoto to the term *kotoba* (words or languages). According to Akinari, the term *mikoto* signified that in the Divine Age the deities "expressed what they thought in words and that everyone followed these words."[55] Akinari thus rewrote the Divine Age narrative as a story that expressed the power of language and narrative to create a sense of community. But he concluded his account of the Divine Age by asserting again that the rise of writing, memory, and history had fundamentally altered the status of storytelling. The *Kamiyo monogatari* ends with the statement that "the reign of [Jinmu] was declared to be the beginning of the Age of Men, and all of those stories that had been told again and again from the [Divine Age] were made inappropriate. This was [the beginning] of what we call 'national history.' "[56] Thus the emergence of orthodox history is portrayed as a silencing of the myriad tales that had been told by a multitude of speakers. Akinari's kokugaku practice aimed to recover the ability to speak and to narrate that had existed before the public realm began to be defined by historical writing.

Akinari's view that the ancient texts were not transparent representations of the past but the traces of relations of power had profound implications for his conception of Japan as community. He rejected Norinaga's assertion that the "natural" community of the ancient age was knowable and therefore recoverable. For Akinari, the "public realm" of Tokugawa society was defined not by the intentions of the deities but by human beings who struggled to gain and maintain control. Their views of the "private realm" differed as well. Like Norinaga, Akinari privileged the "private realm," finding in it the possibility of a new kind of social experience, one not defined by political power from above. But while Norinaga defined the "private realm" as the domain of everyday life in which people should be free to express their emotions and desires, Akinari called for it to be a site of critical production, wherein one could write the stories that would expose the political exigencies that defined social experience. As ordinary subjects began to write "myriad tales," it would be possible to "imagine" the social in ways that problematized the accounts of "orthodox history." It was this that would allow for the production, not the recovery, of new and more authentic forms of community.

Chapter 5

Fujitani Mitsue: The Poetics of Community

Unlike Ueda Akinari, Norinaga's contemporary, Fujitani Mitsue took up the *Kojiki* in the period when Norinaga was well established as the dominant figure in kokugaku practice. He was twenty-three in 1790, the year that saw the publication of the first five chapters of the *Kojikiden*. It is unclear whether the two ever met, but clearly Norinaga heard something of the much younger Mitsue's accomplishments. Writing around 1794, Norinaga remarked approvingly of the work of Mitsue's father, Fujitani Nariakira, who wrote on linguistic theory and poetics, and he went on to praise Mitsue, stating, "Although young, he is working enthusiastically and purposefully to explain the way of our country. I think he is very promising, and I want to know what he is doing and writing." [1] In his late forties, Mitsue reflected on his initial encounter with the *Kojikiden*:

> When I was about seventeen or eighteen, I first looked at the Divine Texts, and I was puzzled by the phrases "chaos" [*konton*, from the *Nihon shoki*] and "begin to open" [*shohatsu*, from the *Kojiki*]. No matter how much I pondered them, I could not understand, and even though I looked at the annotations of earlier scholars, there was no one who took up these questions, and so my doubts became greater. Then I was able to see Norinaga's *Kojikiden*, and I thought he was so learned that surely here I would find answers to my questions. But not only did my doubts remain, I realized that he was very strongly concerned with the surface of the words. Within the Divine Text when he comes to those places that are difficult to understand or concern the deities, he says that one should not use human intelligence to consider such things. [2]

The perception that Norinaga dealt only with the "surface" of the text was the starting point for Mitsue's analysis of the *Kojiki* as well as other early Japanese works. Before his death at the age of fifty-six, Mitsue wrote exegetical texts on the *Man'yōshū*, *Tosa nikki*, *Hyaku'nin isshu*, and the *Kokinwakashū*, as well as the treatise on language *Makotoben* (A Discourse on Poetic Language, c. 1802) for which he is best known today. But it was the Divine Age chapters of the *Kojiki* that preoccupied him.

In 1808, Mitsue published the theoretical treatise he called *Kojiki tomoshibi ōmune* (The Principles of Illuminating the *Kojiki*). From that year until his death fifteen years later, he was engaged primarily in the task of analyzing the first half of the *Kojiki*, a process of revision and rewriting now evident in the series of the texts collectively known as *Kojiki tomoshibi* (Illuminating the *Kojiki*). Ironically, the young man for whom Norinaga had such high expectations did indeed try to "explain" Japan, but his work on the *Kojiki* was critical of almost every aspect of Norinaga's *Kojikiden*. Like Akinari, he questioned the theories of language and text that were the foundation of Norinaga's *Kojikiden* and rejected the notion that Japan was a "natural" community, divinely authorized. However, he went far beyond Akinari in interrogating the relation between the subject and the "public realm," the problem that the *Kojikiden* reading of the Divine Age myth had attempted to deflect.

Also ironic in light of Mitsue's concern for the *Kojiki* is his status within modern intellectual and literary histories. In his own time, Mitsue was a well-known figure in kokugaku circles. In his twenties and early thirties, he published no fewer than six works on Japanese poetry and poetics, and his friends included Kagawa Kageki and Kamo Suetaka, both prominent theorists of poetics.[3] He also appears in the *Heian jinbutsu shi* (A Guide to People of the Capital), a guidebook to scholars in Kyoto, named as a teacher of "Japanese learning" or wagaku.[4] His work on the *Kojiki* attracted the attention of members of Norinaga's Suzuya school, and two of them, Saitō Hikomaro and Ban Nobutomo, wrote attacking him fiercely for his critique of the *Kojikiden*.[5] But in the Meiji period, Mitsue's work was largely forgotten, until Sasaki Nobutsuna devoted a chapter to him in his *Nihon kagakushi* (A History of Japanese Poetics, 1910). In keeping with the theme of this history, Sasaki focused on Mitsue's poetic theory, although he noted that it was linked to his understanding of "the way of the deities." Mitsue's work on poetry, he wrote, "is extremely peculiar [*tokushu*]. His poetics was influenced by his views on Shinto, and since he does not explain the principles of Japanese poetry itself, it is hard to give his theories much credence."[6] At the same time, Sasaki praised the theoretical rigor of Mitsue's argument and its originality.

Sasaki's approach has set the tone for much of the work on Mitsue in the modern period. Mitsue is almost invariably described by means of adjectives such as "peculiar," "unique," and "unusual." A case in point is the title of a recent study, Tada Junten's *Ishoku no kokugakusha: Fujitani Mitsue no shōgai* (The Unique Kokugaku Scholar: The Life of Fujitani Mitsue).[7] In many cases the designation of "peculiar" has been accompanied by a search for the deviant—that is, nonkokugaku—influences that could account for Mitsue's "difference." Some of the possibilities that have been identified are Neo-Confucianism, Taoism, Yoshida Shinto theology, medieval poetics, and Pure Land Buddhism.[8] Like Sasaki, most scholars who have analyzed Mitsue's work have focused on his poetic theory and praised its analytical approach. For example, in the 1920s the literary critic Tsuchida Kyōson wrote of Mitsue: "Of the philosophers and literary critics of our country, Fujitani Mitsue is one of those I respect most. If he were alive in the present, he would probably be a philosopher whose depth of experience and precision of analysis would be above comparison."[9] Since the 1980s Mitsue's work on poetics has gained the attention of a new generation of scholars who have found in it ideas that reverberate with postmodern discussions of poetic language and subjectivity. One such scholar is Kamada Tōji, who has asserted that by refusing to read Mitsue from the perspective of kokugaku discourse, he was able to discover "connections" between Mitsue's discussion of *kotodama* (spirit of language) and Julia Kristeva's theory of poetic language.[10]

In the discussion that follows I take the approach that Kamada criticized and situate Mitsue's work within the kokugaku discourse of the late Tokugawa period. Read in this way, it is evident that Mitsue's work is not as "peculiar" as has been suggested but in fact was directly engaged in the debates that were shaping kokugaku practice. Like Norinaga and Akinari, Mitsue's exploration of community was ordered around issues of language and textuality and attempted to analyze the relationship between "public" and "private" experience. I want to begin by examining Mitsue's theory of poetic language, because this was the foundation of his assertion that the *Kojiki* was not a record of actual events during the Divine Age, but rather was a "teaching" that explained the process that Mitsue called *kaikoku* (establishing the country) and *kyokoku* (unifying the country). For Mitsue, the *Kojiki*, the *Man'yōshū*, the ancient imperial rites, and even the geographic distribution of ancient shrines and temples all signified the same central event, the production of Japan as a community.

A SOCIAL POETICS

When Mitsue began to explore the social value of poetry in the 1790s, he was inserting himself into a long-standing and contentious debate. Norinaga's own poetic theory had taken form in the wake of the *Kokka hachiron* exchanges of the 1740s, in which Arimaro, Mabuchi, and Munetaka had participated. In his early works on poetry, Norinaga, following Mabuchi, rejected the Confucian assertion that poetry was to be an aid to government or to serve the interests of political authorities by imposing ethical constraints on those they ruled.[11] Using the term *mono no aware* to explain the production of poetry, Norinaga had argued that poetic practice was not a tool of governance but an essential form of language by means of which the subject expressed his emotional responses to both the social and natural worlds. Thus the theory of mono no aware privileged an emotive realm of experience within which the subject was "freed" from but also restrained from attempting to shape the rules, norms, and conventions of social experience. In Norinaga's work, poetry then was the means to respond to a social world that was "outside." Within the context of the *Kojikiden*, however, the autonomy of the poetic expression assumed new significance. As Yamato kotoba, it could express the primordial Japaneseness that existed before and beyond the constraints of the social and political world. Like Norinaga, Akinari viewed the poems of the *Man'yōshū* as traces of the consciousness of the archaic Japanese people, but he refused to accept Norinaga's assertion that this way of perceiving the world was recoverable through textual practice. Akinari's concern was for the world "after writing," the world in which those invested with political authority have the power to shape social memory and thus social reality.

Like both Norinaga and Akinari, Mitsue too was concerned with interrogating the relation of the individual to the public realm, but he followed Norinaga in regarding poetic expression as a cultural form of primary and continuing significance. As a young man growing up in Kyoto, Mitsue began to study poetry while in his teens. Much later he recalled, "From the time I was young I studied poetry as my father wished, but one day it occurred to me that if the composition of poetry is nothing more than a pastime, then it is of no benefit to me or anyone else, and if it is of benefit, then it must be pursued avidly, and so I began to consider this in various ways."[12] Mitsue took up the issue of the function of poetry within the context of the Japanese poetic tradition in which the composition of such poetic forms as waka, renga, and haikai occured within varied social settings. Waka were often exchanged within letters and were also composed publicly at parties and competitions. Renga and haikai, two "linked verse" forms, were group compositions that took form as one poet "linked" his verse to that of another. In keeping with this tradition of poetic practice, Mitsue explored poetry as a distinct form of language that was in essence a mode of communication between two people, whom he designated as "I" (ware) and the other (kare or hito). It was in his consideration of the nature of the "I" that composes poetry that Mitsue departed from his predecessors and introduced a new complexity into the discussion of the subject-social relation.

In his earliest work on poetic language, Kadō hiyui shō (On the Special Nature of the Way of Poetry, c. 1797), Mitsue's concern for the interiority of the subject is already apparent.[13] In describing what he called the "the way of the heart" (kokoro no arikata) of the poet, Mitsue wrote:

> When I do something that is wrong, such as being argumentative or speaking ill of someone behind his back or pocketing someone's belongings, I feel that I know completely what I am doing, but afterwards there is a sense of unease. I call that sense of unease magokoro [written with the characters kōshin, literally "public mind"]. I call the mind that is selfish and thinks only of its own rewards hitoegokoro [written with the characters shishin, literally "private mind"]. . . . Far beneath this private mind, there is another "mind" that feels ill at ease when the private mind is allowed to act without restraint. This is the public mind. But hidden far beneath this public mind, there is that which moves the public mind. This is what is called kami [written with the character for "deity"].[14]

This description of human consciousness relies upon the same opposition of public and private that ordered Norinaga and Akinari's analyses. But while "public" was used by Norinaga to designate the social/political world ordered by the "Chinese mind" and controlled by the deities, and by Akinari to signify the social world constituted by political authority, Mitsue viewed "public" and "private" as intrinsic and internalized aspects of every subject. In the Kadō hiyui shō, the term "public mind" demarcated something akin to the moral conscience: it was the "sense of unease" that prevents someone from acting purely in order to gain selfish satisfaction at the expense of another. Mitsue asserted that while the "public mind" is experienced as the product of social rules and norms, this sense of morality was founded upon a more primal "public mind." Hidden beneath the "public mind" that was the product of internalized social rules was what Mitsue termed *kami* (deity). Here, Mitsue used this term to denote an innate sense of morality that both gives rise to ethical principles and makes adherence to them possible. The kami were not transcendent heavenly beings whose will controls events in the human realm, as Norinaga insisted, but rather were the primal aspects of human consciousness, the workings of which we are largely unaware.

At this stage, Mitsue's analysis was still marked by a profound concern for ethicality, and his evocation of innate human morality seems to reflect the Neo-Confucian conception of human nature. But in the five years or more that separate the *Kadō hiyui shō* from the *Makotoben*, Mitsue rethought the nature of subject, abandoning ethicality as a framework once and for all. In *Makotoben* his starting point was again the nature of the subject who speaks through poetry. But he now used the term *kami* to signify not an innate sense of morality but rather the "private thoughts, desires, and emotions" (*watakushi shiyokujō*) that are a part of every human being. Mitsue asserted that in addition to these emotions and desires, human consciousness is also shaped by the internalized rules and norms of society (*kōri*, literally "public principle"). The opposition of public principle and private desire is reminiscent of that of the "public mind" and the "private mind," but no longer is the former understood as moral and the latter as amoral.

In order to convey the relationship between primal desire and internalized social norms, Mitsue employed a series of oppositions: desire is to reason as earth is to heaven, mother is to father, body is to mind, inner is to outer, the hidden to the revealed. In each case it is the productive power of desire that is emphasized. In contrast, "public principle" is characterized not as the expression of innate human morality but rather as a set of restraints, controls, and limits on desire that have been internalized.[15] For Mitsue, human actors had a dual nature: they were simultaneously composed of both a "public body" (*kōshin*) and "private desire" (*shiyoku*).

Why does the subject internalize rather than resist the imposition of social norms? In contrast to Norinaga, who thought of social rules and norms as the product of the "Chinese mind" and argued that they could be stripped away to reveal a more authentic Japanese self, Mitsue regarded social norms as an integral part of every subject. Because the "I" is by nature a communal being, it wants to speak of itself to another and to be understood by the other. Mitsue argued that ordinary language—which he termed "direct speech" (*chokugen*) and "the surface of language" (*kotoba no shōmen*)—is a perfectly acceptable tool for communication when what is communicated is in keeping with established social norms, for after all both "I" and the other have internalized the same rules and norms. The problem is how to communicate "private" desires and emotions to the other. Mitsue termed the state of the subject who wants to express private desires *hitoegokoro* (passion) and *hitaburugokoro* (obsession). He argued that ordinary referential language cannot convey these primal, preverbal, presocial desires and emotions.

The argument that primal desire cannot be expressed by direct language is made in various ways. In good kokugaku fashion, Mitsue cited passages from the *Kojiki* and the *Man'yōshū* that describe Japan as "the country that does not lift up words" (*kotoagesenu kuni*), a phrase that he interpreted to mean the avoidance of direct language. In making sense of these passages, Mitsue argued first that there is a fundamental discordance between the public/social nature of ordinary language and the prelinguistic nature of the kami. As he put it, "Language kills the kami." But equally problematic was another point of disjunction, that between private desire and the social context in which speech inevitably takes place. Mitsue termed this context *toki* (occasion) and offered this explanation: "[Toki is] the situation in which one comes into contact with things and deals with events."[16] Simply put, toki is the social context of any specific speech act, a context shaped by the speaker's gender, age, social status, and so on. Within Mitsue's work, the notion of toki signified a dynamic moment of potential fusion or rupture between the speaker and the social world: "In the toki there is both myself and another. As for me, I am in an emotional state that can disrupt the situation that has prevailed until that point. As for the other, it is those things and events that are different from my thought. But from the perspective of that thought, I too am an other. So toki refers to that which will not submit to my thought."[17]

This statement reveals the complexity of the subject in Mitsue's work. Torn between primal desire and the internalized social norms, he is both "I" and the other. The social world encapsulated in an instance of toki is the catalyst for a struggle within the subject that wants both to communicate and to express the thoughts that are kami. The price for expressing desire without regard to the social context is "to destroy the toki," to break the rules of the social context and to potentially bring harm to oneself. But the inability to express desire gives rise to a state of emotional alienation that Mitsue termed "despair" (*utsujō*), a term that brings to mind Akinari's use of the term *ikidōri* (indignation or rage). But while Akinari characterized "rage" as a response to a social world "outside" the subject, Mitsue used "despair" to describe the internal struggle of someone who is torn between his "public body" and "private desire."

How can a speaker express desire to the other without destroying the toki? Mitsue argued that this was possible through the use of the form of language he called *tōgo*. He discovered this term in the *Nihon shoki* where it appears in the first chapter of the Age of Men section of the text, which describes the exploits of the first human emperor, Jinmu. In the mythohistories, Jinmu is depicted as the descendant of Ninigi, the grandson of the sun deity Amaterasu, and it is his birth that divides the Divine Age from the Age of Men. In the passage that describes how Jinmu subdued the unruly earthly deities and established his reign, there is the statement that "by using poetry and tōgo [Jinmu] subdued the unruly spirits. This was the beginning of the use of tōgo." [18] Mitsue seized upon this obscure term, which appears only in this one instance in the *Nihon shoki* and not at all in the *Kojiki*, and made it the foundation of his interpretive project. It was tōgo, he insisted, that could convey the emotions and desires that could not be expressed in "direct language":

> Within the minds of human beings, there is that which cannot be interrogated. Therefore, since one cannot use direct language to reach that part, in our great country we make use of a miraculous method. When one uses tōgo, the kami are there. . . . Thus, tōgo is the border between speaking and not speaking. The essence of tōgo is when one wants to say what one thinks, but instead says what one does not think. . . . Tōgo is when one takes the spirit [*tama*] of what one wants to say directly and makes a new expression. Then based upon this expression, the other can know what I think.[19]

According to Mitsue, tōgo "is neither public nor private. It mediates between the public body and the private mind and expresses in a benign way how one feels in an any given situation." [20] As a result, the use of tōgo made possible a kind of communication that was impossible in direct speech.

In later works, Mitsue would devote much time to clarifying what forms of linguistic expression were included within the category of tōgo. Perhaps the most concise statement appears in the work *Kadō kyoyō* (The Essence of the Way of Poetry, 1815):

> There are two forms of tōgo. One is metaphor [*hiyu*]. As an example of metaphor, it is when one uses the falling of flowers to convey the

notion of mutability or speaks of the age of the pine tree to express the good fortune of human longevity. But the second form of tōgo is . . . metonymy [soto he sorasu]. For example, instead of saying that I want to see my lover, I write a poem about wishing to see my lover's home; or in order to thank someone for a gift, I talk of how the thing that was given is beyond compare.[21]

But elsewhere he expanded upon this statement, citing examples from classical texts that suggest that paradox, simile, and allegory were also forms of tōgo. He also noted that tōgo was not a characteristic purely of poetic forms such as waka but was to be found in prose as well.[22] As this suggests, Mitsue used tōgo to convey the expressive power of a wide range of linguistic forms in which words were used for other than their strictly referential value. It was "poetic language," in which various forms of semiotic slippage were deployed to convey meaning. Mitsue argued that poetic language was able to express what he called "kotodama." Another term from the ancient texts, kotodama literally means "the spirit of words," but for Mitsue it described the power of metaphor and metonymy to convey the kami within one speaker to another. The result of this kind of communication was the creation of a relationship of "emotional responsiveness" (kantsū) between the I and the other. Mitsue described such a relationship as an almost magical occurrence. It is like, he said, the instant when flint and stone come together to produce fire.[23] For Mitsue, it was based upon this transformative experience that "selfish" subjects came together to constitute the basic node of community.

The debate between Norinaga and Akinari had centered on the representational value of the language of the ancient texts. Norinaga argued that the Yamato kotoba of his kana Kojiki was the language of the transmissions from the Divine Age and that this language conveyed the reality of that age. Akinari, of course, questioned the validity of this claim, asking who wrote and why. But while Akinari pursued these questions in order to question the value of texts for the recovery of the past, Mitsue detached language from the problem of representation in order to explore its communicative function. Thus, in his theory of poetic language, every linguistic expression was viewed as a speech act between two subjects. Tōgo was an extraordinary kind of language that allowed for communication when "ordinary" language failed. This new concern for communication rather than representation fundamentally altered a whole set of relations within Mitsue's hermeneutic project. For one, the relation between the subject and the "public realm" was no longer conceived of solely in terms of submission or resistance. Rather than being something exterior to the subject, social norms became something "within" that necessarily mediated any attempt to speak. Moreover, the conception of language as communication necessarily implied both a speaker and listener. Thus, when Mitsue began to explore the *Kojiki*, he asked, "Who is speaking?" "To whom?" and "Why?"

DISCOVERING THE "METHOD" OF THE *KOJIKI*

In 1808 Mitsue published his theoretical treatise on the *Kojiki*, the *Kojiki tomoshibi ōmune*. The *Ōmune* has been characterized as "a work of Norinaga criticism," and, indeed, it is organized as a refutation of the first chapter of the *Kojikiden*.[24] Like that chapter, the *Ōmune* put forth a textual history of the *Kojiki*, analyzed the nature of its language, and established a set of hermeneutic principles. Norinaga had argued that the language of the *Kojiki* was unlike that of any other text. Free of the influence of alien modes of discourse and unmarked by the mediation of any human author, it was able to represent the events of the Divine Age as they had occurred. It is precisely this conception of the *Kojiki* that Mitsue attempted to deconstruct as he laid out his own theory of the text in the *Ōmune*. His attack, however, began subtly, and the *Ōmune* opened with homage for Norinaga:

> Recently, Motoori Norinaga of Matsuzaka in Ise realized that the *Kojiki* is far superior to the *Nihon shoki*, and he discussed the faults of that prince [Toneri Shinnō, editor of the *Nihon Shoki*]. Indeed, when one reads his theory, it is clear that, as Norinaga stated, there are many places in this work [the *Kojiki*] that reveal the language of our country just as it was. I am indebted to this master, because now without much difficulty I recognize the veracity of the *Kojiki*.[25]

Mitsue's words of praise seem disingenuous in light of the discussion that followed. He immediately turned to reject Norinaga's characterization of the *Kojiki* as a history that recorded the facts of the Divine Age. On Norinaga's insistence that the text be read as a historical record, Mitsue stated, "This is the meaning of the *Kojikiden*, and before [the *Kojikiden*] this was the intent of the *Naobi no mitama*. Because it seems quite reasonable at first glance, there have been many people recently who accepted this. . . . When one considers the evidence for this theory, it seems very strange, no matter how long one reads the Divine Text and thinks about it."[26]

Norinaga's insistence on the historicality of the *Kojiki* had been directed against earlier readers, such as the Suika Shinto scholars, who had attempted to understand the Divine Age narrative in terms of Neo-Confucianism. But he rejected as well the view of readers such as Arai Hakuseki and Tayasu Munetake, who had viewed it as a history, but of events that occurred within human society. For Norinaga, of course, the Divine Age narrative was a chronicle of the events that occurred among the deities, before the beginning of human time. In contrast, Mitsue argued not only that the *Kojiki* did indeed relate a "theory" but also that it was written purposefully with an instructive intent.

According to Mitsue, the Divine Age narrative was authored by the emperor Jinmu in order to explain the method (*shinpō*, literally "method of the mind or heart") of "following the way of the kami" that had allowed him to create a community from the disparate mass of people who had lived on the Japanese islands in ancient times.[27] After he had succeeded in establishing himself as ruler, Jinmu taught the "method" he had used to his subjects, who then replicated it in their families, villages, and elsewhere. For generations this essential social knowledge was conveyed orally and iconistically through the construction of shrines and the establishment of rituals until the early eighth century, when the decision was made to commit it to writing.[28] The writing of the *Kojiki* was just another strategy to diffuse this "method," but it took place as Japanese had become aware of "Chinese" claims of the centrality of their culture. Mitsue argued that the surface narrative of the *Kojiki*, which made Japan the divinely ordained product of a primordial past, was merely a "childish" device inserted to challenge Chinese claims of cultural superiority.[29] But the important aspect of the text was not the superficial remnants of eighth-century culture but the essential knowledge encoded within it.

For Mitsue, the actors in the Divine Age narrative were not anthropomorphic deities, as Norinaga would have it, nor human actors writ large, as Arai Hakuseki and Tayasu Munetake had asserted. Drawing upon the understanding of kami he had put forth in the *Makotoben*, Mitsue argued, "The heavenly deities spoken of in the first section [of the *Kojiki*] are all names given to the divine spirits [i.e., the private thoughts and desires] that exist with the body of the emperor Jinmu, and the earthly deities are all without doubt the divine spirits that dwell within the masses of people under heaven."[30]

The recasting of the deities of the *Kojiki* into representations of the primal emotions and desires within human actors was the founding moment of

Mitsue's interpretaton of the work. He viewed Jinmu and the rulers who succeeded him not as the descendants of heavenly deities divinely authorized to
rule Japan but as human beings of the same nature as those over whom they
ruled. Thus, Mitsue refused to speculate on Jinmu's origins and stated that
it is both impossible and unnecessary to know anything of his background.
What was important was how he had established himself as ruler, for this
was the act that had initiated the process of community formation. According to Mitsue, the *Kojiki*'s description of the events of Jinmu's life made it
clear that the would-be ruler did not resort to conquest to gain political hegemony: "It is obvious that the first section of the *Kojiki* explains the august
way of the kami within Jinmu and the deities within the common people of
the world. Based upon divine acts, Jinmu was able to pacify the people and
make them follow him, [although] in the account of this emperor it is clear
from the way in which the many local leaders submitted that he did not fight
violently against them." [31]

How then was he able to win their compliance? Rejecting Norinaga's
vision of Japan as a "natural" community, Mitsue argued that Jinmu became
ruler because he was able to communicate his desires to those around him
and bring about their submission.

As this discussion suggests, Mitsue used the *Kojiki* to explore the nature
of political power. He was concerned not only with interrogating how rulers
acquired political power but also with understanding how authority could be
sustained without reliance upon force and coercion. In other words, what allowed those who were subject to political power to recognize the authority of
those who ruled? How could affective bonds be established between them?
For Mitsue, a samurai who held an important official post in service to his daimyo, this was clearly an issue of great significance. In *Kaikokuron* (A Theory of
Establishing the Country, c. 1804), Mitsue described the condition of Japan
in his day:

> It goes without saying that this is a time when the world and the coun
> try are in a state of disorder. At present, even though the products of
> the country are many, their cost is high. Moreover, debts are so great
> that even several years worth of the products would not be enough to
> repay the debts. It is just as though there is no government. Moreover,
> the manners of those above and below are not good, and those above
> and below feel no intimacy. The people of our country feel resentful.
> Thus, even though there is one who rules, it is as if he does not exist. [32]

This vision of a society marked by financial woes, declining morals, resentment, and alienation is echoed elsewhere in Mitsue's work. In the poems he wrote during these years, Mitsue spoke of the "spread of great evil" and "this era of suffering."[33] Particularly revealing is his overt recognition of the relations of power that ordered his society: "Rulers collect the land tax, and so their loyal retainers and filial children eat and sleep at night, and there is no one who names this as selfish desire; but if one considers this, then surely it must be recognized as self-interested."[34]

As Mitsue analyzed early Japanese poetry and prose in the first decades of the nineteenth century, he sought to understand the nature of the relationship between the ruler and the ruled. Like Akinari, he probed the context in which these works were written and argued that they reveal the traces of struggles that do not appear on the textual surface. An example of this strategy is Mitsue's commentary on one of the Man'yōshū poems he took up in his work Man'yōshū tomoshibi (Illuminating the Man'yōshū, published 1822). The poem, which is attributed to the workers who built a new palace for the empress Jitō after the capital was moved to Fujiwara in 694, states that the "the people of the empress" rushed to be of service, "forgetting their own homes, with no care for themselves."[35] Mitsue argued that while the surface of the poem expressed praise of the empress and her palace-building enterprise, this was the language of tōgo. Hidden beneath the words of praise was the real intent of its author, who lamented the suffering of those forced to leave their families and their fields to labor in the construction of the new palace: "The people given the duty of moving the capital seem on the surface to have forgotten their homes and their bodies and seem to revere [the empress], but it cannot be that they were in fact happy to leave their homes and exhaust their bodies, so in their hearts they must have resented the duty of moving the capital."[36]

Another classical text that expressed "resentment," according to Mitsue, was the Tosa nikki, the work on which Akinari had based his story "Kaizoku." In his preface to the Tosa nikki tomoshibi (Illuminating the Tosa nikki, c. 1816), Mitsue explored the circumstances that led Ki no Tsurayuki to compose this work by posing as a female member of his own household during the journey from Tosa, where he had been serving as governor, back to the capital of Kyoto. According to Mitsue, the appointment of Tsurayuki, a talented man of letters and an experienced official, to the lowly post of governor of a distant province was evidence of the decline of imperial rule in the late tenth century, as men of ability were passed over in favor of those less qualified but better connected. This, Mitsue asserted, "was the origin of the misfortune of the court and the troubles of the people of the realm." Mitsue argued that the *Tosa nikki*'s surface account of the hardships of the journey back to the capital and the anticipation of Ki no Tsurayuki and his entourage of their return to Kyoto concealed Tsurayuki's real theme, which was to deplore his exile and its cause.[37]

For Mitsue, who was concerned with recovering such traces, Norinaga's insistence that the *Kojiki* narrative be accepted "as it was written" was an issue that transcended the question of how to read this single text. He argued that Norinaga's insistence on the historicality of the *Kojiki* account of the divine origins of "Japan" led to a flawed relation between ruler and ruled: "[According to Norinaga] the purpose of reading this Divine Text is just to ponder how strange and mysterious are the origins of the emperor. As for he who is the descendent of this line [i.e., the present emperor], one is just supposed to serve him reverently and with awe and be content to follow his commands. Thus it seems that no amount of wisdom is of any use."[38]

As this statement suggests, in the *Ōmune*, the relationship of reader to text and subject to ruler came to be linked epistemologically. Mitsue questioned Norinaga's criticism of overt attempts to interpret the *Kojiki*: "Within the *Kojikiden*, it is said that to question deeply those places that are strange or difficult to understand is the 'Chinese mind.' In that case, would it be evidence of the 'Japanese mind' [*Yamatogokoro*] to put these places aside as if one had not heard of them?"[39] Thus, Mitsue refused to accept Norinaga's characterization of attempts to probe the meaning of the *Kojiki* as evidence of the "Chinese mind," and he was equally unwilling to view a stance of "belief" as evidence of Japaneseness. This, he asserted, was part of a problematic conception of community that sought to enhance the power of the ruler by transforming him into a mystified object, which the subject/reader can only regard with fear and reverence. As Mitsue put it, the *Kojikiden* rested upon the assumption that "one cannot understand the ways of the deities, and [thus] it seems that the unfathomable and miraculous acts of the divine ancestors are recorded so that their power to inspire awe would extend to their descendants [i.e., later emperors] in later ages."[40]

Mitsue rejected outright this conception of Japaneseness. He argued that, according to Norinaga's understanding of the "way of the gods,"

> It seems that the way of man is simply to follow the intentions of the
> emperor. However, even the ordinary people, all according to their sta-

tion, have work and family, and always there are various problems that arise. . . . On these occasions what should they do? Moreover, [Norinaga's argument] does not agree with the words from the [Kojiki] passage on yomi [in which Izanagi declares], "You should help the people of reed plains of the middle land when they meet with misfortune or are troubled."[41]

Mitsue cited this passage from the Kojiki several times in the Ōmune. For him it revealed that the "teaching" of the Divine Texts was addressed not only to the ruler but to all the people of the country, regardless of their status. Criticizing Norinaga for "running away" from the concerns of the people by saying the text is "concerned with the deities and the emperor," Mitsue argued that the theme of the Kojiki is nothing more than "the course of human emotions and the way of the world."[42]

It was precisely those aspects of the text that Norinaga described as beyond the limits of human comprehension that for Mitsue revealed the necessity for a reading/political subject who is not sunao (obedient or docile) but a critical and constructing agent. He argued that the inconsistencies and incongruities of the Divine Age narrative recorded in the Kojiki were included purposefully to signify to later readers that this text was not a historical narrative that relates facts that can be passively received.[43] Thus it was necessary to reject the practice of reading employed by others scholars of the Kojiki who "only looked quickly at the text in a general way . . . without the intention of delving into that which is questionable."[44] The form of the text, according to Mitsue, had the aim of forcing the reader to adopt a different stance toward the text. Inscribed in tōgo, the language of metaphor designed to transmit the kami of the speaker, the real meaning of the text is apparent only when the reader moves beyond the surface narrative (variously described as gaiyō and shōmen) to discover meanings that are "within."

Mitsue viewed the creation of harmonious relations of power as essential to every emergent society. He argued that Buddhism in India and Confucianism in China, like tōgo in Japan, took form as attempts to shape disparate and contesting masses of people into orderly communities. However, those two methods were ultimately less successful than tōgo. Buddhism tried to suppress desire by advocating asceticism, while Confucianism attempted to control desire by making the subject adhere to rigidly defined patterns of behavior.[45] Both failed to recognize that primal desire was an integral part of every subject and must be expressed. As these comparisons suggest, Mitsue's work was ordered by a conception of cultural identity reminiscent of that in Norinaga's work. He repeatedly made reference to "the ways of our country" (*mikuniburi*) in explaining the practice of tōgo in Japan. In remarks that are designed to criticize Norinaga's attack on the "Chinese mind," Mitsue stated:

> Even within our own country there are differences according to the province and the village, so of course the customs of China and India and the texts of those countries are different from our country. This is because the teachings were established in accordance with those customs. For our people certainly the teaching that was established in our country is most appropriate. So it is only this teaching that I remember in my heart. But just because Buddhism and Confucianism are not in accordance with our customs does not mean that they are evil.[46]

Here, in explaining Jinmu's discovery of tōgo, Mitsue asserted that even before Jinmu began his act of "establishing the country" there was already something that could be named as "Japanese" rather than "Indian" or "Chinese," even though he at the same time acknowledged the differences in local practices within Japan. By arguing that the teaching of the *Kojiki* discovered and practiced by Jinmu reflected "customs" that predated it, Mitsue suggested that the community instituted by Jinmu was based upon a prior "culture." However, in accounting for the origin of cultural difference, Mitsue made reference not to divine origin but to geography and history, explaining that the situation of Japan was very different from that of China, a large country bordered by non-Chinese people and often under attack by them.[47] Formulated in response to these circumstances, Buddhism and Confucianism were thus appropriate for the people of India and China, but not for the Japanese.

ESTABLISHING THE COUNTRY

Mitsue's analysis of the "establishment of the country" is related in the more than fifteen extant texts that take up various sections of the *Kojiki*. The fragmentary nature of this enterprise is attributable perhaps to Mitsue's premature death at the age of fifty-six—presumably he died before completing this work—but also certainly to the nature of his hermeneutic itself. Convinced that the *Kojiki* was inscribed by means of tōgo, he argued that its meaning could be discovered only by moving beyond the textual surface. No

section concerned him more than the opening passage of the Kojiki, which relates the appearance of the primal deities Ame no Minakanushi, Takamimusubi, and Kamimusubi at the beginning of heaven and earth, followed by
the deities Kami-ashikabi-hikoji and Ame no Tokotachi, and then the seven
generations of deities that concludes with the emergence of Izanami and
Izanagi. For Mitsue, this opening section was the most significant passage
in the Kojiki: he described it as "the great law of our teaching." In contrast,
the remainder of the Divine Age narrative was regarded as exemplary in nature. It provided a series of examples to clarify the principle delineated in
the first section, while in the Age of Men chapters the use of pure tōgo was
abandoned in favor of a mixture of factual information in direct speech and
expressions in poetic language. I want explore Mitsue's analysis of the opening passage of the Kojiki by utilizing one text of the Kojiki tomoshibi. Dated to
1806, it was written at about the same time as the Kojiki tomoshibi ōmune and
only a few years after the Makotoben.[48]

In Mitsue's reading, the Kojiki was transformed into a discourse on the
relationship between superiors and inferiors, an opposition that he used to
characterize every kind of social relationship. According to Mitsue, the opposition of heaven and earth that ordered the textual surface of the Kojiki signified the hierarchical nature of social roles: " 'Heaven' is used to speak of all
those things that stand above. Kings, fathers, husbands, elder brothers, and
teachers, those who are wise, nobility of the first grade within the system of
ranks, and those who stand first in relation to some event or profession, all
of these are termed 'heaven.' "[49]

In contrast, "earth" referred to retainers, children, younger brothers, disciples, and those of limited ability and low rank. The concentration on relations of hierarchy that begins here and extends throughout the Kojiki tomoshibi seems reminiscent of Neo-Confucianism, but for Mitsue, the social
roles of the superior did not derive from, nor were they evidence of ethicality.
Rather, one become a superior by convincing others to follow or submit and
thus of their own volition to adopt the position of an inferior. Moreover, the
performance of multiple social roles in everyday life meant that one moved
in and out of the positions of superior and inferior. Drawing on the text of
the Kojiki as evidence, Mitsue pointed out that the deities Izanami and Izanagi are sometimes referred to as kami (written as "deity," but here "the superior," according to Mitsue) and sometimes as mikoto ("the one who acts
according to the words of a superior," according to Mitsue). He asserted that
they are identified as kami in those instances when they occupy the position

of superior, but when they act in the inferior role—such as when they carry
out the land making on the orders of the heavenly deities—they are termed
mikoto.⁵⁰

Mitsue never succeeded in thinking beyond hierarchy, but he did acknowl-
edge that it was a source of potential conflict. He noted, "The people of the
realm, the samurai, farmers, artisans, merchants, and even the wandering
entertainers, all want greater fortune than is their lot, but all fear officialdom
[ōyake]."⁵¹ The problem then was how to create a relationship of superior
to inferior that was not coercive, not shaped by resentment and fear. The
Kojiki explained how this could be achieved; it related the process by which
community took form as subjects willingly adopted the roles of superior and
inferior.

Mitsue's analysis of the formation of community began with his commentary on the first phrase of the *Kojiki*, "when heaven and earth first opened up"
(*ametsuchi hajimete hirakuru toki*). He focused on the meaning of the character
he read as *hirakuru* (to open up). Norinaga had argued against this reading
and insisted that the phrase means "at the beginning of heaven and earth"
(*ametsuchi no hajime no toki ni*). As I noted in chapter 3, Norinaga's concern
was to suppress the potential significance of the character *hatsu*, which had
been read by his predecessors as *hirakuru* (to open) and *wakareru* (to separate),
and thus he labeled both these readings as evidence of the "Chinese mind."
In contrast, for Mitsue, the term *hirakuru* was vitally important. It signified
that distinctions between superiors and inferiors had come to be recognized,
internalized, and acted upon by the members of the community. Mitsue described this process as involving both the "superior" and the "inferior." As
each acknowledges his own position, he simultaneously affirms the status
of the other. The note on *hirakuru* states, " 'To open up' means that the superior relies upon his own superiority and never imposes private interests
on those below him, and those in the inferior role do not make light of or
despise those above them and never violate those in this role."⁵² For Mitsue,
this process of mutual acknowledgment was the foundation of community.
As he proceeded through the *Kojiki* text, he attempted to explain how and
why it took place.

The next sentence of the *Kojiki* tells of the appearance of the deities, Ame
no Minakanushi, Takamimusubi, and Kamimusubi. Mitsue put great emphasis on the term *minakanushi*, which literally means something like "the
ruler of middle." According to Mitsue, someone is "in the middle" when
he avoids showing bias toward any single person and thus is in an advanta-

geous position to act upon and influence others. The efficacy of this stance is said to be illustrated by the *Kojiki* narrative, which described the emergence, one following the other, of the next two deities, whose appearance is demarcated by the repetition of the term *tsugi ni* (next). According to Mitsue, *tsugi ni* signified an act of "following" or "submitting," and he explained that this represented a relation between "I" and the other based upon "the principle of responsiveness" (*kannō no dōri*). The term "principle of responsiveness" is similar to what was called "emotional responsiveness" in the *Makotoben*. It was the result of an act of communication that succeeded in conveying one speaker's kami to another, producing the kind of transformative union that Mitsue compared to the production of fire from stone and flint. According to Mitsue, the appearance of Takamimusubi and Kamimusubi signaled their recognition of Ame no Minakanushi as a superior and their new willingness to follow and aid him. Like Norinaga before him, Mitsue saw great significance in the fact that while the etymology of the name of Ame no Minakanushi and his emergence as the first deity suggest that this deity was of central importance, he never appears again within the *Kojiki*. In contrast, Takamimusubi and Kamimusubi do appear later in the narrative. For Mitsue, this revealed the proper relationship between inferior and superior. As he explained it, the disappearance of Ame no Minakanushi from the surface narrative signified that that this deity was acting through or by means of the two Musubi deities. Based upon the "principle of responsiveness," they put aside their own interests and acted for Ame no Minakanushi.

The full import of the "principle of responsiveness" becomes apparent in the explanation of the next passage in the *Kojiki* that states, "These three deities all appeared as single deities, and their bodies were hidden." For Mitsue, the term *mi wo kakusu* or *kakuremi* (literally, "to hide the body") was "the great norm that is common to the world and the country, emperors and the common people, the great and the small, in the long run and the short run, for the past and the present."[53] He offered this explanation of its meaning:

> The character *mi* (body) refers to a receptacle that transfers words and actions [to others], so you can understand that generally such things are termed *mi*. "To hide the body" refers to "hiding" one's words and actions depending on the time, place, one's status, and the matter at hand. . . . The way of "hiding the body" is such that if my personal emotions are involved then even if the matter at hand is of a public nature,

> my intentions will become apparent; whereas if I act before the eyes and
> ears of others, based upon receiving the intentions of others, then it is
> not my own intention and so does not appear in my words and actions.[54]

According to Mitsue, the challenge for the one who acts as a superior, be
it the emperor or the head of a household or business, is to somehow make
those beneath him understand his desire and act in accord with it. However,
to directly speak of or act out one's desire—in other words to attempt to
coerce or persuade the other to agree—is to invite dissent. Mitsue argued
that the term "hiding the body" signified the means by which one subject
was able to convey his desires to another but in such a way as not to invite
conflict.

As in the *Makotoben*, Mitsue warned of the dangers of using direct speech
to express desire. Interpreted by the other as coercion, direct speech invited
conflict and struggle. He cited a series of examples from the *Kojiki* as evidence
of this principle. For example, the birth of a deformed child to the deities
Izanami and Izanagi is explained as the result of Izanami's speaking directly
of her attraction to Izanagi. Similarly, the emergence of the evil Magatsuhi
deities is traced to Izanagi's "extreme behavior" in following his dead wife
to the underworld.[55] In both cases, according to Mitsue, it was the direct expression of emotions in words or actions that brought harm not only to the
person in question but also to "the world" as a whole. For Mitsue, the phrase
"hiding the body" signified the need to make use of the linguistic forms he
grouped together as tōgo. By "hiding" his desires, emotions, and intentions
in poetic language, the superior assumed a position "in the middle." The result was the formation of a relationship marked by "responsiveness," as the
inferior recognized that desire and acted in response to it. In this way, the
basic node of community, the relation between "I" and the other, took form
without a sense of resentment on either part.

Mitsue further explored the concept of "responsiveness" in his explanation of the next sentence in the *Kojiki* that describes the "young land" as being
like "floating oil" and a "drifting jelly fish." He characterized these phrases
as metaphors that refer not to the state of the land itself but to the people
(kokumin) of the emergent Japan. The reference to youth was explained as a
description of the state of the people before they observed Jinmu's inaugural
act of "hiding the body." The other two expressions describe the emotional
response of the people to that event. Metaphors of movement and confusion,
they are said to describe the surprise and bewilderment felt by the people

upon observing the refusal of the "superior" to act.[56] Mitsue asserted that the next sentence of the *Kojiki* text—a description of the appearance of the deity Kami-ashikabi-hikoji who emerged from a reed-like object that "sprouts upward"—signified the resolution of the emotional turmoil of the people. Of particular significance for Mitsue was the term "sprout upward" (*kizashinoboru*). It was explained as a description of the excitement or stimulation felt by the people as they put aside the "the habit" of acting on their own desire and began to submit to or to follow the "superior," by recognizing and responding to his desire.[57] According to Mitsue, when the person who was mired in the "mud" of private desires and intentions witnessed the other expressing his desire not directly but through tōgo, he first felt confusion and then excitement. Then "learning from" the other, he "spontaneously forgot his own desires."[58]

Mitsue's analysis of the *Kojiki* continues in this vein. As this summary suggests, in the *Kojiki tomoshibi* the Divine Age narrative became an exemplification of the theory of poetic language he had put forth in the *Makotoben.* Inscribed in tōgo, it also explained the functioning of tōgo, the process by which desiring subjects could communicate and achieve a state of empathy. Mitsue argued that Japan took form as the result of an infinite number of reciprocal acts of "hiding the body" as people began to recognize the desire of others and to act upon them, putting aside their own interests. It was through his mastery of tōgo that Jinmu was able to establish himself as ruler. And throughout history, according to Mitsue, it was the imperial line that embodied this principle. The emperor, he asserted, provided a model for the conduct of all social relations:

> [The *Kojiki*] records the beginning of the imperial line that has ruled this land to the present and which the people have never thought to overthrow. If those who rule a domain, a locality, a village, or a family would learn from this, then how could their descendants not prosper? . . .
> . . . The reason why the imperial line has prospered even until the present generation is based upon the "hiding of the body," . . . and since there is a "heaven" and an "earth" for each locality, for each family, and for each person, if we learn from the happy existence of the emperor and practice the way of "hiding the body," then how can the establishment of the country [*kaikoku sōgyō*] not occur?[59]

As both these passages suggest, Mitsue asserted that the imperial line had succeeded in maintaining its position not because of its divinity but because

of its exemplary practice of the principle of "hiding the body." It was precisely this practice and its reproduction at every level of the community that
was necessary for what Mitsue termed "the establishment of the country."

RECOVERING COMMUNITY

As he pondered the disorder of his own times, Mitsue became convinced that
it resulted because the practice of "hiding the body," the fundamental principle of community formation, had been forgotten. It was possible, he noted,
for "there to be a ruler, and his vassals, and many officials" and yet for there
to be no "country."[60] For Mitsue, the significance of texts such as the *Tosa
nikki* and the poem by the builders of the Fujiwara Palace was that these were
traces of the relationship of "responsiveness" that had existed in the past.
As this suggests, Mitsue's vision of community did not call into question the
uneven distribution of power within the society—he found no fault with the
empress's command that her people construct the palace. What was significant for Mitsue was that they in turn could express their resentment at this
task through poetic language, and that this act of critique was incorporated
into the imperial anthology, signifying that it had been heard and acknowledged. In "recent times," this kind of relationship was no longer possible.
Instead, "superiors" at every level of society relied upon force to achieve their
aims, evoking only fear from those beneath them. The result, as Mitsue put
it in the *Kaikokuron*, was that "those above and below feel no intimacy" and
"the people of our country feel resentful." For Mitsue, the aim of kokugaku
practice was the revival of the practice of "hiding the body" and the recovery
of the "responsiveness" that had once infused the relationship of the ruler
and the ruled with empathy. In light of this, Mitsue came to characterize the
work of Norinaga and his disciples not only as mistaken and misleading but
also as "a great crime." As the notion that the *Kojiki* was a record of actual
events and should not be interpreted became popular, the true meaning of
the work was obscured, and more and more people were adopting a stance
of passive reverence before the emperor.[61] But reverence from the ruled, like
coercion from the ruler, was antithetical to Mitsue's vision of community.

In keeping with his view of the emblematic role of the imperial institution, Mitsue turned to consider how to make it the model it had once been.
Like Norinaga, he never made mention of the possibility of a return to direct
imperial rule, but he became intensely interested in the Ise Shrine, where
Amaterasu, the sun deity and supposed ancestor of the imperial line, is wor-

shiped. The Ise Shrine had become an important focus of popular devotion beginning in the fifteenth century, when low-ranking priests of the shrine known as onshi began to travel from village to village, proselytizing and collecting funds. As they preached the benefits of making a pilgrimage to Ise, associations known as Ise kō began to take form. Members of such societies contributed rice and money to finance a trip each year by one or more of its members, and those who maintained their membership in such associations were assured that at some point their chance to make the journey to Ise would come about. The number of Ise kō increased dramatically during the Tokugawa period, a development revealing that devotion toward the shrine and its deities had become a culture-wide phenomenon. A shrine document from 1777 lists some 439,000 households in seventy-two domains as parishioners.[62] During the especially auspicious years (okage doshi), when the shrine was newly rebuilt, as custom dictated it be every twenty years, pilgrims numbered in the millions. For example between April and August 1771, it is recorded that 2,700,000 people visited Ise.[63]

The Ise cult was especially well established in and around Kyoto, where Mitsue resided his entire life. According to one scholar, "It is no exaggeration to say that every village around Kyoto had an Ise kō."[64] Mitsue himself made the pilgrimage to Ise twice. His first visit was in 1786 at the age of nineteen. Then, more than twenty years later, in 1809, he returned, this time to watch the rituals that marked the completion of the shrine's reconstruction. This visit took place as Mitsue was deeply involved in analyzing the Kojiki; he had published the Ōmune the previous year and had completed the version of Kojiki tomoshibi I examined above. Around the time he made this second pilgrimage, Mitsue wrote a work he called Ise ryō dai jingū ben (An Explanation of the Two Great Shrines of Ise], in which he advocated the revival of the custom of installing in the Ise shrine a woman who was known as the saigū.[65] According to ancient practice, upon the accession to the throne of a new emperor, his daughter or sister was chosen to reside at Ise to act as the "consecrated priestess" in the conduct of the rituals of the shrine. As she traveled to Ise from Kyoto, the newly selected priestess would perform rituals at important shrines along the way. With the death of the emperor or his abdication, she was allowed to return to secular life. This practice of installing the saigū was abandoned in the mid-fourteenth century when, in the aftermath of an abortive attempt at an imperial restoration, the court was split between two contenders to the throne, and it was never resumed.[66]

Mitsue's interest in the institution of the saigū was intimately related to his conception of "hiding the body" as a necessary act for the constitution of community. The saigū was also known as the "hidden priestess" (*imi no miya*). While the emperor was a public figure responsible for the conduct of government, she was secluded in the Ise Shrine. Another term for her was *mitsue shiro* (the substitute staff), which was used to signify her role as an aid or support for the emperor. It was this term that was inspiration for the name "Mitsue," which he adopted in 1811, abandoning the name "Narimoto" by which he had been known to this point. Mitsue came to believe that the institution of the saigū and her relationship to the emperor was a method devised in ancient times to convey to the Japanese people the relation of superior and inferior, the "I" and the other, that allowed for the creation of community. In the *Kojiki tomoshibi ōmune* Mitsue stated that in the age before writing the ancient emperors had propagated the principle of "hiding the body" iconically through the construction of shrines and the establishment of rituals:

> Originally in our country, in the earliest times, since there was no form of writing, in order to make the teaching known to the world, shrines were established in each province and the deities of heaven and earth were worshiped. Its meaning was entrusted to objects and propagated in this way. Now we use the characters of Chinese writing, and since we can write freely, the [earlier] method seems very inconvenient, but whether one entrusts meaning to shrines or to characters, it is the same kind of act.[67]

Years later, in an account of his second visit to Ise, Mitsue related that as he viewed the consecration of the new shrine, he was struck by the manner in which various ritual objects were transferred to the new structure while shielding them from onlookers. Thinking this strange, he questioned a priest of the shrine about the need to conceal these objects but was told only that it was a practice dictated by "ancient transmissions." Mitsue concluded that this too had been a means to convey the principle of "hiding the body" to the people of Japan.[68]

Mitsue seems to have believed that the revival of the saigū, in the context of popular interest in the Ise shrine, would make it possible to diffuse the now forgotten practice of poetic language to the Japanese people. Writing in the *Ise ryō dai jingū ben*, he stated, "If once again we began to respect the saigū then she would be the great master who would reach all the people of the country and instruct them in the teaching."[69] Like Norinaga, Mitsue too was intensely concerned with popularizing his vision of Japan, but he adopted a very different strategy. While Norinaga viewed the expansion of the Suzuya as evidence of "return to the ancient way," Mitsue tried to construct a powerful central symbol that, linked to popular beliefs, would be source of inspiration and edification. In the end, however, his plan met with little support and perhaps overt opposition. During this period Mitsue made a series of visits to members of the nobility, including the imperial prince known as Awada no Miya and the aristocrats who served as the abbots of powerful temples such as Daigoji.[70] He seems to have hoped to win the support of the nobility for his project of reinstating the saigū, but if so, he had little success. Writing to a disciple in 1813, Mitsue lamented, "It is already more than ten years since I have been speaking of the way of the kami and the way of poetics, but I have no success in either and am left with many regrets. . . . The way is great, but the one who explains it is humble and without virtue."[71]

THE REALITY OF HIERARCHY

As his campaign for the revival of the saigū came to nothing and as his views on the *Kojiki* became known, Mitsue became the object of overt criticism. He himself took note of one reader who attacked him for his "baseness" in claiming to have discovered "a great teaching that has been lost for more than a thousand years."[72] Then in 1821, both Mitsue and his son were suddenly deprived of their samurai status by the Tachibana lord of Yanagawa, a devastating loss of both rank and income. While Mitsue at various times counted among his students not only the wives and daughters of the Tachibana lord and those of his fellow retainers but also a number of Kyoto townsmen, his official stipend meant he had not needed to acquire a large number of students to live well.[73] Consequently, after his dismissal he had great difficulty making ends meet and for the first time began a concerted effort to recruit students, a campaign clearly dictated by financial need.[74] Ill and impoverished, just months before his death, Mitsue was reduced to begging for money, writing one of his students that he and his family faced starvation if a loan was not forthcoming.[75]

The reasons for Mitsue's sudden disgrace are not at all clear. The only direct testimony that survives from Mitsue himself are poems such as one that states, "Punished for a crime I did not commit, I am blameless; this is the heart that would speak to my lord."[76] A chronicle of his life composed by one of his students is similarly oblique. It states only that in 1821, "there

was an evil act by those deities over whom the heavenly deities have no control," evoking an understanding of kami that seems more reminiscent of
the *Kojikiden* than the *Kojiki tomoshibi*. Domainal documents record only that
the actions of Mitsue and his son were "not satisfactory."[77] Some scholars
have speculated that this punishment was an expression of official displea-
sure with Mitsue's work as a kokugaku scholar, but there is no concrete evidence to support such a conclusion.[78] More recently, Mitsue's biographer,
Tada Junten, has suggested that Mitsue may have been punished for mis-
handling the sale of domainal rice stores in Osaka. He notes that in the year
before he was sanctioned Mitsue made frequent trips to Osaka and that this
was a time when rice prices were fluctuating rapidly, a situation that created
the possibility for great losses.[79]

Suzuki Eiichi has remarked on the "pathos" of Mitsue's disgrace, given
his conception of toki and his concern for carefully negotiating the relations
of power he saw inscribed in every social encounter.[80] But what this "pathos"
reveals is the engagement of Mitsue's work with the reality of late Tokugawa
society. The opaqueness of his terminology and the often unwieldy attempt
to use the *Kojiki* as a vehicle of expression have led many to dismiss the *Kojiki
tomoshibi* as nothing more than "forced interpretation." Certainly, Mitsue's
understanding of the *Kojiki* has little to do with the intentions of the imperial
official who compiled it in the eighth century, but the same must be said of
the *Kojikiden*.

The significance of the *Kojiki tomoshibi* lies in Mitsue's attempt to rethink
the relations of hierarchy that ordered life in Tokugawa Japan and in his effort
to imagine a community in which "inferiors" could speak to those above and
be heard. This had been the aim of Akinari's use of the monogatari form as
well. Like Akinari, Mitsue took note of the resentment that resulted from
the uneven distribution of power within society, and he explicitly identified
this as the cause of the conflict and disorder he saw around him. But, unlike
both Norinaga and Akinari, he did not regard the "public realm" and "private
realm" as distinct or autonomous. His conception of the subject as the product of both "public principle" and "private desire" made this impossible. And
while Mitsue evoked a notion of cultural identity to explain the rise of tōgo,
he did not make Japaneseness alone an explanation of community. Mitsue's
reading of the Divine Age narrative redefined Japan so that the ordinary subject had a crucial role to play in its production. No longer a natural, much
less "divinely" authorized entity, Japan became a human construct. It took
form from the network of social relations and social encounters embedded

in every day life, as desiring subjects through language came to know, ac-knowledge, and submit to one another. While he never abandoned the notion that social relations were inherently vertical in nature, he made this arrange-ment reciprocal and fluid and called for it to be infused with empathy and responsiveness.

Chapter 6

Tachibana Moribe: Cosmology and Community

In contrast to Akinari and Mitsue, who wrote mainly in response to Norinaga's *Kojikiden*, Tachibana Moribe took up the study of kokugaku in the first decade of the nineteenth century, a contentious era when those who studied the "ancient way" criticized not only or even mainly Confucianists but also their fellow kokugaku practitioners in terms that were harsh and denigrative. After Norinaga's death in 1801, his Suzuya school continued to be a significant force in kokugaku studies under the direction of his adopted son, Motoori Ōhira, but it now focused on the study of poetry and poetics rather than the *Kojiki*. Mabuchi's former students, known as the Edo school, were also active, under the leadership of Murata Harumi. They too focused on the practice of poetry but conceived of its purpose in terms critical of the scholarship of their contemporary Suzuya scholars. Murata in particular spoke out against Ōhira's insistence that poetry was a means to know the "way of the deities," arguing instead that it offered insight into the elegant and forthright "spirit" of the ancient Japanese people, the view of Mabuchi himself.[1]

The divisive nature of kokugaku practice was heightened after 1810, when Hirata Atsutane, who had joined the Suzuya school only after Norinaga's death, began overtly to criticize the scholarship that emanated from it, attacking Ōhira for abandoning the analysis of the Divine Age narrative in favor of poetry. In works such as his cosmological treatise *Tama no mihashira* (The Pillars of the Spirit, published 1813) and his reconstruction of the Divine Age narrative *Koshiseibun* (The True Text of the Ancient History, published 1818), Atsutane began to distance himself from Norinaga's work on the *Kojiki*, although he continued to evoke his disciple status throughout his life. Arguing that the truth of the Divine Age was not revealed in the *Kojiki* alone but dispersed among the ancient texts, he brought together elements from a number of works, weaving them into a narrative that allowed for a new and affirmative understanding of the events of the Divine Age and their significance for the present. His work found an enthusiastic readership among literate villagers, members of the Shinto priesthood, and lower-ranking samurai, and by the time of his death his school, known as the Ibukiya, challenged the Suzuya in size and influence.

Written in the wake of the work of Mabuchi, Norinaga, and Atsutane, Moribe's texts are scattered with statements that, if extracted and viewed in isolation, seem reminiscent of one or another of his predecessors. However, his understanding of the mythohistories departed greatly from those of fellow readers. Through the use of an innovative theory of language, he transformed the Divine Age narrative into a cosmology of two contending dimensions, the "hidden" world of the deities and the "revealed" world of men. By situating Japan at the junction of these worlds, Moribe made the acts of the everyday life of the Japanese people into events of ritual significance and linked them to the imperial rites and ceremonies performed by the emperor. Together, the emperor and his people came to be envisioned as a single "body" that sustained the great cosmic divide. In the discussion that follows, I move beyond the identification of points of resemblance to rediscover the gap that separated Moribe's work from other forms of kokugaku practice. To this end, I begin by exploring the theories of language and text that Moribe relied upon in the early 1830s and then turn to analyze their transformation in the theory of the Divine Age narrative that took form in the 1840s.

LANGUAGE AND THE RECOVERY OF THE PAST

Unlike the work of other figures in this work, Moribe's oeuvre is not easily explainable by terms such as continuity or development. In marked contrast to Norinaga, who spent thirty-five years reading the *Kojiki* in light of theories of language and text he established early on, Moribe's work was shaped by a series of methodological shifts, as he abandoned one approach for another, often without explanation. At the heart of his methodological uncertainty were the issues that every kokugaku scholar confronted: the nature of the language of the ancient period, its relation to the ancient texts, and the status of those texts for the project of recovering the past. Over the course of his career, his work unfolded as a series of attempts to conceptualize this set of relations.

Moribe was in his late twenties when he began his study of the ancient

texts with Shimizu Hamaomi, a student of Murata Harumi. In keeping with
the practice of the Edo school scholars, Moribe's early work was focused on
issues of poetics and poetry composition, and he gained a reputation for
his skill in composing chōka, the "long poems" of the style found in the
Man'yōshū.[2] He was then living in the post-station town of Satte in Musashino province, supporting himself and his family by teaching reading and
writing to children and offering instruction on poetry composition to adults.
The relationship with Hamaomi eventually ended in discord after more than
a decade, but before it did, Hamaomi at some point introduced Moribe to
a group of textile merchants in the towns of Kiryū and Ashikaga. By 1833,
more than twenty of them had enrolled as formal students, and they became
important patrons of Moribe's work. Not only did they provide funds for the
publication of his work, but they also financed his move to Edo in 1829. In return Moribe traveled frequently to Kiryū to offer instruction and wrote texts
specifically with this readership in mind.[3]

It was their support that in the 1830s allowed Moribe to plunge into the
ongoing debate on the nature of the ancient language, when as an unknown
scholar he published his first work, the *Yamabiko zōshi* (Book of the Mountain
God, 1831).[4] Subtitled "Thoughts on Difficult Words," *Yamabiko zōshi* is unlike anything else produced in this period.[5] It is not a dictionary, or a textual
study, or a grammatical treatise, but rather an exploration of semantic content, lexical relations, and the diachronic development of language. Moribe
sought to explain the meaning of words and expressions found in the ancient texts and to suggest the process of evolution by which these "original words" were transformed and new words produced. The organization
of the work reflects this purpose. The 225 entries are not listed in the order
of the kana syllabary, as would be the case in a dictionary or a similar reference work. Rather, they are arranged according to semantic content; that is,
synonymous expressions are grouped together, as are words of common origin. Moribe explained the reason for this unusual approach in the following
terms:

> For those of us born in the later times who wish to clarify the ways
> of earlier ages, if we do not explore the meaning of words, then what
> means do we have to achieve understanding? After the Heian period, the
> world was disordered for a long time, and since people no longer under-
> stood the meaning of words, the way of learning came to be abandoned.
> But since the beginning of the ancient studies, it gradually has become

clear again. But even though many great masters have appeared, why have they not succeeded in discovering the origins of every word?[6]

Within the confines of textual exegesis, the search for "original meaning" was in no sense unorthodox. Many of Norinaga's annotations within the *Kojikiden* are devoted to etymological issues. Moribe's innovation was to abandon the text as an object of analysis. His goal in *Yamabiko zōshi* was not to understand the *Kojiki* or any other single work but to explore "words" themselves, abstracted from a textual context.

The preface of the *Yamabiko*, attributed to an anonymous student but probably authored by Moribe himself, suggested that dissatisfaction with Norinaga's work was at the heart of Moribe's endeavors: "When one tries to interpret the ancient words of the Divine Age, one feels as though stuck in mud up to the neck. And if one attempts to follow the teachings of [Norinaga], then . . . one becomes more and more addled. Thus even those who follow Norinaga have put aside the 'way' that tries to understand [the Divine Texts] and only compose poetry and write prose."[7]

The last sentence seems to be a reference to the fact that after Norinaga's death, the Suzuya school had turned from the analysis of the *Kojiki* to grammatical and poetic studies. Moribe charged that the study of "the ancient way" had been abandoned because Norinaga's method confused and discouraged those who sought to follow it. For Norinaga, of course, it was not words in isolation but their referential value in the narrative of the *Kojiki* that was important. Thus, in the *Uiyamabumi* (First Steps on the Mountain, published 1799), a handbook for students of kokugaku, Norinaga specifically warned, "You should think about the context employed by the ancients rather than search for the original meaning. It is important to know precisely which words were used in what context. If you do not know the context of a word, it is difficult to understand the statement."[8] In contrast, Moribe asserted that it was clarification of language as a semantic chain, detached from any text, that was the means of accessing the past.

Yamabiko zōshi was a controversial work and attracted attention from both established and aspiring kokugaku practitioners. For example, Nakashima Hirotari, a Norinaga disciple living in Nagasaki, wrote to Ban Nobutomo, who was in Edo around 1832, asking, "What kind of man is Tachibana Moribe of Edo? I hear that many works by him are appearing. Please tell me about him." In 1834, Moribe himself received a letter from Tsuda Masanari, a sake brewer living in the province of Owari, who wrote, "In moments when I am free from work, I have been trying to read the work of Motoori and others." However, according to Tsuda, nothing had impressed him as much as Moribe's *Yamabiko zōshi*, which he had read repeatedly, each time with admiration. The letter concluded with a request to become a formal disciple.⁹

But in spite of the interest aroused by *Yamabiko zōshi*, soon after its publication Moribe began to explore the language of the early texts in very different terms. In the three works that together are known as *Sansenkaku* (Three Selections, c. 1832)—*Chōka senkaku* (Chōka Selections), *Tanka senkaku* (Tanka Selections) and *Bunshō senkaku* (Prose Selections)—Moribe asserted that the poems and prose recorded in the *Kojiki*, *Man'yōshū*, and other early work were the traces of speech acts performed long ago. This perspective is reminiscent of that of Fujitani Mitsue, but it did not lead to the same kind of careful consideration of the nature of the subject-other relation. Moribe examined the poems not as acts of individual communication but rather as the traces of forms of community that had existed before writing had created self-conscious, "clever" subject-actors. Thus, within these works, he took up for the first time the opposition of writing and orality that had ordered so much of kokugaku discourse to this point, but he problematized this opposition by introducing yet another, that of koto and *kotobana*. Moribe used the term *koto* (written in kana) to refer to the signifying function of language that linked koto (word) and koto (thing). It was this system of meanings that he had explored in the *Yamabiko zōshi*. But his concern in the *Sansenkaku* was for the new aspect of language he identified as *kotobana*, which became for him the new site of the "difference" of the language of ancient times. On the relation of koto and kotobana, Moribe stated, "In later periods koto and kotoba came to be almost the same thing, but kotoba originally meant kotobana (the flower of language) and kotobana is used to mean that there is *aya* (design, pattern) in language."¹⁰ He went on to explain that in ancient times aya was a part of every utterance, and thus its traces can be found in both the poetry and prose of the past. It was the analysis of kotobana or aya that was the project of the *Sansenkaku*.

What was aya? It did not refer strictly to the syntax of the ancient language. Indeed, Moribe criticized Norinaga's attention to the workings of the particles of te, ni, wo, and ha and the grammatical studies of his successors. In words addressed to "the practitioners of kokugaku of recent times," he stated that "to be only concerned with the workings of meaningless words and the use of particles is like worrying about the number of fingers and toes a man has and not being concerned about whether he has a foolish heart or an ill-formed face."[11] In describing the form of aya, Moribe spoke of "con-nection" (tsunagari), "rhythm" (hyōshi), "the arrangement of words" (koto no narabi), "movement" (hakobi), "phrasing" (ku no tsuzuki), and "the form of phrases" (kukaku). As these terms suggest, aya was used to refer to certain stylistic patterns that Moribe believed characterized the speech of early Japa-nese people—patterns that cannot be reduced to semantic content. Thus, Moribe put aside his earlier concern for the referential function of words and employed the concepts of aya and kotobana to delineate a linguistic level that is not accessible through etymological analysis. This new distinction between words and the form of expression is evident in his comments on the poetry of his contemporaries:

> In recent times, in the poems of those who attempt to bring about the restoration of the past and speak of returning to the way of the past, the lines of seven and five syllables move in the wrong way, and there is a break in the first line or third line. Why is it that they only make use of ancient words and do not think of returning to the ancient form? I, Moribe, think that even if the words follow the current usage, it is the structure that must follow the way of the ancient times since the struc-ture of the poem is its essence.[12]

Revealingly, Moribe makes no mention of his own very recent concern for recovering the ancient vocabulary. But as these remarks suggest, the notion that the imitation of ancient forms of expression was a means of accessing the "ancient way" was shared by many.

Kamo no Mabuchi had argued in the 1760s in the Bun i kō that the prose of the Kojiki and other early texts was characterized by a directness and imme-diacy that was revealing of the "spirit" of the early Japanese people, and he had urged a mastery of that style, suggesting that it would allow for the in-ternalization of the spirit that gave rise to it. As a result, many of Mabuchi's students began to experiment with the imitation of ancient prose. Norinaga was dismissive of much of the writing that resulted from the new fashion of writing in wabun. He pointed out that in many cases it was grammati-cally flawed, intermingling syntactical forms from various periods, and often used vocabulary that was clearly Chinese in origin. In keeping with his view that only authentic Yamato kotoba allowed for the recovery of Japaneseness, Norinaga's prose was marked by a new grammatical and lexical consistency. In contrast to those who saw value in imitating the ancient language, Ueda Akinari had ridiculed this practice, suggesting that so much concern for how to write was an odd preoccupation for those who idealized the orality of the ancient period.

Moribe's position in the *Sansenkaku* recalled that of Mabuchi: he argued that it was the mastery of the aya of the ancient Japanese language that was the key to recovering the past. However, underlying his new concern for the form of expression was the assertion that speech in ancient times had a performative aspect that was lacking—that had been lost—in later times. In *Chōka senkaku*, Moribe asserted that the chōka of the *Kojiki, Nihon Shoki,* and *Man'yōshū* were originally songs that were performed to the accompaniment of music and dance within a communal, festive, or ritual setting.[13] The language of these songs was shaped by the performative setting, the requirements of melody and rhythm, the emotions of the moment, and the interaction of speaker and audience. The repetition of phrases and syntactic inconsistencies that resulted puzzled later readers, who were unaware of the context that produced them. Moribe argued that the recovery of the experience of the ancient period could be achieved by understanding and reproducing the aya: "All books, even the Divine Texts and the histories of the country, are things mediated by human intentions, so one must realize that to sing the poems of ancient times and thus to know the true emotion of following the way of the deities is of vital importance."[14] To speak in the cadences marked by aya was to recall the performative setting of the past with its associations of community, immediacy, and authenticity. It was to put aside the "human intentions" of later times and to "follow the way of the deities." Moribe described the experience of recovery he envisioned in distinctly sensory terms: "If one enters a room of orchids, does not the scent adhere to one's clothes? One should enter into the past and merely wait for it to imbue you."[15] In keeping with this perspective, Moribe's analysis of the ancient songs was twofold. He attempted not only to delineate the nature of the aya that characterize these expressions but also to explore the performative setting that generated them, to explain who was singing and in what context.

In the *Chōka senkaku*, aya is described as an aspect of the "songs" of the *Man'yōshū*, but in *Bunshō senkaku*, nonpoetic utterances too are said to possess aya. In all three of the works that make up the *Sansenkaku*, Moribe employed a set of symbols and a method of graphing to identify the patterns that he believed distinguished the language of the ancient period. As this suggests, his analysis rested upon the uneasy assertion that traces of the speech of the ancient people could be found in the early texts. He insisted that there had been a moment when "the language of ancient times was always inscribed just as it was spoken, and so naturally it was not only speech that had aya."[16] However, in the early Nara period the transparent recording of speech was transformed as writing came to be mediated by what Moribe termed "artificiality" (sakui). As he described this process, "As time passed, men no longer submitted to the spontaneity of the spoken word and began to employ various kinds of artifice; as a result, the aya that the [written] language had possessed was lost."[17] Moribe characterized this new form of writing as "shaped by skill" (takumi ni hikareta) and "seemingly clever" (sakashirageni).[18] Like Akinari before him, he argued that writing was corrupted by the new self-consciousness of the scribe, who began to reflect on and theorize about the act of inscription. The result was that writing began to generate writing, and so too did it begin to influence speech as people "forgot" about orality and the writing that had recorded it. Gradually the patterns that had characterized speech in the communal world of ancient times were lost as people began to speak in syntax marked by the "skill" and "cleverness" that were the products of a new self-consciousness. Unlike Norinaga, however, Moribe never made use of the "Chinese mind" to explain the rise of writing in Japan and the loss of the original orality. Rather, he mentioned China as simply another example of a common pattern. In China, as in Japan, the symbiotic relation of writing and speech that existed in the ancient period was lost as "artificiality" came to replace direct recording.

In spite of his statement that writing had soon ceased to be a transparent inscription of oral expression, Moribe argued that it was possible to discover the traces of orality in the early texts. In Bunshō senkaku, he evaluated a series of examples from the Kojiki, Nihon shoki, and Izumo fudoki, in terms of the presence or absence of aya, the sign of orality. He concluded that "in both the Kojiki and the Nihon shoki, . . . the original form of the divine language was influenced by the Chinese characters and much of the aya was lost."[19] Rejecting Norinaga's valorization of the Kojiki, Moribe complained that in this work in particular "the meaning of the spoken words that Hieda learned and recited was extracted and wrapped in Chinese."[20] The aim of the Bunshō senkaku was to reverse this process, by returning passages available only in "artificial" writing to their "original" form. For example, in analyzing the opening passage of the Kojiki, Moribe stated that the original form of the ancient words recited by Hieda no Are were as follows:

Ametsuchi no hajime no toki ni Takamanohara ni, kami narimashiki.
Sono narimaseru kami no mina ha, Ame no Minakanushi no kami.
Tsugi ni narimaseru kami no mina ha, Takamimusubi no kami.
Tsugi ni narimaseru kami no mina ha, Kamimusubi no kami.
Sono mihashira no kami ha, onomo onomo hitorikami narimashite,
   mimi wo kakushimashiki.[21]

Norinaga had regarded long sonorous phrases to be typical of the ancient transmissions, perhaps based upon his reading of ritual prayers and imperial edicts, and in his kana *Kojiki* had rewritten the *Kojiki* to reflect this. In contrast, Moribe conceived of the style of oral expression in very different terms, as rhythmic prose marked by relatively short phrases and the repetition of key patterns.

The *Kojiki* and *Nihon shoki* are the earliest examples of Japanese prose, and yet, as Moribe recognized, they were already "wrapped in Chinese." And thus the fragile nature of Moribe's attempt to recover aya becomes apparent. No text was ever written in the style he idealized, and the series of examples he took up as evidence of the existence of aya were chosen precisely because they exhibit the patterns of orality as he imagined it. For Moribe, as for Norinaga, the belief that writing had recorded the "orality" of the ancient transmissions was the aporia at the center of his project. However, unlike Norinaga who never wavered from his assertion that through language one could "know" the reality of the ancient period, Moribe shared the uncertainty, if not the candor, of Akinari.

A work called *Tadaka monogatari* (A Tale of Direct Revelation, 1833), written during the same period as *Yamabiko zōshi* and the *Sansenkaku*, is revealing both of Moribe's passion for and his doubts about the recoverability of the past. An attempt at narrative fiction, the work was never finished, but a detailed summary of the plot survives.[22] The story opens by describing the life of a fictional character Fujiwara Katanaru, said to be a student of Kitabatake Chikafusa (1293–1354), a scholar who supported Emperor Go-Daigo's failed attempt to revive the ancient imperial state in the event known as the Kenmu Restoration in 1333. The work Kitabatake authored, *Jinnō shōtōki masukagami* (A Record of the Legitimate Succession of the Divine Emperors), championed Go-Daigo's cause by arguing that Japan's "superiority" derived from its unbroken line of emperors.[23] Living in seclusion in an isolated village in Yamato, Katanaru and his wife, both in their fifties, beseeched the deities to send them a child. Then one day an eagle appeared bearing a small child in his beak. Katanaru killed the eagle and then raised the child, whom he named Hisakata, as his own son. The next event in the plot is the death of Katanaru, who in his last moments called upon his adopted son to carry on his study of the ancient texts. Hisakata vowed to continue, but one day, lamenting the state of his world in which usurpers ruled in the place of the emperor and the people's hearts had turned from the deities toward Buddha, he called on the deity of the Takeiwatatsu Shrine, saying,

> From the time of my father I have deeply lamented this. What is the fate of this world? Let me know. No matter how much I study the ancient ways of the Divine Age, I cannot understand all that is related in the Kojiki and Nihon shoki, and there is much that is questionable to me. What is the truth of this? Please let me know, even if but in a dream. . . . How can I return to the world that has passed?

In response, the deity appeared and granted Hisakata his wish. Over a period of twenty months, he was allowed once each month to leave his body and travel back in time to the Divine Age, first to the time of the primal deities, and then forward to the time of the "seven generations of deities," and finally to the Engi era (901–922). After each visit Hisakata returned to his own time and instructed the people of the village in the ways of the deities. The Tadaka monogatari draws to a close with the statement that the hearts of the people had become like those of the Divine Age.

No doubt Moribe longed, like Hisakata the time traveler, to experience the Divine Age directly, but he could not. During the years that separate Yamabiko zōshi and Sansenkaku from Moribe's next major works, he immersed himself in the reading of the Kojiki and Nihon shoki. But as Moribe sat reading in his home in Asakusa in Edo, Japanese society underwent a series of convulsions. The year 1833 marked the beginning of the great Tenpo famine. As tens of thousands starved, the countryside was rocked by a series of uprisings. Those in the cities suffered as well, as rice prices fluctuated widely and the streets were filled with desperate beggars, developments of which Moribe took note in his letters and other personal writings. In 1837, Ōshio Heihachirō led an uprising in Osaka against the bakufu he served, an event Moribe was moved to memorialize in a long Man'yōshū-style poem. When he began to write on the Divine Age toward the end of the decade, it was to put forth a new theory of the Divine Texts, of how they worked and what they meant.

DECIPHERING THE LANGUAGE OF THE TEXT

In the 1840s Moribe completed in rapid succession *Nan-Kojikiden* (A Critique of the *Kojikiden*, c. 1842), *Itsu no chiwake* (Distinguishing the August Way, 1844), and *Kamiyo tadaka* (A Direct Account of the Divine Age, 1847). All three texts are devoted to the analysis of the narrative of the Divine Age that is related in the *Kojiki* and the *Nihon shoki*. In the *Nan-Kojikiden*, Moribe took up passages from the *Kojiki* and corresponding segments of the *Kojikiden* and tried to prove how the latter was mistaken in light of his own understanding of the ancient texts. The *Itsu no chiwake* was Moribe's annotated text of the *Nihon shoki*, while in *Kamiyo tadaka* he brought together passages of the *Kojiki*, *Nihon shoki*, and other texts to retell the story of the Divine Age. While the form of the three works is different, they all put forth the same understanding of the story of the Divine Age. As in the *Yamabiko zōshi* and the *Sansenkaku*, issues of language were at the center of Moribe's project, but in these three works he took up the ancient language with a new awareness of textuality. Unlike Norinaga, who had argued that the text of the *Kojiki* was a transparent inscription of the oral transmissions from the Divine Age, Moribe problematized the relation of the events and attempts to narrate them. He argued that while the texts did indeed record the oral transmissions of the ancient people, the "events" of the Divine Age and "words" that told of them were not the same. Thus, Moribe's work on the ancient texts now posited a moment of rupture between the Divine Age (*kamiyo*) and the ancient period (*inishie*). While in the *Yamabiko zōshi* and *Sansenkaku*, Moribe had focused on the recovery of the language of the ancient period, his aim now was to filter out that language in order to recover the real meaning of the Divine Age narrative.

The foundation of Moribe's rereading of the *Kojiki* and the *Nihon shoki* was the meaning he attached to the terms *kuji* (ancient words) and *honji* (fundamental words), which he encountered in the preface to *Kojiki*. Describing the circumstances that led to the compilation of the *Kojiki*, the preface related that the emperor Tenmu, having heard that the written records called the *honji* and *kuji* were being altered, ordered Hieda no Are to read and memorize the imperial genealogies and the stories concerning the Divine Age. Thirty years later, the reigning emperor Genmei ordered Yasumaro to record what Hieda no Are was able to recite from memory. In the first chapter of the *Kojiki-den*, Norinaga too had cited this passage, but he attached little significance to these texts, foregrounding instead the scenario he imagined in which Hieda no Are learned to recite the ancient transmissions by hearing them "voiced" by the emperor. In contrast, Moribe took up the question of who wrote these texts and why in order to interrogate their relationship with the *Kojiki* and *Nihon shoki*.

In the *Itsu no chiwake* and *Kamiyo tadaka*, the production of the honji and kuji was explained by means of the textual history that Moribe constructed by piecing together the fragmentary accounts of the introduction of writing into Japan and the writing of the earliest records that appear in the *Kojiki*, *Nihon shoki*, and other works such as the *Kujiki*. The *Kujiki* had already been identified as a Heian-period forgery by Norinaga and others, but Moribe accepted its veracity, arguing that it was compiled using fragments of records that date from the same period as the *Kojiki* and *Nihon shoki*. Moribe used the term *honden* (original transmission) to refer to the narrative of the events of the Divine Age that was passed from the deities to men when the Age of Gods gave way to the Age of Men. In contrast, in his usage kuji referred to the transformation of the original transmission as it came to be embedded in the voices of the Japanese people. On the relation of the honden and the kuji, Moribe wrote, "The ancient transmissions from the Divine Age were not the private possession of the Imperial Court alone. They were recited far and wide under heaven. As for their origin, in the Divine Age they were related from deity to deity and so entered this world. After the original transmission entered this world, from the beginning of the Age of Men they were recited and passed on widely throughout the land."[24]

According to Moribe's account, the kuji were passed down orally for generations, until the time when Chinese characters were introduced from the continent, a process that occurred in two distinct stages. First, beginning perhaps in the reign of the emperor Sujin, who appears as the tenth emperor in the *Kojiki* and *Nihon shoki*, Chinese writing was brought by a series of Korean immigrants who, while unschooled in the Chinese classics, knew how to use writing to create simple records. They transmitted this skill to the Japanese, and at the local level "words" and "events" began to be recorded by means of this form of writing that was, according to Moribe, "sufficient for local uses."[25] These texts, suggested Moribe, were the first attempts to record the oral kuji. It was in the reign of the emperor Ōjin, depicted as the fifteenth emperor of the Age of Men, that Chinese texts—the Confucian classics, dynastic histories, and so on—were brought to Japan, and as a result the way in which the ancient Japanese people perceived and represented the world began to change. Moribe described the period that stretches from the introduction of these texts until the age of the emperor Tenmu as an age of

decline in which the *kamigoto* (divine words) of the oral traditions that told
of the Divine Age began to be forgotten: "The four generations from the emperor Kōgyoku to the emperor Tenchi were a time when the translation of the
divine words of the oral transmissions from ancient times into the style of
Chinese texts flourished." Moreover, in the aftermath of the Taika Reforms,
as state building on the Chinese model began in earnest, "those who recited
the Divine Words of the ancient transmissions all but disappeared."[26]

According to Moribe, the reign of Tenmu marked a turning point in the
process of transformation and loss. The emperor, fearing that the essential knowledge contained in the ancient transmissions would be lost if not
somehow fixed and preserved, ordered that a new record be created. The imperial scribes entrusted with this task experimented with two strategies of
inscripture. The first led to the compilation of the texts known as honji. According to Moribe, the honji were created by extracting and inscribing elements of the kuji according to their relevance to certain externally defined
topics, such as the genealogies of the imperial line and influential clans and
the history of the origin of the imperial regalia. Moribe regarded this kind of
thematic organization as inspired by Chinese models. On the origin of the
honji, he wrote, "Long ago in ancient times, that which had been transmitted
from the Divine Age was, after the Chinese texts came to be known, divided
up and recorded in separate sections as in the histories and other records
of that country."[27] Honji then were compiled in order to foreground certain essential information contained in but obscured by the kuji. However,
Tenmu was dissatisfied with this method, not only because it resulted in a
loss of the "ancient words," but also because this process of transcription
was mediated by an individual—the scribe who extracted and reorganized
the information of the kuji. Eventually, attempts to record the original transmission in honji form were abandoned, and a second strategy was employed,
the recording of the originally oral kuji into writing. However, this method
too was problematic, because the process of oral transmission over many
generations had significantly altered the honden. However, the insertion of
what Moribe called *katarikotoba* (narrating words) during oral transmission
was judged to be less damaging than the "translation" mode of the honji.
Moribe asserted that there were two reasons for the decision to record the
kuji. First, the direct inscripture of the voices of the community would forestall any effort to manipulate the texts for private (watakushi) purposes. Second, the direct inscription of kuji would preserve the narrative syntagm of
the original transmission that the honji destroyed.[28]

Moribe argued that both the *Kojiki* and the *Nihon shoki* were compiled by using the strategy of kuji inscription, but the *Nihon shoki* was the more successful attempt. The *Kojiki*, the first effort to inscribe the kuji, recorded only one version of the ancient transmissions, that which was recited by Hieda no Are. However, the emperor was displeased with this text and ordered it discarded. Moribe asserted that the *Kojiki*, because it related only one version of the Divine Age narrative out of the plurality then in existence, did not escape the potentially biased selectivity that had marred the honji. Thus the compilation of the *Nihon shoki* was ordered in order to improve upon the shortcomings of its predecessor. For this reason, the *Nihon shoki* was compiled by collecting all of the kuji that had been recorded by the various clans and communities when writing was first introduced. This explanation accounted for the complex form of the *Nihon shoki* in which each episode is presented in multiple versions that are labeled issho. According to Moribe, Norinaga's condemnation of the *Nihon shoki* as the product of the "Chinese mind" revealed that he did not understand the intentions of the emperor who oversaw its compilation. In criticizing the *Nihon shoki*, Norinaga had placed far too much emphasis to the version of the narrative that was named in the *Nihon shoki* as the "main text." Moribe agreed that this version was undeniably sinicized, and he suggested that it was named as the "main text" only out of reverence for its status as a court-produced document. In terms of a real affinity to the original transmission, it is the alternate versions of the story, the issho, that are important.

At the center of Moribe's textual history was his conception of katarikotoba as extraneous elements that had adhered to the original transmission. Moribe discovered the term *katarikotoba* in the *Kojiki*, but like Mitsue, he used a single reference to authorize a complex theory of the language of the text.[29] In explaining his conception of "narrating words," Moribe expanded upon the idea of the performative setting that he had taken up in the *Sansenkaku*. He argued that the ancient storytellers had relied upon a number of techniques as they related the story of the Divine Age to those around them. The "narrating words" thus were the residue of the recitation of the original transmission among the ancient Japanese people. Moribe argued that while the collective nature of this process acted as a safeguard against the mediation of any individual, the repeated insertion of "the voices of the people" rendered the original transmission all but incomprehensible to later generations. The result of the use of "narrating words" was that "the distinction between men and the deities was forgotten and the faith of the men of this world was lost."[30] Thus, when Moribe described the "narrating words," he took pains to distinguish between their nature and that of the original transmission. While the latter was to be revered, the "narrating words" reflected *bonryo* (ordinary ideas), *bonyoku* (ordinary desires), *bonzoku no jō* (the emotions of the masses), and *bonjō* (commonplace emotions).[31] As a result, Moribe's exegesis was organized around identifying the "narrating words" found on the textual surface and explaining how to move from them to the original transmission.

Central to this process was the creation of a typology that attempted to explain the various forms of "narrating words," how they took form, and how they functioned. According to Moribe, the most common type of "narrating words" was what he termed *osanagoto* (childish words). He explained that the ancient people who regarded the original transmission as essential knowledge instructed their children in the events of the Divine Age from a very early age. This required that the narrative be rendered comprehensible and amusing to the young, and thus aspects of children's life and language came to be integrated within it. The numerous references in the Divine Texts to body parts, crawling, crying, and excretion are described as examples of "childish words." Moribe regarded these as relatively easy to identify and exclude. A greater challenge to the reader was posed by those cases in which the insertion of "childish words" altered the narrative sequence of the original transmission, that is, when childish stories were used to convey the plot itself. As examples of this, Moribe cited such episodes as Izanami and Izanagi's making of the land by stirring the brine from the floating bridge of heaven, Susanō's insistence on going to the land of his mother, and Ōkuninushi's trials at the hand of Susanō as "adaptations" of the events of the Divine Age to make them interesting to children.[32]

A second form of "narrating words" was termed *katarigoto*. Moribe described this as "the language that naturally adhered [to the narrative] and which was drawn in by the power of language as the stories were being told."[33] It is "like the narration of the tales of later ages, the words of the storyteller."[34] The product of that performative moment, katarigoto refers to the incorporation of figurative language—metaphor, allegory, and rhetorical embellishment—into the narrative. Moribe regarded the descriptions of yomi and ame, portrayed respectively as a dark subterranean world and as the heavenly realm of the deities, as the most pervasive example of katarigoto. The original meaning of yomi as "that which cannot be seen" was transformed through a series of metaphorical extensions until it came to be represented as a dark and foul underworld. Similarly, ame is not really "a world above the heavens with mountains, rivers, trees, grasses, palaces" as the katarigoto describe it.[35] According to Moribe, a pervasive form of katarigoto was the description of the deities of the Divine Age in human terms, when in fact neither the physical restrictions that bind men nor the emotional motivations and responses associated with human behavior could be ascribed to them. Thus he dismissed the image of Amaterasu weaving that appears in the Kojiki as katarigoto, saying, "Do you think that in the other world where the deities reside there are such trivial human pursuits? How ridiculous."[36] Similarly, labeling the account of Ōkuninushi's troubles with his children as katarigoto, Moribe stated, "What kind of mind would think that this kind of petty affair relates to an august deity?"[37]

Moribe delineated a number of other forms of "narrating words," including yogatari (folktales) and the strategies of abbreviation (habukigoto) and implication (fukumegoto). Yogatari referred to what seemed to be popular tales, such as the passage in which the deity Ōkuninushi courts the daughter of an earthly deity, that at some point came to be grafted onto the original transmission but which are in fact completely extraneous to it. Regarding abbreviation and implication, Moribe argued that the collective nature of the narrative, the fact that everyone knew the original transmission and participated in its transmission, resulted in certain things being omitted from the oral text: "Because there was no one who did not know the real meaning of the ancient transmissions, even if things were abbreviated to a great extent, there were no misinterpretations."[38] Like Norinaga and Mitsue before him, Moribe was troubled by the disappearance of the first deity named in the Kojiki, Ame no Minakanushi, from the remainder of the narrative. He evoked the strategy of "abbreviation" to argue that this deity shaped the unfolding of the events in the Divine Age, even though he is not named. Thus, although on the textual surface Izanagi or Amaterasu are described as performing an important act, for example, creating the Japanese islands or deciding to send a ruler to "middle world," the reader must recognize that Ame no Minakanushi too was involved in these events.

As these examples suggest, the various forms of "narrating words" functioned on different levels in relation to the textual surface of the Kojiki and the Nihon shoki. The category of yogatari, discernible on the level of the narrative syntagma, allowed Moribe to simply exclude many sequences within the narrative, while the notions of abbreviation and implication made it possible to insert extratextual material. In contrast, Moribe himself stated that

many of the osanagoto and katarigoto could not be simply extracted, because the original transmission was expressed through them. Like Mitsue,
he insisted that much of the language of the text was metaphorical in nature.
Thus the foundation of Moribe's exegesis was the movement from the literal
meanings of the textual surface that was recorded in "narrating words" to
discover the real meaning of the original transmission they obscured. But of
course this movement was necessarily teleological in nature: the distinction
between "narrating words" and the original transmission was dependent
upon an a priori understanding of what the real meaning of the narrative
was. It is clear that Moribe was well aware that his conception of "narrating
words" was open to question. In each of his three works on the Divine Age,
he made reference to "secret teachings" that allowed him to distinguish the
narrating words from the original transmission. In the autobiography he authored in the mid-1840s, *Tachibana monogatari* (A Tale of Tachibana), Moribe
offered an explanation of the origin of the "secret teachings" upon which he
claimed to base his work.[39]

Tachibana monogatari is unfinished and covers only the first twenty-five
years of Moribe's life, ending long before its author attained any renown
as a scholar. However, within it, Moribe portrayed his role as a kokugaku
scholar as preordained by destiny and descent. According to the autobiography, Moribe was born in Ise in the district of Asake just at the moment of
sunrise and was given the childhood name of Asaiya (literally, "respect for
the rising sun"), because even as an infant only two months old, he had the
habit of bowing his head reverently toward the sun. Moreover, in the genealogy put forth in the text, Moribe claimed to be a descendant of Kitabatake
Chikafusa, the fourteenth-century scholar and imperial loyalist who had figured in the *Tadaka monogatari*. The central event in the *Tachibana monogatari* is
the death of Moribe's father, Iida Motochika, and his deathbed wish that his
son become a scholar. This came soon after the disgrace and exile of Moribe's
family from their native village, a punishment that Moribe attributed to the
wrath of a deity, whom his father had angered by cutting down a sacred tree to
rebuild the family home. In the autobiography, Moribe's father, living proof
of the power of the deities to control man's fate, explicitly ordered his son
not only to take up the study of kokugaku, but also to correct the mistakes
and shortcomings of his predecessors:

> You must study! And you must study the ways of ancient imperial court.
> Now in Matsuzaka there is someone named Motoori Norinaga. He is

well known, but he relies only on his own study and does not know the rules for interpreting the Divine Texts. He just adds to the mistakes that have been made from Azumamaro to Mabuchi. [Aragita] Hisaoya was not strong enough. And the scholarship of my teacher Tanigawa [Kotosuga] was also not correct. You should leave their work alone and discern the original truth. In our family there was an ancient and mysterious oral transmission, but recently it has been lost. . . . There are nothing but a few traces in missing books, but with your talents I think you will be able to understand [the truth].[40]

The invention—for clearly that is what it was—of the "secret teachings" to support his theory of the original transmission was Moribe's attempt to avoid the charge that he was imposing his own views upon the ancient texts. In both the *Sansenkaku* and his history of the compilation of the *Kojiki* and *Nihon shoki*, he had problematized the role of the scribe who through the act of writing acquired the ability to insert his own "human intention" into that which he recorded. The evocation of "secret teachings" allowed Moribe to claim that he did not invent the various categories of narrating words, but merely recovered a bit of lost knowledge. Thus, like Norinaga before him, Moribe tried to conceal his act of interpretation, but with equally little success. In 1853, Mutobe Yoshika, a student of Hirata Atsutane, wrote scathingly of Moribe, "Using his own narrow views, he made additions to and abridged the august ancient transmissions just as he wanted and so established his own groundless theory."[41]

CONSTRUCTING A COSMOLOGY

As Mutobe recognized, Moribe used his theory of the narrating words to construct a new "story" from the surface texts of the *Kojiki* and the *Nihon shoki*. He excised from these accounts of the Divine Age all anthropomorphic references to deities. Identified as extraneous to the original transmission were such well-known passages as Izanami and Izanagi's sexual union and her act of giving birth to the Japanese islands, Susanō's rivalry with Amaterasu and his expulsion from Takamagahara, and Ōkuninushi's subjugation at the hands of the heavenly deities. Similarly, Moribe rejected Norinaga's equation of the deities with the physical phenomena of the natural world. The deity Amaterasu is not the material object, the sun, as Norinaga had insisted in his debate with Akinari, but a "spirit," according to Moribe. The exclusion of the "narrating words" in their myriad forms reduced the complex surface narrative to a far simpler one that told of the relationship of the three concepts that Moribe termed ame, yomi, and kami. He described these as the "mysteries" of ancient texts and stated, "If one does not understand these three things, then one will not be able to understand the meaning of the Divine Texts. They are the source of confusion. They are the source of enlightenment."[42] In the introduction to *Itsu no chiwake*, his exegesis of the *Nihon shoki*, Moribe offered this preliminary description of ame, yomi, and kami:

> Ame and yomi are two names that both exist within kami, and they are not outside of the [apparent] world. I could say they are very near, because above and below, to the left and right, they surround our bodies; only our hands cannot touch them. I could say they are distant, because they fill the cosmos; only our eyes cannot discern them. . . . As for the distinctions, in relation to the gods, one says ame; in relation to the demons, one says yomi. Combining these two, one speaks of kami. Ame aids yomi, and yomi assists ame. They are like husband and wife, night and day, the land and the sea. Eternally helping each other, they maintain the revealed world, and each and every event of the world is planned by the deities within kami. Prosperity and decline, happiness and misfortune, reward and punishment all come from this kami that cannot be seen, so it is the most august of things but also the most fearful.[43]

As this suggests, Moribe rejected the information that appears on the surface text, in which ame (written with the character *ten*, "heaven") is described as the "heavenly world" of the deities and yomi as the dark subterranean world of the dead. He argued that ame and yomi are not "places" as such, but rather are two aspects of the dimension of kami, the realm of the deities that is imperceptible to human senses. Moribe applied the reading kami to the compound written with the characters *yūmei* (the hidden world), arguing that this had become the term for the deities because they originated within this dimension. The immensity of kami was conveyed in both temporal and spatial terms. For example, Moribe argued that the simple temporal markers that appear on the surface text in describing events within kami—words such as "next" and "then"—actually signify gaps of "tens of thousands of years" and "a great expanse of time." Similarly, in describing the size of kami, Moribe stated that "men are made to live in the midst of it, and although they are allowed only a tiny part of the cosmos, their minds conceive of it as a huge world."[44] Moribe called "the tiny part of the cosmos" of which human beings are aware, *arawani*, literally, "that which is revealed."

The description of kami as a dimension of reality that is all around us but beyond human perception—characteristics of the world that Hirata Atsutane termed *yūmeikai*—has prompted some modern scholars to argue that a relationship of influence exists between the work of Moribe and Atsutane.[45] Certainly, Moribe was aware of the cosmology Atsutane put forth in *Tama no mihashira* and *Koshiseibun;* however, he ridiculed it as relying upon the "narrating words" of the surface text, noting that Atsutane oriented his discussion of the location of ame and yomi around the celestial objects, the sun and the moon.

A more significant point of departure, however, was in the two scholars' view of the relationship of the "hidden world" to the human realm. In his work *Things Seen and Unseen*, Harry Harootunian has analyzed Atsutane's work on the Divine Age and its transformation in the hands of his followers during the last decades of the Tokugawa period. Harootunian characterized as Atsutane's "great innovation" the establishment of yomi and the yūmeikai as physically and functionally distinct places.[46] Atsutane agreed with Norinaga that yomi was indeed a place of pollution, as the *Kojiki* narrative implied, but he rejected Norinaga's insistence that it was to this foul site that human spirits were relegated after death. Yomi, according to Atsutane, was forever separated from heaven and earth during the Divine Age; rather, it was the yūmeikai, a hidden realm that was both omnipresent and coterminous with earth, that was the sanctuary of the dead. Atsutane characterized the yūmeikai as spatially contiguous to the human realm—ancestors live close to their descendants but are unseen—and much like the world of the living in all its attributes. Even its system of administration paralleled that of the revealed world: it was governed by the deity Ōkuninushi, the descendant of Susanō, as the human realm was ruled by the emperor, the descendant of Amaterasu. Atsutane's concern for the problem of death and the afterlife was intimately tied to his project. Thus the *Tama no mihashira* began with the statement that "if one desires to strengthen the Japanese spirit, the most important task is to know the destination and resting place of the spirits after death."[47]

In another departure from Norinaga, who had emphasized the absolute power and inscrutability of the deities and termed human beings their "puppets," Atsutane portrayed the relationship of deity and man in more optimistic terms. He was critical of Norinaga's depiction of the deity Magatsuhi as the origin of all the evil in the world and argued instead that Magatsuhi had simply given human beings the capacity to discriminate between good and evil. As this suggests, while Norinaga had emphasized the passivity of human subjects in relation to the divine, Atsutane stressed that men were causal agents whom the deities had endowed with the means to shape the events of their lives.[48] He called upon men to repay this divine trust by acting in accordance with the divine will, that is, by living lives ordered around the intertwined acts of agricultural work and worship. In particular, Atsutane established a link between the "productive" acts of the deities who created the world and the human occupation of agricultural production. Thus, Atsutane's rewriting of the Divine Texts functioned to affirm the lives of Japan's villagers by infusing their work with value and offering them the promise of rest and reward after death.

Revealing of the gap between Moribe's cosmology and that of Atsutane is the differing status of the issue of the afterlife in their works. As I noted above, Moribe placed yomi not outside but within the "hidden world," but even more significantly, he showed little concern for the fate of the departed spirits, mentioning only in passing that "the world of yomi is extremely large, and it is the hiding place not only of the spirits of the dead but also of a host of malevolent deities, as well as demons, vengeful ghosts, and all kinds of apparitions."[49] This is not to say, however, that he characterized yomi as an evil or polluted place in the manner of Norinaga. Rather, Moribe portrayed yomi as existing in a symbiotic relation with ame: "Yomi is second in reverence only to ame. When there is something that must be done, even with the power and good offices of the deities of ame, nothing could be accomplished without the aid of yomi."[50] For Moribe, it was the delineation of the relationship of ame and yomi within the realm of kami and of kami to arawani, the world available to human perception, that was the theme—and the teaching—of the original transmission. It is the delineation of this teaching that became the theme of the narrative that Moribe constructed in varying degrees of specificity in *Itsu no chiwake*, *Kamiyo tadaka*, and *Nan-Kojikiden*.

According to Moribe, the Divine Age began not with a state of primordial chaos as the surface texts suggest but with the dimension of kami already in existence. It was within this vast formless space that the primal deity Ame no Minakanushi appeared. He then "used his power" to bring the two other primal deities, Takamimusubi and Kamimusubi, into existence. "Acting together," these three deities then imparted physical form to part of kami and created not only the revealed world but also the deities who would act within it, a process conveyed by means of the description of the "seven generations of deities." The primal deities then commanded the last pair of deities, Izanami and Izanagi, to create rulers to oversee the hidden world. However, they had difficulty completing this task, until Izanami entered into kami to "borrow" its strength. This allowed for the creation of the rulers of ame, Amaterasu, and of yomi, Susanō. After their appearance, Izanagi too entered the hidden world. Amaterasu and Susanō were then commanded to create a ruler for the revealed world. Amaterasu entered the hidden world, and as a result the two were able to combine the "power" of the hidden world and the revealed world and create Ame no Oshihomimi, who eventually became the father of Ninigi. It was the latter who as the "divine descendant" entered the revealed world to be its ruler. When this was accomplished, Susanō passed into the hidden world. His descendant, Ōkuninushi, was then commanded to prepare the world for the coming of Ninigi. However, as a deity of the revealed world, Ōkuninushi was not strong enough to pacify the unruly deities that invaded it from kami, and so a representative of that realm, Sukunabiko, was dispatched to aid him. After this subjugation was completed, Ninigi entered the revealed world to become its ruler, and Ōkuninushi moved into the hidden world to aid the other deities in overseeing the revealed world, their combined creation.

Within this rewriting of the Divine Age narrative, Moribe depicted the relationship of kami and arawani in ambivalent terms. The deities of the hidden world create the revealed world, they establish a ruler for it, and they continue to protect it "from the shadows." And yet the differences of spirit and form, deity and man imparted a fundamental instability to this relationship. Moribe portrayed the mingling of the two realms as both productive and polluting. The deities in the revealed world turn to kami for aid, but they must also perform rituals of purification after contact. Moribe explained the purification of Izanagi after his return from yomi, the seclusion of Amaterasu in the Iwayado, and the expulsion of Susanō as references in "narrating words" to rituals performed to overcome the pollution that results from the juncture of kami and arawani. He even provided a name for this kind of pollution, calling it *azunai*.[51] A term from the ancient texts, it seems to have referred to certain tabooed acts, but Moribe created a new etymology and argued that *azu* is a corruption of the term *ameutsu* (a combination of *ame* and *utsu*, the latter meaning "visible"). The suffix *nai* makes this an adjective, which describes the result of an intermingling of the two dimensions. According to Moribe, azunai named the polluted state that results when the separation of kami and arawani is not maintained.

In addition, argued Moribe, the realm of kami contained a host of pestilent spirits always ready to flow into the world of men. Such is their virulence, Moribe said, that even the great deity Ōkuninushi could not control them. He portrayed the difference of these two realms as a border or boundary— this, in spite of his insistence that the hidden world and the revealed world are not in fact "places": "From the time of Kamimusubi no Mikoto long ago, the separation of kami and arawani has been considered a very grave matter, because from the border many evil spirits can come through and torment the people of the revealed world."[52] As this statement suggests, for Moribe the problem of maintaining the border was a concern for the present just as in the Divine Age. He stated that the people of this world should "respect and fear" the world of kami above all else, but "since they cannot see it, they think it is far away. However, not to think of [kami] is the height of foolishness."[53] In contrast, the ancient people who knew the teachings of the original transmission regarded kami with such fear and awe that even to speak of it was taboo. According to Moribe, that is why there is so little information on kami on the level of the surface texts: it was conveyed only through multiple levels of "narrating words."[54]

RITUAL AND COMMUNITY

In contrast to Atsutane's affirmative vision of Japan, in Moribe's writings on the Divine Age the image emerges of a society always potentially at risk, always vulnerable to the pollution and marauding spirits that emanate from the border between the hidden and the revealed worlds. It is clear that this vision of humanity's plight predated the cosmology that was constructed to explain it. In 1829 Mitsue wrote a work he called *Taimon zakki* (Scribblings in Answer to Queries) for his Kiryū students. A kind of handbook, it is filled with advice on the management of business and household affairs. Typical of the tone of the work is Moribe's suggestion that information to be conveyed to servants be posted in the toilet, where presumably they would be sure to take notice of it. But interspersed with such homely suggestions are frequent references to the problems of *magagoto* (misfortune) and *wazawai* (evil), which Moribe explained in the following terms:

> In the Divine Texts one finds repeated mention of arawani and kami. Arawani refers to things that can be perceived by our eyes, understood by our minds, and felt by our bodies. Kami refers to things we cannot

see, know, or sense. In the case of harm that comes from arawani, if one moderates the body and acts thoughtfully, it can be avoided, but there is nothing that can done about the harm that arises from kami. The evil that seeps from kami is incomprehensible and inescapable. All that one can do is avoid the places and acts that may attract it or invite it.[55]

In keeping with this view of the origin of misfortune, *Taimon zakki* described how to avoid the places and acts associated with kami. Trees should not be cut down thoughtlessly, and taboos associated with fire should be respected, because these things are linked to powerful deities. For the same reason, one should avoid eating the meat of deer, monkeys, and chickens. Moribe warned his students that spirits from yomi are attracted to lonely places, to the darkness of night, and to dirty houses. Moreover, jokes, the use of inauspicious nicknames, and harsh emotions such as anger could also cause them to emerge and do harm.[56] Like Norinaga, before him, Moribe stressed the inscrutability and incommensurability of the deities, but his point of reference was not the rise and fall of various governments over the course of Japan's history, as it had been for Norinaga, but the mundane practices and emotions of everyday life. Many of the taboos he cited in *Taimon zakki* seem to have originated in the village culture of which Moribe was a product.

In the 1840s, however, when Moribe took up the issue of the harm that arose from kami, it was in new terms that engaged directly with the ongoing debate on the nature of Japan. According to Moribe, the harm that emanated from the hidden world was a problem not for the individual but for Japan as a whole and particularly for the emperor: "Since the harm that comes from yomi usually troubles the virtuous people, it is of great importance that each generation of emperor ensures that the rituals are performed. When the veneration of the deities slackens and the purification rituals are performed carelessly, the Imperial Court declines, and the bad things of the world increase. In order to escape these difficulties, we must always serve the gods of heaven and earth."[57]

As this statement suggests, when Moribe turned to consider the state of his own society in light of his reading of the Divine Age narrative, it was to emphasize the role of the emperor in the management of the cosmic instability of kami and arawani. Moribe argued that the emperor, through his performance of the imperial rituals passed down from the Divine Age, maintained and safeguarded the border between the hidden and revealed worlds.

Describing the role of the emperor in relation to kami, Moribe stated that "after being thrust into the apparent world, the descendant of the deities too cannot avoid all of the dangers that come from kami. . . . There may be people who look upon the fact that [the emperor] cannot overcome kami and thus feel doubts, but they do not understand the distance between kami and arawani."[58] As this evocation of the emperor's vulnerability suggests, within Moribe's reading of the narrative, the emperor is depicted not as the representative of the deities before the people—his place in Norinaga's work—but as the representative of the people before the deities.

But while the emperor is not the equal of the deities, he plays an important mediating role between the dimensions of kami and arawani. Moribe's concern for delineating the role of the emperor can be seen in his treatment of the passage in the *Kojiki* and the *Nihon shoki* that describes Amaterasu's command to her descendants to, in Moribe's terms, enter the revealed world and rule there. In rewriting the command of Amaterasu to her son Ame no Oshihomimi "to descend and rule," Moribe replaced the character *chi* or *shiru* (literally, "to know") that was used to write *shirasu* (to rule) with a sequence of three characters that literally mean "to be the king." He justified this by noting that "these characters appear in two of the alternative texts included in the *Nihon shoki*. The people of the world both low and high should not carelessly overlook the meaning of the Divine Command."[59] Then in annotating Amaterasu's repetition of her command, this time to Ninigi, Oshihomimi's child, Moribe made another substitution and inserted the character *chi*, usually read as *osameru* (to pacify). Since Moribe read both these characters as *shirasu*, it is clear that he was attempting via the significance conveyed by the characters to clarify his vision of what the act of "rule" entailed. Moribe's vision of imperial rule was centered on the acts signified by the term *osameru*. Certainly, *osameru* too can have the meaning of "to rule," but Moribe's substitutions suggest that he wanted to foreground the kind of "rule" conveyed by this term. According to Moribe, in the *Kojiki* and *Nihon shoki*, it was used to refer specifically to the acts of "serving and worshiping the deities" and "restoring order to confusion." In describing the role of the emperor, Moribe stated "Every generation of emperor should remember this [the power of the deities]. If they do not pacify [osameru] the deities of kami, then there may even appear those who will rise up against the country."[60] As Moribe envisioned the emperor's role, it was cosmological in orientation. Standing between kami and arawani, between the deities and men, his offerings of homage and veneration pacify the deities and maintain the revealed world and the country.

A second important moment in Moribe's account of the original transmission is Amaterasu's act of bestowing rice on Ninigi in preparation for his move into arawani, an incident that does not appear in the *Kojiki*. The significance of this addition becomes clear in Moribe's reading of the events at Takachiho, the site to which Ninigi came following his departure from kami. Moribe insisted that this all-important passage was "abbreviated to an extreme degree in the *Kojiki* and the *Nihon shoki*."[61] He argued that the original transmission related how Ninigi planted rice with seed he brought from kami, a gift from the deities. Upon harvesting it, Ninigi made offerings to the deities of heaven and earth and then distributed the rice to those over whom he ruled. This was said to be the origin not only of the Nii'namesai, the imperial rite of the harvest, but of all the imperial rituals.

For Moribe, this was the formative moment of Japanese community. Significantly, it was envisioned as a system of exchanges: the Japanese people offer veneration to the emperor and receive rice in return; the emperor offers veneration to the deities and thus safeguards the integrity of arawani. Thus, within Moribe's account, the daily consumption of rice by the people assumed great meaning. It signified the incorporation and participation of all the Japanese people into the narrative of the Divine Age. Asked by a student for evidence of Japan's superiority to China, Moribe replied that in Japan the people of all classes eat rice, the gift of deities, while those in China eat "inferior" grains such as wheat and millet.[62] In the *Kamiyo tadaka*, Moribe declared, "How gracious! How venerable! From this time forward, even the lowest of the low receive the gift of the delicious rice of the gods. To be able to eat of it until one is full is the joy of having been born in the land of the emperor. But the people of later generations do not realize that this is the gift of Amaterasu and that we receive it because of the good offices of the divine descendant."[63] Moribe argued that even the word for "to eat" (*taberu*) is in fact a corruption of the word for "to receive" (*tamau*). Thus the act of partaking of rice was invested with great meaning: it became a ritual that recalled and recouped the event of the Divine Age.

Moribe referred to this system of relations and the emperor's place within it as the *kokutai* (literally, "the body of the country"). As the corporal metaphor suggests, he envisioned the emperor and the Japanese people as inextricably linked together. The deities in the Divine Age narrative provided models for human behavior. As the deities "aided" and "supported" one another and "combined their strength," so too were the Japanese people called upon to aid and support the emperor. Acting in union with him, they could forestall the evil that threatened to enter from the hidden world. For Moribe, it was this vision of community that constituted the "teaching" of the Divine Texts, and he argued that "it is essential that not only the students of kokugaku, but those who study anything—indeed every single person born in this land— understand the kokutai of our land. If we do not understand it, then there will come a time when [this ignorance] will bring harm to the country."[64]

DIFFERENCE AND INCORPORATION

Moribe's equation of cosmological and political space is reminiscent of that which took place in Norinaga's work, although he defined the Japan that was its product in very different terms. The division between the public/social world defined by political authority and the private world of emotion and desire that was central to Norinaga's work—and to that of Akinari and Mitsue as well—has no place in Moribe's work. Indeed, his vision of the "body of the country" was premised upon the collapse of the "public" and "private." Within the context of Moribe's understanding of the relationship of the "hidden" and "revealed" worlds, the acts of eating rice, lighting fires, failing to clean one's house, or falling into a rage assumed cosmological significance. Thus, although Moribe, like Akinari and Mitsue, came to feel that the narrative inscribed in the *Kojiki* and *Nihon shoki* was not a transparent recording of the events of the Divine Age but was in fact a product of historical time, the Age of Men, this perception did not lead him to the same kind of conclusions. While Akinari concluded that the past was unrecoverable and Mitsue asserted that the narrative had no cosmological significance, Moribe held fast to the notion that the Divine Age was knowable and recoverable.

What then was the place of cultural "others" in relation to the cosmologically constituted "Japan" of which Moribe wrote? In the 1840s, such "others" had become a real rather than conceptual problem, as rumors of foreign ships seeking contact began to spread and as the bakufu issued harsh punishments against scholars of "Dutch learning," the term used to describe knowledge from the West.[65] A belief in original cultural difference had been the foundation of Norinaga's work, and Mitsue too had relied upon such a concept when he attempted to explain the "establishment of the country." Moribe took up the issue of the relation of foreign cultures to Japan in a work called *Jūdan mondō* (Questions and Answers in Ten Passages), which was written during the period when he was writing *Itsu no chiwake* and the other works on the Divine Age. The work takes the form of a critique of Norinaga's use of the term "the Chinese mind" to argue that all things "not Japanese" are a barrier to the recovery of the "ancient way." Moribe asserted that Norinaga "hated Buddhism and Confucianism and made enemies of the foreign lands because of his small, narrow, and twisted mind."[66] This prejudice had prevented him from recognizing that cultural contact was in fact authorized by the ancient imperial practices. Moribe pointed to the chapter on the reign of the empress Jingū in the *Nihon shoki* that told of her conquest of the kingdoms on the Korean peninsula. Here he found the statement that "from this time onward, barbarians from the west unceasingly brought tribute." According to Moribe, the "west" referred to all foreign countries including China, India, and Holland, and "tribute" should be understood as a reference to all things of foreign origin, including Confucianism, Buddhism, and the knowledge that came from the West.[67] Like the original transmission itself, this statement from the Age of Men section became not only a description of what had happened but also an authorization of future practice.

Moribe described the proper relationship between the "teaching" of the original transmission and the knowledge offered by "foreign" systems of thought by a series of metaphors. The ancient way, he said, is like the roots and trunk of a great tree, while the other forms of knowledge are its branches and leaves. The relative roles of the two within Japanese culture are like the foods provided at dinner: rice and fish are enough to fill one's belly, but how much more satisfying it is to have vinegary dishes and seasoned vegetables. In much the same way, a man who already has a wife is still happy upon acquiring a concubine.[68] Confucianism, Buddhism, and knowledge from the West were thus characterized as "supplements" that did not compromise or call into question the authoritative status of the teaching of the original transmission. Moribe pointed to their functional value in the management of human relations. They taught "commonsensical" (*jōshiki*) notions such as the evils of acts of violence and the virtues of restraint, thrift, and chastity—human concerns not taken up in the Divine Age narrative, which focused on defining the kokutai. Confucianism and Buddhism, he argued at one point, are like medicines for the sick: they can do both good and harm depending upon their use.[69]

But in spite of the seeming moderation of such views, Moribe never approached anything like the true relativism of Akinari, who argued that every country had its myths and in each case people accepted their veracity. Like Norinaga, Moribe emphasized the superiority of Japan vis-à-vis other societies and explicitly declared that "our august imperial house" is the ruler of the multitude of countries. He even offered a suggestion of how cultural others could be brought into Japan. Pointing to the sequence of marriages related in the *Kojiki* and *Nihon shoki* in which heavenly deities took as wives the daughters of earthly deities, Moribe remarked that "those from foreign countries" could be counted as Japanese if they were born of a woman who was a descendant of the deities. Then, he declared, "they too can count the gods as their divine parents."[70] Thus, Moribe envisioned a world in which everyone could become Japanese, incorporated into the "the body of the country" through the wombs of Japanese mothers.

The inclusiveness of this vision of Japan, which provided a role for foreign lands, non-Japanese people, and Confucianism and Buddhism, and which aligned the humble practices, acts, and beliefs of everyday life with the great imperial rituals, may explain Moribe's rise to influence in the late 1830s and 1840s. Largely self-educated and with no strong ties to any of the established kokugaku schools, he nevertheless eventually acquired an extensive network of disciples. Unlike Atsutane's work, which attracted large numbers of educated cultivators who responded to his valorization of agricultural work and village society, Moribe's teachings seem to have appealed to diverse groups. While there were of course many merchants, such as those from Kiryū and Ashikaga, there were substantial numbers of cultivators and samurai as well. And more than any other kokugaku scholar, Moribe attracted a large following among the Buddhist clergy.[71] His cosmological vision of community offered all of these groups both a compelling explanation of the disorder and unrest of their time and a solution that was within their grasp and which they were empowered to effect.

Chapter 7

National Literature, Intellectual History,

and the New Kokugaku

The terms of kokugaku discourse were fundamentally altered after the forced opening of Japan in 1854 at the hands of Commodore Perry transformed the political landscape of Tokugawa Japan. The perception that the bakufu stood craven before foreign intruders incited both fear and indignation on the part of many within Japanese society. In the wake of this event, two kokugaku schools in particular, the Hirata school, now under the leadership of Atsutane's adopted son, Kanetane, and that of Ōkuni Takamasa, a student of Hirata Atsutane, took the lead in redefining what was meant by references to the "return to antiquity." In the 1860s, it came to be understood as requiring the overthrow of the Tokugawa bakufu, the expulsion of foreigners from Japan, and the return of the emperor to a position of direct political authority. The complex event that was the Meiji Restoration of 1868 cannot of course be viewed solely from the perspective of the kokugaku movement, but when the antibakufu forces issued a pronouncement on January 3, 1868, declaring in the emperor's name that from this point onward "all things would be based upon the foundations established by Jinmu," many students of kokugaku regarded it as the fulfillment of their dream of recovering the "ancient way."[1]

Historians of the Restoration differ greatly in their evaluations of the role the nativists played in the overthrow of the bakufu and the formation of the new state. Yasuda Yoshio points to the "great gap" that separated the vision of Japan as a modern nation-state that was quickly embraced by Kido Takayoshi and Ōkubo Toshimichi, the two most important leaders of the early Meiji period, and that held by the nativists. He suggests that from the outset the new leadership merely used figures such as Hirata Kanetane to legitimate their creation of an imperial ideology that would support their program of institutional change.[2] Sakamoto Koremaru rejects this view, which he argues reduced the kokugaku scholars to "puppets," and asserts that while the involvement of large numbers of nativists in the central government lasted only a few years, the conception of the imperial system as a "union of worship and rule" that originated with them remained the framework of the imperial state until 1945.[3] Moreover, rejecting Yasuda's characterization of all those associated with kokugaku as obsessed with "a return to antiquity," Sakamoto notes that there were kokugaku scholars such as Konakamura Kiyonori, Iida Takesato, Kimura Masakoto, Kurogawa Masayori who "knew the ancient works" and "were experts as textual research" but wanted to "apply [these skills] to the new social climate."[4]

In this chapter, I want to turn to explore the status of kokugaku discourse in the new social and political context of Meiji Japan, the period marked by profound institutional changes carried out by the modernizing central government, industrialization and urbanization, the establishment of new and often contestatory relations with the countries of Europe and North America, and the beginning of imperial expansion in East Asia. Unlike Yasuda and Sakamoto, however, my aim is not to evaluate the role of kokugaku scholars, whether individually or collectively, in either the overthrow of the bakufu or the establishment of the new government. Rather, it is specifically the fate of the early modern discourse on Japan as community within modern discussions of Japanese nationness that is my topic. What happened to the interpretive strategies, the theories of language, text, and history, the critical vocabulary that took form within the work of Norinaga and the others? What meaning did their attempts to conceptualize "Japan" as the source of individual identity and collective cohesion acquire within the work of modern intellectuals? And what, ultimately, did the attempts by modern intellectuals to deploy, transform, and refigure early modern kokugaku practice reveal about the nature of modern conceptions of Japan and Japaneseness?

These are the questions that order my discussion in this chapter as I explore the analysis that a series of Meiji intellectuals brought to bear on the kokugaku discourse of the late Tokugawa period. At the outset, it is important to recognize that these scholars—Konakamura Kiyonori, Haga Yaichi, Muraoka Tsunetsugu, and others—had a very different relationship with political authority than had Norinaga, Akinari, Mitsue, and Moribe. While the kokugaku scholars of the early modern period were without direct ties to the political authorities of their day or stood only occasionally on the margins of power, Konakamura, Haga, and Muraoka were part of the Meiji intellectual elite. For example, Konakamura served in the Home Ministry and the Ministry of Education, while Haga was a professor at Tokyo Imperial University and thus had the status of an official. Their "new kokugaku," as it came to be termed, abandoned the interrogation of political authority that was at the center of early modern practice and sought instead to explain Japan in terms that affirmed, rather than questioned, state-authorized conceptions of national identity.

ABANDONING RECOVERY

It was in the post-1890 period that kokugaku again became central to discussions of Japan, but before turning to examine the "new kokugaku" of this period, it is necessary to review briefly the struggles that enveloped the "nativists" — as I will now term kokugaku practitioners — in the first two decades following the Restoration. The conflicts of this period reveal the overtly divisive turn that the debate on Japaneseness took after 1868 as those inside and outside of the new government struggled over what was to be "recovered" and how.

It was Yano Harumichi, a student of the Hirata school, who became the most prominent kokugaku scholar in the immediate Restoration era. He had close ties with Iwakura Tomomi, the leader of a group of prorestoration nobles, and soon after the announcement of the Restoration, he submitted a lengthy memorial to the "imperial government," then still an idea, rather than a reality. Called *Kenkin sengo* (Humble Petition of a Fool), it has been described as the "platform" of the restorationist nativists.[5] While Yano in this work and elsewhere referred repeatedly to the need to emulate the "the rule of emperor Jinmu," neither the *Kojiki* nor the *Nihon shoki* offered any hint of what form the "rule" of this mythical figure had taken. Instead, Yano found the precedent he sought in the institutions and customs of the ancient imperial state that took form from the late seventh century. This was the government that Norinaga had dismissed as the product of the "Chinese mind," that Akinari had faulted for its manipulation of history for ideological purposes, and that Mitsue had criticized for its "childish" concern for imitating China. In contrast, Yano portrayed this age in utopian terms as the moment when the rule of the emperor was established through the "union of worship and rule." Thus, in marked contrast to the pre-1850 kokugaku discourse, Yano imagined Japan as a thoroughly emperor-centered theocratic polity. The most important institution was to be the *Jingikan* (Office of Shinto

Worship), which in the ancient imperial state had been the highest organ of government.

When the Meiji leadership announced the revival of the Office of Shinto Worship in 1868, Yano and other members of the Hirata and Ōkuni schools flowed into it, becoming officials of the imperial government. But far from being the vehicle to realize his dream of "recovery," the Office of Shinto Worship became for Yano the site from which he witnessed its demise. The movement of the capital from Kyoto to Edo (now renamed as Tokyo), the decision to abandon the ancient imperial rites and devise new "modern" ceremonies for the enthronement and the central imperial ritual called the Daijōsai, the content of the proselytizing campaign that began during the movement to separate Buddhism from Shinto, the eventual dissolution of the Office of Shinto Worship itself—all marked the formation of a new conception of Japan that owed little to antiquity or to kokugaku.[6] As Meiji leaders such as Kido Takayoshi and Ōkubo Toshimichi became convinced that modernization was necessary for Japan's survival, the slogan of "union of worship and rule" was replaced by "rich nation, strong army." But even before nation building had begun in earnest, some nativists turned against the government whose establishment they had celebrated only a few years before. In 1871 Yano was among the more than 250 people, many of them Hirata disciples, implicated in a plot to take the emperor back to Kyoto by force, an event known as the Offenses against National Affairs Incident.[7] In its aftermath, Yano composed a bitter poem that stated, "The desire to return to the divine age of Kashiwara was nothing but an impossible dream."[8]

In the 1870s the influence of the formal affiliates of the Tokugawa-era kokugaku schools within the new government declined rapidly. But as they were excluded from official posts, the nativists identified a new aim, the creation of an institution of high learning that would institutionalize, maintain, and advance kokugaku. Such a school had, in fact, been created in Kyoto in 1868, only to be abandoned when the capital was established in Tokyo. In 1868–1869, when the nativists petitioned the Meiji leadership to create a government-supported kokugaku school in Tokyo, the government initially responded positively. In 1870, it ordered the establishment of a *daigakkō* (university). According to the edict that authorized its creation, the new institution was "to take kokugaku as its foundation and make Chinese learning a supplement."[9]

But as the Meiji leaders began to abandon the rhetoric of "the return to antiquity," they also backed away from their support of the institutionalization of kokugaku in what was to be the pinnacle of Japan's new educational system. As a strategy to disavow their former support, the Meiji leaders presented a policy statement to the Shūgiin, the assembly composed of former daimyo, that stated that only Japanese texts should be studied at the new university and that the ritual homage traditionally paid to Confucius should be abandoned in favor of rites in honor of the native deities. As expected, the members of the Shūgiin, many who had been educated in Confucianism, roundly rejected this proposal. When the nativists continued to agitate for recognition of the primacy of kokugaku and as the daigakkō was disrupted by frequent, often violent confrontations between Confucian scholars and the nativists, the Meiji government responded by dissolving the institution itself.[10]

After the dissolution of the daigakkō, the government pursued its goal of establishing a modern university by transforming two former bakufu institutions—the Kaiseisho, where "Western learning" had been taught, and Igakusho, a medical school—into modern academic institutions. Foreign professors were invited to teach, the schools were reorganized into departments along Western lines, and new curriculums were established. When the government decided in 1878 to try again to establish a university it was these two institutions that became its foundation, with the result was that within the four Divisions of Law, Letters, Science, and Medicine that made up the new Tokyo University, not only was there no department of Japanese studies, but those of literature and history were devoted to the study of Europe and America. The exclusion of the study of Japan from the new university was a crushing blow for the nativists, and for the next four years they again lobbied hard for the establishment of a department in which kokugaku studies could continue. Yet even with the help of some powerful allies, their efforts met with little success. Although Katō Hiroyuki, in charge of the Divisions of Law, Letters, and Science, submitted numerous requests to the Ministry of Education for the creation of a department of Japanese studies, it was only in 1882 that the government agreed that a department of classics (*koten kōshūka*) could be established—but only as a separate institution associated with the Division of Letters, not as part of the university proper. But even this success was mixed: in 1884, the department was divided into two parts, one devoted to Japanese studies, the other to the study of the Chinese classics. It was not until 1890 that the study of Japan officially found a place in what was now known as Tokyo Imperial University (renamed in 1887) with the creation of the Department of National Literature.

The frustration felt by the nativists with their exclusion from the new university in the 1870s and 1880s is clearly reflected in their efforts to create an institution that would be devoted to the study of Japan.[11] A petition submitted by Sakurai Yoshimi, head of the Bureau of Shrines and Temples, to Matsukata Masayoshi, the home minister, in 1881 reveals the nativists' perspective that kokugaku had an important contribution to make to the new Japan:

> Of all the established nations, is there any that does not study its own classics and scriptures? But in our land in the aftermath of the turmoil of the Restoration, we have made progress our goal and have not had time to study the classics and the scriptures. However, more than ten years have passed, and there is the fear that our children will not know the uniqueness of our good institutions and beautiful customs and will fall into the bad habit of despising the old and competing over the new. Therefore we should establish a school to study the classics and make it a place where the ceremonies, imperial rites, and the ancient way will be studied and illuminated.[12]

Matsukata agreed and authorized the establishment of the Institute for the Study of the Imperial Classics (*Kōten Kōkyūjo*), which in 1891 was enlarged, reorganized, and renamed as Kokugakuin University, a private university.

The creation of the Department of National Literature at the Imperial University and of Kokugakuin University, both with the sponsorship of the Meiji government, was part of a larger transformation taking place in Japan in the late 1880s and 1890s. In her definitive study of late Meiji ideology, Carol Gluck has described the "ideological eruption" that occurred in the aftermath of two decades of bureaucratic nation-making as both inside and outside of government, there emerged the perception that, new institutions notwithstanding, the Japanese people lacked a "sense of nation" and must somehow to be transformed into "citizens of the nation" (*kokumin*).[13] As a result, the Meiji state began a concerted effort to create a sense of nationhood, by utilizing the "divine" emperor as the means to convey to the populace a sense that they participated in a mystical national polity. In public statements and documents, there was frequent reference to the Divine Age myths of the *Kojiki* and the *Nihon shoki* that established, it was said, the emperor's divinely authorized right to rule and revealed the genealogical link between him and the Japanese people. Through the schools, the press, and public ceremonies, the imperial presence was inserted into the daily life of the Japanese people, and the emperor was established as both social benefactor and ancestral patriarch of the nation, as a symbol both of Japan's progress and of the continuity of its traditions.

Within this cultural context, kokugaku gained new prestige as the discipline best able to speak to questions of national polity, cultural identity, and the imperial institution. An example of the new influence of the nativist scholars was their successful campaign to discredit the historians associated with the Bureau of Historical Writing (Shūshikyoku).[14] Created in 1875 as a government agency, the bureau became a part of Tokyo Imperial University in 1888. From its inception, it was dominated by historians trained in the Confucian tradition of historical writing whose research concentrated on the production of narrative histories, rather than the annotation of texts. However, under the influence of Western positivism, historians of the bureau such as Shigeno Yasutsugu, Kume Kunitake, and Hoshino Ko became increasingly critical of the Confucian mode of historical writing that required narrating history from an ethical perspective.

The first nativist assault on the bureau occurred in 1882, sparked by an article written by Shigeno in which he challenged the account of the so-called Northern and Southern Courts that appeared in the *Dai Nihon shi*, the great history of Japan begun under Tokugawa Mitsukuni in 1657 but not completed until 1906.[15] Shigeno argued that the *Dai Nihon shi* relied uncritically on the description of events that appeared in the fourteenth-century chronicle *Taiheiki*, which he characterized as an unreliable source. The article, which cast doubt upon the legitimacy of the imperial line of which the Meiji emperor was the end product, led to a storm of criticism and earned Shigeno the nickname of "the erasing professor" (*massatsu kyōju*) because of the perception that he wanted to reject long-established "facts." The nativist scholars responded by publishing a stream of articles in which they attacked Shigeno's "subversionism."

Tension between the two factions came to a head in 1892, when Kume published an article entitled *Shintō ha saiten no kozoku* (Shintō Is an Ancient Custom of Heaven Worship), in which he argued that in ancient times Shinto was not a "religion" in the modern sense of the word but a primitive cult. Although the article was originally published in the academic journal *Shigakkai zasshi* (Journal of the Association of Historical Studies), it was republished in the popular magazine *Shikai* (Seas of History), with a provocative introduction by its editor Taguchi Ukichi, a historian of "civilization," as histories organized by the theme of universal progress were termed. Taguchi challenged those he termed the Shintoists to listen to Kume and stated:

The problem is not whether it is possible today to abandon the study of the history of ancient Japan. It is whether the people of today can or cannot advance new explanations . . . in addition to the far-fetched interpretations of Norinaga and Atsutane. To offer new explanations — is this to be disrespectful to the imperial house? I do not believe this. . . . What I strongly believe is that the Japanese people must be at liberty to study ancient history without it being regarded as disrespectful of the emperor.[16]

The reaction of the nativists to this challenge was swift and furious. They immediately pressured the Imperial Household Agency, the Ministry of Education, and the Home Ministry to rebuke Kume. Not only was he ordered to resign, but the journals in which his articles appeared were forbidden to be sold.

THE NATION-STATE AND THE NEW KOKUGAKU:
KONAKAMURA KIYONORI

The nativist victory in ousting Kume signaled a resurgence of interest in the kokugaku tradition. Beginning in the decade of the 1890s, the nativist scholars, now firmly ensconced in academic posts and with the explicit support of the Meiji state, embarked on a new enterprise. They began self-consciously to define the meaning of kokugaku in relation to the late Meiji project of creating "citizens of the nation," a project that required the delineation of a new set of meanings from the heterogeneous field of Tokugawa kokugaku. The nativists themselves acknowledged, albeit obliquely, their appropriation of the Tokugawa discourse when they began to speak of their efforts as the construction of a "new kokugaku" (*shin kokugaku*). One of the first expressions of the new interest in kokugaku can be found in Konakamura Kiyonori's remarks at the ceremony marking the establishment of the Department of Classics at Tokyo University in 1882: "The department that we are establishing now is made up of pure and expert kokugaku scholars and thus is a place where the facts of the imperial court, the changes in policy, and the transformation of the language of present and past will be explained. . . . Its primary object and intention is to take what has been gained through study and apply it to the realities of today."[17]

Konakamura (1821–1895) was the nativist scholar who took the lead in defining the meaning of kokugaku for modernizing Japan in early Meiji. Born in

1821, as a young man he became a disciple of Motoori Uchitōshi, the adopted son and successor of Motoori Ōhira. After the Restoration, he served in both the Office of Shinto Worship and the Home Ministry, before joining the Ministry of Education in 1880. He went on to play an active role in the establishment of both Tokyo University's Department of Classics and Kokukaguin University and taught in both institutions. The first scholar to be granted the title of doctor of letters in the Meiji period, he was fiercely protective of the kokugaku tradition.[18] It was none other than Konakamura who led the assault against Kume Kunitake and the Bureau of Historical Writing in the early 1890s.[19]

The need for a "new kokugaku" that would serve the nation was the theme of an essay by Konakamura called "Kokugaku no zento" (The Future of Kokugaku, 1890). In it, he began by attempting to define what constituted true kokugaku practice. His discussion moved in two directions, to dismiss the contemporary and commonsensical understanding of this term and also to delimit the various meanings it had carried before the Meiji period. Konakamura acknowledged that within Tokugawa society the term *kokugaku* had been used to refer to a broad range of scholarly practices that centered on Japan. It encompassed not only the work of those he called the "four great men," Azumamaro, Mabuchi, Norinaga, and Atsutane, who attempted to "know the foundation of the national polity (*kokutai*) and to strengthen the Japanese spirit," but also that of poets, linguists, people with an antiquarian interest in ancient ceremonies and court traditions, and even works by Confucianists like Arai Hakuseki and the historians of the Mito school on Japan.[20] Moreover, according to Konakamura, in recent times "as for ordinary people, most of them think that a kokugaku scholar is someone who composes poetry or is a Shintoist."[21] However, Konakamura rejected such understandings: only the work of the "four great men" should be regarded as kokugaku, and it was their work that should be the foundation of the modern study of Japan.

The term "four great men" and the genealogy of kokugaku it signified were not Konakamura's inventions, but he deployed them in new ways and for a new purpose.[22] The use of intellectual genealogy to legitimate one's work was a well-established practice in kokugaku discourse. Norinaga, of course, had situated his own work in relation to that of Keichū and Mabuchi, and as a result, those associated with both the Edo and Suzuya schools began to speak of the "three wise men" (*santetsu*) of kokugaku in the early nineteenth century. In the 1820s and 1830s, references to intellectual geneal-

ogy became especially prominent as the multiple schools of kokugaku com-
peted against one another for influence, prestige, and students. It was in
this context that Tachibana Moribe had evoked ties to the medieval scholar
Kitabatake to support his understanding of the mythohistory. But it was the
Hirata school, in particular, that embraced genealogy as a legitimating device. In _Tamadasuki_ (c. 1824), Hirata argued that it was not Keichū but Kada
no Azumamaro who was the first true kokugaku scholar, not because of his
scholarly accomplishments, but because he was the supposed author of a
petition to the bakufu to establish an official school of kokugaku.[23] From
fragmented evidence about Azumamaro's life, Atsutane identified a complex set of motivations that he attributed to Azumamaro and declared that
the creation of "the study of the imperial land" began with the work of this
man.[24] Having defined the mission of the discourse in these terms, Atsutane
then identified Mabuchi, Norinaga, and of course himself as the successors
of Azumamaro and dismissed those who focused on poetics, "numerous as
ants" though they were, as people who "did not know the true meaning of
the way."[25]

After Atsutane's death, his student Ōkuni Takamasa added his name to
the genealogy and declared that the "four great men" were responsible for
"the revival of true Shinto." Hirata Kanetane too embraced this genealogy
and went so far as to deify the four, bestowing Shinto-style deity names upon
them. It was this conception of the "great men" that functioned in a ceremony sponsored by the Office of Shinto Worship in the spring of 1870 in
which more than 150 kokugaku scholars, Shinto priests, and government
officials gathered together at the Tokyo residence of the lord of Wakayama
to conduct a ritual (_reisai_) to honor the spirits of Azumamaro, Mabuchi, Norinaga, and Atsutane, who were named as the "four great men of kokugaku."[26]
According to a handwritten account of the ceremony, now preserved in the
library of Kokugakuin University, over the course of several hours, commemorative poems were presented, offerings of food made, and several ritual
prayers intoned, in honor of these men and in praise of their perceived role
in the restoration of the emperor in 1868.

Konakamura's deployment of the genealogy of the "four great men" has a
very different status from these earlier uses. While Norinaga had used genealogy to legitimate his practice in relation to Confucianism, Hirata Atsutane
to valorize his work in relation to other forms of kokugaku, and the officials
in the Office of Shinto Worship to shore up the goal of the "return to an-

tiquity" already under siege, Konakamura's use of the genealogy had the aim of aligning kokugaku with state ideology. By evoking the kokugaku scholars, he concealed the newness of the Meiji conceptions of nation by linking it with the eighteenth-century discourse. It was from this perspective that Konakamura urged the new generation of scholars to emulate "the four great men" and write "good history," history that would prove useful to the nation and the people. Konakamura characterized this project as "academic" and "scholarly" in nature and warned future students of Japanese studies to avoid the excesses of their predecessors who were overly critical of Confucianism and overly concerned with the "religious" matters of Shinto. However, when he described the topics of "good history," it was in the terms of an ideologue, not a scholar. For example, he called for the study of the kokutai, employing the term we encountered in Tachibana Moribe's work, but attaching a very different meaning to it:

> As for the national polity, it is nothing other than the divine commandment of eternal and immutable rule. It is to know the foundation of the august imperial household that is without equal in the cosmos, to know how the nation was established, and to know that our country from the time of the descent from heaven [of the ancestor of the emperor] made a distinction between subject and lord, and thus is as different as heaven and earth from the foreign lands where first there was the people and then the ruler.[27]

For Konakamura, the term kokutai signified not the corporal unity of the emperor and the Japanese people, but the hierarchical relation of ruler and subject, privileged as evidence of Japan's "difference."

In another essay, "Shigaku ni tsuite" (On the Study of History), also published in 1890, Konakamura argued that the writing of this kind of "good" history was essential in Meiji society for three reasons: first, to encourage young people to be patriotic; second, to provide historical models for all aspects of government including diplomacy, military affairs, and policy toward agriculture, business, education, and religion; and third, to ensure that the study of Japan remained the privileged province of Japanese experts. On this last point, Konakamura noted that non-Japanese scholars, such as Basil Chamberlain, William Aston, and Ernst Satow were learning more and more of Japan. It would be a national shame, he declared, for any Japanese to know less about his culture than a foreigner.[28]

JAPANESE PHILOLOGY AND NATIONAL ETHICS:
HAGA YAICHI

If Konakamura defined the terms for the construction of a new kokugaku, the central figure in its expansion and popularization was Haga Yaichi (1867–1927), who became a professor at Tokyo Imperial University in 1899 at the age of thirty-two. Haga's role in making kokugaku into a point of origin for the modern academic discipline of "national literature" has been acknowledged by both his contemporaries and scholars writing in the post–World War II era. In 1911, in his work *Motoori Norinaga*, Muraoka Tsunetsugu, who would later become the first professor of the "history of thought" at a national university, described Haga as "a new kokugaku scholar for the Meiji era," and he praised Haga's description of kokugaku as *bunkengaku*, the translation that Haga chose for the term "philology." Muraoka described his own study of Norinaga as a work of bunkengaku and acknowledged Haga as an important source of inspiration.[29] Some fifty years later, the literary historian Hisamatsu Sen'ichi (1894–1976) echoed this view when he described Haga as "the pioneer" who had "established national literature in the Meiji period" by continuing "the traditions of early modern kokugaku."[30] As these characterizations suggest, Haga, like Konakamura, regarded kokugaku not merely as an object of study, a set of texts, ideas, and methods with implications for understanding the Tokugawa era, but as a still vital intellectual tradition, of which he himself was a part.

Haga was born into a family that had strong ties to kokugaku, Shinto, and politics, and he could not but have been aware of the struggles in early Meiji over the role of kokugaku in the emergent nation-state. His father, Haga Masaki, was a samurai from Fukui who studied kokugaku under Hirata Kanetane as a young man.[31] After the Restoration, Masaki operated a private kokugaku academy for several years before beginning a career in government service in the Home Ministry in 1879. Reflecting on his youth, Haga Yaichi later wrote, "When I look back on the course of my education, I can understand the development of education in Meiji."[32] He noted that he began learning English in elementary school and that even in other courses the textbooks used were translations of British and American works. At the same time, however, his father was instructing him in the kokugaku canon at home. Upon his completion of middle school in Sendai, Haga was sent to Tokyo to attend preparatory school. Then, in 1889, he entered Tokyo Imperial University as a student of the National Literature Department, where his teachers included both Konakamura and one of the foreign experts he feared, Basil Chamberlain. After graduating in 1892, Haga taught at an elite high school until 1898, when he joined the national literature faculty at Tokyo Imperial University. An early glimpse into Haga's future politics comes from his activities during the Sino-Japanese War: he joined the Greater Japan Society, which advocated Japanese expansion in Northeast Asia, and helped found a journal called *Nihonshugi* (Japanism) in 1898. Then, in 1900, Haga was sent to Germany at government expense to research "methods for studying the history of literature." He departed from Yokohama on the same ship as Natsume Sōseki, later the most famous of Meiji novelists, who was journeying to England as a government scholar of English literature.

Haga's first systematic attempt to explain the meaning of kokugaku for modern Japan was put forth in the series of lectures he gave only a few weeks before his departure for Europe, later published with the title *Kokugakushi gairon* (An Introduction to the History of Kokugaku, 1900).[33] Against what he called the "general view" that kokugaku was nothing more than the study of things Japanese and thereby akin to "Chinese studies" and "Western studies," Haga argued that kokugaku was of a completely different status— not only had it played a vital role in bringing about the Meiji Restoration, but it had contributed as well to the emergence of Japan as the only country in Asia "that stands on the stage of civilization together with all the countries of the West."[34] Both the Restoration and the rise of Japan as a modern power were the result of the "mental strength of the Japanese people," and this was fostered by kokugaku discourse from the mid-Tokugawa period onward:

> It was the kokugaku scholars who advocated loyalty and patriotism by discarding that which was new and returning to the foundation upon which the country of Japan was established— [the knowledge] that our country was to be revered, that our county was the land of the gods. This gradually began to move men's hearts, and this was the most important reason why the bakufu was overturned. . . . This shows the power of ideas. When Norinaga wrote *Kotoba no tama no o*, it cannot be viewed simply as work that had significance for only the study of language. When Mabuchi studied the *Man'yōshū* and wrote the *Kanji kō*, he did not only explain the *Man'yōshū*.[35]

It was the attempt to resituate kokugaku as a point of origin for modern Japanese nationalism that becomes the theme of this work. Employing a new vocabulary that owes nothing to Tokugawa kokugaku, Haga characterized kokugaku as the study of "the character of the Japanese nation" (*kokusui*) and "the spirit of the nation" (*kokka seishin*). As he moved chronologically through the history of kokugaku, he demarcated "true" kokugaku by selecting, discarding, and reinterpreting aspects of kokugaku discourse. What was lost in the course of this recycling was precisely the kokugaku attempt to constitute community in ways that resisted and interrogated political authority. Against the heterogeneous discourse on Japan that took form in kokugaku, Haga created a new image of the Japanese nation.

He began by insisting that Keichū should not be considered as a kokugaku scholar, even while acknowledging the rigor of the latter's analysis of the archaic language of the *Man'yōshū*, because Keichū was not a "nationalist" (*kokkashugisha*), a characteristic that for Haga became the defining feature of kokugaku practice. It was Kada no Azumamaro whom Haga identified as the first kokugaku scholar because "relying upon that which he found in the national language and national texts," he "excluded the influence of Buddhism and Confucianism" and was thereby able to reveal "the special nature of the Japanese nation," "the special nature of the Japanese people," and "the pure Japanese thought." [36] The next figure in Haga's genealogy of true kokugaku was Kamo no Mabuchi, who was praised because "to the fullest extent he tried to 'return to antiquity' and for all things he took Japan's ancient customs as his standard. In all things he tried to return to the time before the influence of Confucianism and Buddhism, and so his clothes, meals, and home imitated those of the past, and needless to say his prose and poems were written in the language of the past." [37]

Unfortunately, according to Haga, many of Mabuchi's most prominent disciples failed to grasp their master's concern for the "ancient way." They became mere "men of culture" who treated writing poems in the style of the *Man'yōshū* as a diversion like writing Chinese poetry, and they failed to emulate Mabuchi's rejection of things Chinese. While Haga was an admirer of Akinari's fiction—in 1903 he had edited one of the first modern editions of the *Ugetsu monogatari*—he dismissed Akinari as a *wagakusha*, a scholar who studied Japanese texts but lacked the nationalism necessarily to qualify as a practitioner of kokugaku. This description was applied to Tachibana Moribe as well. [38] For Haga, the next true kokugaku scholar was Norinaga, who was praised as one "who held the nationalist view that the way of the nation must be clarified." According to Haga, it was Norinaga who recognized that "it was the *Kojiki* that wrote of Japan directly" and thereby identified the principle that "the *Kojiki* is the only starting point . . . for leaving behind the theories of the Buddhists and Confucianists in order to speak of pure Shinto."[39] Hirata Atsutane was the fourth and final figure in Haga's genealogy of kokugaku. He was praised for recognizing that the "establishment of the way of the nation must be based upon Japanese texts" and for reading Chinese and Western texts "with Shinto as his perspective."[40]

The genealogy that took form within the *Kokugakushi gairon* was that of Konakamura, but Haga attached new meaning to it. He argued that not only did "true" kokugaku produce information that was of continuing value for modern Japan, but also that its very emergence was important—it signified the rise of national consciousness. Azumamaro, Mabuchi, Norinaga, and Atsutane are praised for their prescient sense of nationalism, but this was equated specifically with their recognition of Japanese "uniqueness" (*tokushitsu*) in relation to cultural others. As we have seen, this way of conceptualizing Japan was one of the most contested aspects of kokugaku practice, rejected in varying degrees by Akinari, Mitsue, and Moribe, but for Haga it became the criterion for determining what was true kokugaku and what was not.

The concept of uniqueness became the foundation of Haga's theory of Japanese national culture. It organized one of his first attempts to conceptualize "national literature." In *Kokubungakushi jūkō* (Ten Lectures on the History of National Literature, 1899), Haga argued that the study of literary history was important because "the thought, virtues, and emotions of the nation's people are reflected in the national literature." By studying literature, "it is possible to recognize that the history of the Japanese people is unique in the world." Employing the familiar opposition of "Japan" and "China," Haga explained Japanese literary production as the product of the interaction of "pure Japanese thought" and Buddhism and Confucianism:

> The ideas of Confucianism and Buddhism were mixed together with pure Japanese thought, and the culture of later eras sprang from this fusion. Since Buddhism and Confucianism were written in Chinese, the study of Chinese became a foundation of knowledge, but the special literature of our people was not lost but continued to be vital. Gradually extending from the court down to the common people, "writing in Japanese" and "writing in Chinese" came together, giving rise to the waka of the Nara court, the monogatari of the Heian court, and the warrior tales and Nō theater of the medieval period. Then at the height of the

Tokugawa period, with the resurgence of the ancient texts, a new popular literature emerged, and this was the foundation of the literature of
the Meiji period.[41]

As this passage reveals, while Haga acknowledged the centrality of writing in "Chinese" in Japan, he also portrayed "Japanese" literature—waka,
monogatari, and other writings in wabun—as the site where "pure Japanese
thought" was preserved. As a result, his history celebrated all writings in
wabun but especially what was termed the "lower-class literature" of the
Tokugawa period, that is, haikai poetry and the various genres of gesaku.
Like the formation of kokugaku discourse, popular writings in wabun too
became evidence that in the eighteenth century "the Japanese people had
come together in a great national union."[42]

In contrast to this affirmative view of the Tokugawa era, Haga regarded
the early Meiji period with ambivalence. He noted that "in the era of Meiji,
learning from the West entered very rapidly and was applied to all things,
so even though people spoke of 'return to antiquity,' in fact, new knowledge came from the foreign countries. As a result, there was the tendency
for some time to discard kokugaku, together with Chinese learning."[43] The
final pages of the *Kokugakushi gairon* take the form of a plea to young scholars to revive and embrace kokugaku as "the study of the nation." Kokugaku,
Haga insisted, was not an outdated remnant of the past, but rather, "what
the kokugaku scholars have done for two hundred years is the philology of
Japan," a term he explained as "what Western scholars call using texts as
the foundation to study the nation." Haga concluded by evoking the popular
state slogan of "rich nation, strong army" and declared that "it is necessary
to establish the study of the nation. If we can do this, then as education in
national language and national literature takes place, the mentality of the
Japanese people will be strengthened, and the wealth and power of the nation
will surely increase."[44]

As these early works reveal, Haga departed for Europe with a vision of kokugaku's significance for Japan already in place. During his eighteen months
at Berlin University, he attended courses on topics such as "comparative literature and the history of the German novel," "methods of literary criticism," and "early modern literature" and sought out contemporary works
on Japanese culture by Europeans. But much of his time was spent reading
works by German philologists such as Wilhelm von Humboldt (1767–1835),
Philip August Böckh (1785–1867), and Herman Paul (1845–1921).[45] By the

time he returned to Japan, Haga had reinterpreted the task he had been assigned. Rather than discovering in European scholarship a method for studying national literature, he concluded that within kokugaku practice there was a method as modern as anything Europe had to offer.

The nature of this reinterpretation is evident in the first public presentation Haga gave upon his return to Japan. In 1904, before an assembly of students at Kokugakuin University, he delivered a talk entitled "Kokugaku to ha nani zo ya" (What in Fact Is Kokugaku?), which was published a few months later. In it he repeated the assertion that the Meiji Restoration was the result of the rise of kokugaku, evoked the work of the "four great men" as true kokugaku, and referred repeatedly to the relationship of kokugaku to such things as "the thought of the Japanese people," "the way of Japan," and "special character of the nation." However, in this work, Haga began by posing new questions: "In the West, what do they call this thing we call kokugaku? Is it permissible to speak of kokugaku over there? From the perspective of today's science, can kokugaku be established as an academic discipline?"[46]

Haga's answer to all three questions was a resounding yes. Arguing that in its aim and method kokugaku resembled the discipline called philology in Germany, he declared, "Kokugaku too is a science."[47] Haga explained the aim of philology by evoking Böckh's famous description of its purpose, "to know what had been known" (*das Erkennen des Erkanten*). According to his account, Böckh recognized that the civilization (*bunmei*) of Europe developed from the culture (*bunka*) of ancient Greece and Rome, and so he took up the study of the languages and texts of these societies as the means to understand how "the ancient people understood not only politics, literature, laws, and music but also all the other aspects of society."[48] Arguing that philology, which he translated variously as *bunkengaku* (textual studies) and *kotengaku* (study of the classics), is not merely the study of language or literature, Haga stated:

> Only by exploring the texts of Greece and Rome is it possible to know the true nature of the civilization of Europe today. It is because scholars pursued that true nature that the foundation of European civilization was established. So the work of the scholar of bunkengaku is very important. And their method is, in fact, exactly like the method employed by the kokugaku scholars of our country, Azumamaro, Mabuchi, and the others. In other words, taking the national language and national literature as a foundation, they tried to explain the country.[49]

In making this distinction between "culture" and "civilization," Haga called into question the understanding of "civilization" that had emerged in early Meiji period, when—as in the popular phrase "civilization and enlightenment"—it was used to advocate the adoption of aspects of Western culture and society. Haga affirmed the distinction between "culture" and "civilization," noting that all societies have a "culture" but not all are "civilized," but he questioned the equation of civilization and Westernization. For Haga, the self-conscious study of culture that philology undertook became the most significant evidence of civilization. As he put it, "As for what is called bunkengaku, it cannot take place in a country that is without civilization." Thus, for Haga, the rise of kokugaku became evidence that in Japan's case "civilization" was indigenous in nature and did not rely upon the imitation of the West.

Haga carried this argument one step forward when he suggested that it was precisely the recognition of the continuity between "culture" and "civilization" that was the "foundation" of the modern European nations. In other words, unlike the Japan where "the things that made the nation unique have gradually been reduced" in the pursuit of Westernization, Europeans had preserved their cultures, and this, according to Haga, was the source of their national strength. The rise of philology was thus explained as the product of the recognition of "the uniqueness of each nation."[50] Needless to say, the description of philology as a discourse on "uniqueness" strayed far from Böckh's conception of ancient Greece and Rome as a common site of origin for all of European culture. Haga himself seemed to realize this was an issue, because he attempted to explain the development of philology in Europe in light of rising concern for discerning the specificity of national culture: "Japanese kokugaku and Western philology have followed the same course. Recently it is said [in the West] that there is value to studying the culture of the individual countries. In the past, they only spoke of ancient studies and studied the culture of Greece and Rome, but now they have progressed one step and have come to speak of England's philology, France's philology, and Germany's philology."[51]

Haga cited with approval Wilhelm von Humboldt's description of philology as *Wissenschaft der Nationalität*, for which he provided the English translation, the "science of the nation." Here he noted, "philology was even named as kokugaku, the study of the nation."[52] But, as Hatanaka Kenji has noted, this assertion in fact ignored the complexity of Humboldt's use of the term "nation." In Humboldt's work, "nation" referred to linguistic "communities," the borders of which were not defined by the political boundaries of modern nation-states. In light of this, Hatanaka, in translating the term "nation" in Humboldt's work, suggests the term minzoku (ethnic group), and he points out that many of Humboldt's contemporaries had begun to use the term Volk in opposition to "nation" precisely in order to foreground the distinction between cultural communities based on language and modern political communities.⁵³

But if Haga's equation of kokugaku and philology rested upon a purposeful misreading of the work of the German scholars he cited, it was equally a manipulation of the kokugaku discourse of the late Tokugawa period. While Haga described the texts that were the object of kokugaku practice as examples of "national language and literature," Norinaga and the others scholars of Haga's genealogy never conceived of the texts they studied as "literary" in nature. For Norinaga, of course, the *Kojiki* stood alone—it was the "Divine Text" that revealed the reality of the Divine Age. In order to render the Tokugawa discourse into a "science," Haga had to suppress the emphasis on the "divine" nature of the mythohistories, a defining feature of precisely the forms of kokugaku he valorized. Ironic as well is the description of Norinaga, in particular, as a practitioner of bunkengaku, when the whole of the *Kojikiden* was organized around the suppression of textual issues and the insistence that the "orality" of *Kojiki* meant that it was a transparent representation of the reality of the Divine Age. In contrast, Böckh warned the practitioners of philology that they are "obliged to go beyond literal meaning" when the literal meaning is "not consonant" with other information, individual, historical, and generic.⁵⁴

Most illuminative of the distance between Haga's new kokugaku, "the science of the nation," and Tokugawa kokugaku is the "knowledge" that Haga presented as the results of his own practice of philology. The most widely read of Haga's works was *Kokuminsei jūron* (Ten Lectures on the National Character, 1908), an attempt to describe the "special characteristics" of the Japanese people. Between 1908 and 1927, this work alone was reprinted twenty-two times, and in this same period Haga published other works on the same theme, including *Nihonjin* (The Japanese, 1912), *Sensō to kokuminsei* (War and National Character, 1916), *Nihon seishin* (The Japanese Spirit, 1917), and *Kokugo to kokuminsei* (National Language and National Character, 1928). According to Shimizu Masayuki, *Kokuminsei jūron* was one of the first in the genre that came to be known as "theories of national ethics" (kokumin dōtoku ron), which filled the pages of both popular and academic journals in the aftermath of the Russo-Japanese War. Hisamatsu Sen'ichi too commented on its significance, stating that "the views of [*Kokuminsei jūron*] greatly influenced the studies of national character that followed. Moreover, it was after the appearance of this work that scholars in every field began to take up the study of national character." [55]

The starting point for the *Kokuminsei jūron* was the assertion that "the character of the citizens of the nation influences the culture of the nation and so it is impressed upon the political system, laws, language, literature, customs, and so on." [56] Haga asserted that the first and most important of the ten qualities that constituted the Japanese character was "loyalty to the emperor and love of country." Pointing to the "unbroken" imperial line, and citing references from the *Kojiki* and *Nihon shoki*, he characterized devotion to the imperial family as a defining feature of the Japanese people and argued that it was the fusion of "devotion to the country" and "devotion to the emperor" that made Japan "the only strong country in Asia." [57] Also characteristic of the Japanese people was "reverence to ancestors and pride in the family name." Describing the Japanese state as a "divine polity," Haga argued that reverence for the emperor, the imperial ancestral deities, and one's own ancestors was central to the Japanese character. Thus, while the societies of the West are collections of individuals, "our nation is a fusion of families." [58]

The rest of the work continues in this vein. Deploying the *Kojiki* and the *Nihon shoki*, as well as other texts, as the sources for anecdotal evidence, and aligning this information with a hodgepodge of references to custom, language, architecture, and popular beliefs, Haga abandons any pretense of textual analysis, historical analysis, or the deployment of Böckh's principle of "knowing what had been known." His description of Japanese national character takes form as a series of oppositions between what is Japanese and what is other. The Japanese are pragmatic and practical, and thus in the mythohistories there is none of the concern for metaphysics that one finds in Christianity, Buddhism, and Confucianism. Unlike the West with its ethos of equality, the Japanese value reputation and politeness, and thus distinctions of status are reflected in their religion, language, and customs. The Japanese love nature, are optimistic and straightforward, and have a love of cleanliness. They are brave and imbued with martial spirit, but not aggressive.

Haga's reduction of Japan to a shared set of attributes based upon the opposition of Japan and an other seems reminiscent of Norinaga's work, although the "West" replaced "China" as the point of reference. But while Norinaga used his theory of innate Japaneseness to preserve the "private" world of emotion and desire from "public" attempts to impose ethical norms, Haga's aim was precisely to authorize a set of politically defined virtues. It was this genre of writing that Haga described as the new koku-gaku that would serve the needs of the nation by inculcating in the people reverence toward the emperor and pride and a sense of allegiance toward the nation, characterized as divine and unique.

KOKUGAKU AS INTELLECTUAL HISTORY:
MURAOKA TSUNETSUGU

Haga's rendering of kokugaku as philology profoundly shaped the modern Japanese understanding of this discourse, defining its canon, its method, and its meaning. One of those who embraced Haga's perspective was Mu-raoka Tsunetsugu, the pioneer of "intellectual history" in Japan. A graduate of Waseda University, where he studied Western philosophy, Muraoka, like Haga, received training in the kokugaku tradition. In his teens, he studied the Japanese classics under Sasaki Hirotsuna and his son Sasaki Nobutsuna. The elder Sasaki was associated with the Suzuya school and his son, Nobutsuna, became an influential scholar of Japanese poetics. At Waseda, Muraoka fo-cused his studies on the philosophy of ancient Greece, but his first major work, written when he was only twenty-six, was *Motoori Norinaga*, published first in 1912 and then reprinted in 1928. At the time he wrote this work, Mu-raoka was working for a German newspaper in Yokohama as a translator. The acclaim it won him was a springboard to an academic career. After hold-ing a series of academic posts, in 1923 he was dispatched by the Ministry of Education to study "cultural history" for two years in England, France, and Germany. Upon his return, he became a professor at Tōhoku Imperial University.[59]

In *Motoori Norinaga*, Muraoka explicitly acknowledged his debt to Haga's understanding of kokugaku, stating that he got a "suggestion" from the latter's "Kokugaku to ha nani zo ya."[60] But his analysis of kokugaku was not merely a reiteration of Haga's stance. While he adopted Haga's description of kokugaku as bunkengaku, Muraoka abandoned the genealogy of "four great men" in favor of "one great man," Motoori Norinaga. According to Mu-raoka, "Norinaga's theories were all the result of his solid research, in which he carefully examined each thing in light of the ancient texts, and he suc-ceeded in his goal of understanding the whole of the ancient period as it really was. One cannot but make comparisons with Böckh's philology."[61] His work

Motoori Norinaga divides neatly into two sections: the first half is biographical in nature, while the second is concerned with organizing and analyzing the content of Norinaga's texts. In a paraphrase of Böckh, Muraoka began part two by stating that his purpose was "to explain the concepts of [Norinaga's] work, that which he himself understood and knew."[62] However, the tone of what follows is complimentary, rather than analytical. Typical of Muraoka's conclusions is his declaration that Norinaga "never lost the scholarly progressive spirit that valued truth, loved truth to the utmost."[63]

But Muraoka went beyond merely praising Norinaga for his "objective" and "analytical" approach to Japan's early texts. He argued that "within his study of the classics, Norinaga is someone who created a discipline [*gakusetsu*]." As Muraoka explained, "unlike the old school of commentators, he did not bury himself in verifying facts and interpreting phrases here and there. His careful and thorough analytical research was always synthesized, so that he never forgot to discern rules, principles, and doctrines from every fact."[64] Muraoka praised this approach as the best means to recover "the consciousness of the ancient people" and coined the phrase *Norinagagaku* (Norinaga studies) to describe it. "Norinaga studies" offered, he asserted, the means to improve upon the discipline of national literature: "If I compare Norinaga studies to national literature, then its objects are almost same as those of national literary studies; however, Norinaga did not confine himself to looking only at language or literature, but was concerned with social life in every perspective, history, law, ethics, religion, customs, policies, and so on."[65]

As this suggests, Motoori Norinaga played multiple roles in the emergent discourse Muraoka would describe variously as *shisōshi* (history of thought) and *seishinshi* (the history of ideas, after the German *geistes Geschichte*): he was at once the object of study and the source of the methodology of that study.[66] In a series of theoretical statements made in the early 1930s, Muraoka turned repeatedly to Norinaga and his kokugaku practice to explain the method and purpose of his own scholarship and the discipline he was founding. For example, in an article entitled "Nihon shisōshi no kenkyūhō ni tsuite" (On the Method for Studying Japan's Intellectual History, 1934), Muraoka stated, "As a discipline of the same nature as the philology of Europe, there is kokugaku or 'ancient learning,' which was produced independently and splendidly realized in our own country, and the one who completed it was Motoori Norinaga, whose accomplishments match those of Böckh. . . . Philology in general terms refers to the intellectual history of the classical period, and kokugaku is the intellectual history of Nara and Heian times."[67]

In addition to serving as an object of study and a methodological inspiration, Norinaga played yet a third role in Muraoka's work. Unlike Haga, Muraoka viewed Azumamaro and Mabuchi not as nascent nationalists but as "men of Confucian culture." In contrast, Norinaga was "a scholar of pure Japanese character":

> When I consider his personality in its entirety, then I think it is possible to say that he was someone who had the representative character of the historical Japanese. Of course, this is true in terms of his spirit of reverence to the emperor, love of country, and the respect he showed to the imperial family, but the other unique aspects of his character—his warmth, naturalness, cheerfulness, optimism, simple straightforwardness—each of these is a unique characteristic of our original national character.[68]

This description of the Japanese national character reiterates the attributes defined in Haga's *Kokuminsei jūron*, which had been published only a few years before. "National character" became an important theme of Muraoka's work in the 1930s and 1940s, when wrote a series of essays on this topic, including "Nihon seishin ni tsuite" (On the Japanese Spirit, 1934) and "Nihon seishinron" (A Theory of the Japanese Spirit, 1943). In his works on national character, Muraoka identified what he called "imperial centrism" (*kōshitsu chūshin shugi*) as the foundation of the Japanese nation. He praised Norinaga's criticism of Confucianism, arguing that the Confucian notion of heaven-sanctioned revolution was antithetical to "the Japanese idea of the national polity."[69]

His commitment to the concept of national character notwithstanding, Muraoka was a very different kind of scholar from Haga Yaichi. He was a dedicated positivist and undertook the kind of close textual research that characterized the German tradition of philology. Moreover, his valorization of kokugaku did not rely upon its easy recoupment as "the study of the nation." In contrast to Haga, Muraoka always characterized kokugaku as the study of the ancient period, and even in his work on national character he attempted to distinguish, sometimes unsuccessfully, his research from "the emotional quality and tendency toward mass psychology" that he asserted characterized much popular writings on this topic.[70] However, this positivism itself worked to conceal not only the ideological nature of Norinaga's work but also the ideological nature of the reinterpretation of Tokugawa ko-kugaku in which Muraoka participated. As a result of this double blind, ideas that were sustained by Norinaga's textual practices—his reconstruction of Yamato kotoba, his conception of "original cultural identity," and the claim that the authentic "Japanese" subject was the passive agent of the emperor and deities—achieved a new status. Now, they were "facts," the product, it was said, of objective, rigorous, scientific study.

It is precisely this problem that Koyasu Nobukuni identified in *Norinaga mondai to ha nani ka* (What Is the "Norinaga Problem"? 1995). His title is phrased as a response to a 1988 newspaper column by the cultural commentator Katō Shūichi. In this brief essay, Katō took up Norinaga's work in light of the then current debate over how to evaluate Heidegger's *Being and Time*, given the author's support for the Nazi Party during the period when he was writing it. According to Katō, Norinaga's work presents a similar problem: "In contrast to the rigorous positivism of his research on ancient Japanese, which marked the beginning of a new era, why did this same scholar, as Ueda Akinari demonstrated, advocate an exclusionary nationalism that was comical and crude?"[71] In response, Koyasu argues that the real "Norinaga problem" is not what Katō calls the "two aspects" of Norinaga's work, but precisely the recoupment of Norinaga's work in modernity, a recoupment that made possible the problematic distinction between his "rigorous positivism" and his "ethnocentricism." It was this distinction that made it possible in the post–World War II period for one such as Saigō Nobutsuna to criticize kokugaku as a source of a deviant nationalism, while embracing Norinaga's claim of the *Kojiki*'s "orality" as the foundation for his own exegesis of the *Kojiki*. As this suggests, Saigō dismissed the "Chinese mind" as ideology but retained the idea of Yamato kotoba, the very thing that sustained the edifice of original cultural identity.

QUESTIONING THE CANON

But the refiguring of kokugaku as philology and national ethics was not without its critics in the period before World War II. Beginning in the late 1910s, both the kokugaku of the Tokugawa period and the Meiji understanding of it began to be addressed by scholars working outside the disciplines of national literature and intellectual history. While Origuchi Shinobu and Tsuda Sōkichi shared the concern of Haga and Muraoka for issues of nationness, they rejected the "genealogy of four great men" and the understanding of kokugaku it made possible. Both men privileged what had come to be designated as marginal forms of kokugaku practice, finding in them the possibility of a national culture that resisted the categories of "national ethics" and "national character."

Origuchi Shinobu graduated from the National Literature Department of Kokugakuin University and in 1922 became a professor there, before moving to Keiō University in 1928. In 1913, Origuchi first met Yanagita Kunio, and the two together are considered to be the founders of Japanese folklore studies. However, while Yanagita's work focused on the analysis of contemporary customs and oral traditions as traces of the past, Origuchi analyzed the early Japanese texts, the *Kojiki*, the *Nihon shoki*, and especially the *Man'yōshū*. In addition, he was a well-known poet: from 1913 to 1917, he was active in the Araragi poetry group, which sought to revive the waka form as a mode of poetic expression, and he wrote poetry throughout his life under the name Chōkū.

Origuchi directly addressed the modern appropriation of kokugaku in three articles. The first of these appeared in the *Kokugakuin zasshi*, a journal published by Kokugakuin University, in 1920. Origuchi's purpose is hinted at in his title, "Iyaku kokugaku hitori annai: Kōno Seizō sokka ni sasagu" (One Man's Guide to a Different Kokugaku: An Offering to Kōno Seizō). Kōno Seizō (1882–1963), at the time a professor of Kokugakuin and one of the editors of *Kokugakuin zasshi*, was an enthusiastic contributor to the discourse on national ethics. In 1917 he had published *Kokumin dōtoku shiron* (A Historical Theory of National Ethics), in which he argued that the foundation for the national character of the Japanese was reverence toward the deities and respect for ancestors. For several years preceding the appearance of this work, Kōno had been lecturing on national ethics to classes at Kokugakuin.[72] Origuchi returned to problem of kokugaku almost two decades later in two essays, "Kokugaku to ha nani ka" (What Is Kokugaku? 1937) and "Kokugaku to kokubungaku to" (Kokugaku and National Literature, 1937). Both addressed the relationship of kokugaku and national literature and Haga Yaichi's role in defining this relation.

Organizing all three works is an awareness of the context in which the discipline of national literature and the discourse of national ethics had taken form. Writing in 1937, Origuchi quoted Yano Harumichi's famous statement that "the desire to return to the age of Kashiwara" had ended as "an impossible dream" and suggested that the two decades of the Meiji period through which he lived must have been all but unendurable for Yano: "The establishment of the Office of Shinto Worship in the first year of Meiji and the policy of 'the union of worship and rule' were purely rhetorical gestures. Until the establishment of Kokugakuin, every dream ended as a dream. For those who thought they had accomplished 'the return to the imperial way,' it must have been bitterly disappointing to find that they were chasing nothing more than a fantasy." [73]

But according to Origuchi, if Yano had cursed the "rising tide of Western culture," there were others who embraced it. He identified Haga Yaichi and the others who established the National Literature Department of Tokyo Imperial University as among "those who had perceived the trend of the Meiji government." But the "national literature" they created from this perspective was not "the literature of the country of Japan" but "a history of literature based upon the method of intellectual history." [74] According to Origuchi, while national literature takes as its objects many of the same things as kokugaku, they are complete different kinds of practice, and "of those who study the literature of our country today, without exception everyone of them is a scholar of national literature, and there is not a single student of kokugaku." [75]

It is this opaque reference to the politicized beginnings of national literature that frames Origuchi's attempt to distinguish between kokugaku and national literature in the two essays from the 1930s. He stated clearly, "As for our image of what a kokugaku scholar is, we cannot find that in Mabuchi and Norinaga. Rather, it comes later. It developed within our study of national literature." [76] In particular, Origuchi criticized the characterization that kokugaku was "exclusionary." He noted that there were many kokugaku scholars who were not critical of Chinese thought and even those, like Norinaga, who were, "borrowed the concepts of Confucianism." Criticized as well was the genealogy of "four great men" that took form within national literature. Rejecting the theme of development that underlies this genealogy, Origuchi asserted that the work of Mabuchi and Norinaga was superior to that of Atsutane, because "their method was based upon literature" and "their theory moved toward literary production." Moreover, he attacked the idea that kokugaku had a "stable essence" in this period that could be recouped via genealogy and identified as important those considered as "departures from the main line" (*bōkei*), such as Ueda Akinari, Murata Harumi, and others. [77]

The same themes are expressed in "Iyaku kokugaku hitori annai," but in contrast to the restrained tone that orders the later two later works, the earlier essay is an overt attack on the discourse of national ethics and the understanding of kokugaku upon which it was founded. The work opens with a call to Kōno to become "a practitioner of kokugaku in its true sense," and it takes the form of a delineation of the failures of the "new kokugaku scholars" of Meiji and Taisho.[78] In a clear reference to Yano's lament on the "impossible dream," Origuchi criticized the attempts in the first years after the Restoration to achieve the "return to Kashiwara" through government, institutions, or policy: this was as a "temporal mistake," a desire to reverse the workings of history. Rejected as well were the efforts of the Meiji nativists to "fix" the "floating" field of Tokugawa kokugaku. According to Origuchi, "They were able to construct the essence of kokugaku in terms of the 'four great men' alone and those around them. But once that has been done, there is no question remaining for our generation, and so there is nothing so meaningless as what we are doing."[79] Origuchi protested not only the creation of the canon but also its use to transform kokugaku into a discourse on national ethics:

> There is the opinion that all of the processes that make up the historical life of the Japanese people can be sacrificed for an ethical viewpoint. This is the same as forgetting to deal with each thing individually and [instead] just falling into utilitarianism. It may seem that there is nothing wrong with focusing on whether or not there is an ethical viewpoint in order to distinguish between the literary schools of wagaku and the pioneers of kokugaku. But is it really all right to dismiss the work of those like Akinari . . . that is of a different nature?[80]

In this way, by alluding to Haga's distinction between wagaku and kokugaku, Origuchi questioned whether meaningful aspects of kokugaku had not been silenced in order to produce the discourse of national ethics.

Against this kind of "new kokugaku," Origuchi posed his own version of "true kokugaku." He argued that the restoration of the past is possible, but it can be achieved only on the level of the psyche (*seishin*). He called upon modern kokugaku scholars to "build upon" the achievements of their Tokugawa predecessors and produce a "history of literature and culture" ordered not by the necessities of modernity but by the "real lives of the ancient people." This would allow, he argued, for a restoration of the "spirit" of the archaic period. In Origuchi's words, "The realization through literature of the Kashiwara Palace would infuse strength and authenticity into the inner lives of our people."[81] In relation to this conception of the task of historical study, it was the work, not of Norinaga and Atsutane, but of Akinari and others such as Murata Harumi and Tachibana Akemi, writers of fiction and poetry, that was identified as important. In them, Origuchi found a reflection of his own project of reconstructing the worldview of the ancient Japanese people. In works such as the novel *Shisha no sho* (The Book of the Dead, 1939), Origuchi tried to imagine the psychological world of the ancient Japanese, an attempt that recalls Akinari's *Harusame monogatari*.

A very different critique of the "genealogy of four great men" orients the work of the historian Tsuda Sōkichi (1873–1961), who was a contemporary of Origuchi. Tsuda differs from the other figures examined in this chapter in that he had no nativist ties. A graduate of Tokyo Senmon Gakkō (later Waseda University) of which he became a professor in 1919, he conducted research on Korean and Manchurian topics for more than ten years as a member of the research division of the South Manchuria Railway under the direction of Shiratori Kurakichi, one of the pioneers of *Tōyō shigaku* (oriental history) in Japan. Founded as a discipline institutionally distinct from national history, Tōyō shigaku had its own ideological agenda, the production of China as "Japan's Orient," as Stefan Tanaka has put it.[82] But another important influence on Tsuda's work was the histories of civilization produced by nonacademic historians such as Taguchi Ukichi, who had championed Kume Kunitake, and Yamaji Aizan, whose works contained a strong element of political critique and activism.[83] When Tsuda turned in the decade of the 1910s to examine kokugaku, he put forth an analysis that was a thorough and explicit rejection of the interpretations that emanated from national literature and intellectual history.

Tsuda's most explicit examination of kokugaku is found in *Bungaku ni arawaretaru waga kokumin no shisō* (Studies in the Thought of Our People as Expressed in Literature, 1916–1921). This massive five-volume work attempted to trace the transformation of "the thought of our people" from the ancient period through the nineteenth century. Like Haga, Muraoka, and Origuchi, Tsuda too was intensely interested in issues of nationness. As he explained the purpose of his work, "As our country tries to establish itself as a nation-state before the world, a strong sense of unity is the most important thing. It was only when we were confronted with the problem of how to deal with the foreign countries that the nation began, as we keenly felt our country to be one nation."[84] From this perspective of Japanese national identity as new, fragile, and undefined, Tsuda explored Japanese literature with the aim of finding ideas, practices, and strategies that could become the foundation of a sense of nationness that emanated not downward from the political authorities but from within civil society. Thus, for Tsuda, the designation of *kokuminteki* (national) was a function of being "public" (*kōkyōteki*), "popular" (*minshūteki*), "of the commoner classes" (*heiminteki*), and "of the citizens" (*kōminteki*).

Waga kokumin no shisō has been called a "harsh and bitter critique of Japanese culture" and a discourse of "negation."[85] As these characterizations suggest, Tsuda's review of Japanese literature had little in common with the celebration of Japanese uniqueness that oriented the discourse of national ethics. In volume 1, which analyzed texts from the eighth through the twelfth centuries including the *Kojiki*, *Nihon shoki*, and *Man'yōshū*, Tsuda concluded that "the nature [of this literature] was aristocratic and there was nothing "national" [*kokuminteki*] in it."[86] Volume 2, on "the period of the warrior literature," explored works from the thirteenth through the sixteenth centuries. Tsuda characterized "warrior culture" as "narrow and rigid" and asserted that "certainly there is nothing within it that could be called public, nor is there anything like national sentiment."[87] The title of the last three volumes, *Heimin bungaku no jidai* (The Period of Commoner Literature), seems to imply that in this period Tsuda found the beginnings of the "nationness" he sought, but in fact his overall perspective is pessimistic. On cultural productions such as haikai poetry and gesaku fiction, Tsuda wrote that such works "were popular, but on the whole the cultivators who are the foundation of national life were excluded from them," and so, "rather than showing the development of national life directly as a whole, they tended to be nothing more than a celebration of urban life."[88]

It was in the context of delineating the limitations of the cultural productions of this period that Tsuda turned to explore the work of the kokugaku scholars. After reviewing the work of Norinaga and Mabuchi, he rejected outright the notion that their scholarship represented in any sense a recovery of the reality of archaic Japan. Instead, according Tsuda, while they tried to establish "the way of Japan" by criticizing Confucianism, their work never succeeded in transcending that discourse. Tsuda asserted that, in spite of the anti-Confucian rhetoric Norinaga and the others employed, their philological method as well as many of their characterizations of ancient Japanese society were borrowed outright from Sorai's "ancient words" school. The concept of the "ancient way," the notion of an "original" human nature, the ideal of "return to antiquity" were, Tsuda insisted, mere adaptations of ideas that circulated within the Sorai school. Thus he characterized the "knowledge" of ancient Japan produced by Norinaga and Mabuchi as of little value for understanding the reality of the ancient people. Throughout *Waga kokumin no shisō*, Tsuda made repeated reference to the reliance of Japanese intellectuals on "Chinese thought" (*Shina shisō*) and suggested that this had been a barrier to the development of a true national culture. For example, in volume 1, Tsuda criticized such *Man'yōshū* poets as Yamanoue no Okura for writing "under the influence of Chinese thought." In contrast, in volume 2, there is a rare moment of affirmation when Tsuda praised warrior codes of honor as indigenous in nature and thus an appropriate "source of pride." [89]

This view that kokugaku was a failed attempt to define Japaneseness orders Tsuda's analysis. He argued that in the Tokugawa period kokugaku was purely an intellectual enterprise that lacked the emotional power to move the people and give rise to a "real patriotism." In Tsuda's words, kokugaku "did nothing more than wantonly call up an empty national pride." [90] He characterized it not as presciently "modern" and "scientific" but as a purely feudal ideology, something that had to be overcome in order for a true sense of nationness to emerge: "This was the Tokugawa period and so [the koku-gaku scholars], without any justification, explained the feudal system and the class system as the proper and best system and rejected the notion of human equality. This was the world of an autocratic government, and so they argued that government is the duty of the ruler who is above and has nothing to do with the people." [91] Tsuda argued that by celebrating this "feudal" conception of the relationship between ruler and subject as authentically "Japanese," kokugaku had in fact hindered the formation of "true" nationalism.

In the 1910s and 1920s as he was writing *Waga kokumin no shisō*, Tsuda was also involved in writing a series of works analyzing the *Kojiki* and the *Nihon shoki*, including *Shindaishi no atarashii kenkyū* (New Research in the History of the Divine Age, 1913), *Kojiki oyobi Nihon shoki no shinkenkyū* (New Research on the *Kojiki* and *Nihon shoki*, 1919), and *Kojiki oyobi Nihon shoki no kenkyū* (Research on the *Kojiki* and *Nihon shoki*, 1924). In these works as well as in *Waga kokumin no shisō*, he argued that it was only the imperial institution — correctly understood — that could serve as a foundation for Japanese nationness, because it was the only cultural form that was both authentically Japanese and an object of popular sentiment throughout history. According to Tsuda, "The imperial institution is internal to our sense of nation, the center of our racial unity, and the nucleus of the national union. . . . This is the fundamental reason why the imperial line has continued. But it is completely different from the tendency of Chinese thought that viewed the emperor and people by means of oppositions such as 'heaven' and 'earth.'"[92] As this passage suggests, Tsuda was by no means a critic of emperor-based theories of nationness, but he wanted to render the imperial institution "public" and "popular," qualities that had defined it, he argued, in the ancient period.

Like Haga, Muraoka, and Origuchi before him, Tsuda made the Tokugawa discourse the site in which to discover the origins of his own analysis, which he characterized as "rational," "critical," and "modern." In his work on the ancient texts, Tsuda identified as the central flaw of Norinaga's exegesis his insistence that the story of the Divine Age recorded in the *Kojiki* is of divine origin and must be accepted in its entirety as fact. In contrast, Tsuda characterized the *Kojiki* text as the product of the court officials in later ages, who "wrote as though certain things had been established by the command of the imperial ancestral deities."[93] The notion that the *Kojiki* was the product of the imperial court seeking to legitimate its own rule had been suggested by Akinari and is now the accepted explanation for the production of the mythohistory, but in the pre–World War II period it struck at the heart of the emperor-centered nationalism. Tsuda insisted, however, that the recognition of the ideological nature of the *Kojiki* and *Nihon shoki* texts must be the starting point for the recovery of the popular emperor-subject relation. Within the context of this project, Mitsue, Akinari, and Moribe were privileged as men of critical insight—and the forerunners of Tsuda's own work:

> As for how to deal with the history of the Divine Age, which contains many irrational elements, there were various views even in this age, but the most common theory was that it should not be regarded as factual. In general terms, there were those who saw it as a metaphorical representation of the traces of the archaic age, such as Akinari in *Kamiyo monogatari*. . . . And there is the theory that [the history] was narrated as legend within which irrational elements had come to be inserted. In both cases, the commentators viewed the deities as real people of the archaic age and so tried to construct a rational interpretation. . . . However, there are also those who see it completely as the creation of a later age, such as Fujitani Mitsue in *Kojiki tomoshibi* and *Kitabe zuihitsu* and Yamagata Bantō in *Yume no shiro*. . . . Moribe's analysis of the [narrative] and his statement that it tells of the unseen deities as though they were men and that allegories, children's stories, and folk stories of the

common people were included within it was a very unusual insight for that time.[94]

Thus, in contrast to Haga who had identified Akinari, Mitsue, and Moribe as insufficiently "national" to be considered practitioners of kokugaku, Tsuda privileged them as evidence of a "rational" historical analysis of the ancient texts. And he argued that it was precisely this kind of practice that would allow for the recovery of an emperor-subject relation that by transcending ideology could serve as a basis for a new more authentic national culture. By 1940, however, Tsuda's attempt to reconceptualize the imperial system through the analysis of the ancient texts had become impossible. In that year, both Tsuda and his publisher, Iwanami Shigeo, were arrested and charged with "infringing upon the dignity of the imperial household." Found guilty, both received two-year suspended sentences.[95]

BEYOND THE GENEALOGIES OF MODERNITY

My examination of the various ways in which kokugaku was appropriated from the 1890s onward, first within the disciplines of national literature and intellectual history and then from outside them, is not intended to valorize one use over another or to argue that Origuchi's and Tsuda's interpretations of kokugaku were somehow closer to the Tokugawa reality than those of Haga and Muraoka. Just as the label philology reflected the exigencies of the Meiji period and not the practice of kokugaku in the early modern era, so too is the antimodernism that infused Origuchi's work wholly his own and not Akinari's. Similarly, Tsuda's attempt to situate Mitsue and Moribe as methodological precursors of his own "rational" historical practice, like Muraoka's use of Norinaga, ignored both the complexity of their textual strategies and the visions of Japan that they sustained. Rather, my goal was to reveal the way in which kokugaku discourse, a heterogeneous field of methods, motives, and ideas, was transformed into a set of competing genealogies, each with its own claim to authenticity, each authorized by a different notion of what Japan was or should be. The modern authors I have examined all operated in the same way, by extracting certain elements of the Tokugawa discourse and organizing them in order to create a "history" for their own projects so that they appeared to be not subjective enterprises rooted in the necessities of the particular political moment, but somehow transcendent, objective, and normative.

Haga and Muraoka used the work of Norinaga to demonstrate that the vision of the Japanese nation they embraced was not the product of the post-1868 context but the culmination of a tradition of shared and unique cultural values that stretched back into time immemorial. At the same time, their valorization of Norinaga's method as "scientific" sustained their concept of the nation in another way: it allowed them to reject the notion that Japan's modernity — its status as a "civilized" society — derived in any way from Western models. The indigenous "rational" philologic practices they "found" in Norinaga became proof of Japan's indigenous modernity. In contrast, Origuchi and Tsuda rejected the visions of nationness that had taken form in the late Meiji period. For Origuchi, it was spiritually empty, a shallow shell incapable of sustaining a vital national culture. Tsuda, too, criticized the artifical sense of nation that had taken form in the Meiji period. It was founded on concepts of Japaneseness that were not authentically popular but rather were merely flawed remnants of feudal culture masquerading as modern. But like those they criticized, both Origuchi and Tsuda looked to kokugaku discourse. Rejecting the genealogy of "great men," they constructed another genealogy and offered it up as proof that alternative and more valid concepts of nationness were available. They found in kokugaku the possibility of another national past and used it to imagine a different present.

Conclusion

Imagined Japan(s)

In this work, I set out to explore the kokugaku discourse of the late eighteenth and early nineteenth centuries with the aim of rethinking both its meaning for Tokugawa society and its relationship with modern conceptions of national identity in Japan. As a strategy to distance myself from the modern narratives that identify kokugaku as a point of origin for Japanese nationness, I abandoned the genealogy and canon created by modern scholarship and explored the discourse as a set of contesting interpretations of a seminal text, the Divine Age narrative that is inscribed in the *Kojiki* and the *Nihon shoki*. The works of the kokugaku scholars I examined—Motoori Norinaga, Ueda Akinari, Fujitani Mitsue, and Tachibana Moribe—represent disparate and, with the exception of that of Norinaga, discontinuous forms of kokugaku that played no great role in the major histories of nationalism. My examination of kokugaku from this perspective revealed the emergence in late Tokugawa period of a complex and contentious discourse on the nature of Japan. By interrogating language, textuality, and history, the kokugaku scholars made the early Japanese texts the means to articulate new forms of community that contested the social and political order of their time. Against divisions such as status, regional affinities, and existing collectivities such as domains, towns, and villages, they began to make "Japan" the source of individual and cultural identity.

In imagining Japan, the kokugaku scholars created a new vocabulary and a new set of epistemological strategies that engaged the social and political divides of late Tokugawa society. First among these strategies was the identification of language as the primary "bearer of identity and difference," to borrow the words of Michel Foucault.[1] While earlier readers of the mythohistories had read the early Japan texts as the exemplification of universal Confucian and Buddhist principles, Norinaga attached new value and meaning to the language of the *Kojiki*. He argued that it was written to preserve the original language of Japan, Yamato kotoba, and that understanding this language was the means to know and recover modes of perception and social relations that were authentically and uniquely Japanese.

Akinari, Mitsue, and Moribe did not share Norinaga's faith that the original transmissions were inscribed intact within the ancient texts, but they too believed that the language of the texts signified something important about the formation of Japan as a community in the distant past. For Akinari, the ruptures and inconsistencies of the language of the texts revealed the irreversible loss of some primal identity and the rise of politically constituted forms of community in which those with power began to write history and thereby create social memory. In contrast, Mitsue argued that the language of the *Kojiki* revealed a special linguistic regime that—when successfully negotiated—allowed social relations shaped by empathy to take form, producing community. Like Norinaga, Moribe argued that "Japan" was the product of a moment outside historical time, but he did this by distinguishing between the "narrating words" of the mythohistories and the cosmology they described. Knowledge of an original and authentic Japanese identity was thus possible through exegesis.

As these kokugaku scholars sought to analyze the "difference" of the language of the ancient Japanese texts by reference to Chinese, they were also drawn into a discussion of the origin and nature of cultural difference—with the result that a new assumption of difference between rather than similitude across cultures took form. For Norinaga, of course, Yamato kotoba itself signified the regime of difference that had once existed in ancient Japan, so that "Japan" took form as an expression of an innate Japaneseness. Moreover, this regime of difference was always envisioned as hierarchical in nature: the Divine Age narrative supposedly signaled the superiority of Japan and its people. No other kokugaku scholars would completely accept Norinaga's conception of original cultural identity, but no one fully escaped it either. Moribe postulated the possibility of incorporation of cultural others into Japan—but it required the forging of a genealogical link with someone really "Japanese." Similarly, Moribe viewed Confucianism, Buddhism, and knowledge from the "West" as merely useful supplements that did not call into question the superiority of Japanese practices. Mitsue, in trying to explain the use of poetic language in Japan in contrast to Buddhism in India and Confucianism in China, took refuge in a nascent conception of "Japanese character" as something shaped by geopolitical factors. Only Akinari resisted easy reference to the idea of original cultural difference, but he characterized the response of the ancient Japanese to ideas that were "Chinese" as confusion and bewilderment, implying that a sense of alienness necessarily accompanied them.

The evocation of cultural difference was implicated in another strategy of the kokugaku scholars, the attempt to rethink the relationship between community and political power. Norinaga made "China" the antithesis of "Japan" and reduced the former to a set of known cultural qualities: it was a group of disparate individuals held together by force and coercion on the part of powerful leaders acting out of self-interest. In his view, the Confucian ethics were not cosmically authorized principles but human inventions designed to legitimate certain forms of political authority. Imagining "Japan" as the negation of "China," Norinaga portrayed ancient Japan as a natural community in which ruler and ruled were joined by the awe and reverence they felt for the ancestral deities who had created them and their land. Cosmology functioned in Tachibana Moribe's discussion of community, as well. Moribe envisioned Japan as the product of the rituals performed by the Japanese people and the emperor. Working together as one "body," they protected and sustained Japan.

Like Norinaga and Moribe, Akinari too made the ancient texts the means to explore the relationship between what were termed the "public" and "private" realms. However, while Norinaga attempted to prove that the *Kojiki* was not the product of any single subject but a transparent representation of a once collective reality, Akinari asserted that all of the ancient texts were inherently political. They were inscribed by human authors who were already part of a politically constituted community. In contrast to Norinaga, who once characterized human subjects as "puppets" of the deities, Akinari viewed them as complex agents in history and tried to uncover how their motives, ideas, and ambitions had been shaped by political forces. Thus, in reading the ancient texts, his intent was to provide a glimpse into what lay beneath the surface narratives, the conflicts and struggles that "orthodox" histories left unrecorded. It was from this perspective that Akinari rejected Norinaga's conception of Japan as a natural community and worked instead to deconstruct the visions of the social put forth in official histories.

Writing in the first two decades of the nineteenth century, Fujitani Mitsue too began by recognizing the political nature of the *Kojiki*. Like Akinari, he began by historicizing the *Kojiki* and making it the product of a human author. However, his work shares something with that of Norinaga as well.

Beginning from a perspective of cultural identity, Mitsue argued that the language of the *Kojiki* was inherently different from that of the Chinese classics. But while Norinaga viewed the language of the *Kojiki* as capable of transparently representing the reality of the Divine Age, Mitsue argued that it revealed the workings of the special kind of linguistic practice he called tōgo. Through metaphor, allegory, and other tropes, a speaker in a public setting was able to convey to another the primal desires and emotions that conflicted with social norms. As this suggests, in Mitsue's work, the subject—as well as the notions of "public" and "private"—acquired a new complexity. Rather than using the "public" to signify external relations of power and situating the "private" as a site outside the public realm, Mitsue argued that for community to take form it was necessary for every subject to internalize a set of social norms, even though he continued to "desire" in ways that conflicted with those norms. Reading the *Kojiki* in light of this theory of language, Mitsue asserted that Japan was produced as ancient rulers skillfully used language to convey their thoughts, desires, and intentions to those beneath him. As a result, the "establishment of the country" occurred as relations of empathy took form throughout society.

The work of Norinaga, Akinari, Mitsue, and Moribe was thus ordered by a concern for interrogating political authority and for recovering community as something distinct from political power and from the Confucian ideology of virtue used to legitimate it in the Tokugawa period. In explaining the nature of Japan, Norinaga idealized emotional responsiveness as the defining feature of Japanese, Akinari called for the writing of stories that contested official representations of community, Mitsue sought to infuse empathy into relations of power, and Moribe sublimated politics to ritual and ethics to cosmology. The kokugaku critique of Confucian explanations of political authority necessarily entailed the creation of a new political vocabulary. A case in point is the rendering of the emperor as a privileged signifier of Japanese cultural identity. Of course, what precisely the emperor meant in relation to Japan was a subject of great debate. While Norinaga made him an emblem of submission to the deities, Mitsue valorized his creation of community through language, and Moribe transformed him into a performer of rites. But all agreed that the emperor had a central role to play in constituting and maintaining Japan. Terms such as *kami* (deity), *sumeramikuni* (imperial land), *kamiyo* (divine age), and *inishie* (the ancient period) have a similar status: all were imbued with new meaning as they became implicated in attempts to define a specifically Japanese community.

THE "COLONIZED" IMAGINATION AND
JAPANESE NATIONNESS

The kokugaku scholars' celebration of language as a site of cultural identity, their articulation of new privileged signifiers of collective cohesion, and their delineation of a new opposition between "Japanese" selves and cultural others all point to an emerging sense of something that seems like nationness in late eighteenth- and early nineteenth-century Japan. But while Norinaga, Akinari, and the others overtly questioned and perhaps thereby began to subvert the social divisions sustained by the Tokugawa political system, they did not conceive of a new political formation that would embody or represent "Japan." Indeed, their concern was to make community something separate from and more authentic than the social that was the product of Tokugawa politics. To preserve and problematize the distinction between late Tokugawa conceptions of Japan and that created by the modern nation-state, I want to continue to reject the use of the term "nationalism" and to adopt Prasenjit Duara's use of "culturalism" to describe the kokugaku discourse on Japanese community that emerged in the late eighteenth century. Duara adapted this term from Joseph Levenson's usage in order to avoid the teleological assumption that premodern conceptions of identity "develop into" modern national identities, while at the same time avoiding the presumption of a radical break of the kind posed by Benedict Anderson and Ernest Gellner, who have argued that the creation of cultural/political identities was a purely modern phenomenon.[2]

The relationship between early modern Japanese culturalism and the nationalism that took form in the late nineteenth century was the topic of the final chapter of this work, in which I explored how kokugaku became implicated in efforts to forge new modern conceptions of nationness within the disciplines of national literature and intellectual history, sites of ideological production for the Meiji state. As we have seen, modern scholars such as Konakamura Kiyonori, Haga Yaichi, and Muraoka Tsunetsugu selected, reorganized, and adapted aspects of kokugaku practice to sustain new conceptions of national character and national culture, a process that necessarily involved attempts to silence concepts of "Japan" that had the potential to challenge the modern vision of the nationness. Moreover, the referencing of early modern kokugaku allowed modern scholars to conceal the historical moment that gave rise to the nation and its political exigencies. In other words, the rise of the Meiji state was portrayed as the result of nationalism, rather than nationalism as the product of the nation-state.

My work then has been a "case study" of how a self-consciously modern nationalism was constructed by deploying existing culturalist notions of community. The particularity of the Japanese case, however, allows reflection on another issue of nationness. In his work *The Nation and Its Fragments*, Partha Chatterjee points to an important aporia that has characterized the theoretical discussion of the formation of modern national cultures. According to Chatterjee, in the work of Anderson and others, the "nation" has been reduced to a set of "modular forms" produced in the West that modernizing elites within the countries of Asia and Africa have attempted to apply, imitate, or in Chatterjee's term, "consume." The result, charges Chatterjee, is the postulation that in the "non-West" even the ability to "imagine" nationness has been "colonized."[3] To be sure, Chatterjee's discussion relies on a problematic reliance on a seemingly homogenous "West," ignoring the complex historical dimensions of the production of "nationness" in European and North American societies, but he forces us to ask whether the "nation" is in its essence a Western concept that has merely been imitated, with greater or lesser degrees of success, by non-Western societies.

It was the desire to create a Japanese nationalism that was on par with but not derived from that of the Western nation-states that motivated the production of the "new kokugaku" of the Meiji period — hence Haga Yaichi's painstaking efforts to construct a narrative of the rise of national consciousness stretching back to antiquity but culminating in the "philologic" practice of Norinaga, a narrative that paralleled but never intersected with those of Western nationalisms. Situated within this narrative, Norinaga's work became presciently scientific, academic, and modern — but still distinctly Japanese. Ultimately, the aim of placing Japan within a universal history of the rise of nation-states oriented Meiji scholarship, even as nationalist concerns required scholars to again and again establish Japan's "difference" vis-à-vis the cultures of the West through reference to the uniqueness of its imperial institution, the superior character of its people, and the distinctiveness of its cultural practices.

Was the modern imagining of the nation in Japan "colonized"? Yes, but never completely. It was precisely the gap between "culturalism" and "nationalism" that enabled the critical perspective of figures such as Origuchi Shinobu and Tsuda Sōkichi, who attempted to "rethink" the nation in the early part of the twentieth century. This same gap has implications for contemporary scholars of Japan. The recovery of the marginalized kokugaku and its uses within modernity point to the need to continue to reassess the intellectual genealogies that have been created within Japanese modernity. If we can identify the exigencies that have created these genealogies, we can begin to question them, to ask what has been silenced, what has been legitimated, and to what end.

Appendix

"Reading" the Kojiki

THE "ORIGINAL" KOJIKI (712)

天地初發之時。於高天原成神名、天之御中主神。次高御産巣日神。次神産
巣日。此三柱神者、並独神成坐而、隠身也。次國稚如浮脂而、久羅下那洲多
陀用幣流之時、如葦牙因萌騰之物而成神名、宇麻志阿斯訶備比古遅神。次天
之常立神。此二柱神亦、独神成坐而、隠身也。上件五柱神者、別天神。

KAN'EIBAN KOJIKI (1644)

Ametsuchi no hajimete hirakuru toki, Takamanohara ni nariizuru kami wo Ama
no Minakanushi no kami to mōsu. Tsugi ni Takamimusubi no kami. Tsugi ni
Kamimimusubi no kami. Kono mihashira no kami ha narabi ni hitori kamu
narimashite, mi wo kakushimasu. Tsugi ni kuni wakakushite ukaberu haragomori no
kurage nasu tadayoheru toki ni, ashikabi no gotoshi kizashi noboru mono
ni yotte, nariizuru kami wo Umashi-ashikabi-hikoji no kami to mōsu. Tsugi ni Ama
no Tokotachi no kami. Kono futahashira no kami tarashi mata hitori kamu to
narimashite mi wo kakushitamaeri.

WATARAI NOBUYOSHI, GŌTŌ KOJIKI (1687)

Ametsuchi hajimete hirakuru toki, Takamanohara ni naru kami no mina ha, Ame
no Minakanushi no kami. Tsugi ni Takamimusubi no kami. Tsugi ni, Kamumimusubi no kami. Kono mihashira no kami ha narabi ni hitori kami narimashite,
mi wo kakushimasu. Tsugi ni kuni ishiku ukaberu abura no gotoku ni shite kurage
nasu tadayoheru toki ni, ashikabi no gotoku kizashi noboru mono ni yorite
naru kami no mina ha Umashi-ashikabi-hikoji no kami. Tsugi ni Ame no Tokotachi
no kami. Kono futahashira no kami mo mata hitori kami to narimashite, mi wo
kakushimasu.

KADA AZUMAMARO, HITTEN KOJIKI (1724)

Ametsuchi *hajimete wakareshi toki*, Takamanohara ni *naru kami no mina wa*, Ame no Minakanushi no kami to nazukemōsu. Tsugi ni Takamimusubi no kami. Tsugi ni Kamumimusubi no kami. Kono mihashira no kami ha *mina hitori kami to narimashite, mi wo kakushitamau*. Koko ni kuni ishiku ukaberu abura no gotoku ni shite, kurage nasu tadayoeru toki ashikabi no gotoku kizashi noboru mono ni yorite *naru kami no mina ha*, Umashi-ashikabi-hikoji no kami. Tsugi ni Ame no Tokotachi no kami. Kono futahashira no kami mo *narabi ni mata hitorikami to narimashite, mi wo kakushitamau*. Kami no kudan no itsuhashira no kami ha *sunawachi*, amatsukami nari.

KAMO NO MABUCHI, KANAGAKI KOJIKI (1765)

Ametsuchi *no hajimete hirakuru toki*, Takamanohara ni *narizuru kami no mina ha*, Ame no Minakanushi no kami. Tsugi ni Takamimusubi no kami. Tsugi ni Kami-musubi no kami. Kono mihashira no kami ha, *narabi ni hitori kami narimashite, mi kakurimashinu*. Tsugi ni kuni ishiku, ukaberu abura nashite kurage nasu tada-yoheru toki ni, ashikabi nasu kizashi noboru moni ni yorite *narizuru kami no mina ha*, Umashi-ashikabi-hikoji no kami. Tsugi ni Ame no Tokotachi no kami. Kono futahashira no kami mo *hitorigami narimashite, mikakurimashinu*. Kami no kudari no itsuhashira no kami ha kotogoto ni amatsukami nari.

TAYASU MUNETAKA, KOJIKI SHŌSETSU (C.1760S)

Ametsuchi *hajimete hirakeshi toki*, Taka-amabara ni *naru kami no mina ha*, Ame no Minakanushi no ōmikami. Tsugi ni Takamimusubi no ōmikami. Tsugi ni Kami-musubi no ōmikami. Kono mihashira no ōmikami ha *narabi ni hitori kami to narimashite, mi wo kakushimashiki*. Tsugi ni kuni ishiku ukaberu abura no goto *nareba*, kurage nasu tadayoheru toki, ashikabi no goto kizashi noboru mono ni yorite *narimaseru ōmikami no mina ha*, Umashi-ashikabi-hikoji no ōmikami. Tsugi ni Ame no Tokotachi no ōmikami. Kono futahashira no kami mo *hitorigami narimashite, mi wo kakushimashiki*. Kami no kudari no itsuhashira no ōmikami ha *wakite* amagami nari.

MOTOORI NORINAGA, *KOJIKIDEN* (1790)

Ametsuchi *hajime no toki*, Takamanohara ni *narimaseru kami no mina ha, Ame no Minakanushi no kami*. Tsugi ni Takamimusubi no kami. Tsugi ni Kamimusubi no kami. Kono mibashira no kami ha *mina hitori gami narimashite, mimi wo kakushitamaiki*. Tsugi ni kuni *wakaku ukiabura no gotoku ni shite*, kuragenasu tadayoheru toki ni, ashikabi no goto moeagaru mono ni yorite *narimaseru kami no mina ha, Umashi-ashikabi-hikoji no kami*. Tsugi ni Ame no Tokotachi no kami. Kono futabashira no kami mo *hitorigami narimashite, mimi wo kakushitamaiki*. Kami no kudari itsubashira no kami ha koto amatsukami.

TACHIBANA MORIBE, *BUNSHŌ SENKAKU* (1832)

Ametsuchi no hajime no toki ni Takamanohara ni, kami narimashiki. Sono narimaseru kami no mina ha, Ame no Minakanushi no kami. Tsugi ni narimaseru kami no mina ha, Takamimusubi no kami. Tsugi ni narimaseru kami no mina ha, Kamimusubi no kami. Sono mihashira no kami ha, onomo onomo hitorikami narimashite, mimi wo kakushimashiki.

Notes

ABBREVIATIONS

FMS   Fujitani, Mitsue. *Fujitani Mitsue shū*. 5 vols. Kokumin Seishin Bunka Kenkyūjo, 1936–1940.

FMZS   Fujitani, Mitsue. *Fujitani Mitsue zenshū*. Edited by Miyake Kiyoshi. 8 vols. Kyoto: Shibunkaku, 1979–1993.

HYS   Haga, Ya'ichi. *Haga Yaichi senshū*. Edited by Haga Ya'ichi Senshū Iinkai. 7 vols. Kokugakuin Daigaku, 1982–1992.

KMZ   Kamo, Mabuchi. *Kamo no Mabuchi zenshū*. Zoku Gunsho Ruijū Kansei Kai, 1977–1992.

MNZ   Motoori, Norinaga. *Motoori Norinaga zenshū*. Edited by Ōno Susumu and Ōkubo Tadashi. 22 vols. Chikuma Shobō, 1968–1975.

OSZ   Origuchi, Shinobu. *Origuchi Shinobu zenshū*. 38 vols. Chūō Kōronsha, 1965–1968.

TMZ   Tachibana, Moribe. *Tachibana Moribe zenshū (Shintei)*. Edited by Tachibana Jun'ichi. 13 vols. 1930. Reprint. Tōkyō Bijutsu, 1967.

TSZ   Tsuda, Sōkichi. *Tsuda Sōkichi zenshū*. 33 vols. Iwanami Shoten, 1963–1989.

UAZ   Ueda, Akinari. *Ueda Akinari zenshū*. Edited by Hino Tatsuo et al. 12 vols. Chūō Kōronsha, 1990.

INTRODUCTION

1   The question of what to call this discourse has been an issue since the late eighteenth century. Motoori Norinaga, for example, resisted the use of the term *kokugaku* and insisted that his work should simply be termed *gaku* (learning) and that work in the Confucian mode should be demarcated as a subcategory within this larger field as "Chinese learning" (*kangaku*). At the same time, the term *wagaku* continued to be used by many. The problem of how to translate the term *kokugaku*, which eventually gained acceptance, continues to be a problem for those who write in English. Traditional translations such as "national learning" and

"national studies" imply continuity between the kokugaku visions of Japan and the modern Japanese nationalism. And the term "nativism," which Harry (H. D.) Harootunian and Peter Nosco (following Harootunian) adopt, suggests that an opposition between Japan and the foreign other that organized Norinaga's work is characteristic of the discourse as a whole. With no other translation to offer, in this work I use the Japanese term. Throughout this work, I give Japanese names in the Japanese fashion, surname first. I also follow the Japanese convention of referring to noted scholars by their personal names in subsequent references.

2 Cornelius Castoriadus, *The Imaginary Institution of Society* (Cambridge, Mass.: MIT Press, 1987).

3 Etienne Balibar, "The Nation Form: History and Ideology," in *Becoming National: A Reader*, ed. Geoff Eley and Ronald Grigor Suny (New York: Oxford University Press, 1996), 138.

4 Roger Chartier, *The Order of Books: Readers, Authors, and Libraries in Europe between the Fourteenth and Eighteenth Centuries*, trans. Lydia G. Cochrane (Cambridge: Polity Press, 1994), 3.

5 For characterizations of kokugaku in such terms, see, for example, Haga Noboru, *Kokugaku no hitobito—sono kōdō to shisō* (Hyōronsha, 1977), 6; James White, *Ikki: Social Conflict and Political Protest in Early Modern Japan* (Ithaca, N.Y.: Cornell University Press, 1995), 115. The place of publication for all Japanese-language works cited in this volume is Tokyo, unless otherwise indicated.

6 For a rendering of this narrative, see Peter Nosco, *Remembering Paradise: Nativism and Nostalgia in Eighteenth-Century Japan* (Cambridge, Mass.: Harvard University Press, 1990).

7 The phrase is from Tetsuo Najita and H. D. Harootunian, "Japan's Revolt against the West," in *Modern Japanese Thought*, ed. Bob Tadashi Wakabayashi (Cambridge: Cambridge University Press, 1998), 207–272. On the Japan romantic school, see Kevin Doak, *Dreams of Difference: The Japan Romantic School and the Crisis of Modernity* (Berkeley: University of California Press, 1994).

8 Maruyama Masao, *Nihon seiji shisōshi kenkyū* (Iwanami Shoten, 1952), translated by Mikiso Hane under the title *Studies in the Intellectual History of Tokugawa Japan* (Princeton: Princeton University Press, 1974).

9 Saigō Nobutsuna, *Kokugaku hihan* (originally published 1948, rev. ed. Miraisha, 1965), 230–284. Saigō later acknowledged the influence of Maruyama upon his own work. He noted that his work on Norinaga was "the result of the impact" of reading Maruyama's work as it was serialized in *Kokka gakkai zasshi*. Quoted in Go Tetsuo, "Kokubungaku/kokugaku hihan," *Nihon bungaku* 523 (January 1997): 11.

10 Matsumoto Sannosuke, *Kokugaku seiji shisō no kenkyū* (Miraisha, 1972), 17–18.

11 Haga Noboru, *Kokugaku no hitobito*, 6.

12 Ibid., 5–7, passim.

13 Ernest Renan, "What Is a Nation?" in *Nation and Narrations*, ed. Homi Bhabha (New York: Routledge, 1990), 19.

14 E. J. Hobsbawm and Terence Ranger, eds., *The Invention of Tradition* (Cambridge: Cambridge University Press, 1983); Benedict Anderson, *Imagined Communities: Reflections on the Origin and Spread of Nationalism* (London: Verso, 1983); Homi Bhabha, "Introduction," in *Nation and Narrations*, ed. Homi Bhabha (New York: Routledge, 1990).

15 Carol Gluck, *Japan's Modern Myths: Ideology in the Late Meiji Period* (Princeton: Princeton University Press, 1985).

16 T. Fujitani, *Splendid Monarchy: Power and Pageantry in Modern Japan* (Berkeley: University of California Press, 1996), 4–9.

17 Prasenjit Duara, *Rescuing History from the Nation: Questioning Narratives of Modern China* (Chicago: University of Chicago Press, 1995), 51.

18 Ibid., 27.

19 Stathis Gourgouris, *Dream Nation: Enlightenment, Colonization, and the Institution of Modern Greece* (Stanford: Stanford University Press, 1996), 7.

20 Balibar, "The Nation Form: History and Ideology," 133.

21 Thanks to Leslie Pincus for suggesting this phrase.

22 This is not to say that a scholarly literature does not exist on these figures. It does, especially in the case of Akinari. However, they are always situated as "peculiar" or "unique" forms of kokugaku.

23 See, for example, Uchino Gorō, *Bungei gakushi no hōhō: Kokugakushi no saikentō* (Ōfūsha, 1974) and *Edo kokugaku no ronkō* (Sōrinsha, 1979). A recent work of a similar stance is Suzuki Jun's *Edo wagaku ronkō* (Hitsuji Shobō, 1997).

24 H. D. Harootunian, *Things Seen and Unseen: Discourse and Ideology in Tokugawa Nativism* (Chicago: University of Chicago Press, 1988).

25 Jean-Luc Nancy, *The Inoperative Community* (Minneapolis: University of Minnesota Press, 1991), 42.

26 The term *fukko* literally means "to return to ancient times" and thus must be distinguished from the term *ishin* (used to describe the political revolution of 1868, the Meiji Ishin), which is also translated as "restoration." The latter means to "start anew," "to reform," or "to renovate." As this suggests, not all those involved in the Restoration or its aftermath embraced the notion of "going back" that oriented kokugaku involvement in the events of 1868.

27 Partha Chatterjee, *Nationalist Thought and the Colonial World* (Minneapolis: University of Minnesota Press, 1995), 1–35.

28 E. J. Hobsbawm, *Nations and Nationalism since 1780: Programme, Myth, Reality* (Cambridge: Cambridge University Press, 1990), 1.

CHAPTER I. LATE TOKUGAWA SOCIETY

1 Miroslav Hroch, "From National Movement to the Fully-Formed Nation: The Nation-Building Process in Europe," in *Becoming National: A Reader*, ed. Geoff Eley and Ronald Grigor Suny (Oxford: Oxford University Press, 1996), 61.

2 Ibid., 66–68, passim.

3 The following is based on Sigeru Matsumoto's biography of Norinaga; see *Motoori Norinaga, 1730–1801* (Cambridge, Mass.: Harvard University Press, 1970).

4 Takada Mamoru provides an overview of Akinari's early years in *Ueda Akinari nenpu kōsetsu* (Meizendō Shoten, 1964).

5 Several works discuss Mitsue's family background and early education. See Hirai Takeo, "Fujitani Mitsue daijin no seikatsu," parts 1 and 2, *Kokugakuin zasshi* 25, nos. 4 and 6 (1919); and Tada Junten, *Ishoku no kokugakusha: Fujitani Mitsue no shōgai* 2d ed. (Kyoto: Shibunkaku, 1996), chap. 1.

6 On Moribe's background, see Suzuki Eiichi, *Tachibana Moribe* (Yoshikawa Kōbunkan, 1972), chaps. 1–3.

7 Bunyō Inshi, "Seji kenbun roku," in *Nihon shomin seikatsu shiryō shūsei*, vol. 8, *Kenbun*, ed. Harada Tomohiko et al. (San'ichi Shobō, 1971), 645, 662. According to Harada's introduction, little is known about Bunyō, but he may have been a "masterless samurai" (*rōnin*) formerly in the service of a daimyō. The preface to the work is dated 1816.

8 Quoted in Aoki Michio, *Bunka bunsei ki no minshū to bunka* (Bunka Shobō Hakubunsha, 1985), 13. Throughout this work, all translations are by the author unless otherwise noted.

9 The discussion that follows is based upon the overview of the process of commercialization offered by Nakai Nobuhiko, "Commercial Change and Urban Growth in Early Modern Japan," trans. James L. McClain, in *Cambridge History of Japan*, vol. 4, *Early Modern Japan*, ed. Marius Jansen (Cambridge: Cambridge University Press, 1991). On the late eighteenth-century, see 579–590. The rise of the rural textile industry is examined by Nakamura Satoru, "The Development of Rural Industry," in *Tokugawa Japan: The Social and Economic Antecedents of Modern Japan*, ed. Nakane Chie and Ōishi Shinzaburō (University of Tokyo Press, 1990), 81–96.

10 David L. Howell, "Hard Times in the Kantō: Economic Change and Village Life in Late Tokugawa Japan," *Modern Asian Studies* 23, no. 2 (1989): 349–371.

11 For a discussion of Tanuma's economic policies, see John Whitney Hall, *Tanuma Okitsugu: Forerunner of Modern Japan* (Cambridge, Mass.: Harvard University Press, 1955).

12 On daimyo commercial policies, see Nakai, "Commercial Change and Urban Growth in Early Modern Japan," 588–560.

13 The transformation of village society and its relation to peasant rebellions is ex-

plored in Stephen Vlastos, *Peasant Protests and Uprisings in Tokugawa Japan* (Berkeley: University of California Press, 1986).

14 Ibid. The statistics are drawn from a chart on page 74 of Vlastos's work, the source of which is Aoki Kōji, *Hyakushō ikki no nenjiteki kenkyū* (Shinseisha, 1966), 36–37.

15 Quoted in Suzuki Eiichi, *Tachibana Moribe*, 163.

16 Sugita Genpaku, "Nochimigusa," in *Nihon shomin seikatsu shiryō shūsei*, vol. 7, *Kikin ekibyō*, ed. Mori Kahei and Tanigawa Ken'ichi (San'ichi Shobō, 1970), 55–86. The third section of the work is found on 68–86.

17 Sugita, "Nochimigusa," 71–72.

18 Ibid., 79.

19 Kikuchi Isao, *Kinsei no kikin* (Yoshikawa Kōbunkan, 1997), 162, 158. A koku was a measure for rice equal to 1.8 liters.

20 Calculated from the data in Aoki, *Hyakushō ikki no nenjiteki kenkyū*, 122–134.

21 Sugita, "Nochimigusa," 83.

22 Herman Ooms, *Charismatic Bureaucrat: A Political Biography of Matsudaira Sadanobu* (Chicago: University of Chicago Press, 1975), 6–7.

23 For an account of the Edo riot, see Yamada Tadao, *Ikki uchikowashi no undō kōzō* (Kōso Shobō, 1984), 267–273.

24 Sugita, "Nochimigusa," 69.

25 Kikuchi, *Kinsei no kikin*, 156–157.

26 Ibid., 154.

27 The phrase is the title of Kabayama's article, "Kikin kara umareru bunka," in *Bakumatsu bunka no kenkyū*, ed. Hayashiya Tatsusaburō (Iwanami Shoten, 1978), 389–420.

28 In the discussion that follows, I draw upon Konta Yōzō's research, especially "Edo jidai no saigai jōhō," in *Edo chōnin no kenkyū*, ed. Nishiyama Matsunosuke, vol. 5 (Yoshikawa Kōbunkan, 1980). The Dewa documents are examined on 174–180.

29 Quoted in Haga Noboru, *Motoori Norinaga: Kinsei kokugaku no seiritsu* (Shimizu Shoin, 1972), 133.

30 Ibid.

31 Ibid. Interestingly, Genpaku also makes mention of these appeals to the emperor in "Nochimigusa." See 84.

32 For an overview of publishing developments in the Tokugawa period in English, see Moriya Katsuhisa, "Urban Networks and Information Networks," in *Tokugawa Japan*, ed. Nakane and Ōishi. Konta Yōzō provides a series of diagrams illustrating the expansion of the publishing industry in *Edo no hon'yasan* (NHK Bukusu, 1977), 92–93. On the phenomenon of "bestsellers," see Takeuchi Makoto, "Shomin bunka no naka no Edo," in *Nihon no kinsei*, vol. 14, *Bunka no taishūka*, ed. Takeuchi Makoto (Chūō Kōronsha, 1993), 17–18.

33 Nagatomo Chiyoji, *Kinsei kashi hon'ya no kenkyū* (Tōkyōdō Shuppan, 1982), 43.

34 Cited in Moriya, "Urban Networks and Information Networks," 115.

35 On the rural book trade, see Nagatomo, *Kinsei kashi hon'ya no kenkyū*, 87–122.

36 On the function of manuscript books in the late Tokugawa period, see P. F. Kornicki, "The Enmeiin Affair of 1803: The Spread of Information in the Tokugawa Period," *Harvard Journal of Asiatic Studies* 42, no. 2 (December 1982): 503–533; Nakajima Takashi, "Hanpon jidai no 'shahon' to ha nani ka," *Kokubungaku* 42, no. 11 (1994): 49–53; Nakano Mitsutoshi et al., "Zadankai: hanpon wo meguru shomondai," *Edo Bungaku* 15 (1996): 2–23.

37 Konta deals with this and other banned works in *Edo no kinsho* (Yoshikawa Kōbunkan, 1981). For a detailed description of this so-called Title Incident, see Ooms, *Charismatic Bureaucrat*, 105–119. The author of *Nakayama monogatari*, Nakayama Yoshitaka, an official in the imperial court, represented the emperor in negotiations with the bakufu over this matter. In the late 1790s, Nakayama was influential in introducing Norinaga's work to the imperial court.

38 Konta, "Edo jidai no saigai jōhō," 193–197.

39 The entire *Ukiyo no arisama*—more than a thousand pages in length—is available in *Nihon shomin seikatsu shiryō shūsei*, vol. 11, *Sesō*, ed. Harada Tomohiko and Asakura Naohiko (San'ichi Shobō, 1971). Moriya Takeshi discusses references to kawaraban in this work in "Shisei no jōhō: *Ukiyo no arisama* wo meguru nōto," in *Bakumatsu bunka no kenkyū*, ed. Hayashiya Tatsusaburō (Iwanami Shoten, 1978).

40 Konta discusses mail delivery services in "Edo jidai no saigai jōhō," 189–193.

41 Ibid.

42 Takeuchi examines the political themes in kibyōshi in "Shomin bunka no naka no Edo," 17–22. Peter Kornicki takes up these works in "Nishiki no Ura: An Instance of Censorship and the Structure of a *Sharebon*," *Monumenta Nipponica* 32, no. 2 (summer 1977): 153–162.

43 Konta, "Edo jidai no saigai jōhō," 232–233.

44 Quoted in Konta, "Edo jidai no saigai jōhō," 249.

45 Quoted in Haga, *Motoori Norinaga*, 135.

46 Ibid., 136–137.

47 Quoted in Suzuki Eiichi, *Tachibana Moribe*, 164.

48 Quoted in ibid., 168.

49 On Ōshio Heihachirō, see Tetsuo Najita, "Ōshio Heihachirō (1793–1837)," in *Personality in Japanese History*, ed. Albert M. Craig and Donald H. Shively (Berkeley: University of California Press, 1970), 155–179.

50 Suzuki Eiichi, *Tachibana Moribe*, 174–175.

51 On Matsudaira Sadanobu, see Ooms, *Charismatic Bureaucrat*. The influence of Neo-Confucian thought on Matsudaira is discussed on 23–48.

52 There is an extensive literature on the Kansei reforms. In English, see Ooms, *Charismatic Bureaucrat*, 49–104. Tsuji Tatsuya, "Politics in the Eighteenth Century," trans. Harold Bolitho, in *The Cambridge History of Japan*, vol. 4, *Early Modern Japan*,

ed. John Whitney Hall (Cambridge: Cambridge University Press, 1991), 467–477; Isao Soranaka, "Kansei Reforms—Success or Failure?" *Monumenta Nipponica* 33, no. 2 (summer 1978): 151–161.

53 Konta discusses these regulations in several works including *Edo no kinsho* and "Jūkyū seiki no media jijō," in *Nihon no kinsei*, vol. 14, *Bunka no taishūka*, ed. Takeuchi Makoto, 269–318.

54 Konta, "Jūkyū seiki no media jijō," 291–295.

55 In 1791, for example, Santō Kyōden was sentenced to fifty days in handcuffs and his works were banned, as punishment for writing of a contemporary scandal in Yoshiwara in one of his works. Shikitei Samba was similarly subjected to handcuffing in 1799 when he was punished for mockingly describing a recent quarrel among Edo's firemen in one of his works. See Kornicki, "Nishiki no Ura."

56 Konta Yōzō, "Hikka to shuppan kikō: Shuppan bunka to Edo bungaku wo meguru shomondai," *Kokubungaku* 42, no. 11 (1994): 33–39.

57 Herman Ooms explores the status of Neo-Confucianism in early bakufu ideology in *Tokugawa Ideology, 1570–1680* (Princeton: Princeton University Press, 1985). He examines the "prohibition of heterodoxy" in *Charismatic Bureaucrat*, 122–150.

58 Ooms, *Charismatic Bureaucrat*, 138.

CHAPTER 2. BEFORE THE KOJIKIDEN

1 For an analysis of the problematic status of kundoku in the eighteenth century, see Naoki Sakai, *Voices from the Past: The Status of Language in Eighteenth-Century Japanese Discourse* (Ithaca, N.Y.: Cornell University Press, 1991), esp. part 3. The kaeriten include a symbol indicating the reversal of the word order of two words; the numbers one, two, and three; and the characters for top, middle, and bottom. They were inserted within the Chinese sentence in order to indicate in what order to read words and phrases. The kundoku operation also made use of furigana to indicate the preferred pronunciation of characters and okurigana to insert particles and other aspects of syntax necessary in Japanese.

2 Saitō Fumiya has illuminated how fluid the kundoku operation was in his article "Kinsei ni okeru kanbun kundokuhō no fukko," in *Kokugo kenkyū*, ed. Matsumura Akira Sensei Kiju Kinenkai (Meiji Shoin, 1993), 296–316, in which he analyzes how key sentences from the Confucian classic, *Rongo* (The Analects), were "read" in kundoku by noted Confucian scholars of the Tokugakwa period.

3 Suzuki Toshio discusses the influence of moveable type in the early seventeenth century in *Edo no hon'ya*, vol. 1 (Chūō Kōronsha, 1980), 3–42.

4 Kōzu Hayato, "Kinsei no Kojiki kenkyū," in *Kojiki taisei: Kenkyūshi hen* (Heibonsha, 1956), 89. The oldest surviving manuscript of the *Kojiki* is known as the *Shinpukuji-bon*, after the Shinpuku Temple where it is stored. It was copied in 1371–1372, and contains no diacritical markers. Another manuscript, the *Ise-bon*

(dated 1422) does contain some markers, as does a third manuscript, the Yūhan-
bon (dated 1522).

5 For ease of comparison, I have included the original kanbun text of this passage
as well as romanized versions of the readings produced in Tokugawa Japan in the
appendix. Donald Philippi has translated this passage as follows:

> At the time of the beginning of heaven and earth, there came into existence
> in Takama-no-hara a deity named Ame-no-mi-naka-nushi-no-kami; next,
> Taka-mi-musubi-no-kami; next, Kami-musubi-no-kami. These three deities
> all came into existence as single deities, and their forms were not visible.
>
> Next, when the land was young, resembling floating oil and drifting like a
> jellyfish, there sprouted forth something like reed-shoots. From these there
> came into existence the deity Umashi-ashi-kabi-hiko-ji-no-kami; next, Ame-
> toko-tachi-no-kami. These two deities came into existence as single deities,
> and their forms were not visible.

From Donald Philippi, Kojiki (Tokyo University Press, 1968), 47. (I have altered
the romanization of the deity names to reflect their pronunciation in standard
modern Japanese.)

6 My romanization is based upon excerpts from the Kan'eiban text that appear in
Tsugita Masayuki, "Kojiki kenkyūshi," Kokugo to kokubungaku 11, no. 4 (1934): 367.

7 The term suika (literally, "grace" and "protection") was derived from a medieval
Shinto scripture. Yoshida Shinto was founded by Yoshida Kanetomo (1453–1511),
a priest of the Yoshida Shrine in Kyoto. Also known as Yuiitsu Shinto, it was a
Buddhist-Confucian-Shinto syncretic sect.

8 For an examination of Ansai's work, see Herman Ooms, Tokugawa Ideology, 1570–
1680, chaps. 6–7.

9 Here I am following Takashima Motohiro, Yamazaki Ansai (Perikansha, 1992), esp.
471–508.

10 Ooms, Tokugawa Ideology, 239.

11 Quoted in Tokumitsu Kyūya, Kojiki kenkyūshi (Kazama Shoin, 1977), 74–75.

12 Tsugita, "Kojiki kenkyūshi," 376.

13 Uematsu Shigeru, "Kinsei shoki no Kojiki kenkyū," Kojiki nenpō 4 (1957): 21.

14 Tetsuo Najita examines the issue of historicism in late eighteenth-century Japan
in "History and Nature in Eighteenth-Century Tokugawa Thought," in The Cambridge History of Japan, vol. 4, Early Modern Japan, ed. John Whitney Hall (Cambridge:
Cambridge University Press, 1991), 596–621.

15 On the compilation of the Dai Nihon shi, see Bitō Masahide, "Mitogaku no tokushitsu," in Nihon shisō taikei, vol. 53, Mitogaku, ed. Bitō Masahide et al. (Iwanami
Shoten, 1977).

16 The Shaku Nihongi, compiled in the late Kamakura period, is a compendium of
the scholarship on the Nihon shoki produced to that point.

Notes to Chapter Two   239

17 Quoted in Kōzu, "Kinsei no Kojiki kenkyū," 96.

18 The discussion that follows is indebted to Kate Wildman Nakai's analysis of the Koshitsū in Shogunal Politics: Arai Hakuseki and the Premises of Tokugawa Rule (Cambridge, Mass.: Harvard University Press, 1988), 243–245.

19 Arai Hakuseki, "Koshitsū dokuhō hanrei," in Arai Hakuseki zenshū, ed. Imaizumi Sadasuke, vol. 3 (Tōkyō Kappan, 1907), 210.

20 The term "euhemeristic" derives from Euhemeris, the fourth-century B.C. Greek mythographer, who argued that the traditional Greek gods were deified mortals

21 Hayden White, The Content of the Form: Narrative Discourse and Historical Representation (Baltimore: John Hopkins University Press, 1987).

22 Nakai, Shogunal Politics, 247–248

23 Motoori Norinaga, "Tamakatsuma," MNZ, vol. 1, 85.

24 Quoted in Ōkubo Tadashi, "Akinari no kokugaku: Sono isō," in Nihon koten kanshō kōza, vol. 24, Akinari, ed. Nakamura Yukihiko (Kadokawa Shoten, 1958), 271.

25 In understanding the Tokugawa debate on kanazukai, I have found Itō Shingo's Kinsei kokugogaku shi (Tachikawa Bunmeidō, 1960) very useful. See 170–198.

26 Nomura Hachirō, Kokugaku zenshi, vol. 1 (Marui shoten, 1940).

27 Keichū, "Seisen hondai shoki," in Keichū zenshū, ed. Hisamatsu Sen'ichi, vol. 1 (Iwanami Shoten, 1975), 192

28 Quoted in Nakai, Shogunal Politics, 225.

29 For translations of Sorai's texts, as well as an analysis of his work, see Tetsuo Najita, ed., Tokugawa Political Writings (Cambridge: Cambridge University Press, 1998).

30 Peter Nosco, Remembering Paradise, 74–75.

31 On Sorai's impact on eighteenth-century Japan, see Koyasu Nobukuni, Jiken toshite no Soraigaku (Seishisha, 1990).

32 Kada Azumamaro, "Kojiki sakki," in Kada zenshū. Vol. 6 (1928–1932: reprint, Meichō Fukyū Kai, 1990), 181.

33 Ibid., 189.

34 Toda Toshihiko, "Kada Azumamaro no Kojiki kenkyū," Kojiki nenpō 4 (1957): 55.

35 The romanization is based upon a passage quoted in ibid., 49.

36 Quoted in Nosco, Remembering Paradise, 81.

37 Ibid., 86–87.

38 Norinaga, "Tamakatsuma," 85.

39 Kamo no Mabuchi, "Manabi no agetsurai," KMZ, vol. 12, 310.

40 My description of Mabuchi's theory of the ancient language owes much to my reading of H. D. Harootunian, Things Seen and Unseen, 50–56.

41 Mabuchi, "Engi shiki norito kai," KMZ, vol. 5, 277.

42 Sasazuki Kiyomi, "Kojiki kenkyū shōshi," in Motoori Norinaga no kenkyū (Iwanami Shoten, 1944), 380.

43 Mabuchi, "Bun i kō," KMZ, vol. 2, 332.

44   Ibid.

45   Kazama Seishi discussed these works in "Hyōgen no kokugaku: Kamo no Mabuchi kara Tachibana Moribe made," *Nihon bungaku* 48 (February 1999): 5.

46   Quoted in Sasazuki, "*Kojiki kenkyū shōshi*," 378 and Kōzu, "Kinsei no *Kojiki* kenkyū," 102.

47   Toda, "Kada Azumamaro no *Kojiki kenkyū*," 49.

48   In summarizing the debate, I have found Imai Jun and Ozawa Tomio's *Nihon shisō
ronsō shi* (Perikansha, 1990) extremely useful; see 274–282.

49   Tayasu Munetake, "*Kojiki Shōsetsu*," in *Tayasu Munetake*, vol. 3, ed. Toki Zenmaro
(Nihon Hyōronsha, 1945), 227–410.

50   Quoted in Tokumitsu, *Kojiki kenkyūshi*, 108.

51   The romanization is based upon the text that appears in Toki, ed., *Tayasu Munetake*, 235.

52   Ibid.

53   Ibid.

54   Ibid., 405–409.

55   On Kotosuga, see Kata Takeo, *Kokugakusha Tanigawa Kotosuga no kenkyū* (Yugawa
Kōbunsha, 1934); and Kitaoka Shirō, "Shisei to Norinaga: Sono gengo kenkyū
no michi," in *Kinsei kokugakusha no kenkyū: Tanigawa Kotosuga to sono shūhen* (Ise: Ko
Kitaoka Shirō Kyōju Ikōshū Kankōkai, 1977).

56   Both Kata and Kitaoka make reference to the influence of the Confucian schools
of "ancient learning" on Kotosuga. Kata, *Kokugakusha Tanigawa Kotosuga no kenkyū*,
27; Kitaoka, "Shisei to Norinaga," 112.

57   This is the conclusion of Itō Shingo in *Kinsei kokugogaku shi*, 339–340.

58   Vols. 1–13 of the *Wakun no shiori* were published in 1777, 14–28 in 1805, and 29–45
in 1830.

59   Quoted in Kitaoka, "Shisei to Norinaga," 123–124.

60   Tanigawa Kotosuga, *Nihon shoki tsūsho*, ed. Kojima Noriyuki (Kyoto: Rinsen Shoten, 1978), 70.

61   Kata, *Kokugakusha Tanigawa Kotosuga no kenkyū*, 22.

62   Quoted in Kitaoka, "Shisei to Norinaga," 126. On Norinaga's letters to Kotosuga,
see 124–127.

CHAPTER 3. MOTOORI NORINAGA

1   Kobayashi Hideo, *Motoori Norinaga* (Shinchōsha, 1977), 555–556.

2   Quoted in Kobayashi, *Motoori Norinaga*, 550.

3   Koyasu Nobukuni, *Norinaga mondai to ha nani ka* (Seidosha, 1995), 45.

4   Chapters 1–5 were published in 1790, 6–11 in 1792, 12–17 in 1797, 18–23 in 1803,
24–29 in 1813, 30–34 in 1816, 35–40 in 1820, 41–44 in 1822. The rapid publication of the *Kojikiden* was aided by the support of Norinaga's affluent and knowl-

edgeable students. On the issue of publication and Norinaga, see Toda Tokutarō, "Kojikiden no shinkō," in *Kojikiden no kenkyū*, ed. Fukuda Hisamichi (Rikugeisha, 1941), 36–39; Okamoto Katsu, "Kinsei shuppan no issokumen: Motoori-ke kankei bunshō wo chūshin ni," *Kinsei bungei* 31 (1980): 43–53; Katsurajima Nobuhiro, "Hirata-ha kokugakusha no 'dokusho' to sono gensetsu," *Edo no shisō* 5 (1996): 83–84.

5 On the status and geographic distribution of the students of kokugaku, see Haga Noboru, *Bakumatsu kokugaku no tenkai* (Hanawa Shobō, 1963), 290–292. For a chronology of the expansion of the Suzuya, see Sigeru Matsumoto, *Motoori Norinaga*, 125.

6 The entirety of book 1 has been translated into English. See Ann Wehmeyer, trans., *Kojiki-den: Book 1*, by Motoori Norinaga (Ithaca, N.Y.: Cornell University East Asia Program, 1997). The translations in this chapter are my own, unless otherwise noted.

7 This is the observation of Yoshikawa Kōjiro. See "*Kojikiden no tame ni*," *Bungaku* 36 (August 1968): 31–36.

8 Tokumitsu, *Kojiki kenkyūshi*, 120.

9 Motoori, *Kojikiden*, in MNZ, vol. 9, 3.

10 Ibid., 4.

11 Ibid., 3

12 Ibid., 6.

13 Motoori, "Kotoba no tama no o," in MNZ, vol. 5, 253. For an analysis of this text, see Kanno Kakumyō, *Motoori Norinaga: Kotoba to miyabi* (Perikansha, 1991), esp. 254–305.

14 Norinaga, *Kojikiden*, 9.

15 Ibid.

16 Motoori, "Tamakatsuma," in MNZ, vol. 1, 48.

17 Ibid., 72.

18 Ibid., 31

19 Ibid., 33.

20 Ibid., 32.

21 Ibid., 33.

22 Ibid., 32.

23 Kamei Takashi, "Kojiki ha yomeru ka," in *Kamei Takashi ronbunshū*, vol. 4, *Nihongo no sugata to kokoro* (Yoshikawa Kōbunkan, 1985), 61. Koyasu Nobukuni discussed Kamei's work in "Kojiki—Kono kanji shoki tekusuto," paper presented at the July 1999 meeting of the Shisōshi Bunka Riron Kenkyūkai (Kyoto, Japan).

24 Kojima Noriyuki, "Kojiki kundoku no shūhen," *Bungaku* 36 (August 1968): 37–41.

25 Nishimiya Kazutami, *Nihon jōdai no bunshō to hyōki* (Kazuma Shobō, 1988), 7–8

26 Ibid., 231–232.

27 Motoori, *Uiyamabumi*, 16.

28 Motoori, *Kojikiden*,122, 133. I have included this passage, along with the examples from chapter 2, in the appendix.

29 Ibid., 121.

30 Saigō Nobutsuna, *Kojiki chūshaku*, vol. 1 (Heibonsha, 1975), 69–70.

31 Motoori, *Kojikiden*, 135.

32 Motoori, "Kamiyo masagoto," in MNZ, vol. 7, 488–489.

33 Motoori, *Kojikiden*, 164.

34 Ibid., 204.

35 Ibid., 161.

36 Ibid., 140. I am grateful to Hijioka Yasunori for suggesting the significance of Norinaga's use of contemporary language within the *Kojikiden*.

37 Norinaga's pursuit of this kind of information from his students was the subject of an exhibition held at the Motoori Norinaga Kinenkan, located in Matsuzaka, in the summer of 1998.

38 For a translation of this passage, see chapter 2, note 5.

39 Motoori, *Kojikiden*, 123.

40 Ibid., 134.

41 Ibid., 151.

42 Ibid., 129.

43 Koyasu Nobukuni, *Norinaga to Atsutane no sekai* (Chūō Kōronsha, 1977), 88

44 Motoori, *Kojikiden*, 130.

45 Ibid., 272.

46 Ibid., 276.

47 Saigō, *Kojiki chūshaku*, 210, 212.

48 Ibid., 293.

49 Ibid., 294–296. In translating this passage, I have not included the commentary that Norinaga inserted parenthetically.

50 My analysis Norinaga's theory of history is informed by my reading of Takahashi Miyuki, "Norinaga no rekishi shisō," *Kikan Nihon shisōshi* 16 (1981): 27–40.

51 On historical consciousness in the Tokugawa period, see Noguchi Takehiko, *Edo-jin no rekishi ishiki* (Asahi Shinbunsha, 1987).

52 Motoori, "Tamakushige," MNZ, vol. 8, 321.

53 Ibid.

54 Motoori, "Kuzubana," MNZ, vol. 8, 155,

55 Ibid., 155.

56 Ibid., 154.

57 The translation is from Sey Nishimura, "The Way of the Gods: Motoori Norinaga's *Naobi no Mitama*," in *Monumenta Nipponica* 46, no. 1 (spring 1991): 32.

58 Motoori, "Kuzubana," 141.

59 Ibid., 442.

60 Motoori, "Tamakushige," 320–321.

61 Motoori, "Kuzubana," 177–178.

62 Ibid., 171.

63 Motoori, "Tamakazuma," 145.

64 Quoted in Sugara Tōru, *Motoori Norinaga* (Tōkyō Daigaku Shuppankai, 1978), 7–9.

65 The text of this document is included in MNZ, vol. 20, 191.

66 Momokawa Takahito, *Uchinaru Norinaga* (Tōkyō Daigaku Shuppankai, 1987), esp. 171–177.

67 For a comparison of the students of a contemporary Confucian academy (that of Minagawa Kien in Kyoto) with those of the Suzuya, see Munesada Isō, "Kyoto no bunka shakai: 'Heian jinbutsu shi' Kasei ban to Kyōjin,' " in *Kasei bunka no kenkyū*, ed. Hayashiya Tatsusaburō (Iwanami Shoten, 1976), 292–292.

68 On the status of the Suzuya students, see Umihara Tetsu, *Nihon no shijuku* (Kyoto: Shibunkaku, 1983), 135–136; Okanaka Masayuki, "Suzumon no kaisō," in *Motoori Norinaga to Suzuya shachū*, ed. by Suzuki Jun, Okanaka Masayuki, and Nakamura Kasumoto (Kinseisha, 1984), 348–352; Haga Noboru, *Henkakuki ni okeru kokugaku* (San'ichi Shobō), 52–53.

69 Umihara, *Nihon no shijuku*, 136–137; Okanaka, "Suzumon no kaisō," 352–355.

70 Quoted in Haga Noboru, *Kokugaku no hitobito—sono kōdō to shisō*, 85.

71 Quoted in Umihara, *Nihon no shijuku*, 194.

72 On the relationship of Ichikawa and Tanaka, see Ogasahara Haruo, *Kokuju ronsō no kenkyū* (Perikansha, 1988), esp. 164–187.

73 Quoted in Imai and Ozawa, eds., *Nihon shisō ronsō shi*, 226.

74 Ibid., 227.

75 Here I am following Nozaki Morihide's discussion of *Magahire*. See Nozaki, *Motoori Norinaga no sekai* (Hanawa Shobō, 1972), 80–87.

CHAPTER 4. UEDA AKINARI

1 Ōkubo Tadashi, "Akinari no kokugaku: Sono isō," in *Nihon koten kanshō kōza*, vol. 24, *Akinari*, ed. Nakamura Yukihiko (Kadokawa Shoten, 1958), 271.

2 The phrase I have translated as "Mr. Kojiki" is "Kojiki Heibei" in the original. "Heibei" was a common male personal name in this period. Ueda Akinari, "Tandai shōshin roku," in *Nihon koten bungaku taikei*, vol. 56, ed. Nakamura Yukimiko (Iwanami Shoten, 1974), 254.

3 For an example of this kind of characterization, see Iwahashi Koyata, *Ueda Akinari* (Yūseidō, 1975), 159.

4 Quoted in Blake Morgan Young, *Ueda Akinari* (Vancouver: University of British Columbia Press, 1982), 2.

5 Quoted in Ōkubo, "Akinari no kokugaku," 274, and also in Haga Noboru, "Murata Harumi no rekishiteki ichi," *Rekishi jinrui* 9 (December 1980): 146.

6 Ueda, "Ihon tandai shōshin roku," in *Nihon koten bungaku taikei*, vol. 56, 273. There

is much debate on the question of when Akinari met Umaki. I am following Takada Mamoru's chronology. See Takada Mamoru, "Umaki nyūmon nendai kō," in *Ueda Akinari nenpu kōsetsu* (Meizendō, 1964), 361–376.

7   The title alludes to a poem Norinaga attached to the end of the work, which states, "He obstructs the way that I have purified, this man from Naniwa. Will no one correct this evil?" A play on words, *Kakaika* means both "to correct the evil" and "to cut through weeds."

8   In 1784, Aragita loaned Akinari chapters 12 and 13 of the *Kojikiden*, as well as *Kara osame no uretamigoto*. See Takada, *Ueda Akinari nenpu kōsetsu*, 123.

9   Ueda, "Kakaika," UAZ, vol. 1, 191–250.

10 Why Norinaga felt it necessary to answer the charges of Akinari, who had yet to produce a significant scholarly work, is a question that has given pause to many contemporary historians, most of whom have relied upon pseudo-psychological explanations: for example, Norinaga was too arrogant to let any criticism pass unnoticed. See Takada Mamoru, "Kakaika ronsō no keisei katei shikkō," in *Ueda Akinari nenpu kōsetsu*, 398. In contrast, I argue that Norinaga recognized that Akinari was attacking the very foundations of his project in the *Kojikiden*.

11 Fukunaga Shizuka, "Akinari to Norinaga no ronsō: Kokugo in'on ron ni tsuite," in *Kyōto Joshidai kokubungaku* 31 (December 1963): 19.

12 Ueda, "Reigotsū," in UAZ, vol. 6, 69–114. The text, dated to circa 1793, seems originally to have consisted of six sections that dealt with specific topics, including deity names, place names, objects, poetic terms, verbs, and kana usage. Only the section on kana usage was ever published (in 1797), and this is the only section of the text extant. Akinari put forth his views by alternately agreeing and disagreeing with a set of opinions attributed to an unknown author. Much of the scholarship of the "Reigotsū" takes the form of attempts to identify this author. Some of those suggested include Katō Umaki, Tayasu Munetake, and Fujitani Nariakira. See, for example, Hashimoto Shinkichi, *Moji oyobi kanazukai no kenkyū* (Iwanami Shoten, 1961), esp. 99–110; and Takeoka Masao, ed., *Fujitani Nariakira zenshū* (Kazama Shobō, 1962), esp. 1201–1215.

13 Ueda, "Reigotsū," 71. Akinari's statement that one should write according to how one speaks has led some to situate him as a Tokugawa precursor to the Meiji movement for the "unity of speech and writing." For two opposing opinions on the "modernity" of Akinari's argument, see Itō, *Kinsei kokugogaku shi*, esp. 195–199, and Iwahashi Koyata, "Reigotsū ron," in *Ueda Akinari*, 178–204.

14 Ueda, "Reigotsū," 76.

15 Ibid., 112.

16 Ueda, "Kakaika," 230.

17 Ibid., 236–237.

18 Ibid., 241.

19 In the secondary literature on this debate, the distance between Norinaga and

Akinari's views has most often been characterized in terms of differences in "attitude" that are described variously as rational versus irrational, skepticism versus faith. See, for example, Takada Mamoru, "Hi no kami ronsō ni tsuite no danshō: Norinaga to Akinari no shisō no taishitsu," and Nakamura Hiroyasu, "Yūkō na honshitsu, mukō na honshitsu: 'Hi no kami' ronsō ni tsuite," both in *Nihon bungaku kenkyū shiryō sōsho: Ueda Akinari*, ed. Takada Mamoru (Yūseidō Shuppan, 1972); Washiyama Jushin, "Norinaga to Akinari: Akinari no Norinaga gakusetsu hihan ni tsuite," *Hanazono Daigaku kenkyū kiyō* 9 (March 1978): 67–81.

20 Ueda, "Yasumigoto," in UAZ, vol. 1, 15–52. Ueda, "Otaegoto," in UAZ, vol. 1, 55–140.

21 Ueda, "Yasumigoto," 51.

22 Ibid., 17.

23 Ibid., 18. In analyzing "Yasumigoto," I have drawn upon my reading of Iikura Yōichi, "Akinari to bundo: *Yasumigoto* shiron," *Bungaku* 54 (July 1986): 88–102.

24 Ueda, "Yasumigoto," 26.

25 Ibid., 25.

26 The first poetic anthology compiled in Japan, it brought together 120 poems written in Chinese. The poems, the earliest of which dated from the reign of Tenchi, were arranged in chronological order.

27 Ueda, "Yasumigoto," 21.

28 Ibid., 49.

29 In reading "Otaegoto," I learned much from Moriyama Shigeo's analysis of this work. See Moriyama Shigeo, *Ueda Akinari: Shiteki jōnen no sekai* (San'ichi Shobō, 1986).

30 Ueda, "Otaegoto," 68.

31 Ibid., 69.

32 Ibid.

33 Ueda, "Yasumigoto," 40.

34 Some scholars have argued that "Otaegoto" is a critique of Confucianism and Buddhism. See for example, Washiyama Jushin, "Ueda Akinari bannen no ju butsu nikyōkan: Sono shiron 'Otaegoto' wo chūshin ni," *Hanazono Daigaku kenkyū kiyō* 6 (March 1975): 135–178.

35 Ueda, "Otaegoto," 78.

36 For a discussion of these gesaku genres, see Donald Keene, *World within Walls* (New York: Grove Press, 1976).

37 Ueda, "Yoshiya ashiya," in UAZ, vol. 5, 477–511.

38 Ueda, "Nubatama no maki," in UAZ, vol. 5, 55–82.

39 Ibid., 61.

40 Ibid., 67.

41 Quoted in Nakamura Hiroyasu, "Akinari no monogatari ron," *Nihon bungaku* 13

(February 1964): 1–22. I am indebted to Nakamura's discussion of the relationship of history and monogatari in Akinari's work.

42 The significance of this term was suggested by Iikura Yōichi, "Akinari no okeru
    'ikidōri' no mondai: *Harusame monogatari* he no isshiten," *Bungaku* 52 (May 1984):
    72–85.

43 Ueda, "Nubatama no maki," p. 61.

44 Ueda, "Yoshiya ashiya," 510.

45 Barry Jackman, trans., *The Tales of Spring Rain* (University of Tokyo Press, 1977), 3.

46 The modern *Harusame monogatari* has a complicated textual history. It was first
    printed in 1907, almost a century after Akinari's death. The printed version, based
    upon a manuscript owned by Tomioka Tessai (1836–1924), contained only five
    stories. In the 1940s, Nakamura Yukihiko discovered five more stories among the
    manuscripts owned by the Tenri Library. Then in the 1950s two complete manu-
    scripts of the work, including ten stories and a preface, were found in private
    collections. See Jackman, *The Tales of Spring Rain*, xix–xxiii.

47 On this point, I am indebted to Hino Tatsuo's analysis of "Kaizoku," in *Norinaga
    to Akinari* (Chikuma Shobō, 1984), esp. 232.

48 Jackman, *The Tales of Spring Rain*, 54.

49 This story and the one that follows, "The Celestial Maidens," have often been
    read as an expression of "anti-Buddhist" and "anti-Confucian" sentiments on
    the part of Akinari, conclusions for which I find little internal evidence. See, for
    example, Shigetomo Ki, *Ueda Akinari no kenkyū* (Bunri Shoin, 1971), esp. 376–401;
    and Morita Kirō, *Ueda Akinari* (Kinokuniya Shoten, 1970), 132–141.

50 Cited in Azuma Yoshimochi, "*Harusame monogatari* 'rekishi shosetsu' no kentō,"
    in *Nihon bungaku kenkyū shiryō sōsho: Ueda Akinari*, ed. Takada Mamoru (Yuseidō,
    1972), 225. The *Ruijū kokushi* was compiled by Sugawara no Michizane who took
    information from the six "national" histories that were commissioned by the
    court and organized it chronologically within thematic chapters. The *Nihon isshi*
    was compiled by Kamo Sukeyuki, a priest of the Kamo Shrine in Kyoto.

51 Jackman, *The Tales of Spring Rain*, 11.

52 Ibid., 12, 14, 21.

53 Ibid., 17.

54 Ibid., 15.

55 Ueda, "Kamiyo monogatari," in *UAZ*, vol. 1, 143–170. Cited in Noguchi Takehiko,
    Akinari gengi (Seidosha, 1989), 311–312.

56 Ueda, "Kamiyo monogatari," 170.

CHAPTER 5. FUJITANI MITSUE

1   Motoori Norinaga, "Tamakatsuma," in *MNZ*, vol. 1, 248. Ueda Akinari wrote of
    Nariakira that "he was one of my haikai friends and we used to meet frequently.

We also shared a love for Japanese poetry and prose." From Ueda Akinari, "Tandai shōshin roku," in *Ueda Akinari shū*, ed. Nakamura Yukihiko, 266–267. Naoki Sakai examines Nariakira's linguistic theory in Sakai, *Voices from the Past: The Status of Language in Eighteenth-Century Japanese Discourse* (Ithaca, N.Y.: Cornell University Press, 1991).

2 Fujitani, "Kojiki tomoshibi (Ikkan)," in FMS, vol. 1, 339.

3 Hirai Takeo, "Fujitani Mitsue daijin no seikatsu," part 1, 66–67.

4 Munesada Isō, "Kyōto no bunka shakai: 'Heian jinbutsu shi' Kaseiban to Kyō-jin," 285.

5 Tada Junten, *Ishoku no kokugakusha: Fujitani Mitsue no shōgai* 2 ed., 5.

6 Sasaki Nobutsuna, *Nihon kagakushi* (1910; reprint Hakubunkan, 1942), 372.

7 A similar evocation of Mitsue's "uniqueness" appears in the *Kokushi daijiten* (Dictionary of National History) entry on Mitsue. Authored by Suzuki Eiichi, it states that "among the early modern Kokugaku scholars, he is conspicuously different." See Kokushi Daijiten Iinkai, ed., *Kokushi daijiten*, vol. 12 (Kodansha, 1992), 147–148.

8 See, for example, Shida Nobuyoshi, "Fujitani Mitsue no gakuteki jiban," and Yamane Yasutaro, "Fujitani Mitsue no shii to sono taidō," both in *Kokumin seishin bunka* 3, no. 1 (June 1937). An extreme example of this approach is Ōta Seikyū's discussion of Mitsue's poetic theory in *Nihon kagaku to Chūgoku shigaku* (Japanese Poetics and Chinese Poetics). Ōta argued that Mitsue's poetic theory was profoundly influenced by that of his uncle, the Neo-Confucian scholar Minagawa Kien, who oversaw his education after Nariakira's death when Mitsue was twelve. To prove that Mitsue's poetic theory was "Confucian," he extracted statements from the work of both scholars and aligned them as proof of resemblance. See Ōta Seikyū, *Nihon kagaku to Chūgoku shigaku* (Shimizu Kōbundō Shobō, 1968), 344–383.

9 Tsuchida Kyōson, "Mitsue no kotodama ron," in *Tsuchida Kyōson zenshū*, ed. Tsunetō Kyō et al., vol. 11 (Nihon Tosho Sentā, 1982), 40.

10 Kamada Tōji, "Shinsōtekina jigen toshite no kotodama: Fujitani Mitsue no kotodama ron," *Shintō shūkyō* 114 (March 1984): 67–70.

11 Motoori Norinaga, "Ashiwake no obune," in MNZ, vol. 2, 3.

12 Fujitani, "Kojiki tomoshibi ōmune," in FMS, vol. 1, 20.

13 Here and throughout this chapter, I am following the dates given by Tada Junten. Miyake Kiyoshi suggests that the work was composed sometime between the end of the Kansei era and the beginning of the Bunka era, that is, between circa 1795 and 1805. See Miyake Kiyoshi, *Fujitani Mitsue* (Sanseidō, 1942). Hatanaka Kenji suggests the significance of the *Kadō hiyui shō* in " 'Makotoben' ni miru Fujitani Mitsue no karon," *Bungei kenkyū* 139 (May 1996): 52–63. The discussion that follows owes much to his analysis.

14 Fujitani, "Kadō hiyui shō," in SFMZ, vol. 4, 491–492.

15 Kamada discusses Mitsue's use of these oppositions in "Shinsōteki jigen toshite no kotodama," 48–76.

16 Fujitani, "Hyaku'nin isshū tomoshibi," in FMS, vol. 2, 353.

17 Fujitani, "Makotoben," in FMS, vol. 2, 211.

18 For the context of this statement, see Sakamoto Tarō et al., *Nihon koten bungaku taikei*, vol. 67, *Nihon shoki* (Iwanami Shoten, 1967), 214.

19 Fujitani, "Kojiki tomoshibi ōmune," 22–23.

20 Fujitani, "Makotoben," 215–217.

21 Quoted in Hamasuna Songi, "Fujitani Mitsue no gengoron," *Kokugakuin Daigaku Daigakuin kiyō* 25 (February 1993): 101.

22 Yamada Takanobu provides a list of references to tōgo from Mitsue's work in "Fujitani Mitsue no shinwa kaishaku," *Nihon bungaku* 40 (October 1991): 29.

23 Fujitani, "Makotoben," 213.

24 Kamada, "Shinsōtekina jigen toshite no kotodama," 54–55.

25 Fujitani, "Ōmune," 6–7.

26 Ibid., 8.

27 Ibid. 13–14.

28 In another text on the *Kojiki* written after the "Ōmune," Mitsue altered this account somewhat. In *Shinten kyoyō*, he explains that for ten generations after Jinmu the "teaching" was passed down only within the imperial family. Then in the age of Emperor Sujin, the "teaching" was transmitted to the populace. In FMZ, vol. 2, 77.

29 Fujitani, "Ōmune," 14.

30 Ibid.

31 Ibid., 18.

32 Mitsue, "Kaikokuron," in FMS, vol. 2, 109.

33 Suzuki Eiichi cites these poems and notes their theme of political critique in his "Fujitani Mitsue no shisō ni tsuite no ikkōsatsu," *Nihon shisōshigaku* 7 (September 1975): 9.

34 Fujitani, "Kojiki tomoshibi, Maki ichi," in FMS. vol. 1, 74–75. This is one text of the *Kojiki tomoshibi*.

35 *Man'yōshū*, trans. Ian Hideo Levy (Princeton: Princeton University Press, 1981), 63.

36 Fujitani, "Man'yōshū tomoshibi," in SFMZ, vol. 2, 278.

37 Mitsue's discussion of both the *Tosa nikki* and the *Man'yōshū* poem is examined by Suzuki, "Fujitani Mitsue no shisō ni tsuite no ikkōsatsu," 7.

38 Fujitani, "Ōmune," 8.

39 Ibid.

40 Ibid.

41 Ibid., 35.

42 Ibid., 10.

43 Ibid., 12.

44 Ibid., 18.

45 Fujitani, "Kojiki tomoshibi," (Bunka 2), in FMS, vol. 1, 160.

46 Fujitani, "Kojiki tomoshibi shinten," in FMZ, vol. 1, 384–385.

47 Fujitani, "Kojiki tomoshibi (Awajishima made)," FMZ, vol. 1:158.

48 Fujitani, "Kojiki tomoshibi," (Bunka 2), 137–208. Most of the variant texts seem to have been written with between 1804 and 1816. Hamasuna Songi notes that in spite of variations in the treatment of individual passages, Mitsue's understanding of the narrative as a whole is fundamentally unchanged. See Hamasuna Songi, "Fujitani Mitsue no shinwa kaishaku," Shintō shūkyō 151 (June 1994): 48, n. 3.

49 Fujitani, "Kojiki tomoshibi," (Bunka 2), 137.

50 Ibid., 146.

51 Fujitani, "Shinmyō hyōdan," in FMS, vol. 4, 598.

52 Fujitani,"Kojiki tomoshibi," (Bunka 2), 140.

53 Ibid., 155.

54 Ibid., 156–157.

55 Ibid., 158–159.

56 Ibid., 163–164.

57 Ibid., 165.

58 Ibid., 165–166.

59 Ibid., 139, 162.

60 Ibid., 139.

61 Fujitani, "Shintō daii," in SFMZ, vol. 1, 903.

62 Miyamoto Tsunekazu, ed., Ise sangū (Yasaka Shobō, 1987), 144–159.

63 Nishigaki Seiji, O-Ise mairi (Iwanami Shoten, 1983), 195.

64 Miyamoto, Ise sangū, 132.

65 Fujitani, "Ise ryō dai jingū ben," in SFMZ, vol. 1, 661–728.

66 The institution of the saigū is discussed in Miyamoto, Ise sangū, 29–39.

67 Fujitani, "Kojiki tomoshibi ōmune," 18.

68 Quoted in Tada, Ishoku no kokugakusha, 182.

69 Fujitani, "Ise ryō dai jingū ben," 722–723.

70 Tada, Ishoku no kokugakusha, 5.

71 Quoted in ibid., 185–186.

72 Fujitani, "Shinten kyoyō," in SFMZ, vol. 1, 878.

73 Hirai discusses Mitsue's activities as a teacher in "Fujitani Mitsue daijin no seikatsu," part 1, 65–66.

74 Hirai, "Fujitani Mitsue daijin no seikatsu," part 2, 37–40.

75 Quoted in Tada, Ishoku no kokugakusha, 328.

76 Quoted in ibid., 225.

77 Hirai, "Fujitani Mitsue daijin no seikatsu," part 1, 67–68.

78 See, for example, Shida Nobuyoshi, "Fujitani Mitsue koden," in FMS, vol. 1.

79 Tada, *Ishoku no kokugakusha*, 238–252.

80 Suzuki, "Fujitani Mitsue no shisō ni tsuite no ikkōsatsu," 11.

CHAPTER 6. TACHIBANA MORIBE

1 On the Edo school, see Uchino Gorō, *Edoha kokugaku ronkō* (Sōrinsha, 1979).

2 Suzuki Eiichi explores Moribe's relations with the Edo school in *Tachibana Moribe*, 29–38. So too does Ōta Yoshimaro in "Tachibana Moribe—Hito to gakumon," TMZ, *Hokan*, 175–242.

3 Moribe's relations with the textile merchants are described in Takai Hiroshi, "Kiryū kokugaku no hasseishi," *Gunma bungaku*, nos. 3, 4, 5, 7, 8 (1957).

4 Tachibana, "Yamabiko zōshi," TMZ, vol. 8, 1–128.

5 Suzuki Kazuhiko makes this observation in his study of *Yamabiko zōshi*. See Suzuki, "Tachibana Moribe no kokugo ishiki: *Yamabiko zōshi* ni tsuite," *Yamanashi Daigaku Gakugeibu kenkyū hōkoku* 13 (1962): 31–40.

6 Tachibana, "Yamabiko zōshi," 65.

7 Ibid., 3. In attributing the preface to Moribe, I am following Suzuki, *Tachibana Moribe*, 96. Throughout this chapter, dates cited for texts follow those given by Suzuki. He notes that Moribe often provided false dates for his own work, making them appear to have been completed years before they actually were. See Suzuki, *Tachibana Moribe*, 121–122.

8 The translation is from Sey Nishimura, "First Steps in the Mountains: Motoori Norinaga's *Uiyamabumi*," *Monumenta Nipponica* 42, no. 4 (winter 1987): 474. The original text is in MNZ, vol. 1, 3–30.

9 The reception of *Yamabiko zōshi* is discussed in Suzuki, *Tachibana Moribe*, 106–112. The quotes are from 106 and 108 respectively.

10 Tachibana, "Bunshō senkaku," TMZ, vol. 2, 181.

11 Ibid.

12 Tachibana, "Tanka senkaku," TMZ, vol. 2, 303.

13 Suzuki Kazuhiko analyzes this work in "Tachibana Moribe no kokugo ishiki—'Sansenkaku' ni tsuite," *Yamanashi Daigaku Gakugeigakubu kenkyū hōkoku* 10 (1959). Hirano Kimihiro discusses Moribe's conception of the ancient poems as songs in *Man'yō hihyōshi kenkyū, Kinseihen* (Miraisha, 1965), 234–256. Another commentary is provided by Ōta Yoshimaro, "Tachibana Moribe to kiki kayō," *Kokugo to kokubungaku* 19 (July 1942): 61–77.

14 Tachibana, "Shinpū mondō," TMZ, vol. 5, 406.

15 Ibid., 402.

16 Tachibana, "Bunshō senkaku," 181.

17 Ibid., 213.

18 Ibid., 274.

19 Ibid., 244.

20 Ibid., 236.

21 Ibid. To compare this reading with earlier ones, see the appendix.

22 Tachibana, "Tadaka Monogatari," TMZ, vol. 12, 361–398.

23 On Kitabatake's work, see Iwasa Tadashi, "Kaisetsu," in *Nihon koten bungaku taikei*, vol. 87, *Jinnō shōtōki masukagami*, ed. Iwasa Tadashi et al. (Iwanami Shoten, 1965).

24 Tachibana, "Itsu no chiwake," TMZ, vol. 3, 30.

25 Ibid., 5–8.

26 Ibid., 10.

27 Ibid., 28–29.

28 Ibid., 12–14, 41.

29 The origin of this term is the note in the *Kojiki* that follows the exchange of poems between Yachihoko no Kami (Ōkuninushi) and Suserihime no Mikoto. It states, "These are the word that tell of the events above."

30 Tachibana, "Nan-Kojikiden," 265.

31 These phrases are scattered throughout Moribe's work. See, for example, "Nan-Kojikiden," 246, 265, 274–276.

32 Tachibana, "Itsu no chiwake," 34–37.

33 Ibid., 38.

34 Ibid., 40.

35 Tachibana, "Nan-Kojikiden," 183.

36 Ibid., 234.

37 Ibid., 251.

38 Tachibana, "Itsu no chiwake," 42.

39 Tachibana, "Tachibana monogatari," TMZ, vol. 12, 340–359. It was written by Moribe's daughter Hamako acting as her father's amanuensis.

40 Ibid., 358.

41 Quoted in Suzuki, *Tachibana Moribe*, 226.

42 Tachibana, "Itsu no chiwake," 44.

43 Ibid., 45–46.

44 Tachibana, "Itsu no chiwake," 57.

45 See, for example, Muraoka Tsunetsugu, *Shintōshi* (Sōbunsha, 1956), 143. Here Muraoka describes Moribe's work as "one branch of Hirata Shinto."

46 Harry Harootunian, *Things Seen and Unseen*, 155. The discussion of Atsutane's work that follows is indebted to Harootunian's work. See particularly 143–168.

47 Hirata Atsutane, "Tama no mihashira," *Hirata Atsutane zenshū*, ed. Hirata Zenshū Kankōkai, vol. 7 (Heibonsha, 1977), 92.

48 Harootunian, *Things Seen and Unseen*, 155.

49 Tachibana, "Kamiyo tadaka," 313.

50 Ibid., 314.

51 Ibid., 351.

52 Ibid., 313.

53 Tachibana, "Itsu no chiwake," 54.

54 Tachibana, "Kamiyo tadaka," 325, 329. On 326, Moribe himself cuts short his commentary on the pledge of Izanagi and Izanami in yomi, explaining that one should not speak too much of such things.

55 Tachibana Moribe, "Taimon zakki," in *Nihon shisō taikei*, vol. 51, *Kokugaku undō no shisō*, ed. Haga Noboru and Matsumoto Sannosuke (Iwanami Shoten, 1971), 94.

56 For these examples, see Tachibana, "Taimon zakki," 90–91, 72, 58, 101.

57 Tachibana, "Kamiyo tadaka," 313.

58 Tachibana, "Itsu no chiwake," 56.

59 Tachibana, "Kamiyo tadaka," 345–346; "Itsu no chiwake," 259.

60 Tachibana, "Nan-Kojikiden," 277.

61 Tachibana, "Kamiyo tadaka," 350.

62 Tachibana, "Shinpū mondō," 403.

63 Tachibana, "Kamiyo tadaka," 351.

64 Tachibana, "Itsu no chiwake," 59.

65 For example, in 1839 the Dutch learning scholar Takano Chōei was arrested and punished by the bakufu.

66 Tachibana, "Jūdan mondō," TMZ, *Hokan*, 12.

67 Ibid.

68 Ibid., 21.

69 Ibid., 22.

70 Tachibana, "Kamiyo tadaka," 342.

71 On the makeup of the Atsutane's school, see Haga, *Bakumatsu kokugaku no tenkai*. Of Atsutane's 524 students, 156 were cultivators, 140 were Shinto priests, and 163 were lower-ranking samurai. Suzuki provides a similar analysis of Moribe's disciples in *Tachibana Moribe*, 292. His 181 known students included 24 samurai, 20 cultivators, 41 merchants, 11 physicians, 37 Buddhist priests, 2 Shinto priests, 6 *bunjin*, and 39 people of unknown occupation. While Atsutane, like Norinaga, compiled a comprehensive roll of students, Moribe did not. Thus, Suzuki's figures are best regarded as estimates.

CHAPTER 7. THE NEW KOKUGAKU

1 On the activities of Hirata disciples in Kyoto, see Anne Walthall, *The Weak Body of a Useless Woman: Matsuo Taseko and the Meiji Restoration* (Chicago: University of Chicago Press, 1999), 113.

2 Yasumaro Yoshio, "Kindai tenkanki ni okeru shūkyō to kokka," in *Nihon kindai shisō taikei*, vol. 5, *Shūkyō to kokka* (Iwanami Shoten, 1988), 501–502.

3 Sakamoto Koremaru, "Meiji shonen ni okeru kokugakusha no seijiteki dōkō—Saisei itchi kokka no kōsō wo megutte," *Kokugakuin zasshi* 40 (August 1992): 2–3.

4 Sakamoto, *Meiji Ishin to kokugakusha*, 16–17.

5 Tanaka Sōgorō, *Meiji Ishin taiseishi* (Chikura Shobō, 1941), 27. The text of *Kenkin sengo* is included in Haga Noboru and Matsumoto Sannosuke, eds., *Nihon shisō taikei*, vol. 51, *Kokugaku undō no shisō* (Iwanami Shoten, 1971), 548–585.

6 For a detailed examination of the struggles in the Jingikan, see Sakamoto Koremaru, *Meiji Ishin to kokugakusha* (Daimeidō, 1993). J. L. Breen contrasts the views of Ōkuni disciple Fukuba Bisei with those of Yano in "Shintoists in Restoration Japan (1868–1872): Towards a Reassessment," *Modern Asian Studies* 24, no. 3 (1990): 579–602. Takashi Fujitani examines the decision to move the capital and the formation of new ceremonies in *Splendid Monarchy: Power and Pageantry in Modern Japan*. James Ketelaar describes the campaign against Buddhism in *Of Heretics and Martyrs in Modern Japan* (Princeton: Princeton University Press, 1990). The struggle over the content of the "teachings" to be diffused via the Great Promulgation Campaign is explored in Fujii Sadafumi, *Edo kokugaku tenseishi no kenkyū* (Yoshikawa Kōbunkan, 1987), 42–64.

7 Walthall, *The Weak Body of a Useless Woman*, 300.

8 Quoted in Sakamoto, *Meiji Ishin to kokugakusha*, 5.

9 Quoted in Iwai Tadakuma, "Nihon kindai shigaku no keisei," in *Iwanami kōza Nihon rekishi*, vol. 22 (Iwanami Shoten, 1963), 63.

10 The events surrounding the establishment of Tokyo Imperial University are discussed in many works, including Tōkyō Daigaku Hyakunenshi Henshū Iinkai, eds., *Tōkyō Daigaku hyakunenshi* (Tōkyō Daigaku Shuppankai, 1984); Uchino Gorō, "Kōten kōkyūjo to koten kōshūka no sōsetsu" in *Ishin zengo ni okeru kokugaku no shomondai*, ed. Kokugakuin Daigaku Nihon Bunka Kenkyūjo (Kokugakuin Daigaku Nihon Kenkyūjo, 1983), 1–34. On the clash between the nativists and the Confucianists, see Ōkubo Toshiaki, *Ōkubo Toshiaki choshakushū*, vol. 4, *Meiji Ishin to kyōiku* (Yoshikawa Kōbunkan, 1987), 257–314.

11 The history of Kokugakuin University is related in Kokugakuin Daigaku Hyakunenshi Henshū Iinkai, ed. *Kokugakuin Daigaku hyakunenshi* (Kokugakuin Daigaku, 1982).

12 *Kokugakuin Daigaku hyakunenshi*, 20–21.

13 Carol Gluck, *Japan's Modern Myths: Ideology in the Late Meiji Period* (Princeton: Princeton University Press, 1985), 25. The discussion that follows is indebted to Gluck's analysis.

14 On the Bureau of Historical Writing, see Iwai Tadakuma, "Nihon kindai shigaku no keisei," 59–103; Ōkubo Toshiaki, *Nihon bunka shi*, vol. 4, *Nihon rekishi no rekishi* (Shinchōsha, 1959), 38–55.

15 In 1336, in the aftermath of the Kemmu Restoration, the emperor Go-Daigo sought to reassert imperial authority, but Ashikaga Takauji selected a new em-

peror from a branch of the imperial family in Kyoto. Go-Daigo escaped to Yo-shino, south of Nara and formed the "southern" court, in opposition to the "northern court" in Kyoto. The southern court survived until 1392.

16 Taguchi Ukichi, "Shintōsha shōshi ni tsugeru," in *Nihon bunka zenshū*, vol. 15, ed. Yoshino Sakuzō (Nihon Hyōronsha, 1929), 544. Kume's article is also included in this work, 527–543.

17 Quoted in Haga Noboru, *Hihan kindai Nihon Shigaku shisōshi* (Kashiwa Shobō, 1974), 82. The entire text of "Kokugaku no zentō" is included in Konakamura Kiyonori, *Yōshunro zakkō*, vol. 8 (Yoshikawa Hanshichi, 1898), 1–12.

18 Konakamura's career is discussed at length in Ogawa Shigeo, *Kokugakusha denki shūsei* (Dai Nihon Tosho Kabushiki Kaisha, 1905), 1620–1624.

19 Ōkubo, *Nihon rekishi no rekishi*, 48–49.

20 Konakamura, *Kokugaku zentō*, 16–19.

21 Ibid., 19.

22 Uchino Gorō has written extensively on the formation of the kokugaku geneal-ogy. See for example, *Bungei gakushi no hōhō: Kokugakushi no saikentō* (Ōfūsha, 1974), esp. 90–97. The discussion that follows is based upon Uchino's account, and the quotations from Hirata and Ōkuni are from 92 and 96 respectively.

23 A translation of this document is included in *Sources of Japanese Tradition*, vol. 2, comp. Ryusaku Tsunoda, William De Bary, and Donald Keene (New York: Colum-bia University Press, 1964). The authenticiy of the petition has been questioned by a number of modern scholars. In his authoritative study of Azumamaro's life and work published in 1942, Miyake Kiyoshi argued that the petition was probably a late eighteenth-century forgery by one or more members of the Kada school. See Uchino, *Bungei gakushi no hōhō*, 98–105. Uchino himself suggests that the peti-tion may have been forged by members of Atsutane's school. In contrast, Peter Nosco accepts that authenticity of this document, and his discussion of Azuma-maro mirrors Atsutane's assessment of his significance. See Nosco, *Remembering Paradise*, 90–95.

24 Uchino Gorō, *Edoha kokugaku ronkō* (Sōrinsha, 1979), 60–61.

25 Ibid., 61.

26 The description that follows is based on Sakamoto Ken'ichi, *Meiji shintōshi no ken-kyū* (Kokusho Kankōkai, 1973), 184–185; Sakamoto Koremaru, "Meiji san-nen no kokugaku yondaijin reisai," *Kokugakuin Daigaku Nihon bunka kenkyūjo johō* 140 (1988): 5–7. The latter cites the Kokugakuin University document.

27 Konakamura, "Kokugaku no zento," 22.

28 Konakamura Kiyonori, "Shigaku ni tsuite," *Shigaku zasshi* 1, no. 1 (December, 1890), 5–10.

29 Muraoka Tsunetsugu, *Motoori Norinaga* (1911; reprint, Iwanami Shoten, 1942), 345,

30 Hisamatsu Sen'chi, "Kaisetsu," in *Meiji bungaku zenshū*, vol. 44 (Chikuma Shobō, 1928), 428.

31 On Haga Masaki, see Fujii Sadafumi, "Haga Yaichi Sensei no kokugaku no genryū," in HYS, vol. 1, 327–329.

32 Quoted in Saitō Michiko, "Haga Yaichi to fōkuroa—sono senkateki sokumen," *Kokugakuin Daigaku Nihon bunka kenkyūjo kiyō* 70 (1992): 85.

33 *Kokugakushi gairon* is based upon a talk Haga gave in August 1900 at the Institute for National Language (Kokugo Denshūjo). It was published in December of the same year after Haga had left Japan for Germany. It is included in HYS, vol. 1, 5–55.

34 Ibid., 6.

35 Ibid., 8.

36 Ibid., 14–15, passim.

37 Akinari is discussed on 21; Moribe, on 40.

38 Ibid., 24–25, passim.

39 Ibid., 31, 26.

40 Ibid., 35–36.

41 Haga Yaichi, "Kokubungaku jūkō," in HYS, vol. 1, 317.

42 Ibid., 197.

43 Haga, *Kokugakushi gairon*, 42.

44 Ibid., 45–46.

45 Saitō, "Haga Yaichi to fōkuroa," 87.

46 Haga Yaichi, "Kokugaku to ha nani zo ya," in HYS, vol. 1, 147.

47 Ibid., 154, 159.

48 Ibid., 155.

49 Ibid., 152–153. The quotes that follow in this paragraph are also from 152.

50 Ibid., 161.

51 Ibid. 153.

52 Ibid., 159.

53 Hatanaka Kenji, "Kokugaku to bunkengaku," *Nihon shisōshigaku* 30 (September 1998): 171.

54 Philip August Böckh, "Philological Hermeneutics," in *The Hermeneutic Reader: Texts of the German Tradition from the Enlightenment to the Present*, ed. Kurt Mueller-Volmer (Oxford: Basil Blackwell, 1985), 141.

55 Shimizu Masayuki, "Nihon shisōshi to kaishakugaku—Haga Yaichi to Muraoka Tsunetsugu," *Ronshū* 4 (1985): 117. Hisamatsu Sen'ichi, "Kaidai," in *Miyake Setsurei, Haga Yaichi, Nihonjinron*, ed. Ikimatsu Keizō (Toyama Shobō, 1977), 1.

56 Haga Yaichi, *Kokuminsei jūron* (Toyamabō, 1908), 2.

57 Ibid., 7.

58 Ibid., 37.

59 For a discussion of Muraoka's work at Tōhoku University, see Tōhoku Daigaku Henshū Iinkai, ed., *Tōhoku Daigaku gojūnenshi*, vol. 2 (Tōhoku Daigaku, 1960), 1266–1272. For biographical information, see Yamada Takao, *Nihon rinri shisō* (Daimeidō, 1981), 435–438.

60 Muraoka, *Motoori Norinaga*, 343. Here, Muraoka gives the title of Haga's work as "Kokugaku ni tsuite," but as Hatanaka notes, the dates and content of his remarks suggest that the work in question was "Kokugaku to ha nani zo ya." See Hatanaka, "Kokugaku to bunkengaku," 163.

61 Ibid., 362–363.

62 Ibid, 175.

63 Ibid., 181.

64 Ibid., 238.

65 Ibid., 340.

66 Discussion of Norinaga's place in Muraoka's "history of thought" can be found in Umezawa Iseizō, "Nihon shisōshi gakusha toshite no ko Muraoka Tsunetsugu Kyōju no gyōseki," in *Shintōshi kenkyū* 4, no. 1 (1942): 89–102.

67 Muraoka Tsunetsugu, "Nihon shisōshi no kenkyūhō ni tsuite," in *Zoku Nihon shisōshi kenkyū* (Iwanami Shoten,1939), 32.

68 Muraoka, *Motoori Norinaga*, 527–528. Quoted in Shimizu, "Nihon shisōshi to kaishakugaku," 121.

69 Muraoka Tsunetsugu, *Zoku Nihon shisōshi kenkyū*, 7–8.

70 Muraoka Tsunetsugu, *Nihon shisōshi kenkyū* 4 (Iwanami Shoten, 1949), 188–189. Quoted in Hatanaka, "Kokugaku to bunkengaku," 167.

71 Katō Shūichi, "Yūyō bōgo," *Asahi shinbun* (evening edition), March 22, 1998. Quoted in Koyasu Nobukuni, *Norinaga mondai to ha nani ka* (Seidosha, 1995), 19.

72 For an account of Kōno's work on national ethics, see Yamada Takao, *Kindai Nihon rinri shisō* (Daimeidō, 1981), 388–391.

73 Origuchi Shinobu, "Kokugaku to ha nani ka," in OSZ, vol. 20, 280.

74 Origuchi Shinobu, "Kokugaku to kokubungaku to," in OSZ, vol. 20, 296–298, passim.

75 Origuchi, "Kokugaku to ha nani ka," 279.

76 Origuchi, "Kokugaku to kokubungaku to," 292–293.

77 Origuchi, "Kokugaku to ha nani ka," 281 and 284.

78 Origuchi Shinobu, "Iyaku kokugaku hitori annai Kōno Seizō sokka ni sasagu," in OSZ, vol. 20, 261.

79 Ibid., 264.

80 Ibid., 275.

81 Ibid., 269.

82 Stefan Tanaka, *Japan's Orient: Rendering Pasts into History* (Berkeley: University of California Press, 1993).

83 On the influence of "popular histories" on Tsuda, see Ienaga Saburō, *Tsuda Sōkichi no shisōshiteki kenkyū* (Iwanmi Shoten, 1972), 13–31.

84 Ibid., 780.

85 Ozeki Motoaki, "Tsuda Sōkichi ni okeru tennō," *Ritsumeikan bungaku* 498 (December 1986): 950; Kawamura Sō, "Tsuda Sōkichi—Hitei no shigaku," *Bungei* 26, no. 2 (1987): 268.

86 Tsuda Sōkichi, *Bungaku in arawaretaru waga kokumin no shisō*, vol. 1, *Kizoku bungaku no jidai*, in TSZ, bekkan 2, 221.

87 Ibid., vol. 2, *Bushi bungaku no jidai*, in TSZ, bekkan 3, 277.

88 Ibid., vol. 3, *Heimin bungaku no jidai, Jo*, in TSZ, bekkan 4, 160.

89 Quoted in Ozeki, "Tsuda Sōkichi ni okeru tennō," 952–953.

90 Tsuda, *Heimin bungaku no jidai*, 414–415.

91 Ibid., 416.

92 Tsuda, "Shindaishi no atarashii kenkyū," in TSZ, bekkan 4, 123.

93 Ibid., 398.

94 TSZ, bekkan 4, 408–411.

95 Ienaga Saburō discusses the trial and its outcome in *Nihon no kindai shigaku* (Nihon Hyōron Shinsha, 1957), 161–202. He notes that Tsuda insisted, evidence from his own work notwithstanding, that his intention had not been to question the authenticity of the imperial genealogy related in the *Kojiki* and *Nihon shoki*.

CONCLUSION

1 Michel Foucault, *The Order of Things: An Archaeology of the Human Sciences* (New York: Vintage Books, 1994), 282–283.

2 Prasenjit Duara, "Historicizing National Identity, or Who Imagines What and When," in *Becoming National: A Reader*, ed. Geoff Eley and Ronald Grigor Suny, esp. 153–157.

3 Partha Chatterjee, *The Nation and Its Fragments* (Princeton: Princeton University Press, 1993), 3–5.

Works Cited

Note: The place of publication for all Japanese-language works is Tokyo, unless otherwise indicated.

PRIMARY SOURCES

Arai, Hakuseki. "Koshitsū dokuhō hanrei." In *Arai Hakuseki zenshū*, edited by Imaizumi Sadasuke. Vol. 3. Tōkyō Kappan, 1905.

Böckh, Philip August. "Philological Hermeneutics." In *The Hermeneutic Reader: Texts of the German Tradition from the Enlightenment to the Present*, edited by Kurt Mueller-Volmer. Oxford: Basil Blackwell, 1985.

Bunyō, Inshi. "Seji kenbun roku." In *Nihon shomin seikatsu shiryō shūsei*, vol. 8, *Kenbunki*, edited by Harada Tomohiko et al. San'ichi Shobō, 1971.

Fujitani, Mitsue. *Fujitani Mitsue shū*. 5 vols. Kokumin Seishin Bunka Kenkyūjo, 1936–1940.

———. *Fujitani Mitsue zenshū*. Edited by Miyake Kiyoshi. 8 vols. Kyoto: Shibunkaku, 1979–1993.

Haga, Yaichi. *Haga Yaichi senshū*. Edited by Haga Yaichi Senshū Iinkai. 7 vols. Kokugakuin Daigaku, 1982–1992.

———. *Kokuminsei jūron*. Toyamabō, 1908.

Hirata, Atsutane. "Tama no mihashira." In *Shinshū Hirata Atsutane zenshū*, edited by Hirata Atsutane Zenshū Kankōkai. Vol. 7. Meicho Shuppan, 1977.

Kada, Azumamaro. "Kojiki sakki." In *Kada zenshū*. Vol. 6. 1928–1932. Reprint. Meicho Fukyū Kai, 1990.

Kamo, Mabuchi. *Kamo no Mabuchi zenshū*. Edited by Inoue Minoru et al. 28 volumes. Zoku Gunsho Ruijū Kansei Kai, 1977–1992.

Keichū. "Seisen hondai shoki." In *Keichū zenshū*, edited by Hisamatsu Sen'ichi. Vol. 1. Iwanami Shoten, 1975.

Konakamura, Kiyonori. "Kokugaku no zento." In *Yoshunrō zakkō*. Vol. 8. Yoshikawa Hanshichi, 1898.

———. "Shigaku ni tsuite." *Shigaku zasshi* 1, no. 1 (December 1890): 5–10.

Man'yoshu. Translated by Ian Hideo Levy. Princeton: Princeton University Press, 1981.

Motoori, Norinaga. *Motoori Norinaga zenshū*. Edited by Ōno Susumu and Ōkubo Tadashi. 22 vols. Chikuma Shobō, 1968–1975.

———. *Kojiki-den: Book 1*. Translated by Ann Wehmeyer. Ithaca, N.Y.: Cornell University East Asia Program, 1999.

Muraoka, Tsunetsugu. *Motoori Norinaga*. 1911. Reprint. Iwanami Shoten, 1942.

———. *Nihon shisōshi kenkyū 4*. Iwanami Shoten, 1949.

———. *Shintōshi*. Sōbunsha, 1956.

———. "Tachibana Moribe no gakusetsu." In *Nihon shisōshi kenkyū*. Iwanami Shoten, 1940.

———. *Zoku Nihon shisōshi kenkyū*. Iwanami Shoten, 1942.

Nishimura, Sey, trans. "First Steps in the Mountain: Motoori Norinaga's Uiyama-bumi." *Monumenta Nipponica* 42, no. 4 (winter 1987): 449–493.

———, trans. "The Way of the Gods: Motoori Norinaga's *Naobi no mitama*." *Monumentia Nipponica* 46, no. 1 (spring 1991): 21–42.

Origuchi, Shinobu. *Origuchi Shinobu zenshū*. 38 vols. Chūō Kōronsha, 1976.

Philippi, Donald, trans. *Kojiki*. Tokyo University Press, 1968.

Sakamoto, Tarō, et al., eds. *Nihon koten bungaku taikei*. Vol. 67, *Nihon shoki*. Iwanami Shoten, 1967.

Sugita, Genpaku. "Nochimigusa." In *Nihon shomin seikatsu shiryō shūsei*, vol. 7, Kikin ekibyō, edited by Mori Kahei and Tanigawa Ken'ichi. San'ichi Shobō, 1970.

Tachibana, Moribe. *Tachibana Moribe zenshū (Shintei)*. Edited by Tachibana Jun'ichi. 1930. 13 vols. Reprint. Tōkyō Bijutsu, 1967.

———. "Taimon zakki." In *Nihon shisōshi taikei*, vol. 51, *Kokugaku undō no shisō*, edited by Haga Noboru and Matsumoto Sannosuke. Iwanami Shoten, 1971.

Taguchi, Ukichi. "Shintōsha shoshi ni tsugeru." In *Nihon bunka zenshū*, edited by Yoshino Sakuzō. Vol. 15. Nihon Hyōronsha, 1929.

Tanigawa, Kotosuga. *Nihon shoki tsūsho*. Edited by Kojima Noriyuki. 3 vols. Kyoto: Rinsen Shoten, 1978.

Tayasu, Munetake. "Kojiki shōsetsu." In *Tayasu Munetake*. Vol. 3. Edited by Toki Zenmaro. Nihon Hyōronsha, 1945.

Tsuda, Sōkichi. *Tsuda Sōkichi zenshū*. 33 vols. Iwanami Shoten, 1963–1989.

Ueda, Akinari. "Harusame monogatari." Translated by Barry Jackman as *Tales of the Spring Rain*. University of Tokyo Press, 1975.

———. *Nihon koten bungaku taikei*. Vol. 56, *Ueda Akinari shū*. Edited by Nakamura Yukihiko. Iwanami Shoten, 1974.

———. *Ueda Akinari zenshū*. Edited by Hino Tatsuo et al. 12 vols. Chūō Kōronsha, 1990.

———. *Ugetsu monogatari*. Translated by Kenji Hamada as *Tales of Moonlight and Rain*. University of Tokyo Press, 1971.

Ukiyo no arisama. In *Nihon shomin seikatsu shiryō shūsei*, vol. 11, Sesō, edited by Harada Tomohiko and Asakura Naohiko. San'ichi Shobō, 1971.

Yano, Harumichi. "Kenkin sengo." In *Nihon shisō taikei*, vol. 51, *Kokugaku undō no shisō*, edited by Haga Noboru and Matsumoto Sannosuke. Iwanami Shoten, 1971.

SECONDARY SOURCES

Anderson, Benedict. *Imagined Communities: Reflections on the Origin and Spread of Nationalism.* London: Verso, 1983.

Aoki, Kōji. *Hyakushō ikki no nenjiteki kenkyū.* Shinseisha, 1966.

Aoki, Michio. *Bunka bunsei ki no minshū to bunka.* Bunka Shobō Hakubunsha, 1985.

Azuma, Yoshimochi. "Harusame monogatari 'rekishi shosetsu' no kentō." In *Nihon bungaku kenkyū shiryō sōsho: Akinari*, edited by Takada Mamoru. Yūseidō Shuppan, 1972.

Balibar, Etienne. "The Nation Form: History and Ideology." In *Becoming National: A Reader*, edited by Geoff Eley and Ronald Grigor Suny. New York: Oxford University Press, 1996.

Bhabha, Homi. "Introduction." In *Nation and Narrations*, edited by Homi Bhabha. New York: Routledge, 1990.

Bitō Masahide. "Mitogaku no tokushitsu." In *Nihon shisō taikei*, vol. 53, *Mitogaku*, edited by Bitō Masahide et al. Iwanami Shoten, 1977.

Breen, J. L. "Shintoists in Restoration Japan (1868–1872): Towards a Reassessment." *Modern Asian Studies* 24, no. 3 (1990): 579–602.

Castoriadis, Cornelius. *The Imaginary Institution of Society.* Cambridge, Mass.: MIT Press, 1987.

Chartier, Roger. *The Order of Books: Readers, Authors, and Libraries in Europe between the Fourteenth and Eighteenth Centuries.* Translated by Lydia G. Cochrane. Cambridge: Polity Press, 1994.

Chatterjee, Partha. *The Nation and Its Fragments.* Princeton: Princeton University Press, 1993.

———. *Nationalist Thought and the Colonial World.* Minneapolis: University of Minnesota Press, 1995.

Doak, Kevin. *Dreams of Difference: The Japan Romantic School and the Crisis of Modernity.* Berkeley: University of California Press, 1994.

Duara, Prasenjit. "Historicizing National Identity, or Who Imagines What and When." In *Becoming National: A Reader*, edited by Geoff Eley and Ronald Grigor Suny. New York: Oxford University Press, 1996.

———. *Rescuing History from the Nation: Questioning Narratives of Modern China.* Chicago: University of Chicago Press, 1995.

Foucault, Michel. *The Order of Things: An Archaeology of the Human Sciences.* New York: Vintage Books, 1994.

Fujii, Sadafumi. *Edo kokugaku tenseishi no kenkyū.* Yoshikawa Kōbunkan, 1987.

————. "Haga Yaichi Sensei no kokugaku no genryū." In *Haga Yaichi senshū*, edited by Matsuo Saburō. Vol. 1. Kokugakuin Daigaku, 1982.

Fujita, Tokutarō. "*Kojikiden* no shinkō." In *Kojikiden no kenkyū*, edited by Fukuda Misamichi. Seibunkaku, 1941.

Fujitani, T. *Splendid Monarchy: Power and Pageantry in Modern Japan.* Berkeley: University of California Press, 1996.

Fukunaga, Shizuya. "Akinari to Norinaga no ronsō: Kokugo in'on ron ni tsuite." *Kyōto Joshidai kokubungaku* 31 (December 1963): 7–19.

Gluck, Carol. *Japan's Modern Myths: Ideology in the Late Meiji Period.* Princeton: Princeton University Press, 1985.

Go, Tetsuo. "Kokubungaku/kokugaku hihan." *Nihon bungaku* 523 (January 1997): 10–17.

Gourgouris, Stathis. *Dream Nation: Enlightenment, Colonization, and the Institution of Modern Greece.* Stanford: Stanford University Press, 1996.

Haga, Noboru. *Bakumatsu kokugaku no tenkai.* Hanawa Shobō, 1963.

————. *Henkakuki ni okeru kokugaku.* San' ichi Shobō, 1975.

————. *Hihan kindai Nihon shigaku shisōshi.* Kashiwa Shobō, 1974.

————. *Kokugaku no hitobito — sono kōdō to shisō.* Hyōronsha, 1977.

————. *Motoori Norinaga: Kinsei kokugaku no seiritsu.* Shimizu Shoin, 1972.

————. "Murata Harumi no rekishiteki ichi." *Rekishi jinrui* 9 (December 1980): 135–169.

Hall, John Whitney. *Tanuma Okitsugu: Forerunner of Modern Japan.* Cambridge, Mass.: Harvard University Press, 1955.

Hamasuna, Songi. "Fujitani Mitsue no gengoron." *Kokugakuin Daigaku Daigakuin kiyō* 25 (February 1993): 99–118.

————. "Fujitani Mitsue no shinwa kaishaku." *Shintō shūkyō* 151 (June 1994): 29–51.

Hardacre, Helen. *Shinto and the State, 1868–1988.* Princeton: Princeton University Press, 1989.

Harootunian, H. D. *Things Seen and Unseen: Discourse and Ideology in Tokugawa Nativism.* Chicago: University of Chicago Press, 1988.

Hashimoto, Shinkichi. *Moji oyobi kanazukai no kenkyū.* Iwanami Shoten, 1961.

Hatanaka Kenji. "Kokugaku to bunkengaku." *Nihon shisōshigaku* 30 (September 1998): 156–172.

————. "Makotoben ni miru Fujitani Mitsue no karon." *Bungei kenkyū* 139 (May 1996): 52–63.

Hino, Tatsuo. *Norinaga to Akinari.* Chikuma Shobō, 1984.

Hirai, Takeo. "Fujitani Mitsue daijin no seikatsu," part 1. *Kokugakuin zasshi* 25, no. 4 (April 1919): 58–67.

————. "Fujitani Mitsue daijin no seikatsu," part 2. *Kokugakuin zasshi* 25, no. 6 (June 1919): 33–42.

Hirano, Kimihiro. *Man'yō hihyōshi kenkyū.* Miraisha, 1965.

Hisamatsu, Sen'ichi. "Kaidai." In *Miyake Setsurei, Haga Yaichi, Nihonjinron*, edited by Ikimatsu Keizō. Toyama Shobō, 1977.

———. "Kaisetsu." In *Meiji bungaku zenshū*. Vol. 44. Chikuma Shobō, 1928.

Hobsbawm, E. J. and Terence Ranger, eds. *The Invention of Tradition*. Cambridge: Cambridge University Press, 1983.

———. *Nations and Nationalism since 1780: Programme, Myth, Reality*. Cambridge: Cambridge University Press, 1990.

Howell, David L. "Hard Times in the Kantō: Economic Change and Village Life in Late Tokugawa Japan." *Modern Asian Studies* 23, no. 2 (1989): 349–371.

Hroch, Miroslav. "From National Movement to the Fully-Formed Nation: The Nation-Building Process in Europe." In *Becoming National: A Reader*, edited by Geoff Eley and Ronald Grigor Suny. Oxford: Oxford University Press, 1996.

Ienaga Saburō. *Nihon no kindai shigaku*. Nihon Hyōron Shinsha, 1957.

———. *Nihon shisōshi no shomondai*. Saitō Shoten, 1968.

———. *Tsuda Sōkichi no shisōshiteki kenkyū*. Iwanami Shoten, 1972.

Iikura, Yōichi. "Akinari ni okeru 'ikidōri' no mondai: *Harusame monogatari* he no isshiten." *Bungaku* 52 (May 1984): 72–85.

———. "Akinari to bundo: *Yasumigoto* shiron." *Bungaku* 54 (July 1986): 88–102.

Imai, Jun, and Kozawa, Tomio, eds. *Nihon shisōshi ronsō shi*. Perikansha, 1990.

Itō, Masao. *Kinsei no waka to kokugaku*. Ise: Kogakkan Daigaku Shuppanbu, 1979.

Itō, Shingo. *Kinsei kokugogaku shi*. Osaka: Tachikawa Bunmeidō, 1928.

Iwahashi, Koyata. *Ueda Akinari*. Yūseidō Shuppan, 1975.

Iwai, Tadakuma. "Nihon kindai shigaku no keisei." In *Iwanami Kōza Nihon rekishi*, Bekkan I. Iwanami Shoten, 1963.

Iwasa, Tadashi. "Kaisetsu." In *Nihon koten bungaku taikei*, vol. 87, *Jinnō shōtōki, Masukagami*, edited by Iwasa Tadashi et al. Iwanami Shoten, 1965.

Kabayama, Kōichi. "Kikin kara umareru bunka." In *Bakumatsu bunka no kenkyū*, edited by Hayashiya Tatsusaburō. Iwanami Shoten, 1978.

Kamada, Tōji. "Shinsōtekina jigen toshite no kotodama: Fujitani Mitsue no kotodama ron." *Shintō shūkyō* 114 (March 1984): 38–76.

Kamei, Takashi. "Kojiki ha yomeru ka," In *Kamei Takashi ronbunshū*, vol. 4, *Nihongo no sugata to kokoro*. Yoshikawa Kōbunkan, 1985.

Kanno, Kakumyō. *Motoori Norinaga: Kotoba to miyabi*. Perikansha, 1991.

Kata, Takeo. *Kokugakusha Tanigawa Kotosuga no kenkyū*. Yugawa Kōbunsha, 1934.

Katō Shūichi, "Yūyō bōgo." *Asahi shinbun* (evening edition), 22 March 1998.

Katsurajima, Nobuhiro. "Hirata-ha kokugakusha no 'dokusho' to sono gensetsu." *Edo no shisō* 5 (1996): 83–95.

Kawamura, Sō. "Tsuda Sōkichi—Hitei no shigaku." *Bungei* 26, no. 2 (1987): 268–274.

Kazama, Seishi. "Hyōgen no kokugaku: Kamo no Mabuchi kara Tachibana Moribe made." *Nihon bungaku* 48 (February 1999): 1–11.

Kedourie, Elie. "Introduction." In *Nationalism in Asia and Africa*, edited by Elie Kedourie. London: Weidenfeld and Nicolson, 1970.

Keene, Donald. *World within Walls*. New York: Grove Press, 1976.

Ketelaar, James. *Of Heretics and Martyrs in Modern Japan*. Princeton: Princeton University Press, 1990.

Kikuchi, Isao. *Kinsei no kikin*. Yoshikawa Kōbunkan, 1997.

Kitaoka, Shirō. "Shisei to Norinaga: Sono gengo kenkyū no michi." In *Kinsei kokugakusha no kenkyū: Tanigawa Kotosuga to sono shūhen*. Ise: Ko Kitaoka Shirō Kyōju Ikōshū Kankōkai, 1977.

Kobayashi, Hideo. *Motoori Norinaga*. Shinchōsha, 1977.

Kojima, Noriyuki. "Kojiki kundoku no shūhen." *Bungaku* 36 (August 1968): 37–41.

Kokugakuin Daigaku Hyakunenshi Henshū Iinkai, eds. *Kokugakuin Daigaku hyakunenshi*. Kokugakuin Daigaku, 1982.

Kokushi Daijiten Iinkai, ed. *Kokushi daijiten*. 15 vols. Yoshikawa Kōbunkan, 1979–1997.

Konta, Yōzō. "Edo jidai no saigai jōhō." In *Edo chōnin no kenkyū*, edited by Nishiyama Matsunosuke. Vol. 5. Yoshikawa Kōbunkan, 1980.

———. *Edo no hon'yasan*. NHK Bukusu, 1977.

———. *Edo no kinsho*. Yoshikawa Kōbunkan, 1981.

———. "Hikka to shuppan kikō: Shuppan bunka to Edo bungaku wo meguru shomondai." *Kokubungaku* 42, no. 11 (1994): 33–39.

———. "Jūkyū seiki no media jijō." In *Nihon no kinsei*, vol. 14, *Bunka no taishūka*, edited by Takeuchi Makoto. Chūō Kōronsha, 1993.

Kornicki, Peter. "The Enmeiin Affair of 1803: The Spread of Information in the Tokugawa Period." *Harvard Journal of Asiatic Studies* 42, no. 2 (December 1982): 503–533.

———. "Nishiki no Ura: An Instance of Censorship and the Structure of a *Sharebon*." *Monumenta Nipponica* 32, no. 2 (summer 1977): 153–162.

Kōzu, Hayato. "Kinsei no Kojiki kenkyū." In *Kojiki taisei: Kenkyūshi hen*. Heibonsha, 1956.

Koyasu, Nobukuni. *Jiken toshite no Soraigaku*. Seidosha, 1990.

———. "Kojiki — Kono kanji shoki tekusuto." Paper presented at the July 1999 meeting of the Shisōshi Bunka Riron Kenkyūkai (Kyoto, Japan).

———. *Norinaga mondai to ha nani ka*. Seidosha, 1995.

———. *Norinaga to Atsutane no sekai*. Chūō Kōronsha, 1977.

Maruyama, Masao. *Nihon seiji shisō no kenkyū*. Iwanami Shoten, 1952.

———. *Studies in the Intellectual History of Tokugawa Japan*. Translation of *Nihon seiji shisō no kenkyū* by Mikiso Hane. Princeton: Princeton University Press, 1974.

Matsumoto, Sannosuke. "Bakumatsu kokugaku no shisōshiteki igi." In *Nihon shisō taikei*, vol. 51, *Kokugaku undō no shisō*, edited by Haga Yaichi and Matsumoto Sannosuke. Iwanami Shoten, 1971.

———. *Kokugaku seiji shisō no kenkyū*. Miraisha, 1972.

Matsumoto, Sigeru. *Motoori Norinaga, 1730–1801.* Cambridge, Mass.: Harvard University Press, 1970.

Miura, Hiroyuki. *Nihonshi no kenkyū.* 1930. Reprint. Iwanami Shoten, 1981.

Miyake, Kiyoshi. *Fujitani Mitsue.* Sanseidō, 1942.

Miyamoto, Tsunekazu, ed. *Ise sangū.* Yasaka Shobō, 1987.

Momokawa, Takahito. *Uchinaru Norinaga.* Tōkyō Daigaku Shuppankai, 1987.

Morita, Kirō. *Ueda Akinari no kenkyū.* Kinokuniya Shoten, 1970.

Moriya, Katsuhisa. "Urban Networks and Information Networks." In *Tokugawa Japan: The Social and Economic Antecedents of Modern Japan,* edited by Nakane Chie and Ōishi Shinzaburō. University of Tokyo Press, 1990.

Moriya, Takeshi. "Shisei no jōhō: Ukiyo no arisama wo meguru nōto." In *Bakumatsu bunka no kenkyū,* edited by Hayashiya Tatsusaburō. Iwanami Shoten, 1978.

Moriyama, Shigeo. *Ueda Akinari: Shiteki jōnen no sekai.* San'ichi Shobō, 1986.

Munesada, Isō. "Kyōto no bunka shakai: 'Heian jinbutsu shi' Kasei ban to Kyōjin.' " In *Kasei bunka no kenkyū,* edited by Hayashiya Tatsusaburō. Iwanami Shoten, 1976.

Nagatomo, Chiyoji. *Kinsei kashi hon'ya no kenkyū.* Tōkyōdō Shuppan, 1982.

Najita, Tetsuo. "History and Nature in Eighteenth-Century Tokugawa Thought." In *The Cambridge History of Japan,* vol. 4, *Early Modern Japan,* edited by John Whitney Hall. Cambridge: Cambridge University Press, 1991.

———. "Ōshio Heihachirō." In *Personality in Japanese History,* edited by Albert M. Craig and Donald H. Shively. Berkeley: University of California Press, 1970.

———. *Visions of Virtue in Tokugawa Japan.* Chicago: University of Chicago Press, 1987.

———, ed. *Tokugawa Political Writings.* Cambridge: Cambridge University Press, 1998.

Najita, Tetsuo, and H. D. Harootunian. "Japan's Revolt against the West." In *Modern Japanese Thought,* edited by Bob Tadashi Wakabayashi. Cambridge: Cambridge University Press, 1998.

Nakai, Kate Wildman. *Shogunal Politics: Arai Hakuseki and the Premises of Tokugawa Rule.* Cambridge, Mass.: Harvard University Press, 1988.

Nakai, Nobuhiko. "Commercial Change and Urban Growth in Early Modern Japan." Translated by James L. McClain. In *Cambridge History of Japan,* vol. 4, *Early Modern Japan,* edited by Marius Jansen. Cambridge: Cambridge University Press, 1991.

Nakajima, Takashi. "Hanpon jidai no 'shahon' to ha nanika." *Kokubungaku* 42, no. 11 (1994): 49–53.

Nakamura, Hiroyasu. "Akinari no monogatari ron." *Nihon bungaku* 13 (February 1964): 1–22.

———. "Yūkō na honshitsu, mukō na honshitsu: Hi no kami ronsō ni tsuite." In *Nihon bungaku kenkyū shiryō sōsho: Akinari,* edited by Takada Mamoru. Yūseidō Shuppan, 1972.

Nakamura, Satoru. "The Development of Rural Industry." In *Tokugawa Japan: The Social and Economic Antecedents of Modern Japan,* edited by Nakane Chie and Ōishi Shinzaburō. University of Tokyo Press, 1990.

Nakano, Mitsutoshi, et al. "Zadankai: Hanpon wo meguru shomondai." *Edo Bungaku*
    15 (1996): 2–23.
Nancy, Jean-Luc. *The Inoperative Community.* Minneapolis: University of Minnesota
    Press, 1991.
Nihon Shisō Kenkyūkai, eds. *Nihon ni okeru rekishi shisō no tenkai.* Yoshikawa Kōbun-
    kan, 1965.
Nishigaki, Seiji. *O-Ise mairi.* Iwanami Shoten, 1983.
Nishimiya, Kazutami. *Nihon jōdai no bunshō to hyōki.* Kazuma Shobō, 1988.
Noguchi, Takehiko. *Akinari gengi.* Seidosha, 1989.
——. *Edojin no rekishi ishiki.* Asahi Shinbunsha, 1987.
Nomura, Hachirō. *Kokugaku zenshi.* Vol. 1. Marui Shoten, 1940.
Nosco, Peter. *Remembering Paradise: Nativism and Nostalgia in Eighteenth-Century Japan.*
    Cambridge, Mass.: Harvard University Press, 1990.
Nozaki, Morihide. *Motoori Norinaga no sekai.* Hanawa Shobō, 1972.
Ogasahara, Haruo. *Kokujū ronsō no kenkyū.* Perikansha, 1988.
Ogawa, Shigeo. *Kokugakusha denki shūsei.* Dai Nihon Tosho Kabushiki Kaisha, 1905.
Okamoto, Katsu. "Kinsei shuppan no issokumen: Motoori-ke kankei bunshō wo chū-
    shin ni." *Kinsei bungei* 31 (1980): 43–53.
Okanaka, Masayuki. "Suzumon no kaisō." In *Motoori Norinaga to Suzuya shachū*, edited
    by Suzuki Jun, Okanaka Masayuki, and Nakamura Kazumoto. Kinseisha, 1984.
Ōkubo, Tadashi. "Akinari no kokugaku." In *Nihon koten kanshō kōza*, vol. 24, *Akinari*,
    edited by Nakamura Yukihiko. Kadokawa Shoten, 1958.
——. "Akinari to Norinaga: ronsō no kei'i to tairitsu no imi." *Kokubungaku* (August
    1967): 121–126.
Ōkubo, Toshiaki. *Nihon bunka shi.* Vol. 4, *Nihon rekishi no rekishi.* Shinchōsha, 1959.
——. *Ōkubo Toshiaki choshakushū.* Vol. 4, *Meiji Ishin to kyōiku.* Yoshikawa Kōbunkan,
    1987.
Ooms, Herman. *Charismatic Bureaucrat: A Political Biography of Matsudaira Sadanobu.* Chi-
    cago: University of Chicago Press, 1975.
——. *Tokugawa Ideology, 1570–1680.* Princeton: Princeton University Press, 1985.
Ōta, Seikyū. *Nihon kagaku to Chūgoku shigaku.* Shimizu Kōbundō Shobō, 1968.
Ōta, Yoshimaro. "Tachibana Moribe—Hito to gakumon." In *Tachibana Moribe zenshū*
    (Shintei), Hokan, edited by Tachibana Jun'ichi. Tōkyō Bijutsu, 1967.
——. "Tachibana Moribe to kiki kayō." *Kokugo to kokubungaku* (July 1942): 61–77.
Ozeki, Motoaki. "Tsuda Sōkichi ni okeru tennō." *Ritsumeikan bungaku* 498 (December
    1986): 256–283.
Plemenatz, John. "Two Types of Nationalism." In *Nationalism: The Nature and Evolution*
    of an Idea, edited by Eugene Kamenka. London: Edward Arnold, 1976.
Renan, Ernest. "What Is a Nation?" In *Nation and Narrations*, edited by Homi Bhabha.
    New York: Routledge, 1990.
Saigō, Nobutsuna. *Kojiki chūshaku.* Vol. 1. Heibonsha, 1975.

————. *Kokugaku no hihan.* 1948. Reprint. Miraisha, 1965.

Saitō, Fumiya. "Kinsei ni okeru kanbun kundoku no fukko." In *Kokugo kenkyū,* edited by Matsumura Akira Sensei Kiju Kinenkai. Meiji Shoin, 1993.

Saitō, Michiko. "Haga Yaichi to fōkuroa—sono senkakuteki sokumen." *Kokugakuin Daigaku Nihon bunka kenkyūjo kiyō* 70 (1992): 83–104.

Sakai, Naoki. *Voices from the Past: The Status of Language in Eighteenth-Century Japanese Discourse.* Ithaca, N.Y.: Cornell University Press, 1991.

Sakamoto, Ken'ichi. *Meiji shintōshi no kenkyū.* Kokusho Kankōkai, 1973.

Sakamoto, Koremaru. *Meiji Ishin to kokugakusha.* Daimeidō, 1993.

————. "Meiji san-nen no kokugaku yondaijin reisai." *Kokugakuin Daigaku Nihon bunka kenkyūjo johō* 140 (1988): 5–7.

————. "Meiji shonen ni okeru kokugakusha no seijiteki dōkō—Saisei itchi kokka no kōsō wo megutte." *Kokugakuin zasshi* 40 (August 1992): 1–21.

Sasaki, Nobutsuna. *Nihon kagakushi.* 1910. Reprint. Nakabunkan, 1942.

Sasazuki, Kiyomi. "Kojiki kenkyū shoshi." In *Motoori Norinaga no kenkyū.* Iwanami Shoten, 1944.

Satō, Miyuki. *Ayatari to Akinari to.* Nagoya: Nagoya Daigaku Shuppankyoku, 1993.

Shida, Nobuyoshi. "Fujitani Mitsue no gakuteki jiban." *Kokumin seishin bunka* 3, no. 1 (June 1937): 7–22.

————. "Fujitani Mitsue no koden." In *Fujitani Mitsue shū.* Vol. 1. Kokumin Seishin Bunka Kenkyūjo, 1936.

Shigetomo, Ki. *Akinari no kenkyū.* Bunri Shoin, 1971.

Shimizu, Masayuki. "Nihon shisōshi to kaishakugaku—Haga Yaichi to Muraoka Tsunetsugu." *Ronshū* 4 (1985): 111–124.

Soranaka, Isao. "Kansei Reforms—Success or Failure?" *Monumenta Nipponica* 33, no. 2 (summer 1978): 151–161.

Sugara, Tōru. *Motoori Norinaga.* Tōkyō Daigaku Shuppankai, 1978.

Suzuki, Eiichi. "Fujitani Mitsue no shisō ni tsuite no ikkōsatsu." *Nihon shisōshigaku* 7 (September 1975): 1–12.

————. *Tachibana Moribe.* Yoshikawa Kōbunkan, 1972.

Suzuki, Jun. *Edo kokugaku no ronkō.* Sōrinsha, 1997.

Suzuki, Kazuhiko. "Tachibana Moribe no kokugo isshiki: *Sansenkaku* ni tsuite." *Yamanashi Daigaku Gakugeibu kenkyū hōkoku* 10 (1959): 21–29.

————. "Tachibana Moribe no kokugo isshiki: *Yamabiko zōshi* ni tsuite." *Yamanashi Daigaku Gakugeibu kenkyū hōkoku* 13 (1962): 31–40.

Suzuki, Toshio. *Edo no hon'ya.* Vol. 1. Chūō Kōronsha, 1980.

Tada, Junten. *Ishoku no Kokugakusha: Fujitani Mitsue no shōgai.* 2d. ed. Kyoto: Shibunkaku, 1996.

Takada, Mamoru. "Hi no kami ronsō ni tsuite no danshō: Norinaga to Akinari no shisō no taishitsu." In *Nihon bungaku kenkyū shiryō sōsho: Akinari,* edited by Takada Mamoru. Yūseidō Shuppan, 1972.

————. *Ueda Akinari kenkyū josetsu.* Nara Shobō, 1968.

————. *Ueda Akinari nenpu kōsetsu.* Meizendō Shoten, 1964

Takahashi, Miyuki. "Norinaga no rekishi shisō." *Kikan Nihon shisōshi* 16 (1981): 27–40.

Takai, Hiroshi. "Kiryū kokugaku no hassei shi." *Gunma bunka,* nos. 3, 4, 5, 7, 8 (1957).

Takashima, Motohiro. *Yamazaki Ansai.* Perikansha, 1992.

Takeoka, Masao. "Ueda Akinari to no kankei." In *Fujitani Nariakira zenshū,* edited by Takeoka Masao. Kazama Shobō, 1962.

Takeuchi, Makoto. "Shomin bunka no naka no Edo." In *Nihon no kinsei,* vol. 14, *Bunka no taishūka,* edited by Takeuchi Makoto. Chūō Kōronsha, 1993.

Tanaka, Sōgorō. *Meiji Ishin taiseishi.* Chikura Shobō, 1941.

Tanaka, Stefan. *Japan's Orient: Rendering Pasts into History.* Berkeley: University of California Press, 1993.

Toda, Tokutarō. "Kojikiden no shinkō." In *Kojikiden no kenkyū,* edited by Fukuda Hisamichi. Rikugeisha, 1941.

Toda, Toshihiko. "Kada Azumamaro no Kojiki kenkyū." *Kojiki nenpō* 4 (1957): 48–62.

Tōhoku Daigaku Gojūnenshi Henshū Iinkai, ed. *Tōhoku Daigaku gojūnenshi.* Sendai: Tōhoku Daigaku, 1960.

Tokumitsu, Kyūya. *Kojiki kenkyūshi.* Kazama Shoin, 1977.

Tōkyō Daigaku Hyakunenshi Henshū Iinkai, ed. *Tōkyō Daigaku hyakunenshi.* Tōkyō Daigaku, 1984.

Tsuchida, Kyōson. "Mitsue no kotodama ron." In *Tsuchida Kyōson zenshū,* edited by Tsunetō Kyō et al. Vol. 11. Nihon Tosho Sentā, 1982.

Tsugita, Masayuki. "Kojiki kenkyūshi." *Kokugo to kokubungaku* 11, no. 4 (1934): 357–409.

Tsuji, Tatsuya. "Politics in the Eighteenth Century." Translated by Harold Bolitho. In *The Cambridge History of Japan,* vol. 4, *Early Modern Japan,* edited by John Whitney Hall. Cambridge: Cambridge University Press, 1991.

Uchino, Gorō. *Bungei gakushi no hōhō: Kokugakushi no saikentō.* Ōfūsha, 1974.

————. *Edo kokugaku ronkō.* Sōrinsha, 1979.

————. "Kōten kōkyūjo to koten kōshūka no sōsetsu." In *Ishin zengo ni okeru kokugaku no shomondai,* edited by Kokugakuin Daigaku Nihon Bunka Kenkyūjo. Kokugakuin Daigaku Nihon Kenkyūjo, 1983.

————. *Shinkokugaku ron no tenkai.* Sōrinsha, 1983.

Uematsu, Shigeru. "Kinsei shoki no Kojiki kenkyū." *Kojiki nenpō* 4 (1957): 1–34.

Umezawa, Iseizō. "Nihon shisōshi gakusha toshite no ko Muraoka Tsunetsugu Kyōju no gyōseki." *Shintōshi kenkyū* 4, no. 1 (1953): 89–102.

Umihara, Tetsu. *Nihon no shijuku.* Kyoto: Shibunkaku, 1983.

Vlastos, Stephen. *Peasant Protests and Uprisings in Tokugawa Japan.* Berkeley: University of California Press, 1986.

Walthall, Anne. *The Weak Body of a Useless Woman: Matsuo Taseko and the Meiji Restoration.* Chicago: University of Chicago Press, 1999.

Washiyama, Jushin. "Akinari to Umaki." *Hanazono Daigaku kenkyū kiyō* 8 (March 1977): 121–134.

———. "Norinaga to Akinari: Akinari to Norinaga gakusetsu hihan ni tsuite." *Hanazono Daigaku kenkyū kiyō* 9 (March 1978): 67–81.

———. "Ueda Akinari bannen no ju butsu nikyōkan: Sono shiron *Otaegoto* wo chūshin ni." *Hanazono Daigaku kenkyū kiyō* 6 (March 1975): 135–178.

White, Hayden. *The Content of the Form: Narrative Discourse and Historical Representation.* Baltimore: John Hopkins University Press, 1987.

White, James. *Ikki: Social Conflict and Political Protest in Early Modern Japan.* Ithaca, N.Y.: Cornell University Press, 1995.

Wilson, George. *Patriots and Redeemers in Japan: Motives in the Meiji Restoration.* Chicago: University of Chicago Press, 1992.

Yamada, Tadao. *Ikki uchikowashi no undō kōzō.* Kōsō Shobō, 1984.

Yamada, Takanobu. "Fujitani Mitsue no shinwa kaishaku." *Nihon bungaku* 40 (October 1991): 25–34.

Yamada, Takao. *Kindai Nihon rinri shisō.* Daimeidō, 1981.

Yamane, Yasutarō. "Fujitani Mitsue no shii to sono taidō." *Kokumin seishin bunka* 3, no. 1 (June 1937): 41–55.

Yamashita, Hisao. *Motoori Norinaga.* Iwanami Shoten, 1992.

Yasumaro, Yoshio. "Kindai tenkanki ni okeru shūkyō to kokka." In *Nihon kindai shisō taikei*, vol. 5, *Shūkyō to kokka.* Iwanami Shoten, 1988.

Young, Blake Morgan. *Ueda Akinari.* Vancouver: University of British Columbia Press, 1982.

Yoshikawa, Kōjiro. "Kojikiden no tame ni." *Bungaku* 36 (August 1968): 31–26.

Index

Susan L. Burns is Associate Professor of History at the
University of Chicago.

Library of Congress Cataloging-in-Publication Data
Burns, Susan L.
Before the nation : Kokugaku and the imagining of
community in early modern Japan / Susan L. Burns.
p. cm. — (Asia-Pacific)
Includes bibliographical references and index.
ISBN 0-8223-3183-7 (cloth : alk. paper) —
ISBN 0-8223-3172-1 (pbk. : alk. paper)
1. Kokugaku. I. Title. II. Series.
B5243.K6B87 2003
320.54'0952'09034—dc21   2003010583